TRAFALGAR
CAPTAIN

DURHAM OF THE DEFIANCE

ABOUT THE AUTHOR

Hilary Rubinstein is a Fellow of the Royal Historical Society and the co-editor of the *Newsletter of the Navy Record Society*, Britain's premier society devoted to naval research. She was born in Portsmouth and has a lifelong interest in the history of the Royal Navy. She lives in Aberystwyth.

TRAFALGAR CAPTAIN

DURHAM OF THE DEFIANCE

HILARY L. RUBINSTEIN

TEMPUS

In memory of
Peter Carlton Jones
(1945–2004)

First published 2005

Tempus Publishing Limited
The Mill, Brimscombe Port,
Stroud, Gloucestershire, GL5 2QG
www.tempus-publishing.com

British Library Cataloguing in Publication Data.
A catalogue record for this book is available from the British Library.

ISBN 0 7524 3435 7

Typesetting and origination by Tempus Publishing Limited
Printed in Great Britain

Contents

of water 237 years earlier. He was among the most illustrious of the young 'star captains' – to quote the phrase used by naval historian Tom Wareham in his eponymously titled book (London, 2001) – entrusted by an admiring Admiralty with the command in succession of two of the largest and finest frigates in commission. Before Durham's death as a very senior admiral it was suggested that he had captured more enemy vessels than any of his peers; he certainly took a considerable number and amassed a fortune in prize money. He achieved the first and last surrenders of the tricolour flag in the conflict of 1793–1815. He was the only British naval officer decorated for valour by the restored French monarchy. He was married to the sister of the famous Lord Elgin who brought to Britain the Parthenon Marbles, and, following her death, to a cousin of the celebrated Admiral Lord Cochrane. Well known among his contemporaries, including George III, as a liar and storyteller, Durham left behind a widely cited naval memoir, ostensibly authored by his sister's grandson, Alexander Murray.

Durham enjoyed a naval career of uncommon length and triumph. During Britain's wars with revolutionary and Napoleonic France he was almost continuously afloat, whereas the majority of officers were 'beached' on half-pay. After 1815 this gallant and enterprising Scot enjoyed, in effect, a second career as an entrepreneurial Lowland laird, embroiled in disputes, supporting illegitimate children, fending off sponging relatives, and making money. Amid all that he served as a member of Parliament, and as commander-in-chief of Britain's premier naval port, Portsmouth, and had ill health not intervened he would almost certainly have taken command of the Mediterranean fleet at the age of seventy-seven. His story is worth telling for a number of reasons. It rescues a brave, astute, colourful and exceedingly fortunate officer from the obscurity that gradually overtook his memory. By drawing on sources never previously utilised it augments our knowledge of Trafalgar and of other naval campaigns and incidents. It amplifies such scholarly works as Michael Lewis's *A Social History of the Navy, 1793–1815* (London, 1960; reprinted 2004) and similar subsequent studies by shedding further light, through Durham's social origins, naval patrons and appointments, upon the inner workings of the Royal Navy's officer corps and of the Admiralty during the zenith of Britain's naval supremacy. Although, for reasons of space and emphasis, the fascinating story of the final thirty years of his life can only be hinted at, it helps to illuminate such works as Michael Lewis's *The Navy in Transition, 1814–1864* (London, 1965), by indicating how, following the wars when, unless they reinvented themselves, naval officers faced redundancy or, at best, under-employment, one of their number achieved success on land as well as sea.

My work draws in large part on manuscripts in the National Archives of Scotland, particularly the Henderson of Fordel papers. Those contain such of Durham's personal documents as he saw fit not to destroy and many of his naval ones, as well as a wealth of relevant correspondence from the pens of his second wife and her circle. Very profound thanks are due to the wonderful staff of the two register houses in Edinburgh for their truly outstanding helpfulness and efficiency. I am also deeply grateful to the staffs of the National Library of Scotland, especially the curators of manuscripts, and the University of Edinburgh Special Collections; I made extensive use of both these repositories. I am indebted to the Earl of Elgin, and to Durham's collateral descendants, Mrs Althea Dundas-Bekker and Mrs Myfanwy Baldwin, for making primary and pictorial source material in their possession available to me. That material included, centrally, the Durham of Largo and Dundas of Arniston papers, and material pertaining to the Bruce family. In addition I most warmly thank the Countess of Elgin and Mrs Mary Donnelly for making my research visit to Broomhall a pleasant and productive one. Without R.W. (Bob) O'Hara's unsurpassed knowledge of the naval (and military) holdings of the Public Record Office this study could not have proceeded. I also drew on manuscripts in the possession of the National Maritime Museum, from ships' logs to officers' letters, and, especially for Durham's father's background, the University of St Andrews' Muniments. The James Dennistoun papers in the Beinecke Rare Book and Manuscript Library at Yale University also yielded primary material, as did the Stirling and West Sussex Record Offices, while the London Library proved a rich source of subsidiary material. I thank their staffs for their assistance.

I owe special debts of gratitude to my publisher, Jonathan Reeve of Tempus, as well as to Alan Brotchie, Charlotte L. Cowe, Caroline Gerard, Dr Irene Greatorex, Rear-Admiral Richard Hill, Professor William (Bill) Rubinstein, Emeritus Professor David Stevenson and Dr Tom Wareham. Others to whom I express sincere appreciation are: Pamela Clark (Royal Archives, Windsor), Lavinia Cohn-Sherbok, Robert Fenwick, Professor Henry Fulton, Professor Robert Havard, Commander J.E. Holt RN, David Jenkins, Susanna Kerr (Scottish National Portrait Gallery), David MacLeod, Michael Martin, Richard Overell, Michael Phillips, Cassie Pugh, Professor Nicholas Rodger, Dr Malcolm J. Turnbull, and Miss J.M. Wraight (Admiralty Librarian). Thanks are due to Gill Parry for expertly typing the manuscript.

Regrettably, a good friend of mine, Peter Carlton Jones, bibliophile and collector, who generously insisted on lending me a copy of a very rare edition of an old book on the *Royal George* that he cherished, so that I might compare it to other editions, did not live to see the present biography, in which he took an interest. It is in Peter's memory, and to his widow Lesley and sons Benjamin, Rupert and Timothy, that I dedicate this work.

Hilary L. Rubinstein

I

Seaborne

He that will view the country of Fife must… go round the coast.
Daniel Defoe

There he sits on a high-backed chair upholstered in rich red velvet: James Calderwood Durham (1732–1808), laird of Largo, prince of good fellows, and raconteur extraordinary. In that warm-toned portrait, the black-browed, white-haired Fife landowner holds a scrolled document over his heart, and above his encircling fingers can be seen a single word: Trafalgar. There is no mistaking the old man's pride in the achievements of his third son, Philip Charles, who had commanded the navy's fastest sailing 74, the *Defiance,* at Lord Nelson's final and greatest triumph, had taken two enemy ships, and narrowly avoided losing a leg.

It was the apex of a naval career that had seen Captain Durham survive the worst marine disaster ever to occur in British home waters and evolve rapidly from an unemployed young lieutenant with an illegitimate child to support into one of the country's most illustrious frigate captains, an officer who enjoyed 'a remarkable career of victory' and who has been aptly described as 'one of the luckiest men' in the Georgian navy.[1]

Even a century after his death, into the 1940s, old salts in his home region around the shores of the Firth of Forth were talking of Durham's naval deeds. His reputation as an outstanding officer was such that when, to mark the centenary of Trafalgar in 1905, the naval correspondent of *The Times,* historian Sir William Laird Clowes, wrote a book called *Trafalgar Refought,* ascribing Nelsonian tactics to an imaginary fleet of ironclads in battle against a latter-day foe, Durham featured as a principal star. Today, naval historians remember Durham of the *Defiance* as, so to speak, 'the captain who refused to miss Trafalgar'. As we shall see, he was lucky to be at the battle.[2]

Philip Charles Durham was born on or about 29 July 1763 (the day of his baptism) in the now ruined Adam-designed family seat, Largo House, situated on high ground overlooking Largo Bay and the Forth. He was named after his father's maternal uncles, Sir Philip and Charles Anstruther of Balcaskie; the Durhams of Largo were linked by either blood or marriage to most of the gentry families of Fife. An unlikely great-grandfather for the convivial and rollickingly good-humoured James Durham – whose gregariousness made him an enthusiastic member of a bawdy club with bizarre masturbatory ritual to which most of the male notables of the district belonged – was a famously dour Covenanting professor of divinity whose preaching impressed Cromwell. Either James Durham's father or grandfather had coined Edinburgh's celebrated nickname, 'Auld Reekie'. Long located in Forfarshire, the family had been settled at Largo since shortly after the Restoration, for the estate had been purchased in 1662 by Sir Alexander Durham, Charles II's Lyon King of Arms.

Anne Calderwood Durham, the future Trafalgar captain's mother, was the daughter of a lawyer, Thomas Calderwood of Polton near Dalkeith, and his wife and estate manager Margaret. Mrs Calderwood, whose father, the baronet Sir James Steuart of Goodtrees and Coltness, had been Scotland's solicitor-general, descended from figures prominent in Scottish history, including Sir Thomas Hope of Craighall, Charles I's long-serving lord advocate (a position roughly equivalent to attorney-general in England) and Viscount Stair, whose son helped to plan the notorious massacre at Glencoe. She had studied under the professor of mathematics at Edinburgh University, and her business acumen enabled her to restore the prosperity of her husband's estate at Polton. It had been acquired by his father, William Calderwood, who sat as a lord of session with the designation

Lord Polton. Mrs Calderwood also wrote a rumbustious Fielding-like novel, *The Adventures of Fanny Roberts*; unlike her vivid letters from the Low Countries, written to her daughter Anne during the 1750s when she was visiting her own brother, political economist and Jacobite exile Sir James Steuart of Coltness, this remains unpublished.[3]

Coincidentally, the shades of two local mariners haunted Philip Durham's childhood. Sir Andrew Wood was a famous fifteenth-century Scottish admiral whose exploits against the English had been rewarded with the lands and barony of Largo; there were reminders of his prior ownership everywhere on the estate and he lay buried beneath the parish church. In the fishing village of Lower Largo, abutting the bay, was the birthplace of the ruffianly Alexander Selcraig, whose exploits when marooned on an island in the Pacific had been immortalised by Defoe in *Robinson Crusoe*. Durham's brothers, James (b.1754), who became an officer in the dragoons like his two Calderwood uncles, Thomas (b.1756), who followed his elder brother's example after considering a career in law, and William (b.1764), who studied law at their father's alma mater, St Andrews University, were educated at Edinburgh's Royal High School. But there is no evidence that Philip went there; perhaps a seafaring career had been picked out for him early in life and his studies were of a more mathematical kind. Although he enjoyed a gross annual income from his lands of £4,694, the laird of Largo had outlaid heavily making improvements to his property, and was sliding into debt. By sending his third son into the navy he was saved the expense of purchasing him a military commission.[4]

The brown-eyed, curly-haired Philip was not the first of his family to enter the Royal Navy. His mother's cousin Thomas Erskine, the future lord chancellor, a son of Margaret Calderwood's sister the Countess of Buchan, had once served as a midshipman. Durham's father's younger brother, Robert, had been prepared for the service at the Royal Naval Academy within Portsmouth Dockyard, only to die shortly after completing his course. The law, the Church, the army, the Royal Navy and the East India Company offered openings for younger sons obliged to make their own way in the world. Rough and dangerous though it was, the senior service held out the prospect of eventually making an officer's fortune through prize money. An eighteenth-century ditty observed:

Sailors, they get all the money
Soldiers they get none but brass[5]

Personal gain, enveloped by patriotism, was the spur to heroics, and no officer would exemplify this more than Durham himself.

Although there were plenty of exceptions, most naval officers came from landed and middle-class families, and in a century where patronage governed placement the possession of influential friends helped a man's prospects; it could secure him a post-captain's rank early and could obtain for him command of a ship. Owing to the outbreak in 1776 of war with the rebellious American colonies, ships were being hurried into commission, including the *Trident,* 64, which early in 1777 began filling her complement of 500 men. Her captain was John Elliot, from a Roxburghshire family with professional links to Anne Durham's. He had an enviable reputation as the victor of an action between his frigate squadron and a more powerful French one off the Isle of Man during the Seven Years' War, and now he accepted Philip Durham as one of his young protégés with the notional rating 'able seaman'. At the end of July, when he turned fourteen, Durham joined the ship, then lying in the Downs, and in April 1778, with Elliot flying a commodore's pennant, she set sail for New York with a team of peace commissioners aboard. In effect headed by the husband of Elliot's niece, sister to the future Earl of Minto, these were empowered to offer terms to the rebel colonists.[6]

The remarkable luck for which Durham became noted was soon foreshadowed. At dawn, shortly before the ship was due to sail, an act of sabotage was fortunately discovered. The collar of the mainstay (the rope extending forward from the head of the mainmast and providing that mast's chief support) had been severed; so had the gammoning, or rope lashing, which held the bowsprit down against the upward tug of the forestay (the rope stretching from the head of, and crucially supporting, the foremast). Somebody, working under the cover of darkness, sought to prevent the commissioners reaching their destination. If the damage had gone unnoticed the masts would have been carried overboard in the first strong wind, incapacitating the vessel, and if a severe gale had developed she would almost certainly have foundered. Elliot's captain, John Inglis, immediately announced a reward of 100 guineas (about £6,000 in today's money) for the apprehension of whoever was responsible. But to no avail.[7]

About a month into the voyage the *Trident,* informed by a homeward-bound vessel that both the British military commander-in-chief in North America, Sir Henry Clinton, and his naval counterpart, Lord Howe, were stationed at Philadelphia, changed course. The peace commissioners wished to confer with the pair before communicating with the president of the Congress of the newly formed United States. They were dismayed to learn, on arrival in June, that Clinton had ordered the military evacuation of Philadelphia to proceed within a fortnight, and would not change his mind.

Some days after the ship's arrival the newly posted Anthony Molloy, previously in command of a sloop, replaced Inglis (who was only a commander) as captain of the *Trident* in a straight swap. Molloy was a singularly unpleasant character, and when Durham was sent aboard the sloop to collect Molloy's baggage he received his first inkling of this. 'I wish you joy of him', volunteered the first lieutenant. 'He is one of the most tyrannical, overbearing fellows I ever met with. He led my predecessor such a life that the poor fellow cut his own throat.'[8]

At the end of the month the *Trident,* with the rest of Howe's squadron, arrived off New York and the commissioners disembarked; their peace overtures were to culminate in failure. The squadron's attention was now focused on a nearby French squadron under Comte d'Estaing, which eventually steered for the West Indies. Meanwhile Commodore Elliot invalided, leaving his crew to Molloy's tender mercies. The squadron, now under Vice-Admiral Byron, sailed for Barbados and in December Molloy rated Durham midshipman.

With Elliot gone, Molloy revealed himself to be a stereotypical martinet: 'punishments increased, and all happiness seemed at an end', wrote Durham. 'Molloy's tyranny had by slow degrees worked upon the crew', resulting in a mutinous disturbance off Guadeloupe in the spring of 1779. The men refused to carry on with their work, ran below, and blocked the hatchways. Molloy armed his officers, as well as Durham and another midshipman, Graham Moore. With the two youngsters at his heels he rushed angrily to one hatchway and then another. The men seized his ankle and tried to pull him down the fore-ladder. Somebody shouted that he be tossed overboard. Durham and Moore managed to drag him to safety, and the marines arrested the ringleaders.

Both Durham and Moore resented Molloy, and 'with great difficulty' Durham obtained a discharge and left the ship in June. He thus missed participating in Byron's disastrous action against d'Estaing, fought off Grenada in July with very heavy casualties on both sides. He arranged to return to Britain aboard a storeship, and deposited his sea-chest aboard. As he rowed out to join her she blew up before his startled gaze, her magazine having been ignited. His clothes, nautical textbooks and instruments would have to be replaced. But at least he was alive – and free of Molloy. Sharing the gunner's cabin aboard a sloop, he arrived at Spithead in August.[9]

At Woolwich he joined the *Edgar*, 74, commanded by his former captain, Elliot, and shortly after Christmas she, as part of Rodney's fleet, sailed to relieve the starving occupants of besieged Gibraltar. On 16 January 1780 Rodney, with his twenty-one ships of the line, defeated a smaller Spanish force under Langara amid hazardous conditions – a raging gale, nightfall, and treacherous shoals to leeward: 'few actions have required a higher degree of intrepidity, more consummate naval skill, or greater dexterity of seamanship'. The *Edgar* had narrowly missed the same fate as a Spanish 70 that she was engaging, which blew up with the loss of all aboard; realising that this enemy had caught fire, Elliot hauled off in the nick of time. Once again, Durham was very lucky. In February Rodney left for the Leeward Islands, and Elliot, displaying a commodore's pennant, was left in charge of what little naval shipping remained in Gibraltar Bay. At the end of April the *Edgar* outwitted five Spanish ships of the line blockading the bay, and joined the Channel Fleet under the command first of the old and doddery Admiral Geary and then of Vice-Admiral Darby. Durham soon came to the attention of the junior flag-officer in the fleet, Rear-Admiral Kempenfelt, who in November 1781 transferred from Darby's flagship, aboard which he had been assisting his chief, to the *Victory*.[10]

Now in his early sixties, Richard Kempenfelt was a tall, stooped, deeply religious bachelor, with a grave contemplative air that intrigued and amused his crew. He was devising a new signalling system based on a numerical flag code; it was intended to remove uncertainty during battles by leaving captains in no doubt as to precisely what their admiral or commodore required. It says much for Durham's perceived capability that this fair yet demanding, cerebral admiral appointed him signal officer, responsible for displaying the appropriate flags aboard the *Victory*, interpreting those flown by other ships – and, crucially, comprehending Kempenfelt's innovations and explaining them to others. For even senior captains such as John Jervis and Adam Duncan were perplexed, which reduced Kempenfelt to tears of frustration in Durham's presence.[11]

In December Durham stood beside his admiral making the necessary signals during manoeuvres off Ushant, when Kempenfelt, with a squadron that included twelve sail of the line, intercepted and partially routed a large convoy escorted by a far more powerful squadron under the Comte de Guichen, bound for the French West Indies with reinforcements of vessels, troops, armaments and stores. Although George III expressed dissatisfaction with the number of prizes taken, Kempenfelt had, against all the odds, thwarted French intentions, enabling Rodney to defeat the Comte de

Grasse off Dominica the following April. Durham regarded the action with de Guichen as 'one of the most daring deeds of Kempenfelt's life', and history's verdict has been equally laudatory. Not until Trafalgar would the *Victory* take part in another truly notable encounter.[12]

Lord Howe succeeded Darby as commander-in-chief of the Channel Fleet in 1782, hoisting his flag aboard the *Victory*, and Durham followed Kempenfelt onto a majestic three-decker, the *Royal George*, 108, as signal officer and acting lieutenant. Every ambitious young man hoped to be noticed approvingly by a flag-officer, with his prerogative of placing his followers in commissioned vacancies that occurred aboard his own ship or another in his squadron: usually, the Admiralty routinely confirmed an admiral's appointees. With Kempenfelt as his patron Durham was hopeful of a fairly swift rise to the position of 'master and commander' (an officer captaining a non-post-ship, typically a sloop) once he had passed his lieutenant's examination. But then tragedy struck.

On 29 August 1782 the *Royal George* lay at anchor about a mile off the entrance to Portsmouth Harbour with her bow facing Cowes, waiting with the rest of Howe's fleet to sail imminently to yet another relief of Gibraltar. Shortly before daylight a lighter (victualling vessel) drew alongside, and her 300 bags of bread began to be unloaded. Soon another lighter arrived carrying casks of rum, and the ship's captain, Martin Waghorn, ordered that these should be cleared once all the bread was aboard. The ship's starboard feedpipe was faulty and needed replacing, and while the stowing of the cargo was in progress she was heeled, by running her starboard guns and balls of shot across to larboard, in order for the carpenter and his mates, assisted by artificers from Portsmouth Dockyard, to perform the work.

At eight o'clock Durham took over as officer of the watch, and was assured by the first lieutenant, George Sanders, that the casks of rum were being directly lowered into the hold. Neither officer realised that some of the casks were, in fact, piling up on the larboard side of the lower gundeck. This, together with the weight of the men unloading them and of water driven through the half-open larboard ports – which Sanders assumed were shut – had brought those ports almost level with the sea. Everyone on the quarterdeck was oblivious to the very subtle sensation of the ship listing further, and when the carpenter, Thomas Williams, a man who habitually erred on the side of caution, reported that a worrying amount of water had seeped into the hold and that the ship should be righted, he was treated as an alarmist. When he returned, repeating his fears, Sanders snapped at him.

Just then artificers slung on a platform over the starboard side yelled 'Avast, avast heeling! The ship is rising out of the water!' and the ship's master, Richard Searle, who had been ashore, clambered aboard warning that she was about to sink. Waghorn ordered the drummer to beat to quarters so that the guns could be re-housed, and Durham made for the forecastle to superintend operations there.

But before any guns were shifted the ship took what Durham would describe as 'a sally or tremulous motion'. No sooner had this 'great jerk or crack' been felt by people below than seawater rushed through the larboard ports of the lower gundeck and everyone stationed there stampeded for the starboard ports to try to escape. Durham, still on the quarterdeck, looked up at the masts, and saw that they 'continued to fall over', proving that the ship was listing further. He caught sight of the captain trying in vain to open the door of Kempenfelt's cabin; the admiral, blissfully unaware of impending danger, had been at his desk writing.

Tearing off his coat, Durham leapt overboard. Being 'a bad swimmer' he was grateful to get astride of a large hammock which drifted past, knowing that, if properly lashed, it would be able to support his weight for a considerable time. A drowning marine grasped him by the waistcoat and twice dragged him under, but Durham kept his legs tightly gripped around the hammock and managed to unbutton the waistcoat and discard it. He held onto a floating spar and was carried into the wake of the capsized ship, where he clutched the signal halyards, attached to the head of the mizen topmast. A seaman who could swim well voluntarily took hold of the halyards and towed Durham to the mainmast. Cannon near the entrance to Portsmouth Harbour had fired distress signals, and craft from the shore soon joined boats from the fleet in rescuing survivors. Durham sat on the masthead for about an hour while those in more obvious peril were picked up, and directed the first boat that came towards him to rescue Waghorn, whom he spotted 'hanging to the weather mizen top-sail yard-arm, supported by a seaman'.

The boat that eventually rescued Durham also picked up the half-drowned carpenter. It took them to the *Victory*, aboard which Durham recuperated and Williams died. An immediate list of survivors contained 331 names. No doubt some pressed men who survived had taken the opportunity to desert. There had been some 1,200 persons aboard the ship, for in addition to her complement of over 800 and the Dockyard men, there were visitors: women, children, and traders. The majority had perished. Most survivors had been on deck; only about seventy of those below had managed to escape. The dead included Kempenfelt, Sanders and another lieutenant, the master, several marine officers, the surgeon, and at least twelve midshipmen.[13]

In accordance with standard practice a court martial on the survivors was held on 9 September, to enquire into the cause and circumstances of the loss of the ship. Durham was a principal witness, and it is noteworthy that no blame was laid on him as officer of the watch, nor was any attempt made to scapegoat Sanders, who of course was unable to defend himself. There was no robust interrogation of the thirteen summoned to testify, few of whom were asked to clarify their answers. The court, presided over by Vice-Admiral Barrington, concluded that the ship 'was not overheeled', that as soon as she was found to be settling Waghorn and his ship's company 'used every exertion' to right her, and that her fate was due to 'some material part of her Frame' suddenly giving way owing to 'the general state of the Decay of her Timbers'. The defendants were exonerated.[14]

In fact, the ship appears to have capsized because the initial angle of her heel – a commonplace 8 degrees – was increased by the weight of the piled-up casks and of seawater in the larboard scuppers. Although unnoticed by the crew, this brought the angle to 'the danger mark'. Once the angle passed 10 degrees it was inevitable that, being deeply laden with stores for the voyage (six months' supply of assorted provisions had already been stowed), the ship foundered.[15]

If there was a culprit in all this it was surely Sanders, who was in charge of the routine running of the vessel. But James Ingram, a survivor who, decades later, wrote a vivid account of events, and had heard Sanders haughtily rebuff Williams, had forgotten Sanders' name and muddled him with another lieutenant, whom he could only identify as a hectoring, organ-playing 'good-sized man, between thirty and forty years of age' whom the men dubbed 'Jib-and Fore-sail-Jack'. The organ-player was Monins Hollingbery, whom a modern historian, taking Ingram's narrative at face value, erroneously blamed for the disaster. In fact, Hollingbery was still in his twenties, and although he survived he was not called to give evidence, having no active duty that fateful morning. In an article in a popular historical magazine, Durham, by contrast, has been identified as Ingram's villain; as the writer who himself so eagerly traduced Hollingbery commented, its author 'owes the shade of Durham an apology'.[16]

Delayed by the court martial, Howe's fleet, which included thirty-four ships of the line and a huge convoy, sailed for Gibraltar on 11 September. Acting Lieutenant Durham had initially been absorbed into the *Victory's* complement, but was now filling in for the indisposed junior lieutenant of the *Union,* 90. Coincidentally or not, her captain, John Dalrymple, was related to Durham's mother.[17]

Hampered by contrary winds and bad weather, the fleet took a month to enter the Straits. On 19 October, having provided the British garrison with reinforcements and supplies, it was homeward bound when it sighted a Franco-Spanish force of fifty ships of the line under Cordova, which had previously harassed it but scattered during a gale. A long-range action began the following day at sunset off Cape Spartel, lasting until ten o'clock that night. The *Union,* in the rear of Howe's force, had 'a severe engagement' with a future Trafalgar combatant, the mighty *Santissima Trinidad,* 112, during which Durham took the first lieutenant's place on deck in order to assist Dalrymple with the signalling system that Howe had developed out of Kempenfelt's. Howe's flagship sustained no casualties, whereas the *Union,* with five killed and fifteen wounded – none of them officers – recorded a higher 'butcher's bill' than any other British ship bar two. In the indecisive action sixty-eight Britons were killed and 208 wounded; corresponding figures for the enemy were sixty and 320.[18]

Howe decided that the action could be renewed only if he pursued the flown enemy for an indefinite period along 'the Barbary shore'. This was precluded by the precarious state of provisions aboard a number of his ships. Having victualled and watered, he took most of the fleet into Spithead. The *Union,* however, formed part of a detachment under Rear-Admiral Hughes, which sailed to Barbados to join the Caribbean squadron of Admiral Pigot. There, in December, Durham passed his lieutenant's examination and obtained his commission.[19]

In March 1783 he became fourth lieutenant on the *Raisonable,* 64, commanded by Lord John Augustus Hervey, the twenty-five-year-old son of the Earl of Bristol. In June, when, having arrived at Spithead, she was ordered round to Chatham to be paid off, a mutiny erupted. The mutineers defied the captain and his lieutenants, appointed their own 'officers', and attempted to fire a gun to summon a pilot to guide the ship into Portsmouth Harbour. They desisted only when Hervey vowed to put to death whoever proceeded. After several days of stalemate, Hervey called the ship's company together on the pretext of having a statement to read to them; no sooner had they assembled than Durham and the other officers, heavily armed, overpowered the twelve ringleaders. The officers cut the ship's cable and forced the chastened crew to make sail for Chatham, where, following a court martial, four of the ringleaders were hanged and four flogged. Durham believed that the instigators of the mutiny were dealers from the shore who wanted the ship paid off locally for obvious reasons. However, it seems that there was at the time openly expressed widespread bitterness among seamen over pay and conditions, and perhaps some of this had infected elements in the crew and led to their irrational behaviour.[20]

In October, despite the advent of peace, Durham was lucky enough to be appointed to the *Unicorn,* a small frigate lying at Plymouth bound for the African coast. But before she sailed he was forced to invalid, and found himself on half-pay. Upon his discharge from the naval hospital early in the New Year he joined his parents and only sister Margaret (b.1760) at Bath, where the rheumaticky Mr Durham was taking the waters. Since 1777 Philip's appearance had altered and he had grown considerably, so that at first his father failed to recognise him. Indeed, perhaps like his tall and well-built brother Jamie, he was above average height; tall genes ran in his mother's family. He returned with his family to Largo, but the novelty soon wore off and he grew restless. With little hope of immediate employment he travelled to France with a midshipman friend from Fife, Peter Halkett. Determined to learn the language, Durham boarded for about a year at Bourges, in the Loire Valley, before moving on to the spa of Bourbonne-les-Bains. There a French naval officer, the Comte de La Touche-Treville, and other aristocratic visitors were fascinated by the story of the loss of the *Royal George.* The Duc de Bourbon's nubile sister, Princess Louise-Adelaïde, styled the Mademoiselle de Condé, took a fancy to Durham. In Paris, she introduced him to the cream of French society, and he mixed with Jacobite expatriates and their families, including his relatives Ladies Marie and Lucie Stuart of Traquair.[21]

Shattered by the death in March 1786 of his brother William, newly qualified as a lawyer after a prize-winning undergraduate career, he returned home, and was next appointed third lieutenant of the *Salisbury,* 50, taking Commodore Elliot to Newfoundland as governor and naval commander-in-chief. The wardroom included fine officers: the first lieutenant, George Westcott, was destined as a captain to fall at Nelson's victory at the Nile; the second, Edward Riou, immortalised by the poet Campbell, would perish as a captain at Nelson's victory at Copenhagen; the fourth, Robert Stopford, son of an Irish peer, would, like Durham, enjoy a long and distinguished career.

In September 1786 the *Pegasus,* 28, commanded by Prince William Henry (the future William IV) anchored in St John's Bay alongside the *Salisbury.*

During his brief stay, the young 'sailor prince', an ebullient carouser, made Durham his 'bosom friend'. Perhaps their relationship consisted of the 'wine, women, more wine, more women and the occasional bawdy song' that characterised the prince's friendship with his ensuing favourite, an army lieutenant at Nova Scotia. For Durham could be a boon companion. He had inherited his father's highly sociable and imaginative nature; indeed, he became so notorious for yarn-spinning that whenever George III heard an anecdote of dubious veracity he would quip 'That's a Durham!' In the wake of the *Royal George* disaster several versions of a joke based on Durham's reputation for embroidering facts made the rounds of naval circles: its punchline had his father, or some other recipient of a letter from him assuring them that he had survived the tragedy, pondering whether this can in fact be true, since he 'is such a [damned] liar that one never believes anything he says!'[22]

2

Earning a Reputation

[The Royal Navy is a] lottery-like service… Naval people may be considered, more
than any other class, the sport of chance.
Admiral Sir Thomas Byam Martin

Newfoundland was a wild and gloomy place, and Durham was glad to return home in 1788, spending time with his parents who were staying in London. There the laird of Largo unsuccessfully petitioned the Lords to recognise his claim to an abeyant Scottish title, Lord Rutherford; both parents had their portraits painted by Romney; and Mrs Durham, who was interested in India because her soldier son Tom and her daughter Margaret (wife of East India Company official James Strange) were based there, attended the trial of Warren Hastings, 'a poor little thin man who wears spectacles and writes all the time'. She described her son Philip as 'the best company here'. But, being again on half-pay, Durham began to fret that the rank of master and commander, the usual stepping-stone to a coveted post-captaincy, still eluded him. He was convinced that, had Kempenfelt lived, 'he would have been well taken care of as he was his Signal Officer the last two years of his life and a great favourite'.[1]

From Fife, his parents and other relatives petitioned Scotland's most powerful figure and principal dispenser of patronage, Robert Dundas (later first Viscount Melville) on his behalf. Dundas was personally acquainted with Durham's father; they both owned townhouses in Edinburgh's George Square. Dundas, a Tory who was ever ready to help a fellow Scot regardless of party, seemed the ideal person to plead Durham's case with the first lord of the Admiralty, Lord Chatham. Hearing a rumour early in 1789 that a general naval promotion was imminent Durham wrote on a blank visiting card that he 'wishes to be put in the line of Promotion at home, or First Lt. of Flag Ship going a broad [sic]'. His father enclosed it in a letter to Dundas, telling him: 'My son... thinks of nothing but the sea service'. Dundas gladly put in a good word with Lord Chatham, who, however, advised that no promotions would be immediately forthcoming.[2]

In the enforced idleness that he hated, Durham had an affair with a twenty-one-year-old Burntisland-born Largo lass called Christian Dick and got her pregnant. He left for London, renting a room in Suffolk Street off the Haymarket to be near the Admiralty, and set about lobbying for a ship. Christian, whom he had no intention of marrying, stayed behind, and sometime during the winter of 1789–90, in Edinburgh, she gave birth to a daughter, Ann, who was raised by and generally used the surname of Christian's mother, Ann or Hannah Bower, from Dunfermline. (Mrs Dick followed Scottish custom by retaining her maiden name as an alternative to her married one.) When Christian returned to Largo she was hauled before the local Kirk Session, confirmed what Durham had already admitted, that he was the father of her child, and was ordered to do public penance at Largo parish church on three successive Sundays for her sin of 'fornication'. She absconded, but when she reappeared in Largo five years later the Kirk exacted its punishment. Either because he was the laird's son, or, being a sailor, was considered a non-resident of the parish, her erstwhile lover was spared similar humiliation.[3]

Durham was optimistic regarding his employment prospects. A major diplomatic rift had occurred with Spain, which had refused to apologise or make reparations for impounding a number of British-owned trading vessels at the Nootka Sound region of what is now Vancouver Island (whose thriving colonial economy, based on the pelts of the sea otter that were highly prized in Asia, had, incidentally, been pioneered by Durham's brother-in-law, James Strange, before he took up the lucrative position of paymaster at Tanjore in the Madras presidency). 'The din of war ran through the country like wild-fire, and was hailed by we candidates for promotion as a most auspicious event', one hopeful would recall. A formidable fleet – known as 'the Spanish Armament' – was assembled in June 1790 under Lord Howe, and Durham determinedly pursued his professional ambitions. There were rivals aplenty: 'We have nobody in London but officers of the Navy'. He enlisted the support of his former captain, 'Old Dalrymple', and was tenacious in his quest: 'I think of nothing but promotion and you may depend upon it I shall put myself in the best situation for it', he told his mother. This would mean appointment as a lieutenant – preferably a first lieutenant – on a flagship, were his cherished goal of master and commander to be denied him straight away. John Elliot had offered to take him on board his ship as soon as he got one, but it appeared that accord with Spain might be reached. 'I give you my word I should have been on board a ship long a go [*sic*]', he assured her, 'but we are in hourly expectations that something will be settled'.[4]

To Durham's relief, those expectations proved abortive, and on 29 June Admiral Barrington, in the replacement *Royal George*, 100, sailed from Portsmouth with fifteen ships of the line and several frigates, bound for Torbay. On 8 July an allied Dutch squadron of eleven assorted vessels under Vice-Admiral van Kinsbergen anchored at St Helens on the Isle of Wight. Two days later at Spithead Lord Howe hoisted the old Union flag on board the *Queen Charlotte*, 100, as commander-in-chief of the joint force. 'This flag, a naval distinction second only to that of the Lord High Admiral of England, has not been hoisted upward of 40 years, Sir John Norris being the last admiral who wore so distinguished a flag.'[5]

Elliot warmly supported Durham's yearning for higher rank: 'I am much obliged to Admiral Elliot for the many handsome things he sayd [*sic*] of me to Mr Dundas'. That gentleman, too, genial and obliging – especially to a fellow Scot – was on his side: 'My Lord Chatham is very kind and told me his friend Mr Dundas has recommended me very strongly but [that] I must consider that he [Chatham] had not made a captain as yet'. (In other words, no other current aspirants to master and commander's status had been advanced – and they were numerous.) 'Although I have been solicited by no captain to go with them', Durham toyed with the idea of joining a 'Privat [*sic*] ship' – meaning a non-flag ship – that was fitting out, 'in case the first lord may think it necessary that I should be in employment' to secure promotion. But he decided not to do so, since Chatham assured him that 'my present situation is considered as service'. 'I have not seen any

Person but Admirals and Mr Dundas', he told his mother a little later. 'I have spent all my time in looking out for promotion'.[6]

There were occasional respites from this dogged routine. He travelled to Brighton to show 'the Lions' to a naval colleague who had just returned from the West Indies, and spent a few days with another friend in Tunbridge Wells. He paid social calls on Scottish friends and relatives who were staying or living in London. His mother's cousin Thomas Erskine, who was returned as Whig member of Parliament for Portsmouth that year, was installed in a residence overlooking Hampstead Heath with his wife and children. With her adamant opinions and tales of the Jacobites, whom she idolised, Durham's sister's feisty and loquacious mother-in-law, wife of the celebrated engraver Sir Robert Strange, made a memorable table companion. Best of all, Durham's brother Jamie, who had left the dragoons for an infantry regiment, had returned from a continental sojourn with his wife Elizabeth. Durham caught up with them as they were on their way in June's heatwave ('by much the hottest days I have felt in England the thermometer was at 85 in the shade', scribbled Durham) to the fashionable spa of Tunbridge Wells before heading north.

By his marriage in 1779 with Elizabeth Sheldon, daughter and heiress of a deceased English army colonel, Jamie had acquired the estate of Flitwick Park in Bedfordshire, as well as thirty-six acres in Bethnal Green that he would sell to developers. Elizabeth, a religious lady who doted on dogs, was known to family and friends as 'Little Mrs Durham'. To Jamie's 'great joy', Durham noted, her 'heart is set on Polton at present', and she 'thinks of nothing but settling in Scotland'. (His mother had acquired Polton in 1787 on the death in Lausanne of her only surviving brother, Lieutenant-Colonel William Calderwood, and although she strictly entailed the property so that her second son Tom would inherit it, she intended that while Tom remained in India Jamie should live there.)[7]

These pleasurable jaunts that he was undertaking, combined with the proximity of Suffolk Street to theatres and various other wonders and temptations of the capital, filled Anne Durham with fears that her son was frittering his half-pay on trivial amusements. But not to worry. 'You are much mistaken in my going to public places', Durham informed Anne in words guaranteed to tug at her heart, 'for I have just money enough to get my dinner and at this moment not even that.' Having entered a lottery he mislaid his ticket. He instructed her to sell his mount at Largo and send him whatever sum the animal fetched, but subsequently had a change of heart. 'You had better not despose [of] my mare, as [I] shall not get so good a one for the money I shall get for her'. But he was possibly too late.[8]

While this exchange of letters was taking place, all was bustle in active navy circles. On 10 August Lord Howe left Spithead with six sail of the line and anchored at Torbay, where Barrington had been joined by reinforcements from Plymouth. The fleet under Howe's supreme command consisted of thirty-one sail of the line as well as nine frigates and a few unrated vessels. Three regiments of foot had been embarked in it to serve as marines. In addition to Howe and Barrington there were four flag-officers: Rear-Admiral Leveson Gower was with Howe in the *Queen Charlotte* along with Captain Roger Curtis as captain of the fleet; Rear-Admirals John Jervis, William Hotham and Richard Bickerton flew their flags aboard the *Barfleur*, *Princess Royal*, and *Impregnable* (all of 90 guns) respectively. The dreaded Captain Anthony Molloy, now married to Rear-Admiral Sir John Laforey's daughter, commanded Elliot's old ship, the *Edgar*, and Durham's former bosom companion, Prince William, Duke of Clarence, captained another 74, the *Valiant*.[9]

He should have been with the fleet that left Torbay on 17 August on a cruise, for he had been appointed first lieutenant of the *Barfleur*, intended as Elliot's flagship. However, things had fallen through, leaving him still unemployed. 'We have lost the chance of going to sea with the fleet', he lamented in a letter to his father. 'My commission was ready as first of the *Barfleur* but that is all over and Lord Hood told me he had no ship that would be ready for Admiral Elliot under six weeks.' At the end of June Elliot had 'sent a list up to Lord Hood' – like Leveson Gower, whom Durham also lobbied, Hood was one of the lords commissioners of the Admiralty under Lord Chatham – 'I am first Lt. on that list but am much affraid [*sic*] of a change, as I think William Elliots friends will be disappointed and will get him [John Elliot] to change in some manner or other.'[10]

William Elliot became a lieutenant in December 1787 and was therefore junior to Durham on the lieutenants' list by five years. He had, however, the advantage of being a nephew of Admiral Elliot. The admiral, who had been briefly a Whig member of Parliament over thirty years earlier, was detained in Scotland voting in an election, and his failure to return to England when summoned cost his first lieutenant dear. For when Durham, unaware of what was transpiring, reached Portsmouth expecting to take up his position aboard the *Barfleur* he was told by Howe that he 'might go home again' since Jervis now had the ship and someone else was first lieutenant. Everyone, not least Lord Chatham, was 'much surprised' at

Elliot's 'not coming to town the Moment he was sent for', commented Durham ruefully. 'This matter is a strange history.'[11]

He cursed 'this Murtheren [i.e. tormenting] Peace', dearly wishing that war would definitely break out and improve his prospects. 'I think I shall be made if we are to befriend great men', he declared, apparently reflecting that if war did not eventuate he would need to cultivate highly placed patrons beyond those in the navy and at the Admiralty. Meanwhile, he pinned his hopes on the opportunity to sail with Elliot as first lieutenant, and busied himself referring to the admiral seafaring friends and contacts, mainly from Fife, who wished to be considered for inclusion in the crew. By the beginning of August his outlook had brightened, for he had learned that on her return from her cruise with Howe, the *Barfleur* was to be turned over to Elliot. 'I am in high spirits', he told his mother.

> The Admiral [Elliot] is in town and all settled. I have not the smallers [*sic*] doubt but I shall be made Captn the first opportunity and have been with Lord Hood. Mr Dundas has done all in his power... I beg my kind love to my Father – tell him if [I] get on I shall only be oblige[d] to him, as it will be through Mr Dundas.[12]

Meanwhile, a large fleet assembled at Spithead under the command, in Howe's absence, of Lord Hood: it was allegedly intended for the Baltic, presumably to intimidate Catherine the Great's Russia, which was proving uncomfortably successful in hostilities with Turkey and threatening the balance of power in Europe. 'The despatch used in equipping this fleet was almost unparalleled in the history of the navy', wrote a contemporary.[13] On 4 September Hood hoisted his flag on board the *Royal Sovereign*, 100, and Elliot hoisted his on board the *Bellerophon*, 74. Since this was to be his flagship only temporarily, Elliot (who took charge of this fleet the following day when Hood struck his flag) did not bring Durham or his other followers aboard. He was unwilling to disturb arrangements already existing under his flag-captain, Thomas Pasley. This suited Durham very well: 'It is now the same to me if I remain on shore – for I can expect nothing by going to sea, but the pleasure of going with Mr Elliot which is to me a very great one. You can have no Idea of the attention he has paid me – and with what pleasure he has taken by the hand all those I have recommended to him – he has trusted to my care everything that I could wish.'[14]

Also living at the Suffolk Street address was one of the admiral's relatives, Hew Elliot, whom Durham pronounced 'much the pleasants [*sic*] of all

Elliots knowing nothing of Scotland nor his relations...'. As for William Elliot, Durham's arch-rival for the position of first lieutenant, he had sailed on the *Lion*, 64, as fourth lieutenant, but would also be joining the *Barfleur*. 'I do no[t] know as yet which of us is to be the first Lt.' Durham wrote home to his mother. 'I was in the last arrangement but [they] may change it, as we are to all have new commissions – I have had all the trouble [i.e. of dealing with potential recruits].' Moreover, he had learned that 'Lord Chatham had cut from Mr Dundas's list of officers that he wished to be promoted. I was the first on it – say nothing about this.' He had informed Admiral Elliot of this unwelcome development, but still seemed optimistic about his immediate prospects.[15]

It is obvious that Durham enjoyed finding men and fledgling officers for the *Barfleur*. He asked his parents to recommend to him any connections or contacts wishing to make the navy their career. Among those who entered this way was his relative Philip Charles Anstruther: 'a fine lad, but not as I believe much of a seaman' was Durham's initial verdict on this future lieutenant, from the Balcaskie family. One acquaintance, who had decided not to join, was 'a great foole – he will not have such an opportunity again'. Durham took particular pleasure in finding berths for those his mother nominated. 'I have it but seldom in my power to shew you my gratitude for the many obligations I am under to you', he explained, in what was almost certainly an oblique reference to financial help towards the support of his daughter. He also clearly relished the task of liaising with Elliot and with the Navy Board on behalf of her recommendations, and was proud of the little taste of power that his placements gave him. Having got one of them appointed surgeon's mate on the *Barfleur*, for instance, he declared: 'if the War goes on, I will get him made a Surgeon'. He was even prouder that on the eve of the ship's expected arrival Elliot requested him

> to get all the Mids. and people together – the Captn is in the West of England, and I am the only one to do every thing. But I have one happiness that the Admiral is very much pleased with my attention – and has take[n] with great pleasure every body that I have mentioned to him – and they are not a few... I believe the people [i.e. the crew] think I command the *Barfleur*.

His mother, concerned for her son and his long-term future, seems to have broached the painful subject of what he would do were peace to be declared, but he refused to be drawn: 'as to what I am to do at the peace I have not once thought of it [n]or shall I until it is made – I only think of the war.'[16]

Howe's ships, meanwhile, cruised for just under a month, keeping frequent watch off the strategically important port of Brest, whose splendid harbour could hold a very large naval force, in case the French were up to mischief. Among the fleet that assembled at Spithead on 21 September was the *Barfleur*, commanded by the strict disciplinarian Robert Calder, Jervis's flag-captain, who now became Elliot's. On 24 September Durham went aboard and six days later Calder discharged into another vessel, having been succeeded by Captain Robert Carthew Reynolds. As Durham had been half expecting, William Elliot (described by one of the midshipmen as 'sickly and proud') had been appointed first lieutenant of the *Barfleur*, and he had to be content with second place. William Chantrell ('A very droll and strange fellow' according to that same midshipman) was third lieutenant. There were eight in all.[17]

To coincide with the assembling of the fleet a large promotion took place, across all commissioned ranks: of relevance to Durham was the fact that twenty men who had attained the rank of master and commander before the end of 1782 were posted, and twenty lieutenants who had been made before the end of 1780 became masters and commanders.[18] That this promotion did not include Durham may not have been particularly disappointing for him: he could see that only men senior to him were eligible, and he might have reasoned that, with twenty rivals now given their step up, his own promotion would not be much longer delayed. Nevertheless, it must have been an anxious time.

By mid-October a huge naval force lay at Spithead. That no fewer than ten admirals' flags – including those of Howe, Barrington, Elliot, and Jervis – flew simultaneously was a historic record. 'I got the shirts you was so good as to send me', Durham told his mother on 23 October. 'We have no news now but extraordinary preparations for War... this Country never had such a fleet as they have at present'. However, despite what she might have read in the newspapers, they were not about to set sail for the West Indies (although four days later six ships of the line under Rear-Admiral Samuel Cornish sailed there with troops aboard, intent on an assault against the Spanish colony of Puerto Rico): 'we have no orders of any kind'.[19]

Durham's praise for the fleet echoed Elliot's: 'it is the finest I really believe that ever was in the whole world not for numbers but prodigious fine ships, all in healthful and well-man'd neither Sickness, Desertion, nor even a murmur to be heard from one end to the other of it but one man try'd at a Court Martial since the first of the Armament and not one flog'd for one hundred that used to be...'.[20]

But so near was peace in Elliot's view that he took leave and went up to Scotland. While he was there a dispute broke out between the ship's lieutenants and the purser, who being a stickler for the very letter of an Admiralty standing order of 1761 had steadfastly refused to supply the lieutenants with the extra liquor they considered their prerogative. 'It is, or ought to be well known to every Officer in the Navy, the Spirits (whilst Ships are employed in Channel service) can only be issued when Beer is expended, and never whilst in Port', he observed. On 26 October Durham and the other lieutenants sent him the first of what he termed 'two extraordinary Notes'. It reminded him 'that it is the general custom in the Fleet for Pursers (on liberal terms) to issue any Quantity of Spirits for the immediate use of the Wardroom Mess that may be wanted'. The second, sent the following evening, was worded 'in such arrogant and threatening Stile' that it was 'arbitrary, oppressive and unbecoming [to] the character of Gentlemen and Officers'. Adding insult to injury by having it delivered to his home in Gosport by a black servant of theirs (who for all he knew had shown it round the ship making him a laughing stock), the lieutenants advised that they had unanimously resolved that if he did not immediately 'treat the Gentlemen his Messmates as is Customary for a Purser to do' they would retaliate by 'scratching out his Name from the Mess Book of the Wardroom'. The purser retorted that 'they quite mistake his Character to suppose that their Threats' could intimidate him; he had as much right to occupy the wardroom as they did and 'his Life is not to be made unpleasant by the hasty resolutions of young officers'. In the end he sought Elliot's intervention, and pointed out that the admiral's nephew, being first lieutenant, 'bears so capital a part in these transactions' and therefore was 'the first of whom I have reason to complain'.

The admiral conceded that he had a right to refuse the spirits to the wardroom no matter what other pursers customarily did, but declined to remonstrate with the lieutenants. He stressed that everybody aboard should view Lieutenant Elliot 'in the same light as I do, as an officer only, and I should for ever despise him, both as such and as a relation as well as everyone in the Wardroom Mess' were the purser's harsh characterisation of the notes true: yet although he did not approve of the notes he could not agree that they reflected on the lieutenants' standing as 'Gentlemen and Officers'. As for them being 'young', they were 'all deemed old enough in the opinion of their Superiors, and fully adequate to the stations to which they are appointed'. It was the first case of its kind that Elliot could recall, and might have been nipped in the bud had the purser, instead of sulking ashore, bothered to come aboard to tell him of it sooner.[21]

While the wardroom of the *Barfleur* was embroiled thus in squabbling, on 28 October an agreement between Britain and Spain (known as the Nootka Convention) was implemented. Spain agreed to reparations for the seizure of the British vessels. It acknowledged that it had no rights to claim sovereignty over areas that it did not actually colonise, thereby recognising that the British could occupy and trade in any part of the Americas not occupied by Spain. Although peace did not properly arrive until January 1794 when formal terms were signed in Madrid giving both countries free access to Nootka Sound, the immediate threat of war was averted. Durham's prospects for promotion, however, had not dimmed. The advancement of twenty men to the rank of master and commander on 21 September had rewarded certain deserving or especially well-connected men. But the Admiralty, having dealt with their claims, still had it in mind to promote men of merit and influence further down the lieutenants' list. Between 21 October and 3 November several were promoted, not all of whom had been commissioned lieutenants earlier than Durham. But on 12 November he followed suit, along with another promising young officer, John Woodley. By the end of the month a number of other advancements to master and commander had occurred: those favoured included Durham's former shipmates Joseph Yorke and Graham Moore, Molloy's brother-in-law Francis Laforey, and William Elliot.[22]

It was one thing to have the rank he coveted; it was quite another to be given a ship. But Durham's star was now in the ascendant. Through Henry Dundas's good offices he obtained temporary command of a small post-ship, the 20-gun sixth-rate *Daphne*, earmarked for Alan Hyde Gardner, a newly posted captain on the West Indian station, with orders to sail to Barbados and deliver despatches to Admiral Cornish telling him of the agreement with Spain and thus aborting the planned attack on Puerto Rico, and to Jamaica with similar information for the governor, the Earl of Effingham. Durham was overjoyed. Word of his elevation, and of his new command, obviously reached him ahead of the official announcement. He was the 'friend who will be made a Captn. in a few days... in a Frigate going to Jamaica', of whom Elliot wrote privately on 8 November. And on 11 November he discharged from the *Barfleur* together with several of his associates who had entered as volunteers and now followed his fortunes, including the future lieutenant Philip Charles Anstruther; another relative and future lieutenant, Philip Anstruther, had discharged the previous day.[23]

Durham managed to attract so many volunteers to the *Daphne*, including people who had served with him on the *Royal George*, that he was able to dismiss all the pressed men aboard. His aim of manning the frigate with volunteers delayed sailing, but not for long. 'This day the *Daphne* is reported ready for sea', he wrote to his mother from Plymouth on 24 November:

and I flatter myself the first [i.e. best] man'd ship in the Navy, all *volunteers*... all the officers are good – and the people all my old ship mates – fine Fellowes – *if it was but a war*. Send me nothing out until I write again – you may depend I shall take great care of myself – and only think of being made Post – a terrible experience... [his emphasis]

His parents had forwarded money for his immediate expenses, and somehow he managed to spend the hefty sum of £100 in a single day: 'the first fitting out is the Devil but having a Command of [a] Frigate is the great thing – that is the feather in my cap above all those who made captains and don't on half pay'. James and Anne Durham were too happy about his promotion to begrudge the money. They fully realised how significant this command was to the progress of his career. As he pointed out, 'the great advantage is to have a ship particularly a frigate – as many officers that have none have no claims on the Admiralty – and they like to send people on Service that have served'. Anne observed that although the unhealthy West Indies station had laid many a sailor low, her son had thrived there previously. Disappointment and idleness affected him more adversely than the climate. His loyal, warm, considerate nature won him friends wherever he went.[24]

At Barbados Cornish gave Durham despatches which he took to Jamaica. There, in January 1791, he relinquished command of the *Daphne* to Captain Gardner, and transferred into the 18-gun *Cygnet* on Cornish's station. He was ultimately sent home with despatches describing the progress of a slave revolt, which had broken out in the north of the French colony of Santo Domingo (now Haiti) in August 1791 and spread to other regions. In December 1792 the *Cygnet* reached Britain and was paid off.[25]

He was not long on half-pay. In November 1792, to the Pitt government's consternation, the revolutionary regime in France had abrogated treaty rights guaranteeing the Dutch exclusive navigation of the river Scheldt, and had proceeded to offer military assistance to any countries wishing to be rid of monarchical rule. On 1 February 1793, ten days after the guillotining of Louis XVI, the French republic declared war on Britain as a result of Pitt's protest, and also on Holland. Pitt, who had hoped to maintain peace, had no option but to fight. A coalition was formed with Prussia, Austria,

Spain and Holland. These allies, subsidised by British wealth, bore the brunt of the armed struggle on land against the French. Meanwhile, the Royal Navy, mindful that the enemy had put into commission thirty ships of the line and twenty frigates, valiantly endeavoured to maintain Britain's maritime supremacy. Naval vessels protected Britain from invasion, kept watch on French ports, undertook blockades, provided convoy escort to British and Britain-bound foreign commercial ships, and backed up military expeditions abroad.[26]

As always, the Channel Fleet – with which Durham was to be long associated – formed Britain's primary defensive shield. One of its major functions was to prevent a French naval force from leaving Brest to attempt an invasion, reinforce France's presence in the Mediterranean and elsewhere or protect French convoys. The Channel Fleet was also active in fulfilling the key objective of Britain's naval strategies during the course of the war: securing British commerce.

France's aim of controlling the Scheldt, combined with French privateering activity, materially encouraged by the revolutionary government through favourable terms (including the waiving of its claim to a share of prize money and the exemption of prize goods from import duty), threatened to disrupt Britain's trade. This posed dire consequences for economic prosperity and even national security. If France gained a stranglehold on the Scheldt she could bring Britain's trade with the continent to a virtual standstill. And if not thwarted the captains and crews of the French privateers – privately-owned armed vessels preying on the British merchant marine – would work their mischief again and again. They were audacious raiders and tenacious fighters, fiercely resisting capture. In these circumstances Durham was given command of the *Spitfire*, a sloop built nearly ten years earlier as a fireship, supposed to have fourteen maindeck guns but equipped with only eight, with orders to cruise the Channel coast in quest of privateers and French coastal craft. On 12 February he arrived at Spithead and took over from her previous commander, John Woodley, who had been posted to a 28-gun frigate.[27] In the little *Spitfire*, fast-sailing like others of her class, Durham would give the Admiralty a taste of what he could do: he began by bringing home the first prize of the war.

At half-past twelve in the afternoon of 15 February the *Spitfire* weighed and rounded the Isle of Wight. Her new captain had two lieutenants under him, but the ship was far short of her complement of about 100 men: a vessel of her size was not so attractive to volunteers as a frigate. (How he must have wished he could have taken advantage of the Fife bounty to seamen, patriotically initiated at a meeting in Cupar on 4 February of 'the Noblemen, Gentlemen, Freeholders, and Heritors of the County', which guaranteed two guineas to every able seaman and one guinea to every ordinary seaman and able-bodied landman who presented for service at Leith before 1 June.)[28]

At one o'clock, off Culver Cliff to the north of Sandown Bay, the brig *Provident*, of Sunderland, informed Durham that she and two others had been chased and fired upon by 'a French cutter privateer' three or four leagues south-east of nearby Dunnose Point. Durham immediately steered in a south-easterly direction, and two hours later the enemy was observed from the masthead. At six he caught up with her and she struck her colours, proving to be *L'Afrique*, of Le Havre (known in those days as Havre de Grace), with a crew of twenty-two and an arsenal of what Durham described as 'Blunderbusses, Musquets, Daggers, &c'. That evening the *Spitfire* anchored at St Helens, overlooking Spithead, in order to land the prisoners taken from the prize and to await the much-needed men who took her into harbour. Durham shared with the commander of the brig *Childers*, who that same day off the coast of northern France took the privateer *Le Patriote*, of Dunkerque, the honour of capturing the conflict's first prize. *L'Afrique*'s 'was the first tri-coloured flag that was taken into an English port, and was looked upon as a great curiosity by the inhabitants of Portsmouth'.[29]

True, *L'Afrique*, like *Le Patriote*, was only a small vessel. Durham in his underarmed sloop could hardly compare with Captain Edward Pellew, of the *Nymphe*, 36, who in June would capture the first frigate of the war, *La Cléopatre*, also 36, for which feat he was immediately knighted.[30] But it heralded a string of captures in quick succession by the gallant young Scot and the start of his reputation as one of the navy's most talented officers; the lords commissioners of the Admiralty would have cause to take notice.

Wasting no time in setting sail again, Durham learned that 'a large armed cutter' was about to depart from Saint Valéry-en-Caux, near Dieppe. On 17 February he fell in with a vessel answering her description and gave chase. After a few hours she ran on shore to the east of Cap d'Antifer, and since it was 'blowing hard' with 'a great swell' from the north-east he had no option but to let her go. 'I have every reason to believe that from the situation I left her in, the vessel is entirely lost – the crew saved.' The following morning, close to the French coast, he chased a large sloop which soon went aground about a mile east of Dieppe. 'I sent my Boats on board of her and found her to be deeply laden with a very valuable Cargo, but from the tide ebbing so rapidly, and the arrival of 2 or 3 Regiments with field pieces, which considerably annoyed the Boats employed, I was obliged to desist, and set her on fire.'[31]

On 21 February, off Beachy Head, he took a pilot on board since the *Spitfire*'s master proved 'totally ignorant' of the French coast, and a week later captured the *Saint Jean*, a schooner from Dunkerque 'loaded with manufactured Tobacco', as well as a small cutter from Le Havre, *L'Aimable Rose*. Durham immediately sent the schooner to Portsmouth, but detained the cutter 'as a Decoy Duck'. On 5 March he arrived at Spithead, having taken, off Le Havre, 'a large Lugger deeply laden', the *Sainte Marguerite*. His success in taking small vessels and recapturing British craft that had fallen prey to the French soon came to the attention of the London-based Committee for Encouraging the Capture of French Privateers, newly formed by a number of City merchants worried for the safety of their cargoes. On 14 March they voted to reward Durham for his 'signal services in the capture and destruction' of several enemy privateers. The following day their chairman, Beeston Long, wrote to tell him so:

> I am directed by the committee... to transmit to you the inclosed Extract from the minutes of their meeting yesterday requesting your acceptance of a Piece of Plate as a Testimony of your meritorious Exertions, and I am extremely happy, at the same time, in having this opportunity to acknowledge how much the Commerce of this Country has been promoted by your particular activity in this service.[32]

Durham was the first recipient of such an award, valued at 100 guineas, and naturally enough he was delighted. 'It is always so very agreeable to a British officer to have his Conduct approved by his Countrymen that I cannot sufficiently express how very much I am gratified by the flattering mark of attention shewn me by so respectable a Body as the Merchants of London who have been pleased to consider the services I have endeavoured to render my King and Country as worthy of their particular notice,' he told Long. 'With singular satisfaction I accept their mark of approbation and beg you will have the goodness to assure them of my continued zeal and attachment to their Interests and to the service to which my Life is devoted.'[33]

Shortly after this, Captain James Saumarez of the frigate *Crescent*, 36, delivered to Durham an order from Rear-Admiral Sir Hyde Parker to escort from Jersey as far as Dartmouth, Devon, a number of Newfoundland-bound merchantmen. But they proved unwilling to settle for anything less than a direct convoy across the Atlantic. He thus took under his command several small commercial craft needing an escort from Jersey to Southampton, and then returned to the more exciting and potentially lucrative – because it held out the possibility of prizes – task of scouring the Channel. On 14 April he captured a French privateer, the *République*. She escaped during the night, but he kept possession of her British prize, the *King George*, which had been on her way to London from Charleston, South Carolina, with 'a very valuable Cargo' when taken four days earlier. She and her captor were within one hour's sailing distance of a French port when the *Spitfire* bore down to her rescue.[34]

Towards the end of April Major-General David Dundas, commanding at Guernsey, informed Durham that the neighbouring island of Jersey had almost certainly been attacked by a French squadron. He had sent a sloop home with despatches to that effect to the government and the port-admirals of Portsmouth and Plymouth. Durham swiftly investigated, and found that it was a false alarm: panic had set in on the island when three enemy frigates and an armed brig were sighted nearby. He believed they were on their way from Brittany to Cherbourg and Le Havre. Anchoring at St Helens, he landed twenty French prisoners of war brought from Guernsey and sent his boats ashore with letters to the Admiralty and to the two port-admirals contacted by Major-General Dundas, to assure them that news of an attack was 'without foundation'. He also informed the Admiralty of his narrow escape from capture by two ships on 25 April, when chased from morning until evening to 'within two leagues' of Saint Aubin on the south coast of Jersey. 'We had the good fortune to escape them by our superior sailing and a fortunate change of wind – one of them being within a mile of us for six hours.' He left them at Saint Aubin at eight o'clock 'standing off and on'.[35]

While cruising near the French coast on the afternoon of 27 April he exchanged several broadsides with two enemy brigs, of 16 and 12 guns respectively. They did 'no material damage' to the *Spitfire*, and he pluckily proceeded to chase them under the fort at Cherbourg. But after about half an hour he was obliged to withdraw for fear of running aground. He duly reported to Captain Peter Rainier, whose 74-gun *Suffolk* hove into view, that in the harbour he had seen the two ships which had almost taken him a couple of days earlier, anchored there alongside two small frigates, an armed sloop, and several merchantmen.[36]

On 3 May he captured an American vessel, the *Columbus*, on her way from Lisbon to the principal trading port of the northern French coast,

Le Havre, with a cargo mainly of cotton, but also of indigo, cochineal, the medicinal herb ipecacuanha, and hides. With his sights set squarely on prize money he asked Andrew Lindegren, an agent at Portsmouth, 'to obtain a speedy condemnation and give such hints as you may think necessary for my interest'. Aboard the captured ship had been the French ambassador to Lisbon, whose papers Durham confiscated. He delivered them to Major-General Dundas, to be forwarded to London. That same day he retook the *Two Brothers*, a galiot laden with salt, which had been sailing to Ostend when captured by a French privateer the previous day. He requested the underwriters at Lloyd's Coffee House to 'allow me the usual salvage, on a fair valuation'. When they had done so the vessel, in charge of John Saumarez, an agent at Guernsey, 'shall be immediately allowed to proceed on her voyage'.[37]

Three weeks later he wrote to the Admiralty asking that, 'Her present force being only 8 Four pounders which is perfectly inadequate to the force of the French privateers', the *Spitfire* 'be fitted with 19 Eighteen pound Carronades' like the sloops *Josephine* and *Pluto*. He was restless and ambitious, thinking of what he might achieve with a greater armoury of guns, and, with characteristic energy and initiative, took himself off to the ordnance office in Portsmouth without waiting for a reply to see what was in stock. Finding no guns of the kind he wanted, he altered his request to 'Eighteen 12 pound Carronades'. The Admiralty, however, now felt that this active and enthusiastic officer had proven his worth and deserved a ship more suited to his potential. On 24 June 1793, having brought from Guernsey to Spithead a convoy and about forty French prisoners of war, he achieved his cherished dream – he was made a post-captain. He very briefly held command of the *Narcissus*, a 20-gun frigate like the *Daphne*, and then paid a short visit to Scotland.

He had, since he was last at Largo, lost another sibling. His sister, Margaret Strange, had died at Tanjore on 15 March 1791, news broken to their parents by Tom Durham on his arrival in Britain the following month. Margaret lay buried close to a monument erected by her husband, which paid tribute to her 'distinguished and amiable talents'. Her only child, Isabella, lived in England with Sir Robert and Lady Strange, who had received the small girl during Margaret's fatal illness. They sent periodic reports to her other grandparents, and it was of some comfort to the Durhams that in her pretty looks and winsome disposition she was the image of her mother. Fanny Burney described Belle as 'a delightful little Creature... handsome & open & gay'.[38]

Tom Durham had returned from India for good, apparently no richer. Since his arrival he had begun courting Elizabeth Young of Netherfield, whom he would marry in June 1793. Jamie and his wife were at Polton. In what Anne Durham condemned as a concession to 'folly and fashion' they had commenced their tenure by removing the family portraits from the walls. Anne was incensed at this insult to a likeness of her revered mother ('It deserves the first place in any home that is *mine*'), one of her late brother, William ('He had no equal in our esteem'), and one of her distinguished grandfather, Lord Polton ('the man who raised the family by his industry and talents'). 'I wrote to you when you were abroad, that I was happy to have a room to place these pictures in, and I do not believe any consent was given to take them away'.[39] She insisted on them being restored to their accustomed locations, and advised that she intended to send a portrait of her 'angelic brother James' as a companion piece to that of William.

Unlike his brothers, Philip Durham lacked a settled home of his own and had no prospect of a permanent country property. In contrast to Jamie and Tom, the heirs to Largo and Polton respectively, he had no choice but to make his own way in the world. Around the time of his visit his 'beloved mother' was not in good health, and he would be 'very happy' to learn, some months later, that she was 'so much better, and has been so little affected by the winter'. In the meantime, on 20 October 1793, he was appointed to the frigate *Hind*, with twenty-eight 9-pounders and a complement of 200 men, which was fitting out at Sheerness prior to Channel service. Three days later he received £20 sterling from the indulgent Anne to help with his expenses. In the *Hind* he would really get to know the splendid isolation of command, a virtual prince in his own domain.[40]

20 guns apiece, were hardly considered genuine exemplars of the class (they came to be classed as corvettes). Nor, for that matter, were those with 24. Most frigates carried between 28 and 38 guns, firing 12 or 18 pound shot. Those with 36 and 28 guns were becoming standard.

Nelson called frigates 'the eyes of the fleet', and they were the ideal multi-purpose vessels, assigned a variety of tasks. They were sent ahead as scouts on lookout for the enemy; they cruised on reconnaissance missions gathering intelligence about enemy fleet preparations, strength and movements; they assisted in military operations with land forces; they escorted convoys of merchantmen and transports; and sometimes they went on cruises 'under Admiralty orders', independent of the commander-in-chief of a station. In battle a frigate's main role was to communicate between vessels, repeating the admiral's signals to ships ahead and astern of the flagship which might therefore otherwise miss them, towing disabled ships to safety, and securing the crews of prize vessels. Custom dictated that a ship of the line did not fire upon a frigate, with her vastly inferior broadside capability and much weaker hull scantlings, unless she attacked first, but by the 1790s this convention had begun to break down.[1]

A frigate was always expected to engage an enemy counterpart irrespective of the number of guns the latter carried. Successful frigate duels caught the public imagination, giving rise to laudatory songs and to artists' impressions in the windows of print shops; some victorious frigate captains, such as Edward Pellew and Philip Broke, won enduring celebrity. The daring of frigate captains and the bravery of their crews, of course, has proved persistent as a staple of maritime fiction.

'In wartime', observed a colleague, 'captains always seek the command of a frigate with small pay, in preference to a ship of the line with larger pay.'[2] The young Philip Durham was no exception. A frigate captain did not receive equal pay with a captain of a ship of the line and his crew was smaller and his responsibility correspondingly less. He had, however, a far greater chance of accruing prize money and could, if very successful, make a fortune. Until readjustments in 1808 the captain's share of the prize money was three-eighths of the total: if his vessel was 'under Admiralty orders' he kept that entire amount, since he did not relinquish the one-eighth that was normally due to a commander-in-chief. Every member of a ship's crew picked up some of the prize money, although the captain and his senior officers obtained the lion's share. A frigate captain with a proven record of taking enemy vessels attracted more volunteers, and therefore had less need of the press gang, than an unsuccessful one or the average captain of a ship of the line with his larger complement to fill. 'Most frigate captains were relatively junior', one naval historian has explained, 'but since so much of their work called for individual initiative, they were an elite within the officer corps.'[3]

Another scholar confirms the accuracy of that perception. They were 'the Georgian equivalents of modern media stars' and 'always seem to have been regarded as dashing and brave, cast in the heroic mould...The crucial factor seems to be that the frigate captains not only offered a role model, they also delivered the required deeds in time of war, something that the captain of a ship of the line had less opportunity to do'. Frigate captains tended to be the cream of the naval crop, who merited and typically enjoyed what today would be termed 'fast-track promotion':

> Contrary to popular imagination, frigate command was not just the domain of the young, freshly promoted captain, although there was always a desire to have men of ability in command of frigates – indeed the nature of the job absolutely demanded it. The problem for the Admiralty was that by 1793 few of the men available had sufficient experience. With little fresh blood brought in during the peacetime years, a significant number of those promoted in the first two years of the war were older men – but these were also men of outstanding ability. Once these had been put into position the Admiralty began to 'cherry pick' from what were likely to be the most promising younger men.[4]

Durham had joined a select company.

On 4 December the *Hind* arrived at the Nore from Spithead. Such were his contacts among seamen along the Forth, as well as his growing reputation, resting upon the string of captures by the *Spitfire*, that her eager new captain informed the Admiralty that she was 'now sufficiently mann'd to navigate her to Leith Roads where in a very short time I have not the smallest doubt of completing her Complement'. He was loyal to, and supportive of, those whose work merited it, and therefore attracted followers, especially fellow Scots.[5]

Although his observations about people were often laced with 'caustic sarcasm', he was known for his 'easy pleasant manners' which made him 'the very picture of good nature'. His humane trait was in evidence at the commencement of his command of the *Hind*. Believing that forty pressed seamen who had been sent aboard from the holding tenders had been unjustly treated by the impressment officers, who had not bothered to give them an opportunity to volunteer and thereby collect the bounty owed to those who joined of their own volition, he put up a tenacious fight on their behalf. Although sometimes hotheaded, he was, like all sensible captains, fair and compassionate and devoted to the welfare of his ship's company. It became his practice to give his crews 'a Glass of Spirits to refresh them, in extreme bad Weather, when the Ship has been in danger and the Men have continued wet for a considerable time'.[6] And while he was that necessary and respected figure, 'a taut hand', he was no indiscriminate flogger. 'No monarch is more despotic, as far as respects the power of inflicting corporal punishment short of death, than the captain of a ship of war', observed a contemporary, the pioneering naval historian William James.

> Captains there have been, and captains there are, who seemingly delight in such work; and who were the cruise long enough, would not leave a sailor belonging to the ship with an unscarred back.
>
> Such men, however, are but exceptions. Moreover, they are, for the most part, cowards at heart... The brave officer punishes one man that he may not have to punish 20... When he goes into battle, his men fight like lions, and should they at any time be drawn aside from their duty, they, looking up to him as a father, listen attentively to his admonitions.[7]

If the logs of the ships Durham commanded provide an accurate record of punishments aboard, such occurrences were relatively infrequent. The sorts of penalties he imposed were standard and unremarkable: twelve lashes to a seaman for striking a marine, two dozen for theft, and so on.

His prize-taking in the *Spitfire* had left him richer by several thousand pounds. But in the *Hind* he had, to his obvious disappointment, little opportunity to augment that sum, for he found himself on various escort duties. On the morning of 10 January 1794, returning to Spithead from Guernsey, where he had transported a regiment, he was chased by 'six large French frigates and a cutter'. One closed within range and she and the *Hind* exchanged a few broadsides. Realising that answering the enemy's fire slowed his vessel down, he soon desisted, trusting that she could outsail her pursuers. With two men killed and four wounded, his foresail in tatters from French shot, and his rigging and tackle very badly damaged, he ordered his crew to protect themselves from further onslaught by lying down on deck. Only he, the first lieutenant and the master remained standing as visible targets as the ship ploughed onwards.

The French, however, gained on him, and it was with relief that he noticed two British ships of the line to leeward, off Portland Bill. In a report to the Admiralty, he suggested that the sight of these two vessels probably convinced his pursuers to abandon the chase. His memoir – and we may make of this what we will – tells a more dramatic story. In dire peril of being captured, he made distress signals, but the British ships failed to respond. He therefore sent an officer to remonstrate with them. Since the ship's tackle was virtually destroyed, the boat could not be lowered. Fortunately, however, he had recently bought a lightweight gig, which was lifted out by hand. When the officer got aboard the larger of the two British ships, the *Impregnable*, 90 (Captain George Westcott, Durham's former shipmate), he learned that she and the *Majestic*, 74 (Captain Charles Cotton) were on their way from Plymouth to Portsmouth. The vessels were newly fitted out and inadequately manned, and consequently kept close inshore. When the *Hind* signalled, they had suspected that she was a French decoy attempting to lure them within range of the squadron's guns. They now hauled their wind and bore down to his assistance, and the enemy sheered off. The *Hind*, it is certain, had been very lucky, and on the afternoon of 14 January she put into Spithead for repairs.[8]

Durham then received orders to proceed to Dover. George III's seventh son, Prince Adolphus Frederick (later Duke of Cambridge), had recently been appointed a colonel in the Hanoverian army and required passage to Ostend. But when the *Hind* arrived at Dover Durham found that the prince had already sailed, and he returned to Spithead. It seemed that he was destined for Ostend after all, for the Admiralty ordered him to escort transports carrying several cavalry regiments to that port. But their arrival at Portsmouth was delayed.[9]

While awaiting fresh instructions Durham contacted the relevant authorities requesting that the *Hind* 'be supplied with Sky Rockets and false fires' and that she 'be filled with Midship bolts for the trains of the Guns. As also with a Barricade on the Forecastle.'[10] He also wrote to his mother's frequent correspondent, the sharp and opinionated old Aunt Betty, who kept her letters going with the aid of her great-niece, of a 'black secretary', and of a local schoolmaster. She showed great pride in Durham's achievements. 'When I had the pleasure of seeing you at Coltness, you was so good as to express a wish to see the letters sent me by the committee of merchants in London', he now reminded her.

I have the satisfaction to enclose our correspondence. I am in hopes of sailing in a few days on a cruise, and hope to be more fortunate than in the last – in taking prizes – although I must own we were particularly lucky in escaping from

the French frigates. They are making every preparation on the coast of France
for landing in this country, but [you should] have no idea they will be so mad as
to attempt it. I am well convinced that if they do not one will ever return." [11]

However, to his dismay, on the immediate horizon there proved to be no
rich prizes, only merchantmen and transports needing escorts. In company
with the *Fox*, 32 (Captain Thomas Drury), the *Hind* soon set sail for the
Mediterranean with a convoy. In June, having revictualled at Gibraltar, she
joined the *Fox* and the *Thalia*, 36 (Captain Richard Grindall), in sailing
from the Gulf of Cadiz with a convoy of 157 cargo-laden vessels bound
for the Downs. Both Drury and Grindall were considerably more senior
to and experienced than Durham. Drury had been posted in 1782, and
Grindall, destined to command a ship of the line at Trafalgar, in 1783.
Yet before the convoy reached the Channel they had by some mischance
parted company with it, so that the responsibility of bringing the huge
and valuable convoy through the most hazardous part of the voyage, past
a coast teeming with enemy privateers, devolved upon Durham. It was a
formidable strain for the young captain, and a stern test of his ability, but
he succeeded in bringing them all safely into the Downs. The merchants
at Lloyd's, suitably impressed and profoundly grateful, suggested to the
Admiralty that he be somehow rewarded. [12]

More convoy duty ensued. The *Hind* accompanied transports of troops
to Guernsey and to Flushing in August and September. During these
procedures Durham and the 80th Regiment's young lieutenant-colonel, the
Hon. Henry Paget, heir to the Earl of Uxbridge, had the honour of dining
with William Pitt and Henry Dundas at Walmer Castle, near Deal, and
joining them in a shooting party. Over dinner there were intimations that
he would soon have a small squadron of frigates under his command, but
rather than get his hopes up only to have them dashed he wisely remained
sceptical. However, a wonderful tribute to his ability was on the way. [13]

Several factors convinced the Admiralty, earlier that summer, to
supplement the 38s, the heaviest frigates in service since their introduction
during the American War of Independence, with counterparts to France's
new *rasées*, powerful frigates which were cut-down small 74s. There was,
for instance, Durham's narrow escape in January from six frigates defined
as 'large'; there was the taking in April of one of them, the *Pomone*, 44, the
first French frigate armed with 24-pounders to fall into British hands, a
ship described by her captor, Sir John Borlase Warren, as 'supposed to be
the finest frigate' the enemy possessed; and there was the narrowly averted

defeat in June by four French frigates, two of them *rasées*, of Sir James Saumarez's frigate squadron, consisting of three vessels based at Guernsey. Added to all that, there were fears that French frigates hunting in squadrons would mean aggravated danger for British merchant ships.[14]

Accordingly, three crack new British frigates, the *Anson*, the *Indefatigable*, and the *Magnanime*, all mounting 44 guns, and each having an establishment of 310 men, were converted from 64s. Launched in 1781 by the celebrated Georgiana, Duchess of Devonshire, the *Anson* as a ship of the line had taken part in Rodney's victory in April the following year. At the beginning of October, when the cut-down *Anson* was being fitted out and nearing completion at Chatham, the *Hind* put into the Downs, 'riding by the sheet anchor which is the only one that is trustworthy on board'.[15] Command of the *Anson*, as of the other crack frigates, was keenly sought by a number of senior captains. While shipwrights put the finishing touches to her she attracted a great deal of attention. There were twenty-six 24-pounders on her upper deck. On her quarterdeck she carried eight 12-pounders and four 42-pounder carronades; on her forecastle there were four 12-pounders and two 42-pounder carronades. Little did Durham realise, as he made his way to London, that he was about to obtain command of her – and without marshalling any supporters to solicit it for him. The appointment, in no small measure his reward for succeeding where Drury and Grindall had failed, was a triumph for a man who had been a post-captain for just sixteen months. After all, command of the *Indefatigable* would go to no less an officer than the great Sir Edward Pellew, who like Warren commanded a frigate squadron stationed on the coast of Cornwall. Pellow had been posted in May 1782 while Durham was still a midshipman, and the Honourable Michael de Courcy, posted in 1783, would get the *Magnanime*, destined for the Irish station under Vice-Admiral Robert Kingsmill. All this showed how highly esteemed Durham's seamanship had become in the boardroom of the Admiralty.

As he excitedly explained to his mother, Lord Chatham in a personal interview had offered him command of the *Nonsuch*, of 64 guns:

but I thought her a bad ship and I declined her. He then told me my service deserved any ship he had to give, even the *Anson*, that sixteen old Officers had applied for. Of course I begged his Lordship would have the goodness to give her to me, which he did by return of post, and told me he would man her for me. You may suppose my getting command of this ship has given offence to a number of Officers. I have not had any person to ask his Lordship. I left myself in his hands, from the time he made me a Master and Commander. I find a good friend in Sir Charles Middleton, by what means I know not.[16]

Durham's reluctance to accept the *Nonsuch* was understandable. The 64s had not been highly thought of as ships of the line for nearly two decades, for their limitations in battle, compared to more powerful vessels, had become appreciated during the American War of Independence, and Britain had built no more since that time. They were, as a modern expert comments, 'always a weak link in the battle line and a source of concern to the admiral commanding'.[17] The *Nonsuch* had been launched in 1774, seen service in the Channel, the Bay of Biscay, and at the battle of the Saintes, but would, not long after Durham's rejection of her, be relegated to the function of floating battery. He might have added that not only did he consider her 'a bad ship' but if he were her captain he would have far less scope for amassing prize money than as captain of a frigate, especially a large one. The *Anson* offered the main chance of making his fortune. As for Vice-Admiral Middleton (later Lord Barham), a lord commissioner of the Admiralty, his distant family connections to Durham cannot have been disadvantageous to the young captain. Middleton's great-uncle, the first Earl of Middleton, had married Grizel, sister of Alexander Durham, Lyon King of Arms; his mother, a Dundas of Arniston, was first cousin to Henry Dundas.[18]

Since Chatham had signed an order for the crews of the *Nonsuch* and the *San Fiorenzo* to transfer into the *Anson*, Durham felt he could afford the luxury of dissuading his mother from sending him any men. He had avowedly become disillusioned with fellow Scots among his crews, who seem to have traded on their common nationality with him: 'I do not wish to have any countrymen, they expect more and do less than any set of people.' With characteristic efficiency he had, by December, got the *Anson* fully ready to join Borlase Warren's frigate squadron, which was operating out of Falmouth under Admiralty orders independent of Lord Howe's Channel Fleet. In the *Anson* Durham 'displayed consummate gallantry, and exercised the soundest judgment, which led to the most glorious results'.[19]

Warren, his new chief, came from Nottinghamshire gentry stock, and had inherited a baronetcy. Ten years older than Durham, he had been intended for the Church, had (most unusually for a member of the fighting services) taken a degree at Cambridge, and was urbane and literary-minded, with 'much the air and appearance of a man of rank and fashion', according to a naval colleague. He 'was very popular and deservedly so; for his services were generally successful and he was a man of benevolent feelings and cheerful temper'. St Vincent observed that he 'knows nor fears dangers of any kind'.[20]

Like an admiral of an earlier generation, the Cornishman Edward Boscawen, Warren urged Falmouth's merits as a naval base. Owing to trade with Portugal, to its pilchard fisheries, and its status as the base for packet vessels sailing to the Iberian peninsula and to America, Falmouth had established itself as a commercial port. Warren knew that with a westerly wind his ships could reach Brest from there in twenty-four hours. He appreciated Falmouth's outstanding natural harbour, guarded by the castles of St Mawes and Pendennis. It provided a snug and extensive anchorage for the Royal Navy in any wind. It was from there that the ships of his squadron, soon to have the *Anson* among them, made their forays along the French coast.[21]

Durham was glad that 'every Officer on the ship are my own people, and all come by my application'. All who saw her agreed with him that the *Anson* was the finest frigate ever fitted out in Britain. 'If she does but sail', they usually added; 'which I have no doubt of', he countered (perhaps mindful that all the 64s chosen for conversion to frigates had been selected owing to their good sailing reputations). Alas, appearances were deceptive. In January 1795 the ship arrived at Falmouth 'after a boisterous passage' from the Downs that saw her rolling very deeply. Part of the problem was that she was equipped with masts and spars suitable not for a ship of her original class but for a 50-gun vessel. When Durham got to Falmouth he found an interrogator waiting. Since work on the *Indefatigable* was not yet complete, Sir Edward Pellew was anxious to discover how the *Anson* handled, and 'made particular enquiry' of Durham regarding her 'behavior at Sea, and of her capacity in carrying her Masts and Sails'. He found Durham and all the officers 'firmly of the opinion that the Ship is in her present state under Masted, and that her rolling would be much easier under her present Masts and Sails'. He asked the Admiralty to direct that the *Indefatigable* be rigged with the appropriate masts, but in vain.[22]

On 12 February the *Anson*, with the rest of Warren's squadron, sailed for the coast of Brittany. But two days later, amid 'fresh breezes and a heavy sea', a mishap occurred which had her 'drifting considerably to leeward'. As Durham informed the Admiralty, 'from labouring so very hard' in that sea, her maintopmast and topsail yard were carried away, her fore topmast and fore and main crosstrees were sprung, and some of her chain and futtock plates were lost. 'The misfortune which happened to the *Anson*', lamented Byam Martin, who was acting captain of another of Warren's ships, the

Artois, during the sick leave of Captain Sir Edmund Nagle, 'prevented us making very large fortunes, for being obliged to assist her led us away from a convoy that consisted of three corvettes.'[23]

Durham put into St Mary's Road in the Scilly Isles to repair, but since it proved impossible to correct the vessel's defects at sea he was ordered by Warren to take her round to Plymouth. There a court martial took place on the *Anson*'s gunner, who was found guilty of neglect of duty and drunkenness and dismissed the ship. Durham, meanwhile, wrote a strong letter to the Navy Board, which had rejected his request for additional iron ballast and told him him to make do with more shingle instead. He pointed out that he had on board 70 tons of iron, whereas the *Magnamine* had 120. 'As for taking in more Shingle, that is out of our power having taken in at different times 200 Tons (in order to bring the ship down to the Water Line, expressed in the plan from the Board) which has filled the ship so full that it was impossible to get a single thing down the Hatchway.' On arrival in Plymouth her hold had been emptied, in the expectation of receiving the requested iron ballast:

> but finding you are not inclined to grant it, it has totally overset the plan, and she is being ordered immediately to sea. I must proceed to stow her, which I am sorry to find will be exactly the same as on her arrival. The consequences of which I am much afraid will not be more fortunate than the last cruise.

Durham was to find repeatedly that, being 'deep in the Water', she sailed 'much better when leaving a port' than she did after several days continuously at sea, a failing that he attributed to insufficient ballast.[24]

Around this time the Admiralty sought further information regarding the *Anson*'s masts and spars. It requested Durham to furnish 'a particular account' of the damage she had sustained. After all, she and the other crack frigates had been especially created to perform vital functions in the current emergency, and it made no sense to tolerate defects which compromised their efficiency. The essential obstacle was reluctance to withdraw them from service in order for the requisite modifications to be carried out. One by one, though, each ship was refitted with the masts and spars of a 64. It was the *Indefatigable*'s turn in the spring of 1795, the *Anson*'s during the late summer of that year, and the *Magnamine*'s in the autumn. Nevertheless, as a modern expert on the ships of Nelson's era has pointed out:

Unfortunately, there is evidence that even the enlarged spar-plan never entirely solved the problem. The *Anson* certainly retained a reputation as a poor heavy-weather ship, and continued to roll her spars out...

These characteristics restricted the suitable employment for the ship, making the close-blockade duties often assigned to the big frigates decidedly dangerous.[25]

Several weeks before the refitting of her masts was carried out, the *Anson* took part in a celebrated expedition to the coast of France masterminded by a Breton nobleman, Comte Joseph de la Puisaye, in conjunction with an initially sceptical British government. Puisaye aimed at a huge concerted operation in Brittany against the revolutionary government by royalist *émigrés* like himself and local insurgents known as Chouans, who took their name from a founder's secret call, imitating that of the screech owl. Consisting largely of guerrilla bands of poorly equipped, half-starved peasants, using farm tools as makeshift weaponry, the Chouans had participated in the originally promising but ultimately ruthlessly crushed insurrection in La Vendée during 1793 protesting the government's persecution of priests and relatives of *émigrés*, as well as its introduction of heavy taxation to finance the war. Vendéan rebels remained active, however, under Nicolas Stofflet, a former professional soldier who had become gamekeeper to a nobleman, and joined the cause when his master's chateau was destroyed by revolutionary troops.

Barbarities and rumoured barbarities perpetrated by Robespierre's regime helped to keep the rebellion alive: wholesale destruction of homes and farms, so-called 'republican weddings', whereby a man and woman were tied together naked and put to death, and 'patriotic bathing', in which royalist sympathisers were towed out to sea in boats with false bottoms and drowned. Stofflet kept up a guerrilla campaign in the woods. Moreover, a truce between the regime's military representative, General Lazare Hoche, and the dashing royalist commander François-Athanase Charette, a young man of middle-class origin who for a time had been a naval lieutenant, soon broke down.

Pitt had been deeply hesitant about embroiling Britain in a venture of the kind proposed by Puisaye, which was that a descent of *émigré* forces would take place in Brittany during the summer of 1795, landed by a British squadron and financed by Britain. But he was persuaded by the signs of profound discontent among the French populace with their new republic. Robespierre's reign of terror had been followed by an alarming counter-terror: the currency was devalued; the cost of living soared; wary peasants hoarded corn and there were bread shortages; unemployment among artisans was rife. In these circumstances Puisaye's proposal seemed to offer the best prospect of restoring stable government to France, and with it the onset of a just and honourable peace. Puisaye assured Pitt that as soon as the British squadron bringing the *émigré* forces appeared off the French coast the disaffected would rise up in droves to throw in their lot with the royalist cause.

Five *émigré* regiments were therefore formed. There was the 600-strong Regiment d'Hector, named after the expected commander of the venture, Comte Charles-Jean d'Hector, who had enjoyed a distinguished career at sea; it consisted mainly of officers of the old French navy, who of course had been made redundant at the Revolution. There was the Regiment d'Hervilly, named after the Comte d'Hervilly, a distinguished army officer who played a prominent part in organising the expedition; its 1,287 members belonged mainly to a royalist regiment which had been based at Toulon and was evacuated from that port by Lord Hood in 1793 when he was British naval commander-in-chief in the Mediterranean. There was the Regiment du Dresnay, composed of some 526 Bretons; the Regiment La Chatre, consisting of 472 troops led by Comte Claude Louis de la Chatre, who would one day serve as France's ambassador to the court of St James; and the 500-strong Regiment Rotalier. Supplementing these were about twenty artillerymen from Toulon.[26]

Plenty of officers had been found for these regiments, but not enough rank and file. Unwisely, therefore, recruits were obtained from among French prisoners of war in British custody. Faced with this serendipitous route to freedom many feigned new-found monarchist sympathies and were accepted: 'a measure', Durham recalled, 'which nearly proved fatal to the expedition, as they exhibited a spirit of mutiny almost immediately after the fleet sailed'.[27] This fleet – or rather squadron – was commanded by Warren, hoisting a broad pennant aboard the *Pomone*, 44, which he had captured from the French the previous year. (Like the *Babet*, 22, captured by the British at the same time, she had apparently been one of the five frigates that had almost captured the *Hind*.) In addition to Durham's *Anson*, and several gunboats and cutters, Warren's vessels and their captains were: the *Robust*, 74 (Edward Thornbrough), *Thunderer*, 74 (Albemarle Bertie), *Standard*, 64 (Joseph Ellison), *Arethusa*, 38 (Mark Robinson), *Artois*, 38 (Sir Edmund Nagle), *Concorde*, 36 (Anthony Hunt), and *Galatea*, 32 (Richard Goodwin Keats). Such secrecy surrounded preparations that even Vice-Admiral William Cornwallis, commanding a squadron off Ushant, was unaware of it all.[28]

Having taken aboard stores at Spithead, the *Anson* anchored in the Solent on 11 June with the rest of the squadron. The regiments were due to embark at Lymington the following day. Since Durham spoke fluent French, Warren gave him the delicate task of explaining to Comte d'Hector that the secretary at war, William Windham, wished to see him in London urgently. The count, who was seventy-three, rightly guessed that this sudden summons was a ploy by the British government to detain him while the force sailed. With tears in his eyes he told Durham that he knew exactly what Windham's message meant: 'I am not to command the expedition.' Indeed Puisaye and d'Hervilly would now be in charge, the former having supreme control once the troops reached France.[29]

The regiments embarked as scheduled. They apparently consisted of at least 3,405 men – Warren would later report 4,574 – and 300 horses. Durham's ship received an entire regiment and fourteen officers, including d'Hervilly and de la Chatre. On the afternoon of 14 June the squadron set sail from Yarmouth Roads, Isle of Wight, for Quiberon Bay. Attached to it was a convoy of up to fifty transports carrying clothing, arms and ammunition for 16,000 insurgents. The main body of the Channel Fleet, commanded by Howe's deputy, Lord Bridport, provided the expedition with an escort between Ushant and the Pointe de Penmarch. Then Bridport's ships hauled their wind northward, expecting to find a French fleet under Rear-Admiral Louis-Thomas Villaret-Joyeuse at Brest.[30]

Villaret had the previous year been defeated by Lord Howe in the Atlantic on what has gone down in Britain's annals as 'The Glorious First of June'. It was the opening great sea-battle of the war, a hard-fought and bloody engagement which was to stand as Britain's biggest triumph of the contest against revolutionary and Napoleonic France until Trafalgar. It also broke the career of Durham's old nemesis, Captain Molloy, who in the fast-sailing *Caesar*, 80, had led the British line into action. Apparently preferring to attack his French counterpart from her weather quarter, he had made no attempt to attack her stern or pass behind her to leeward. Instead, soon after battle commenced, he dropped astern and brought-to more than 500 yards to windward. At his subsequent court martial he explained that, as he tried to take the weather quarter, the starboard quarter-block of the tiller-rope became jammed in the sheave owing to the effects of an enemy shot, which prevented the rudder from moving. He was cleared of cowardice, but convicted of not taking his proper station, and dismissed from his command.[31]

But now, unbeknown to Bridport, Villaret had sailed to save a French convoy from capture by Cornwallis's squadron of four 74s and two frigates.

There had been a confrontation on 17 June, following which Cornwallis had undertaken a successful and highly-praised retreat to Plymouth to warn that the enemy was at sea, and Villaret, during a gale, had taken shelter at Belle-Île, the largest of the islands off the Breton coast, due south of Quiberon. On 18 June Warren's look-out vessel, the *Arethusa*, sighted Villaret's 'thirteen sail, three razées of two decks, eight or nine frigates, two brigs and a cutter'. The *Anson*, stationed between Captain Robinson's *Arethusa* and the rest of the squadron, relayed the news to Warren, who immediately made the signal to tack and formed his ships in line to protect the transports. A despatch vessel (a *chasse-marée*) under the order of Captain Keats of the *Galatea*, as well as the *Experiment* lugger and the *Thunderer*, were sent in search of Lord Bridport.[32]

Alerted to the situation by the despatch vessel, Bridport and his fleet steered to Warren's aid. On the morning of 22 June the French and British fleets came within sight of one another: 'saw a strange fleet in the ESE, and Lord Bridports fleet between us and the strange fleet crowding all sail in chace [sic] of them', noted Durham's log. Warren sent his three ships of the line to Bridport, as the latter ordered. He instructed the convoy to remain to windward, 'and went down with the four frigates to give all the assistance in my power'.[33]

Villaret was outnumbered; his officers, replacements for those employed under the *ancien régime*, lacked experience, and his crews were a poorly trained and ill-disciplined rabble. He hoped for a calm and orderly retreat to Lorient (a naval bastion which had been formerly the shipping hub of France's equivalent to the East India Company), but given the circumstances this did not occur. By daylight on 23 June, as the French were rounding the steep-sided rocky coast of the Île de Groix, about four miles from Lorient, Bridport's van caught up with their rear. A partial engagement took place that morning from a quarter to six until half-past nine, in which, wrote Warren, 'I could only be a spectator, though very near'. He did, however (reputedly by the trick of disguising the *Pomone*'s figurehead 'with a huge red Cap of Liberty, decked with a tricolor cockade') get close enough to the French frigate *Tribune*, 36, to fire 'two or three broadsides' into her. He also 'was fortunate enough... to intimidate' another enemy vessel, which 'considered us as the advance-ship of our fleet, and instantly cut and ran' into Lorient. Battle ended with Bridport's capture of the *Alexandre*, *Formidable*, and *Tigre*, all of 74 guns; the latter two were fine new vessels. The other French ships escaped towards Lorient. For some hours, however, low tide prevented them from anchoring in the harbour, and Bridport could almost certainly have destroyed them had he not considered it inadvisable to risk his fleet so close in shore.[34]

After the action Warren's squadron kept company with Bridport's fleet as far as Belle-Île. As they approached that island's southern tip on 25 June 'the fog came on so thick with rain' that Warren had never experienced a situation 'so difficult'. That evening the *Pomone*, *Anson*, and their consorts came to in eighteen or nineteen fathoms of water near the rocky shore of Hoëdic, a tiny island between Belle-Île and the mainland. The following afternoon they anchored in Quiberon Bay, on the sheltered eastern side of the nine-mile-long Quiberon peninsula. Protected from the westerly and south-west gales that regularly assailed the other coast of the peninsula, and out of range of the district's forts, this secure and spacious anchorage was an ideal spot for disembarking the troops. That evening Warren conferred with Puisaye and d'Hervilly about a precise spot to land, and at daybreak on 27 June the troops were put ashore by the boats of the squadron near Carnac. Nearby was the narrow isthmus of Penthièvre, a sandy strip linking the peninsula to the mainland. Watched by crowds of supporters on shore – 'a ragged-looking set, armed with cutlasses, muskets, pikes, &c.', recalled Durham – the Comte d'Hervilly and thirteen other officers aboard the *Anson* were the first to disembark, for Warren had directed Durham and Keats to lead the operation. Overcome with emotion at being again in France, these *émigrés* knelt and kissed their native soil.[35]

A body of 200 revolutionary troops put up a token attempt to foil the landing, fleeing when a British gunboat opened fire. Thirty of them were killed by a company of 700 Chouans marching to the rendezvous under the command of Chevalier Vincent de Tinteniac, who had gone ahead of the *émigrés* to forge links with local people. The only loss to the expedition so far were forty horses, which had succumbed to cold weather during the voyage. In the days immediately following embarkation the squadron was preoccupied with landing the great stores of arms and ammunition. 'I never saw so affecting a scene as the reception of the troops', Warren told Bridport. 'Old men and young cried; and men, women and children brought butter, eggs, milk, bread, wine and whatever they had, both to our people and the troops, and would not receive a farthing in payment.' The Quiberon peninsula, he would later inform Spencer, was 'large enough to hold an encampment of 20,000 men, and unites all the advantages of a port'. By 29 June he had distributed weapons to 'ten or twelve thousand Chouans, and they are still coming in, and the beach resembles a fair'. He was 'happy to say that from every appearance the business will succeed if properly sustained and protected by the British government'.[36]

The last point needed to be made, for there were problems. Although the Chouans were 'numerous and zealous' they were 'as wild as Indians', and 'like all irregulars they are uncertain for any distant expedition'. The married men were prone to return home from time to time, 'in shoals'. The expedition needed the support of regular troops to withstand 'the best forces' that the authorities would 'undoubtedly assemble against us'. The cannon for the artillery was inadequate, 'there being no howitzers or 12 pounders'. Horses were extremely scarce locally, and would have to be imported from Britain 'to penetrate with celerity into the interior parts and also take possession of some port'.[37]

'Situated as we are now, I shall endeavour to do the best I can, if the fleet from L'Orient or Brest are kept from molesting me', Warren advised. 'I have anchored our small force in the strongest position possible to repel the enemy if they should escape Lord Bridport, and to guard the transports that are with us.' He wished that he had more unrated craft, and he felt keenly the absence of his 'best' small vessel, the lugger *Experiment*, which having gone in quest of Bridport when Villaret was sighted, had failed to rejoin the squadron. He also required more frigates 'for the different services of blocking up Belleisle, the business of convoying powder to Monsieur Charette, and the various expeditions that must take place every day'.[38]

In preparation for Puisaye's objective of taking the peninsula, the *Anson* and Captain Nagle's *Artois* on the morning of 30 June attempted to demoralise the defenders by pounding Fort Neuf near Port Haliguen, at the southern tip of Quiberon. The attack lasted for an hour and a half to 'good effect'. Three days later Warren landed Puisaye, with about 150 men from one of the regiments, 1,300 Chouans, and 250 marines belonging to the squadron, at 'a sandy bay on the east side' of the peninsula near the isthmus. Joining d'Hervilly's waiting forces, Puisaye's men advanced against the garrison at Fort Penthièvre ('Fort Sans Culottes') which, besieged on all sides, hoisted a white flag.[39]

Warren moved eight 9-pounders and four 32-pounders from the squadron into the captured fort. He told Spencer that with the addition of 'some guns of large calibre' the stronghold would be made 'inaccessible on the land side'. There were now some 20,000 royalists on the peninsula: 10,000 were 'as yet undisciplined Chouans', 4,000 were other troops, and the remainder were women and children fleeing from Hoche's republican forces. For while the over-cautious d'Hervilly hesitated, Hoche had wrested the old walled town of Vannes at the head of the Gulf of Mobihan out of royalist hands. To feed the influx Warren had to purchase the cargoes of several American merchantmen. He urgently sought provisions from home, requested more ammunition, and reiterated the need for regular troops.[40]

Charette, with 22,000 followers, was nearing Nantes, Warren believed, while Charles Sapinaud, a Vendéan leader, was heading towards Quiberon with 15,000 men and Tinteniac was in the vicinity with 8,000 Chouans. Warren met with tempered optimism the intelligence that Charette was preparing to strike at the Île de Noirmoutier, along the coast south of Quiberon. On 11 July 5,000 men, including 3,000 Chouans who in Warren's words 'behaved with much steadiness and intrepidity', launched an attack upon republican outposts and a camp by the isthmus, inflicting light casualties. 'It is certain all the people are with us wherever we go; but it is difficult to form an army, however well inclined, at once', Warren reported. 'It now depends upon our support from home to route these fellows, and if once put into disorder the whole province must follow.'[41]

Five days after the attack on 11 July, d'Hervilly, at the head of 3,000 *émigré* troops and a corps of Chouans, made an assault on the right flank of Hoche's army entrenched on the heights of Saint Barbe. But he was decisively repulsed, suffering heavy losses, and was himself badly wounded. The young Marquis Charles Virot de Sombreuil – 'the only active man since d'Hervilly's misfortune' – now assumed command. Warren covered the royalist retreat into Fort Penthièvre by firing from five launches stationed close to the shore, each armed with an 18- or a 24-pounder. After this setback desertions to the republican side became frequent, especially among the prisoners of war who had volunteered for the expedition. Such defectors provided Hoche with useful intelligence about the state of the garrison. Moreover, the royalist leaders were hopelessly disunited: intrigue, innuendo, and mutual suspicion plagued their relationships with one another and undermined their cause.[42]

On 19 July Durham and Keats went ashore to assess conditions in the royalist camp. Accustomed to order and discipline, they were appalled to find all the equipment unguarded and strewn about in disarray. The officers were sitting around playing cards, evidently oblivious to danger. The two British captains warned them to be especially vigilant during the early hours, particularly at two o'clock when the tide would be at its lowest, and the enemy would be able to cross the isthmus. 'The exertions... made by the artillery and others putting things in a state of defence were slack beyond measure', Warren accordingly reported, 'and, notwithstanding every exertion and assistance on our part, it was impossible to get things forward, or to have them take necessary precautions.'[43]

Convinced that an assault on the ill-defended royalist position was about to occur, Durham, before turning in for the night, instructed the *Anson*'s officer of the watch to call him at the first sign of activity ashore. At half-past two in the morning the officer reported that gunfire could be heard, and flashes of musketry glimpsed through the rain-filled darkness. As Durham had anticipated, Hoche had attacked Fort Penthièvre at low tide. An advance guard of d'Hervilly's 1,600-strong regiment had deserted, and with cries of 'Vive la République!', turncoats inside the garrison fired upon their comrades and let the enemy inside the fort. Pandemonium reigned. To make matters worse, many royalist regiments, lacking tents, had been billeted in the neighbouring villages and consequently 'could not arrive in time, and were not able to unite', as a dejected Warren noted.[44]

Although the squadron stood only three miles from the coast it was impossible to get close, owing to a buffeting wind at north-west that blew directly off-shore. Nothing could be done until first light, when Warren signalled his ships to slip their cables and ease towards the south-east of the peninsula, which appeared to offer access. But no sooner had they begun this manoeuvre than a messenger from Sombreuil rowed out to the *Pomone* to inform the commodore that all was lost: the fort had been taken, and Sombreuil requested that, while he covered their retreat, the troops be re-embarked. The *Anson* and the other frigates now worked up to the designated spot, and their boats, supervised by Keats bearing a flag of truce, brought off 1,100 troops and 2,400 royalist sympathisers. 'It is impossible to describe the terror and confusion that prevailed in the whole royalist army; they could make no resistance, being wholly unprepared,' remembered Durham. 'Hundreds rushed into the sea to try to swim to the boats, and were drowned in the attempt; while the republicans were giving no quarter on shore'.[45]

Warren estimated that only 139 *émigré* officers and 740 men belonging to the expedition escaped, along with 1,327 peasants capable of bearing arms, making 2,206 persons in all. 'The remainder are either killed or taken prisoners', he explained in a melancholy despatch to Spencer. The officers and men in his squadron had been 'indefatigable in the cause' and he had 'saved near one thousand troops, and one thousand four hundred Chouans, including all the generals and three hundred and fifty of the artillery. As nothing was embarked from the last transports, everything remains, and all the trains of artillery and powder.' But ammunition, as well as vast quantities of shoes and clothing, had been left behind, and six transports laden with

rum, brandy, and provisions that arrived the evening before the betrayal
of the fort also fell into enemy hands. 'I never suffered more in the whole
course of my life than from the effects of this disastrous affair', admitted
Warren. The 'bloody fiasco' at Quiberon, as one historian has rightly called
it, resulted in the slaughter of what Durham termed 'the flower of the
French noblesse'. In violation of the terms of the surrender negotiated with
Hoche, the brave Sombreuil and many other leaders of the uprising were
marched to Nantes, put on trial, sentenced to death, and shot.[46]

Aboard the *Anson* supplies were getting low. In the formalistic words of
her purser, beer had been found to be 'so Sour and stinking as to be unfit
for Men to drink' and cheese 'so rotten and stinking as to be unfit for Men
to eat'. Her crew were suffering from scurvy, and Warren now authorised
her return to Plymouth. He gave Durham despatches for first lord of the
Admiralty Earl Spencer, telling the captain that he must relate the grim
details of the disaster to relevant ministers in person, as he found enlarging
upon his written outline too daunting. The *Anson* arrived at Plymouth on
28 July and the sickest members of her company were admitted to hospital;
six gallons of lemon juice were sent to her surgeon for the benefit of the
remainder. It was now that the Admiralty directed that her masts and yards
be changed for larger ones.[47]

The day after she anchored, Durham delivered Warren's despatches
to Earl Spencer, and in a specially convened meeting he apprised the
prime minister, Pitt, the secretary at war, Windham, and the master-
general of the ordnance, Lord Cornwallis, of all that had occurred. He
could not help being emotionally involved with its harrowing outcome:
of the fourteen *émigrés* whom he had transported to Quiberon only
two had re-embarked (one was the seriously wounded d'Hervilly). In
this sensitive state Durham was struck by the fact that whereas Pitt and
Windham asked him wide-ranging questions, Cornwallis (Vice-Admiral
Cornwallis's brother) was not at all concerned with the human cost of
the expedition: adhering strictly to his portfolio he inquired only about
the fate of the artillery.[48]

A plan to send a British force under Lord Moira to assist the French
insurgents was still under consideration. 'Though very much chagrined
and mortified at the unfortunate events of the 21st, the account of which
reached me by Captain Durham... we are still willing to hope that matters
may not be quite so desperate as to make it necessary to give up all ideas
of further offensive proceedings on the coast of Brittany, &c.', wrote
Spencer to Warren on 31 July. 'The loss, however, of a post so favourable

as Quiberon, with all its attendant circumstances, was so discouraging an event, as might well be supposed capable of causing some little hesitation or at least some deliberation on what was next to be done.' Lord Bridport had been instructed to give Warren's squadron all the aid he could, but since intelligence reports indicated that at Brest there were only five French sail of the line ready for sea he did not believe that a naval attack on Warren's squadron was imminent.[49]

Warren now quietly took possession of the islands of Houat and Hoëdic, which he garrisoned with *émigré* troops, and then disembarked at Lorient 2,000 Chouans, who had requested to be landed there. These disappeared into the Breton countryside, leaving 500 Chouans with the squadron. Twelve French officers shared his cabin aboard the *Pomone*, another fourteen were with his officers below, and he badly needed 'all kinds of eatables'. His crews, he advised Spencer, would be coming down with scurvy unless replenishments of beer, water and cattle for fresh beef were immediately forthcoming. Owing to diminishing supplies he had sent 1,300 royalist civilians – women, children and elderly men – back to their homes. Warren blamed Bridport for not taking possession of the Île de Groix, a straightforward undertaking which would have ensured a supply of water and vegetables to the squadron as well as 'blocking the enemy'. He despatched Captain Ellison of the *Standard* to Belle-Île, asking its governor to deliver up the island to the royalist cause; a derisive reply resulted, the governor noting that since his garrison was well supplied with provisions and artillery, it was more than ready for a British fleet.[50]

Spencer reasoned that the temporary absence of the *Anson* would not be too inconvenient for Warren, who now had the *Venus*, 32, and *Leda*, 38, with him. Four revenue cutters and four gunboats were also sent out as reinforcements. During August and into September the *Anson* lay in the Hamoaze undergoing repairs and the long-awaited modifications. Her captain's presence in London attracted notice. Not long after his meeting with Pitt, Windham and Cornwallis, he dined with William Douglas, fourth Duke of Queensberry, a fellow Scot who was nicknamed 'Old Q'. Queensberry was an immensely wealthy, irrepressibly rakish septuagenarian bachelor, renowned for his love of women, horseracing, and the gaming table. His other guests included several French royalists, including a former court physician, Père Elysée. Inevitably Durham's account of the gloomy Quiberon affair dominated conversation. Durham always enjoyed being the centre of attention at such gatherings, especially those at which his anecdotage could be given free rein. On this occasion, as so often when he held strong opinions about a subject, he jettisoned tact. His scorn for the way the expedition had been organised reached ministerial ears, and, as he would later put it, he 'soon received a hint to join his ship'. He was not entirely sorry to be rid of London, for many friends and relatives of men slain on Quiberon sought him out to seek news: their grief affected him deeply.[51]

Meanwhile, at Quiberon Bay Warren was growing increasingly fretful. By mid-August scurvy had broken out aboard Captain Thornbrough's *Robust*, but Warren could not order her home because Captain Bertie's *Thunderer*, the other 74 in the squadron, had not returned from refitting. Warren's ships had only three weeks' worth of provisions left, and there were the remnants of the *émigré* regiments, the 500 Chouans, and local royalists aboard sixteen coastal craft to feed. 'I have remained in anxious expectation of receiving orders to send back the [*émigré*] troops here, who are in a miserable state, and to blow up the forts at these islands [Houat and Belle-Île], and to return home, or to have seen Lord Moira with the British Army', he advised Spencer at the end of the month. Scurvy would soon be rife among his crews, he reiterated. A fever had spread among the troops, claiming lives and putting another 115 or so in hospital. The constancy of many of the troops could not be counted on: 'I am persuaded they would not stand a second fire, and many of them join the enemy.'[52]

To add to Warren's vexations, Bridport, whose fleet was watching Lorient, pulled rank and sharply berated him for remaining in the bay. Warren jealously guarded his status as an independent commander answerable not to the chief of the Channel Fleet but to the Admiralty. More to the point, he was convinced that his presence was necessary. 'I have harassed the enemy by frequent attacks at Quiberon with the small launches of the squadron, into which I had put an 18-pounder carronade; and... in the night by being inshore the alarm has been general and constant along shore, and the effect has been the means of cutting off many of the enemy's troops.' Morale was still high among the Chouan resistance movement, and he was doing his utmost to keep it so. Although he urgently required 'lemon juice... greens, beer, and live stock', he was managing to prevent a general outbreak of scurvy by netting the fish that abounded in the bay. He was hard at work on a navigational survey of the bay and the two passages leading into it, which might greatly assist British captains. He had only three gunboats, vessels 'useful beyond measure in all desultory expeditions, disembarkations, &c', and knew the French were building several at Nantes. One of his gunboats did not perform as well as the others. He had no sloops and a single cutter.[53]

Warren had learned from Durham, early in September, that the *Anson* was ready for sea. He awaited her return with impatience. Recent setbacks for British interests in the Caribbean meant that all but a fraction of the 14,000 infantry and 3,000 cavalry that had been due to land in Brittany under Lord Moira were now deployed to the West Indies. On 11 September, the day Durham sailed from Plymouth with livestock, vegetables, and other provisions for the squadron, four regiments under Major-General John Doyle, an old associate of Moira, arrived off the French coast from Spithead: 'thank Heaven, at last', was Warren's comment when he saw the huge convoy on the horizon. But his optimism was unjustified. 'We were to have been made up to 1,000 each', observed Colonel Thomas Graham (later Lord Lynedoch), commanding the 90th Regiment of Foot (or 'Perthshire volunteers') on the eve of sailing, 'but the fresh drafts sent us were so execrable that more than one-half were rejected, and we do not consist of more than 2,800 men. What so small a force can accomplish I am at a loss to guess.' The expedition aimed 'to throw upon the coast of La Vendée a considerable supply of field artillery, arms and ammunition to Charette', he wrote. 'The first rendezvous was in Quiberon Bay, and the intention was to land the troops and stores in the Presqu'ile [peninsula] of Nourmoutier'. France's rightful king, the Comte d'Artois, who on 16 August had embarked on board the 38-gun frigate *Jason* (Captain Charles Stirling), was to land in La Vendée to rally the royalists; he had been warned that if he failed to do so morale would collapse. The Comte had become heir-presumptive to the French throne on the death of his nephew, the ten-year-old Dauphin (Louis XVII to the royalists) in custody amid suspicious circumstances on 10 June. Having been conveyed to Britain shortly thereafter Artois was among the *émigrés* whom Durham had met in London. He was accompanied on the passage to France by 'a large suite', which included the Duc de Bourbon, brother of Durham's sometime admirer, the Mademoiselle de Condé.[54]

When Doyle and his officers saw the planned landing place they baulked, for, to quote Graham again, 'generally speaking, the tide which covered the sands connecting Noirmoutier with the mainland did not bring a depth of more than two or three feet of water, while at low tide the communication was uninterrupted for about... three quarters of a mile'. The republicans, who had recently wrested possession of Nourmoutier from Charette, were too well entrenched. Once landed, therefore, the tempting stores would be vulnerable to attack and seizure by 'the overwhelming force which it was in the power of the republican generals to bring'. The British accordingly asked Charette whether he would undertake to be on shore at a given date, when they could land the stores on Nourmoutier and he could carry them off into the countryside. But he declined, 'stating the impossibility of his exposing himself on an open beach to the attack of the superior force of the republicans'.[55]

In view of all this Doyle and his troops occupied Île d'Yeu, three leagues from the mainland. Their plan was to throw supplies piecemeal into the shore at night, whenever Charette signalled that he was in a position immediately to collect them. He had to be able, of course, to be on that beach across the sandy strip connecting Nourmoutier to the coast. Playing this waiting game, the British took possession of the island on 27 September. But the choice of Île d'Yeu displeased Warren. When gale-force winds blew to the north-west or north-north-west it was a dangerous anchorage, with its rocky shoals and no port in which the squadron could shelter. The squadron in such conditions would have to put in at Houat and Hoëdic, where one or two of its vessels were always stationed. In fair weather it would lie off Île d'Yeu, protecting Doyle's troops from nine or ten enemy men-of-war based at Rochefort. While mindful that the island seemed 'impregnable if attacked by anything less than 40,000 men', Warren believed that Normoutier would have been far preferable in every way: for one thing, the squadron would have been able to liaise more readily with both Doyle's force and Charette's. He also felt that Doyle had too few infantrymen to attempt 'anything that is hazardous, and without some risk in a war like this nothing can be done or expected to succeed'. Knowing that the treacherous coast of the mainland would soon be lashed by wintry gales, Warren was anxious to land them there – along with the *émigré* troops, Chouans and stores aboard his vessels – before the winter set in.[56]

The *Anson* rejoined the squadron on 17 September off Houat and Durham went soon afterwards aboard the *Jason* to pay his respects to 'Monsieur', as the Comte d'Artois was called. The latter was, according to Durham, in petulant mood, grumbling in French about his accommodation, and about the frigate's captain, Charles Stirling, who had for some reason failed to meet the Comte's exacting standards of gentility. Monsieur allegedly complained to Durham that Stirling 'was not a man bred at court' and that 'he had that morning knocked his cook's eye out'. When Durham reported this conversation to Warren the Comte was removed, as he had wished, to more spacious quarters aboard a ship of the line.[57]

But not for long. The Comte proved to be a trial to the enterprise, for he could not make up his mind whether to land in La Vendée or not. While he dithered, he and his retinue were accommodated on Île d'Yeu. It was a bleak place, consisting of a few peasant cottages. Although fertile, yielding some crops, it had been stripped of its farm livestock and provisions by the enemy, so that saltmeat and biscuits had to be severely rationed. There was little pasture and forage for the 2,000 horses belonging to the expedition. The men had to camp in the open air, and many of them died of exposure. The young, daring and devotedly royalist Comte de la Rivière was a frequent intermediary between Charette and the British force, and carried out several highly dangerous missions to Paris. But little was accomplished, and the military spent their time on the Île d'Yeu in what Graham described as a 'tiresome and inactive state'. When, on 23 November, Durham anchored off the island following a reconnaissance cruise as far as Quiberon Bay, he received by boat a message from one of the Comte's aides. Artois, it advised, was enduring a dismal existence and was nearly out of food: down, in fact, to his last cup of coffee and sprinkling of sugar. Durham, whose command of the French language and whose recent appearance among the *émigrés* in London made him a favourite naval contact of Artois and his party, sent the Comte what provisions he could spare from his own private store, and later called on him in person. The Comte, living spartanly in a little cottage with a bare stone floor, put a brave face on things, assuring Durham that he could cope. However, the Duc de Bourbon wished desperately to be taken back to Britain. Next morning the discontented duke and an entourage of eleven were received on board the *Anson*, and to Durham's relief were shortly afterwards transferred from that overcrowded vessel to the *Robust* with which she fell in, and conveyed home. Soon Artois, too, would elect to return.[58]

Cruising along the French coast, the *Anson* was involved in a largely cloak-and-dagger operation. She delivered consignments of arms and ammunition to the Chouans, and in a single drop one night landed weaponry for 5,000 men together with £30,000. By prearrangement, a prominent insurgent leader (Durham had no idea which one) signed the receipt with an authorised pseudonym, 'Jacques des Chemins'. The frigate also conveyed intelligence reports which regularly arrived from royalists in Paris for their Vendéan comrades and British allies. These documents, hidden at night beneath a certain stone in a wood, were collected under cover of darkness. Sometimes wily republicans managed to foil the escape routes of the couriers, a number of whom were on various occasions saved from capture and death by being taken on board the *Anson*. Durham claimed to have warned Midshipman John Wesley Wright, who with Captain Sir

Sidney Smith was liaising on behalf of the British government with the counter-revolutionaries, that he was in grave danger of being rumbled. Wright paid no attention, was captured in April 1796, and like Smith was confined in the Temple, a forbidding medieval keep in Paris, until May 1798 when the pair escaped. From prison Wright allegedly wrote a note to Durham, thanking him for the unheeded warning; he placed it under the door of his cell, and miraculously it reached its intended recipient.[59]

At the end of November Warren ordered Durham to attack the fort on the island of Nourmoutier. The navigation of that coast, made so perilous by seasonal high winds and heavy seas, was relatively unfamiliar to the master of the *Anson*. An *émigré*, therefore, was welcomed aboard to pilot the vessel. He was Comte Pierre-René-Marie de Vaugiraud, a respected naval officer under the monarchist regime, who had served with de Grasse in the West Indies. Unfortunately, as Durham reported to the Admiralty, 'the ship unavoidably got aground, and remained there for some hours, during which time she repeatedly struck so very hard as to induce me to believe that part of her false keel or copper are much damaged'. The operative word seems to have been 'unavoidably'. But when the *Anson* struck, Durham lost his temper. He told Colonel Graham and other military officers who were aboard that they had better prepare to abandon ship, and snarled to Vaugiraud that he had a good mind to hang him. Durham was particularly worried because the ship was in danger of being hulled by shot from the fort. However, his luck returned, for she got refloated with the return of the tide.[60]

The Comte d'Artois's decision not to land in La Vendée – he sent Charette a sword of honour instead – effectively killed the uprising (though Charette heroically fought on, only to be captured and put to death the following year). The Comte returned to Britain as he had come, aboard the *Jason*. On Warren's orders the *Anson* arrived off Quiberon Bay to land troops from the La Vendée expedition, in conjunction with the *Robust*. Aboard Durham's vessel were three companies of Lieutenant-Colonel Harvey Aston's 12th Regiment of Foot, most of the camp equipage of Colonel Graham's 90th, thirteen military officers, thirty women, twenty children, and about £25,000 in gold and silver. He had instructions to rejoin Warren as soon as he had disembarked them, provided he received no contradictory ones from Rear-Admiral Henry Harvey, whom Bridport, having returned to Spithead with a few vessels, had left in charge of the Channel Fleet watching the movements of the enemy at Brest and Lorient. However, frequently missing stays, the *Anson* struggled to follow the *Robust*

that the ship be supplied with forty extra tons of iron ballast. Having learned
from Pellew that the *Indefatigible's* complement had the previous September
been raised to 330, since a crew of twenty less was 'inadequate to the task
of working the Ship from her having 64 Guns Ships masts' and that the
number of men aboard the *Magnamine* had been similarly increased, Durham
requested, and in February received, parity for the *Anson*.[1]

It has been remarked that the Royal Navy 'touched mystic chords' in
the hearts of Britons which surpassed 'reason'. The sails of a frigate on the
horizon, the sight of a sailor inland, with his 'tarry breeches and rolling
gait', and the grand spectacle of Britain's fleet 'lying at anchor in one of her
white-fringed roadsteads', had for British men and women 'the power of a
trumpet call'.[2] Nevertheless, towards press-gangs, on the prowl in ports for
mariners of all descriptions to seize for His Majesty's service, there was often
demonstrable antagonism, as Durham found on occasion. A number of his
crew had been taken ill during the abortive Nourmoutier expedition and he
was obliged to sail for Falmouth without them. Although Sir Peter Parker,
the port-admiral at Portsmouth, had been directed to lend the *Anson* thirty
landsmen from vessels in harbour for the forthcoming cruise, the ship was
still short of complement, and Durham put in at Plymouth where, he had
learned, over 150 idle seamen were 'straggling up and down'. But the town's
mayor, courting popularity with those inhabitants who came to jeer at the
Anson's press gang, made a public pretence of refusing to accept the validity
of its impress warrants. Encouraged by the mayor's stance, the bystanders
scuffled and traded blows with the gang, releasing nearly twenty impressed
seamen from its grip. To add insult to injury, four of Durham's men were
arrested and thrown in gaol, with a charge of assault hanging over their heads.
Their indignant captain, protesting that they were 'very badly used', was
compelled to intercede with the Admiralty to obtain their freedom.[3]

Durham was placed briefly under Pellew's orders, during a spell of sick
leave that Warren had after the Nourmoutier episode. On his return to
duty Warren was instructed by the Admiralty to help cripple France's trade
by concentrating on raids against her merchantmen. On 15 February 1796
the *Pomone*, *Anson* and *Galatea*, with the hired 14-gun lugger *Valiant* in
company, sailed from Falmouth and joined up with the *Artois* three days
later. About half-past five in the morning of 20 March, Bec du Raz bearing
north by east at a distance of four miles and the squadron having just tacked
from the Saintes with the wind east by south, several enemy vessels were
spotted from the masthead of the *Pomone*. Warren immediately made the
signal for a general chase, the convoy proving to be up to seventy French

merchant and storeships steering for the shore. Escorted by one frigate of 40 guns, commanded by Commodore François-Henri-Eugène Daugier, three of 36, a 20-gun corvette, and two smaller armed vessels, they were apparently taking provisions to the fleet at Brest. At about ten o'clock the two leewardmost of the enemy, both merchant brigs, were brought to by the *Pomone* and *Artois*, and about thirty minutes later a ship and a brig were similarly seized. The four vessels were guarded by the *Valiant*, which later took them into Plymouth.

The six largest of the French armed vessels were now drawn up in a line leeward of their convoy. Shortly before one o'clock Warren's squadron, which had responded by forming in line on the larboard tack, gave chase. Some two hours later they were within half a pistol-shot of the French, whose van bore down to support the rear. The two squadrons, except for the corvette which remained on the starboard tack to windward, now engaged as they passed each other on opposite tacks. Being the rearmost as well as the smallest of Warren's frigates, the *Galatea* came off worst, with one midshipman killed, four seamen wounded, a maindeck gun dismounted, and her rigging badly cut. The *Artois*, penultimate in the British line, sustained no casualties, but had her maintopmast stay and some of her rigging cut away. At ten to four, the British tacked, and repeated the manoeuvre half an hour later, when a shore battery fired two shots at them, both of which missed.

Having now gained the wind, Warren hailed the *Galatea*, directing Captain Keats to lead the squadron through the French line, cutting off van from rear. At half-past five the rearmost of these French vessels, the armed storeship *Etoile*, of 28 long eight-pounders and 159 men, struck after a brief exchange of shots with the *Galatea*, which lost one seaman and had another as well as an acting lieutenant wounded. Durham sent a petty officer and ten men to help secure the prize. The remaining French ships stood among the rocks in the narrowest part of the passage du Raz. Since nightfall loomed, and he was unfamiliar with the difficult navigation of the passage, Warren called the chase off rather than risk his ships.[4]

A few days later, back in Falmouth, Durham advised Warren of his continuing difficulties with the *Anson*. 'From the amazing alteration for the worse in her sailing, and which must be evident to the whole squadron, my reasons for supposing her bottom damaged are by no means diminished', he wrote. 'I would therefore esteem it as a particular favor [sic] if you will represent her situation to their Lordships and request they will be pleased to order her to be taken into dock and an additional false keel and gripe to be given her; or such alteration to be made as their Lordships may think will make her hold a better wind.'⁵

These representations at last bore fruit. The *Anson* was refitted at Plymouth Dock in June and her false keel enlarged. Early in August Durham told the Navy Board of his 'very great satisfaction' in being able to inform them that she was 'so much improved' that he could hardly believe she was the same vessel. In fact:

> she is by much the best sailing Ship (large) in the squadron (the *Pomone* not excepting), Sails remarkably well by the Wind in smooth Water, carrys her Weather Helm, and staying almost in any weather, and remarkably easy in a Sea. The only point in which she is yet deficient, is under a low Sail with a Swell upon the Bow. I find great difficulty in keeping her to, and ... [she] drifts much to leeward, and [I] should be much flattered in having the opinion of the Board on that point of sailing. I can only attribute the late improvement in the *Anson* to the Alterations made while last in Dock, as she is stowed in every respect with the greatest nicety, in the same manner that she was before being docked, at which time I will venture to say that she was the worst sailing ship in the Navy.⁶

In their reply, the board's trio of officials recorded their 'great pleasure' at hearing that she had behaved so well, 'and that your Judgment and Abilities have produced the good effects you describe in her Sailing'. They continued: 'as it can scarcely be expected that large Bodies can be weatherly under low sail, and a Swell upon the Bow, we must leave it to you at these times to take such Steps as you shall think proper; though at the same time we would recommend your getting the Ship a little more by the head'.⁷

Durham had, in the meantime, suffered a devastating personal loss: his mother had died on 14 May in Edinburgh, in her sixty-second year. She was devoted to him, and he to her, remembering her decades later as 'a sincere and pious Christian' whose 'desire to promote the welfare of her fellow citizens was unbounded'. In her 'cordial sympathy and benevolence' Largo's poor 'found a never failing help'; she was 'the happy instrument under Providence of raising many of the children of her humbler neighbours to stations of life which enabled them to follow her good example'.⁸ She had been, through their correspondence, almost certainly his closest confidante; he would miss her letters, her faith in him, and her pride and delight in his successes.

On the morning of 22 August 1796, with the wind from the north-north-west, the *Anson* and the rest of Warren's ships were stationed off the mouth of the river Gironde, the approach to the important commercial port of Bordeaux. A squadron of four French frigates had been cruising successfully in the area, and at ten o'clock one of them, the 36-gun *Andromaque*, was sighted in the south-south-west, standing in towards the entrance of the Gironde. Captain Keats's *Galatea*, being close in-shore and far ahead of her consorts, crowded sail to cut her off from the river. By flying French signals Keats tricked her into anchoring near the Pointe de Grave. But she soon realised her mistake, cut her cable, and made all sail to the southward, with the *Galatea* in pursuit. The *Artois* and the *Sylph* had been detached to investigate two strange sail seen to the south-west, but the *Pomone* and *Anson* followed the *Galatea*.

By eight that evening Keats's ship was only about two miles astern of the enemy, but, like the other two British vessels, she shortened sail when a ferocious storm erupted an hour later, and lost sight of her in the darkness. When the weather eased at ten o'clock the *Pomone* and *Anson*, assuming that the *Andromaque* had hauled her wind to the northward, stood in that direction. The *Galatea*, however, continued southward, and was rewarded at eleven o'clock when the *Andromaque* came into view. Keats gave chase, and at seven the following morning was joined by the *Artois* and *Sylph*, whose own quarry had proved to be two American vessels from Bordeaux bound for Boston. Meanwhile, by cutting away her three masts in quick succession, the enemy had run on shore within five leagues of Arcachon. Since she had hoisted neither ensign nor pennant, Keats surmised that she would make no resistance, and he therefore merely fired three shots before sending the boats, commanded by his first lieutenant, to destroy her. The boats of the *Artois* and *Sylph*, commanded by the former's first lieutenant, assisted. Heavy breakers prevented most of the boats reaching the shore, but at length, with the ebbing of the tide, the French frigate's captain, several of his officers and a few seamen were taken prisoner. The rest of the crew, warned that their ship would be destroyed, managed to wade ashore. The *Artois* and *Galatea* were two miles away, and the *Pomone* and *Anson* in the offing, as Captain White's 18-gun *Sylph* fired into the ship which, after several hours and despite some interference from her crew, was eventually set totally ablaze. By steering north neither Warren nor Durham were in sight when the major part of this operation occurred. Warren's failure, in his official despatch, to give the officers and men of the *Galatea* and *Sylph* the credit they deserved was inexplicable, reflected badly on him, and seems to have caused lasting bitterness.[9]

In April 1797 a general mutiny broke out in the Channel Fleet at Spithead over the issues of seamen's pay, prize money, provisions, and shore leave. This development had been foreshadowed in petitions to Lord Howe, its commander-in-chief, at Bath a few weeks earlier. But against his better judgment these had been dismissed as hoaxes designed to discredit the government. Now, while the men defied their officers and prevented them from leaving their ships, delegates were elected from each vessel, and on 18 April petitions to the Admiralty and to Parliament were drawn up. Framed in respectful, reasoned language, these asked that the pay of seamen (unaltered since the reign of Charles II and typically in arrears) be raised and given out promptly, that their share of prize money be increased, their food allowance when in port improved, and time ashore granted after voyages. Following talks in Portsmouth with seamen's representatives the Admiralty caved in, and it seemed as if the alarming paralysis of much of Britain's naval war effort was over.

At this time Lord Howe, who had been ailing for some time and was increasingly troubled by deafness, was formally replaced by his second-in-command, Lord Bridport. Appointed in 1793, Bridport, who at seventy was less than a year younger than Howe, had been commander-in-chief in all but name since 1795 owing to Howe's declining health. On 7 May, when he gave the order to weigh, the seamen refused to co-operate, believing that the government intended to renege on the concessions wrung from the Admiralty. Aboard the *London* Vice-Admiral Sir John Colpoys, on the basis of Admiralty instructions of 1 May directing that further disturbances should be suppressed and their perpetrators punished, resisted this fresh outburst of mutiny. In the resultant affray several seamen were shot dead and the first lieutenant only escaped being hanged in reprisal when Colpoys announced that he, in fact, was responsible for the men's deaths, having given the order to fire. The ship's officers were immediately confined to their cabins and Colpoys, half expecting the noose, allegedly made a will in which he left annuities to the widows of the dead seamen. He and the ship's captain were eventually put ashore.

When this renewed trouble was reported to the government it acted quickly, rushing through a bill granting additional pay and allowances to the seamen. Lord Howe was dispatched to Portsmouth on 14 May with the king's proclamation of this legislation and a full pardon for the mutineers. With that, the men returned to their duty, a number of captains and lieutenants who had made themselves odious to the men owing to excess tyranny having been removed at the request of their crews. Next day a joyful parade took place in Portsmouth, where Howe, on coming ashore, received a tumultuous welcome.[10]

The Spithead mutiny was a good deal more justified and restrained than that which broke out at the Nore on 10 May, and persisted long after the Spithead mutineers had achieved for seamen most of what they wanted. Sinister influences were apparently at work among the Nore fleet, whose mutiny was ascribed to Irish malcontents and Jacobin agitators, as well as to intrigues by anti-government activists opposed to the war. It proceeded along intemperate lines, culminating in the executions of its ringleaders. Warren's squadron, now – like Pellew's, and to the disgust of both commodores – under Bridport's broad command and no longer strictly autonomous, was not immune from the spirit of unrest. During a long cruise off Brest mutinous behaviour broke out in the squadron, which obliged Warren to put in at Cawsand Bay, an anchorage which his new chief preferred to Falmouth. Warren wrote Bridport an explanatory letter, but before it arrived the admiral sent him a sharp and deeply hurtful rebuke for leaving his post.[11]

Owing to the disaffected attitude of its crews, the squadron idled away the month of May at Plymouth. There is no hint of this episode in Durham's memoir, and his log provides, in the nature of such records, only snatched glimpses of the situation on the *Anson*. He and his officers were deprived of their authority, but good order and discipline continued to be maintained. On 10 May a memorandum was read 'concerning the Augmentation of Seamens Wages'. Fifteen days later the port-admiral, Sir Richard King, came aboard with Rear-Admiral Sir John Orde, Warren, and several captains: 'the King's Pardon to the Ships Co was read upon which the Command of the Ship was delivered up to the Officers'. King and Orde were, it seems, impressed with the overall conduct of her crew. Finally, on 5 June, having fired the customary 21-gun salute to mark the queen's birthday, the *Anson* set sail.[12]

Complying with Bridport's orders the squadron, awaiting reinforcements but for the time consisting of the *Pomone, Artois, Anson,* sloop *Sylph,* and hired armed cutter *Dolly,* cruised off Ushant until 16 July. On that evening the sound of distant gunfire attracted it southwards. At dawn the next morning three French armed vessels, the frigate *Calliope,* 36, a corvette and a brig, were discovered in Audierne Bay with a convoy of fourteen sail. These were taking ordnance, provisions and naval stores to the French fleet at Brest. The corvette and brig hauled their wind to the southward and escaped round the Pointe de Penmarch. Unable to follow them, the frigate, after cutting away her masts and jettisoning other equipment to make herself lighter, deliberately ran ashore. A brig, carrying naval stores, dropped anchor near her. About seven o'clock the *Anson* anchored with a spring on her cable, and opened fire on the two vessels. She could not get near enough to do them much mischief, and at half-past nine the *Sylph* ran in between her and the *Calliope,* which he subjected to a cannonade that seriously damaged the hull. At half-past eleven the *Anson* weighed and made sail, to return to the *Pomone* and *Artois,* but the *Sylph* continued a remorseless fire until recalled by signal at six o'clock. Next day the *Calliope* was found to be 'totally destroyed, having separated in the midship body and part of her sunk'. Her crew of 250, having evacuated, were encamped nearby. As many of her stores as possible were salvaged by the British, who had captured eight of her convoy: four *chasse marées,* three brigs, and one transport ship. In addition, the brig that had anchored near the *Calliope* was sunk and a vessel laden with timber set alight; the latter had been deliberately driven aground by her crew, who got away in their boats.[13]

A blow to the squadron occurred on 31 July when Captain Nagle's *Artois* struck upon rocks on the French coast. Her rudder was carried away, she was holed in the bilge, and despite the best efforts of her officers and crew she could not be brought off. Nagle and his ship's company, with all the boat's stores aboard, were saved, and taken by Durham into Plymouth. On the voyage, on 7 August, he recaptured the *Fair American,* a cargo vessel that had been on her way to Philadelphia from London when taken by a French privateer.[14] On 3 September Captain John Duckworth, soon to hoist a broad pennant, praised the 'most officerlike manner' in which, the previous day, Durham and Captain Charles Hamilton of the *Melpomene,* 38, had led Duckworth's *Leviathan,* 74, and Captain James Vashon's *Pompee,* 80, far in towards Brest to ascertain French numbers there.[15]

Bridport was autocratic and difficult. He had often failed to keep Howe informed of his movements when second-in-command, and as commander-in-chief his relations with the Admiralty steadily deteriorated. Pellew and Warren, no longer independent, chafed under his control. He objected to officers of their seniority being captains of frigates, and whereas Pellew stubbornly continued to command the *Indefatigable,* the thinner-skinned Warren in September 1797 transferred from the *Pomone,* her frame weakened after running aground, to the 74-gun *Canada.*[16] Seven months earlier when Warren, miffed at the prospect of being placed under Bridport's orders, requested that his squadron be 'favoured with a cruise off the island of Madeira that we may be thrown into Fortune's way',[17] he was easily rebuffed. As the first lord, Earl Spencer, had observed privately, 'The naval service... is and always must be a lottery as to profit', but the station where Warren and Pellew were, 'from the opportunities it frequently affords of meeting with objects of pursuit and capture has ever since I have been at this Board been looked upon by all the officers in the navy as the most desirable in my appointment and accordingly scarce a day passes that I have not some application or other from officers to be placed upon it'.[18] With this potential for prize money Durham was indeed a lucky man.

Reconnoitring the coast of north-west France, gathering information about enemy ships and their movements, was an integral aspect of his work, in which his fluent French came into its own, for he obtained much of his information from local mariners and fishermen as well as captured sailors. On 27 November 1797, for instance, he sent a lengthy report to Lord Bridport, who was stationed at Torbay, and to whom, since Warren's transfer, he now reported. The nephew of France's minister of marine had been appointed naval commander-in-chief at Guadeloupe, and would be sailing in a brand-new frigate which, with two other frigates and a corvette, was fitting out at Rochefort, wrote Durham. Large numbers of seamen, discharged from French sail of the line, were entering the privateer service. Six privateers were almost ready for sea at La Rochelle. Owing to differences between the government and merchants, France had abandoned the idea of fitting out frigates as privateers. Having been 'very particular in inquiring into all the Instructions from the owners of the Privateers to the Captains', he had ascertained that many intended to run up towards Ireland to intercept British coastal craft plying between Bristol and Liverpool, while others were to cruise westward of Madeira on the look-out for British transatlantic merchantmen.[19]

That same day he entered Cawsand Bay, where the squadron's prizes were brought, with the recaptured brig *Edinburgh* of Leith; as part of a convoy bound for Quebec she had been taken by the French. Durham always had an eye on the main chance, and now that the testy Bridport was in overall command he evidently decided that a few well-chosen words would not go amiss. 'Your Lordship must feel much Satisfaction', he wrote flatteringly, 'with the Number of Captures or Recaptures made by the very judicious arrangement of your Lordships Frigates; they have afforded more protection to the Mercantile Interest of this Country during the last 3 months than all our Cruizers stationed on that Coast had done for the last two years.'[20]

Fears of mutiny lingered, it seems. On 3 December Captain Keats, who had been appointed during the summer to the new 38-gun frigate *Boadicea*, informed Plymouth's port-admiral Sir Richard King that 'The Ship is perfectly quiet and under my Command which I will be answerable to maintain, and execute any Orders that you may please to honor [*sic*] me with, provided our Neighbours (particularly the *Anson*) are in discipline.'[21]

Shown Keats's letter by King, Durham immediately wrote to the Admiralty to defend himself:

> I beg leave to observe to their Lordships that in my opinion [the] *Anson* under my command is in as high discipline as any other Ship... and I feel great satisfaction in informing their Lordships, that I believe, there is not a better disposed, or a more regular Ships Company in His Majesty's Service, as I have had repeated proofs thereof during the Three years I have had the honor of Commanding them, particularly during the late disturbances in the Fleet, and which is well known to Sir Richard King and Sir John Orde, who have had the goodness publickly to approve of their regular and good Conduct; and having no reason notwithstanding the representations that have been made to the contrary to change my opinion, and feeling that the reflections insinuated by Captain Keats may be injurious to me in the opinion of their Lordships.

He requested that a formal enquiry be instituted, should Keats's remark 'make any unfavourable impressions on their Lordships respecting the Discipline' on board the *Anson*.[22] But that proved unnecessary, and at the turn of the year the *Anson* was cruising in the Bay of Biscay in company with the 32-gun frigate *Mermaid* (Captain James Newman) and the 38-gun frigate *Phaeton*. The latter's captain, Robert Stopford, was senior to his old shipmate Durham, as well as to Newman, who were thus under his orders. On the evening of 29 December, off the Ile de Ré opposite La Rochelle, Stopford signalled that an enemy ship could be seen in the south-west, steering east-south-east. 'The moment it was dark', Durham duly told Stopford, 'I bore up, and steered the course I thought most advisable to cut off the Enemy, and have much pleasure in informing you that I had the good fortune to cross upon her during the Night; having exchanged a few Shot she struck'. She had five men killed and several wounded, but the *Anson* had minimal damage – merely a few shot through her sails. To Durham's surprise the surrendered ship was none other than the *Daphne*, of which he as a newly made commander had briefly held the acting captaincy.[23]

Captured three years earlier almost to the day, she had been the first, and so far the only, British frigate to fall into enemy hands (though the Admiralty was to reclassify her as a corvette). Her captain, William Cracraft, had escaped from the castle near Brest where he was being held in appalling conditions, only to be apprehended when he reached the coast disguised as a *matelôt*, and reincarcerated. Among the 276 people that Durham found on board were thirty passengers of various kinds, including Citoyens Jacquelin and Lacaize, two French government officials carrying despatches to Guadeloupe and Martinique. They saved the documents from Durham's grasp by throwing them overboard.[24]

'The alacrity with which she [the *Daphne*] was discovered ahead, and taken possession of, upon a lee shore upon the Coast of Arcasson [Arcachon] reflects... much credit upon Captain Durham', wrote Stopford to Bridport. It was a justifiable remark. Being a coastline onto which the wind is directly blowing, a lee shore is notoriously hazardous for sailing vessels, which risk being driven onto it and wrecked; furthermore, that part of the French coast, being rocky and treacherous, had a fearsome reputation. As soon as the wind was favourable the *Anson*, having taken the prisoners of war on board, escorted the prize into Cawsand Bay.[25] On the way there Durham made several small captures of a sort to which he was well accustomed, and on 8 February 1798, back at sea, he seized the copper-bottomed armed vessel *Jason*, of 12 guns and with a crew of 108, only two days out of her home port of Nantes. Shortly afterwards he recovered an American merchantman from Baltimore with a very large and costly cargo of sugar; she had been making for Amsterdam when a French privateer snatched her. He also captured a French brig laden with brandy and wine.[26] Prizes of this kind were par for the course for the active frigate captain that Durham was, swooping with practised cunning like some voracious and vigilant aquatic predator.

While the *Anson* was undergoing routine maintenance in May at Plymouth Dock, Durham must have had a sense of *déjà vu*. The *Anson's* press gang, on duty in Saltash, was waylaid by drunks, who viciously beat one of its members 'without exchanging a syllable', as Durham explained when asked about the incident by the Admiralty. The principal assailant was 'a Notorious fellow who keeps a disorderly house', and who might have killed his victim had not his shipmates come to his aid. The town's mayor proved more co-operative than his counterpart in Plymouth had done a couple of years previously; as Durham related, he observed that the 'respectable Tradesmen and Dock volunteers should not have been in such infamous company, staggering about the streets almost at the break of day, and obstructing Gentlemen on duty'. (When the incident occurred Durham was ashore himself, quite possibly enjoying a genteeler version of that 'disorderly house' and its ruffianly host.)[27]

On 2 September 1798, sailing in company with Stopford, he learned from a passing vessel that the frigate *Flore*, 32, had put to sea from Bordeaux. He sighted her on a stormy afternoon five days later, and set off in pursuit. At eight the following morning, seeing her topgallant mast carried away, he beat to quarters and his bow chasers fired the opening shots of a brisk action that lasted until she struck at a quarter past nine. Having taken her into Cawsand Bay, he joined Bridport off Brest, who sent him to his old station off the Pointe de Penmarch.[28]

Four years earlier, in 1794, when volunteer corps were being recruited to meet the national emergency, Durham's cousin John Anstruther (who had suffixed Thomson to his last name) raised and became major commanding a fencible regiment of Fife cavalry. Two other Anstruthers and the brother, apparently, of Durham's friend Peter Halkett (posted that same year) were among its officers. Concurrently, a fencible regiment of infantry was raised in Fife by Durham's brother Jamie. Each recruit received ten guineas from the government in bounty money, but it cost Jamie £5,000 to organise the regiment. He borrowed much of the sum from Durham, who was able to spare it out of the prize money he had made while captain of the *Spitfire*. By the end of March 1794 the regiment, with Jamie as colonel and his brother Tom as lieutenant-colonel, had its full complement of 1,000 men. It was sent to Ireland and quartered at Londonderry.[29]

Troubled Ireland was perceived as the weak spot in Britain's defences against France. Largely owing to the influence of Jacobinism, and to the failure in 1795 of an attempt to achieve the emancipation of Ireland's Catholics, the 'United Irishmen' movement founded by Wolfe Tone had become radical and separatist. Tone's overtures to French leaders encouraged them to strike directly at Britain by sending an invasionary expedition to Ireland in the expectation that it would foment an anti-British uprising. Tone constantly stressed that to be effective a French force of between 10,000 and 15,000 men would be needed, and on 16 December 1796 a fleet of forty-eight ships commanded by Vice-Admiral Justin Morard de Galles left Brest with 13,000 troops under General Hoche. It evaded the Royal Navy vessels, which had been blockading the port for months, since they had been blown off-station in atrocious weather. But the following day, amid dense fog, five of the French fleet, including the ship carrying Morard and Hoche, lost contact with the rest. Command therefore devolved upon Rear-Admiral François-Joseph Bouvet, who pushed on towards the intended destination, Bantry Bay. There, a severe prolonged storm and other mishaps robbed the would-be invaders of the chance to land, and they returned to Brest.

Yet the continuing assumption that help would be forthcoming from France buoyed Irish radicals, and the nationalist leader Napper Tandy, more hot-headed than Tone, endeavoured to persuade the French that if they landed they would be able to count upon the assistance of 30,000 insurgents. In 1798 uprisings, abetted by French agents, broke out in several parts of Ireland, during which Durham's brother's regiment was moved to Belfast. The uprising in Wexford was crushed in June by General Gerard Lake at Vinegar Hill. A third, in Connaught, received French assistance, for in July the Directory approved a three-pronged plan: Wolfe Tone would land with 3,000 troops under General Felix-Jean Hardy; his brother Matthew would accompany 1,000 commanded by General Jean-Joseph-Amable Humbert; and the Irish-born General Charles Edward Kilmaine would lead another 4,000.

Kilmaine was on the staff of Napoleon, preoccupied with the Egyptian campaign, and his involvement never materialised. But on 22 August, undetected by the Royal Navy, a squadron of four frigates sailed from Rochefort. Commanded by Commodore Daniel Savary, it landed Humbert and 1,150 troops, four field-pieces, four wagons loaded with ammunition, 30,000 pounds of gunpowder, and uniforms and equipment for 3,000 Irish rebels. Within a few days the squadron weighed, and made it safely back to France.[30]

Humbert attracted recruits, though not as many as anticipated. He enjoyed immediate success against the locable fencibles, capturing Killala and Ballina in swift succession and engendering widespread panic when he seized Castlebar from a defending force of 4,000 militia and dragoons. Expecting reinforcements from France, he took his little Franco-Irish army of some 1,600 men towards Sligo, intending to link with insurgents in Ulster. But at the village of Coloney he was checked by the 300 men of the Limerick militia, commanded by Lieutenant-Colonel Charles Vereker, who was seriously wounded. In the mistaken belief that Vereker's force constituted the advance guard of Lake's army he changed direction and marched towards Granard. He hoped to strike at Dublin, which lay vulnerable since most of its garrison had been sent to Connaught. However, British troops under Marquis Cornwallis, the recently appointed Viceroy and commander-in-chief in Ireland, were closing in on him. On 6 September, at Drumkeerin, he rejected Cornwallis's terms for surrender, only to be decisively defeated two days later at Ballinamuck in County Longford.

Several days later, General Hardy, unaware of Humbert's surrender, put to sea from Brest with 3,000 troops, a large train of artillery, and some battery cannon, in a squadron commanded by Commodore Jean-Baptiste Bompart. Hardy and Wolfe Tone (whose brother Matthew had been hanged following his capture at Ballinamuck) embarked aboard Bompart's line of battle ship, the *Hoche*, leading eight frigates and a cutter. Initially, Bompart intended to sail between Ushant and the Black Rocks, but the sight of Bridport's fleet intimidated him. He got away on the night of 16 September, for despite a strong wind blowing off-shore from the north-east, Bridport had taken his ships northward to Ushant, giving Bompart the opportunity of sailing southward through the passage de Raz unchallenged. Determined to avoid the Royal Navy's Channel cruisers, and to bear down on the north-west coast of Ireland from an unanticipated quarter, the French commodore charted a circuitous course, as Savary had done. It saw him sweep widely to the westward, as if he was bound for the Caribbean, and thence to the north-east. But unlike Savary he failed to evade Bridport's detachments. On the morning of 17 September, when clear of land, he was seen about five leagues off in the east-south-east, steering west-north-west, by the inshore squadron commanded by Captain Keats in the *Boadicea*, 38. With the onset of a light breeze the French hauled their wind to south-south-west and made sail. Keats steered northwards to alert Bridport, leaving the *Ethalion*, 38 (Captain George Countess) and Captain White's *Sylph* to monitor the movements of the enemy. Very early the next day these two vessels were joined by the *Amelia*, 38 (Captain the Honourable Charles Herbert).[31]

Countess was several years professionally senior to Durham. Consequently, when the *Anson* joined the little squadron on the morning of 20 September off Belle-Île, Durham came under his orders. He would in due course pay tribute to Countess's 'indefatigable perseverance' in tracking the enemy, 'notwithstanding the foggy and unfavorable weather' that persisted during an operation that would last for almost three weeks. At noon on the day the *Anson* joined Countess the French were nearly hull-down in the south-west by south; forty-eight hours later, with the British within eight or nine miles of them, they were steering west-north-west. Next day, being now virtually certain of Bompart's destination, Countess despatched the *Sylph* to warn Vice-Admiral Kingsmill at Cork.[32]

On the morning of 26 October Bompart's ships tacked, and for a time chased the *Anson* and her consorts; when the pursuit was abandoned around noon the British immediately shortened sail, and again stood to the south-west after the enemy. The wind grew fiercer the following day and the sea consequently so rough that all the vessels were under their topsails and courses, yet Countess's frigates maintained their position about four miles on the enemy's lee quarter. Finding that the fierce weather had abated, the French gave chase about seven o'clock in the morning of 29 October. Three of Bompart's frigates came up fast, the British prepared to fire their stern-chasers, and the *Anson* sprung her main topmast. Two hours into the chase the *Hoche* sprung hers, and one of the French frigates carried away a topsail yard. The chase was called off. Convinced he would never be rid of the dogged British vessels, no matter how hard to strove to bluff them, Bompart decided to steer openly for Ireland. His ships therefore wore on the starboard tack, facing to the north-west, a manoeuvre swiftly imitated by Countess's squadron. On 1 October the French commenced steering a more northerly coast and increased their distance from the British. The next day, off Cape Clear on the south-west Irish coast, Durham wrote to British officials in Ireland to tell them of Bompart's proximity.[33]

In the meantime Captain Keats, on Bridport's orders, had arrived home with the news that the French had left Brest and Vice-Admiral Sir Alan Gardner, at Cawsand Bay, had sent Sir John Warren, aboard the *Canada*, in search of them. With Warren were the *Foudroyant*, 80 (Captain Sir Thomas Byard), the *Robust*, 74 (Captain Edward Thornbrough), and the *Magnanime*, 44 (Captain Michael de Courcy). Setting sail on 23 September, Warren arrived at Cork in the face of bad weather, and was instructed by Kingsmill to proceed northwards along Ireland's western coast and try to fall in with the *Doris* (Captain Lord Ranelagh) and *Melampus* (Captain Graham Moore). These two 36-gun frigates had been searching for the privateer-brig *Anacréon*, which had put out of Dunkirk with Napper Tandy aboard, landed him on the Donegal coast, and re-embarked him a few hours later, he having learned of Humbert's surrender. Bearing northwards to avoid Kingsmill's cruisers, the *Anacréon* had captured two small British merchantmen. When Captain Edward Brace of the brig-sloop *Kangaroo*, belonging to Kingsmill's station, informed Warren that Bompart's squadron was apparently making for Blacksod Bay, County Mayo, the commodore, evidently assuming that Bompart would land where Savary had, remained for some days with his ships at Achil Head. However, unaware of the fate of Humbert's army, Bompart had decided to put in at Lough Swilly in Donegal.[34]

The *Doris* and *Melampus* joined Warren on 10 October. He sent the former to scout for Bompart between the Rosses and Tory Island, and the latter to spread the news of Bompart's approach along the Irish coast. But a gale from the north-west made it too dangerous for the *Melampus* to steer inshore without a pilot, so she remained with Warren, and that same evening the *Amelia* joined his squadron. About ten o'clock the following morning the *Anson, Ethalion* and *Sylph* did the same, and two-and-a-half hours later either the *Amelia* or, according to Countess and Durham, the *Anson*, signalled that the enemy were in sight. They lay north by west about half a point on the *Amelia's* weather beam. Meanwhile, the *Robust* and the *Magnanime* stood on her weather quarter, on the larboard tack like herself, while the rest of Warren's squadron were on the starboard tack, a considerable distance from her lee beam. Warren immediately made the signal for a general chase and to form a line in succession as his ships came up with the enemy. At about half-past two that afternoon the *Canada* and ships near her wore on the larboard tack and made all sail to the east-north-east. The chase lasted all day, in vile and boisterous weather. As the French were so far to windward – about ten or twelve miles – and there were very deep troughs between the crests of the waves (a 'hollow sea'), it proved impossible to catch up with them.[35]

During the night the British continued on their trail, and the *Anson*, as the vessel charged by Warren with keeping them in sight, ploughed on ahead under full sail. Durham had been dogging Bompart for almost three weeks, 'during gales of wind, darkness by night, &c. &c.', and his men were spoiling for a fight, and for victory's rewards, and it seemed that they would shortly be in a position to engage the sternmost vessel. But the night was one of heavy wind accompanied by hail and rain, during which several of Warren's ships split their sails. At half-past nine, just as the *Anson* was 'closing, in high style' with her anticipated victim, her mizenmast was carried away, and as it fell it took the mainyard and main topsail yard with it. 'Here was a sad disappointment! In a moment all was gloom and despair!'[36] The ship was prevented from continuing the chase and Bompart and his squadron disappeared over the inky horizon. 'Your Lordship will be better able to judge than I can possibly express', Durham subsequently lamented to Bridport, 'what my feelings and those of the officers and Ships Company must have been at that critical moment, after all the many anxious hours we had passed in keeping sight of so superior an Enemy, and to be disabled at the moment we were flattering ourselves of being sufficiently repaid for all our fatigue and anxiety'.[37]

Bompart's squadron had its share of trouble that night. Its progress was impeded when the *Hoche's* main topmast fell, smashing away the fore and mizen topgallant masts and tearing the mainsail virtually to shreds. Then the frigate *Résolue*, 40, sprang a leak which at first appeared so hopeless that

Bompart ordered her captain to run her aground and send up rockets and burn blue lights in an attempt to decoy the British – a procedure which, for reasons that are unclear, was not undertaken. By half-past five in the morning on 12 October, when Bompart's ships were again sighted by Warren's, the wind blew, as before, from the north-north-west but had lost its ferocity; its sudden drop had prevented Bompart running to leeward as quickly as he had expected. The crippled *Hoche*, with a newly bent mainsail, stood in the centre of one of the two lines, some distance from each other, into which the French ships were loosely formed. Approximately four miles away, directly astern, were the *Robust* and *Magnanime*, and somewhat further off, about a point on the lee quarter, stood the *Amelia*, with the *Melampus* a little further forward. Slightly before the lee beam, at a distance of perhaps eight miles, was the *Foudroyant*, and the *Canada* stood about a mile nearer, on the lee bow. The previous day's chase had left his vessels so widely separated from one another that it was one-and-a-half hours before Warren signalled the *Robust* to lead the attack and the other vessels to form a line in succession. The Rosses were then bearing from the *Canada* south-south-west at a distance of five leagues. Although, 'from indefatigable exertions', the men of the *Anson* had cleared the debris left by the crash of her mast and yards 'and by day-break got the ship in the best state for service', she was too disabled to come up. At twenty minutes past seven she was a barely visible speck on the horizon to the south-east, trying vainly to join her squadron, her captain and crew straining their eyes to watch in frustration the signs, far away, of an action commencing.[38]

With the wind in the north-west, Bompart, surrounded, had found his escape blocked in every direction except the south-west, towards which he was already steering. He had, therefore, formed his ships in an irregular line ahead. The *Robust*, closely followed by the *Magnanime*, now made for his rear, but light winds and the swell impeded their approach. When they finally got within gunshot they were greeted by fire from the stern-chasers and quarter-guns of the 40-gun frigates *Embuscade* and *Coquille*, protecting the *Hoche*. After returning fire the *Robust* hauled up her mainsail and took in her spanker, intent on reaching Bompart's ship. At ten minutes to nine she got close enough to engage, having in the process exchanged passing shot with the *Embuscade* and *Coquille*. The two French frigates now came under a heavy broadside from the *Magnanime*, and in putting her helm hard a-starboard to avoid running foul of the *Robust* she, like the latter, became the target of a raking fire from the *Loire*, 46, *Immortalité*, 42, and *Bellone*, 36, which bore up out of the line to come to their commodore's assistance.

They were, however, soon driven away by the *Magnanime's* well-directed broadsides as well as by more distant shots from the *Foudroyant*, and sailed off to the south-west. Putting her helm hard a-port, the *Magnanime* got into a raking position ahead of the *Hoche*, which was also attacked on her stern and larboard quarter by the *Amelia*. The *Melampus* directed a destructive fire just as the headmost French frigates were preparing to flee, and the *Hoche's* larboard quarter was assailed from a distance by the *Canada's* bow-guns. With numerous casualties, twenty-five of her guns dismounted, five feet of water in her hold, her hull peppered with shot, her masts swaying precariously, and her standing and running rigging cut to bits, the *Hoche* struck her colours at about eleven o'clock. She was taken possession of by the boats of the *Robust* and the *Magnanime*, to the first lieutenant of which Bompart surrendered his sword. Warren later sent the first lieutenant of the *Canada* to take command of the prize. Aboard was Wolfe Tone, who before the action had refused to transfer to the fast-sailing schooner *Biche*, which would manage to return to France safely.[39] (Subsequently sentenced to death, Tone cheated the noose by committing suicide.)

Seeing their commodore's ship strike, the French frigates endeavoured to escape, with the British in immediate pursuit. The badly damaged *Embuscade* soon dropped astern, to be taken possession of by the *Magnanime*. After about an hour's chase and a spirited resistance the *Coquille* surrendered, and was secured by Captain de Courcy's ship too. The *Melampus*, coming up with the *Bellone*, fired a broadside but was damaged in the sails and rigging by a return of fire and fell astern, to be overtaken by the *Ethalion*. For an hour and a half Captain Countess continued to chase, his ship being subject to an unrelenting assault from the *Bellone's* stern-chasers. But most of the shot passed over the *Ethalion's* masts, and by maintaining a steady course, not yawing to fire, she got abreast of the fast-sailing French ship at about two o'clock. What Countess described as 'an obstinate resistance' ensued for nearly two hours, before the *Bellone*, with several feet of water in her hold and most of her sails shot away, capitulated. The loss to the *Ethalion* was one man killed and four wounded; her opponent's casualties were far higher.[40]

The remaining five frigates were all standing to the west-south-west, with the *Loire* leading by nearly a mile and a half. In their path was the *Anson*, some seven miles from the nearest ship of Warren's squadron. Warren afterwards wrote that he signalled Durham 'to try to cut them off, and harass their van', something not mentioned either in the *Anson's* log or by Durham himself. In any case, Durham needed scant urging, for he had cleared the ship for action at two o'clock. The *Loire* now shortened sail, expecting that her four consorts would join in a concerted attack upon the *Anson*. Finding that they seemed to hang back, the *Loire's* captain, Adrien-Joseph Ségond, hoisted the British flag over the French, a ploy that seems to have fooled Durham, who allegedly hailed the enemy frigate. He was soon undeceived, however, when the ship failed to shorten sail. Now, at about four o'clock, as the *Anson* stood isolated with the French frigates coming directly towards her, Durham displayed a coolness and courage that won the admiration of his squadron. His friend Captain Moore of the *Melampus* described the scene in his official journal:

> At this time we saw the *Anson* directly to leeward, and in the track of the flying enemy, without her mizen mast. She stood for the headmost of the five ships, in the handsomest manner, and endeavoured to close with her, but the enemy's ship, which we have since found was *La Loire*, not being at all disabled, by carrying a great press of sail, passed the *Anson*, the two ships engaging as she passed. The *Anson* then stood for the van of the four other French ships, and engaged them, keeping up a tremendous fire. The sternmost of the four hauled up astern of the *Anson*, and passed her to windward, firing at her as she passed. The three others were engaged with the *Anson*, until some time after dark; but from the disabled state of that ship, she could not close with any of them, and they at length all passed her.[41]

'At 4', noted the *Anson's* log, 'brought the headmost Frigate to Action, three other Frigates coming up in close order; ¼ past they opened their fire upon us and continued a running fight. A fifth coming up on our weather quarter firing at us in passing, which we returned, our Sails, rigging, yards shot to pieces'. Firing ceased at ten minutes to seven: the 'severe struggle', as Durham termed it, had lasted about two-and-a-half hours, 'the whole of the time within half pistol shot'. The first lieutenant, John Hinton, was slightly wounded, the boatswain dangerously so, and a quartermaster, four seamen and a marine were also injured. In a letter to Bridport Durham praised his crew's 'great gallantry'. In despatches Warren was to praise the *Anson's* intrepidity, and he observed that her captain had behaved 'in a very gallant manner, bearing down on the first ship, and sustaining the fire of the others'.[42]

With her stump of a mizenmast, her main yard and main cross trees missing, and now her bowsprit and foreyard shot through in several places, the *Anson* was in no condition to chase the retreating frigates. But Durham was confident that he had inflicted 'considerable damage' on them. In the gathering darkness the *Canada*, *Foudroyant* and *Melampus*, pursuing the five fugitives, which were making off to leeward, passed his stricken vessel. At nine o'clock the *Canada* sighted one of the frigates, the *Romaine*, 46, standing into Donegal Bay, and an hour and a half later was only one mile to the northward of her. Shortly afterwards came a fall in the breeze, which hampered the *Canada*'s progress. At eleven, getting very near to the land, she shortened sail and hauled to the wind. About this time the *Melampus* saw the *Immortalité* and the 40-gun *Résolue* bear up towards the land, while the *Loire* and the *Sémillante*, 36, hauled their wind to the westward. At dawn the next day, with the wind at about west-south-west, the *Canada* and *Foudroyant* stood near each other, the *Melampus* to leeward. The *Anson* was about nine miles off in the north-north-east: being so disabled she 'was unavoidably separated from the Squadron... and driven a great way to the coast of Ireland', her captain duly explained to Bridport. Later that day the badly leaking *Résolue* surrendered to Captain Moore after a brief token resistance. The *Immortalité* got away in the dark, only to be captured a week later off Brest by Captain Byam Martin of the *Fisgard*, 38, following a brief contest during which the French captain was killed.[43]

In the days immediately following her encounter with the five frigates the *Anson*'s crew was employed in knotting and splicing the rigging, and bending new sails while the sailmaker repaired the torn canvas of the old ones. At one o'clock on the squally afternoon of 16 October a strange ship was sighted to the east. Still basically unmanoeuvrable, the *Anson* bore up in her direction. Durham did not know it but she was the *Loire*, the first of the five to engage the *Anson* four days previously. At half-past three he noticed a frigate and a brig-sloop in pursuit of her. These, it would transpire, belonged to Kingsmill's squadron. They were the *Mermaid* (Captain James Newman), mounting thirty-two standard 12-pounders, and Captain Brace's *Kangaroo*, mounting sixteen 32-pounder carronades and two long 6-pounders. Newman, who had recently married Brace's sister, had been sailing towards Blacksod Bay on 15 October when, at eight in the morning, he saw 'two large ships bearing north'. Finding no response to his signal he chased, in company with the *Revolutionnaire*, 38 (Captain Thomas Twysden) and, far astern, the *Kangaroo*. He soon realised, from the tacking of the strange ships and their efforts to get away under a press of canvas, that they belonged to Bompart's squadron. Gaining on them considerably before sunset, he hoped to bring them to action that evening. In the early stages of the chase the French kept their wind, but gradually edged away, and by evening they and the British were before the wind with all sail set.

Then the *Loire* and the *Sémillante*, having signalled and spoken to each other, separated and set different courses, the *Mermaid* pursuing the former and the *Revolutionnaire* the latter. By seven o'clock, in 'thick and squally weather', Newman had lost sight of Twysden's ship, and shortly afterwards of the *Loire* too. He hauled his wind on the larboard tack, wind north by east, and soon afterwards was joined by the *Kangaroo*.

At daylight the following day the two ships again fell in with the *Loire* and gave chase. Not long afterwards Durham spotted them on the horizon. In mid-afternoon, the little *Kangaroo* got close to the considerably more powerful enemy vessel and bravely engaged. But her fore topmast was shot away and her foremast damaged by the *Loire*'s stern-chasers, compelling her to retire. The *Mermaid* continued the chase alone, never losing sight of the *Loire*. Early the next morning, with both frigates steering north-east, which was nearly before the wind, the *Loire* shortened sail in obvious readiness for action. Firing started at about a quarter to seven, and 'soon became very warm on both sides'. By masterly handling of the helm the *Mermaid* foiled an attempt to board her, and, since she was stationed on her adversary's starboard bow she took advantage of a sudden shift in wind from west-south-west to south-south-west to harass her considerably with relative impunity. Then, through repeatedly bearing away and luffing up, the *Mermaid* closed within pistol shot of the *Loire* and with deadly aim brought down her fore topmast and cross-jack yard. Fire from the French frigate's guns now slackened, but volleys of musketry persisted from all over her. At a quarter past nine her main topsail yard crashed down, and Captain Newman had just given orders to run athwart her hawse and rake her when the *Mermaid*'s mizenmast was carried over the side, temporarily rendering the cabin and the quarterdeck guns inaccessible. There had scarcely been time to clear the wreckage when the main topmast also went by the board, sweeping to his death the carpenter, who was over the side stopping a shot-hole. By this time the ship's stays, backstays, shrouds, tacks, sheets and all her running rigging had been virtually destroyed. She was making a rather worrying amount of water, having received a number of shot in her hull, including a potentially lethal one in the breadroom, and there were others in her wing transom. The foremast seemed about to fall. Two of her guns were out of action. All this convinced Captain Newman to cease the engagement. He had the satisfaction of knowing that the big *Loire* 'was equally disabled with ourselves' and he believed she 'must have maintained an immense slaughter, as we mowed down the troops [like most of Bompart's ships, the *Loire* had hundreds of Hardy's soldiers aboard] with round and grape, and they were perceived throwing overboard the killed in great numbers'.[44]

The leaking, dismasted *Mermaid*, all her bread ruined and her supply of drinking water dwindling, anchored in Lough Swilly on 19 October after enduring the worst gale that her captain had ever experienced. In addition to the carpenter she had lost three killed and thirteen wounded. Her adversary, whose name Newman had not discovered, since her stern had been blackened by firing at the *Kangaroo* the previous day, had been as thankful as he was to haul off from action. Putting before the wind, the *Loire* was soon out of sight. Her manner of steering made Newman wonder whether her rudder had been harmed, and he thought her mainmast would shortly topple, which it did during the night. His ship had been, theoretically, no match for a vessel pierced for fifty guns but mounting forty-six, comprising twenty-eight long 18-pounders, twelve long French eights, and six brass 24-pounder carronades. Despite that, he had given her a battering which lasted about two-and-a-half hours. The *Kangaroo*, meanwhile, had refitted herself with a fore topmast to replace that shot away during her own encounter with the *Loire*. At eight o'clock in the morning of 17 October she had fallen in with the *Anson*, and Durham learned that the frigate he had seen in chase was the *Mermaid*, though at this stage Brace knew nothing of her ensuing duel with the *Loire*. In view of the *Anson*'s defects Durham, feeling that the sloop might prove useful, ordered Brace to remain with him. Shortly afterwards the *Kangaroo* pursued and brought to an American ship under Danish colours bound for Guinea.[45]

On 18 October at daylight, while the *Anson* and *Kangaroo* were together in thick squally weather between Inniskea Island and Achil Head off the entrance to Blacksod Bay, the *Loire* was sighted. 'I discovered a large ship to leeward', Durham reported to Lord Bridport; he added, in view of the damage sustained by the *Anson* a few days earlier, 'fortunately for me with the loss of her Fore and Main Top Masts'. The account in Durham's memoir claims that he 'beat to quarters, bore up, and poured in a broadside in less than six minutes'. But this is not supported by the log, which shows that the two ships did not engage until eleven o'clock. There followed 'one hour and fifteen minutes warm work' in an action that was 'most gallantly disputed' by Captain Ségond. The *Loire* struck at a quarter past twelve, two minutes after her mizenmast was shot away. Both frigates, already crippled, had taken a terrible pounding. The *Anson* lost a quartermaster and one seaman, and among her thirteen wounded were her first lieutenant of marines and two midshipmen.

Her opponent fared far worse, with forty-eight killed and seventy-five wounded. (Badly hurt on board the *Anson* was a young midshipman, John Chrystie, who had a musket ball shot through his left cheek. This fact was cited by Lord Nelson, when Chrystie was an acting lieutenant aboard the *Victory* in 1805, in recommending him to the Admiralty.)[46]

As Durham informed Bridport, the *Loire* was 'one of the largest and finest Frigates belonging to the Republic, presented by the City of Nantes, quite New, and never before at Sea'. She carried, counting her crew, 664 persons according to Durham: her officers, when examined in the prize court, would place the figure at forty less. On board were several military officers, as well as clothing for 3,000 men, 1,020 muskets, 200 sabres, twenty-five cases of musket ball cartridges, and other equipment and weaponry, including a brass field-piece. Durham acutely empathised with Captain Ségond in defeat; their vessels had both been so vulnerable, and the contest so closely fought, that the roles of victor and vanquished could so easily have been reversed. Ségond had, coincidently, been captured by Durham earlier, when in command of a small corvette, the 16-gun *Zéphyre*; he had broken his parole at Falmouth and managed to return to France. In what was perhaps one of his vintage tall stories, Durham later claimed that one of the military officers aboard the *Loire* – no less a person, it seems, than Napoleon's aide-de-camp, Antoine Marie Chamans, Comte de la Valette – told him that just before the ship struck a dejected yet defiant Ségond had declared that he would blow her up rather than surrender, and was about to fulfil his vow when he was bodily restrained.[47]

'I beg leave particularly to acknowledge the steady and good behaviour of my Officers and Petty Officers, and cannot avoid recommending to your Lordship's notice my First Lieutenant Mr. John Hinton whose conduct not only upon this occasion but many others has met with my fullest approbation', Durham informed Bridport. Encomiums of this sort were customary after an action and could lead to promotion. But unlike the first lieutenants of the *Canada*, the *Robust* and the *Ethalion*, which had taken a full part in the central engagement of 12 October, and the first lieutenant of the *Fisgard*, whose duel with the *Immortalité* was considered by Bridport to be 'one of the most brilliant single actions that ever adorned the naval page of England's history', Hinton did not receive his step up to commander.[48] This was no reflection on Durham: there were simply too many hopefuls seeking preferment. It was yet one more vicissitude of naval life.

Durham also paid tribute to other officers by name, including Captain Brace, whose *Kangaroo* towed the prize as far as Bray Head, south of Dingle

Bay, when the tow-rope broke, and the *Anson* took over. 'I am much indebted to him for the services he has rendered me in taking possession of *La Loire*', wrote Durham, in words which would return to haunt both men. Like all the best officers, Durham was touchingly grateful to his own crew: 'as to my Ship's Company they have been my faithful Companions during 4 years in pretty active service, and whose conduct upon all occasions merits my warm approbation'. Meanwhile Brace was writing to the Admiralty: 'I trust that it will appear from Captain Durham's Letter, that the *Kangaroo*'s Situation on the 18th was close under *La Loire*'s stern, and that she did… manifest the Zeal and Exertions of [her] Officers and crew… which I hope will in some measure recommend them to their Lordships' notice.'[49]

Although Durham missed the main action off Tory Island on 12 October, his heroism in the face of the five fleeing frigates and his capture of the *Loire* amply compensated for it. 'Your judicious conduct upon this occasion', wrote Bridport, 'as well as the spirited conduct of your officers and men, gives me the highest satisfaction, and is approved of by me, as I am confident it will be by the Admiralty and the public, and I am much pleased with your activity and success'. A little later Bridport was 'highly satisfied with your conduct, not only on occasion of the Loire, but in accompanying the French squadron to the coast of Ireland'. Only three of Bompart's ships, the *Sémillante* (vainly pursued by Captain Twysden), the *Romaine*, and the *Biche*, evaded capture. Warren's victory was the toast of Ireland, and inspired a couple of patriotic ballads, one of which rhetorically asked:

> But who dare to oppose
> Britain's heroes upon their own ocean?[50]

While the *Anson*, having taken the *Loire* into Cawsand Bay, was refitting and awaiting further orders, Durham went to London and to court. It was not the first time that he had been to one of the gatherings regularly held at St James's Palace for, as protocol demanded, he had kissed the king's hand on receiving each of his commands. On this occasion the man who had once, so fleetingly, been his boon companion, Prince William, Duke of Clarence, paid him a handsome tribute before the assembled throng. 'Captain', declared the prince, 'attending that French squadron for seventeen [sic] days as you did and your capture of the *Loire*, after your action with the five frigates, was a fine piece of service, and does you great credit.' With that, the prince took off his belt and sword and presented them to Durham who, seldom if ever prone to bouts of false modesty, undoubtedly revelled in the accolade.[51]

For averting the invasion of Ireland Warren and his captains, including Durham, each received a gold medal. On 21 November 1798 the House of Lords passed a resolution thanking the officers of the squadron 'for their Bravery and Gallant conduct in the Defeat of that [the French] Armament' and – a sad distinction this – the seamen and marines 'for their good behaviour' on that occasion. Similar resolutions were passed by the Commons. These were read to the mustered ship's company of the *Anson* on the morning of 6 December as requested by Warren, who declared his happiness 'in conveying to you so pleasing a Mark of Public approbation, as well as my own Gratitude for the exertions of the *Anson* on that day'. The Irish parliament also recorded its thanks. Perhaps the most lavish praise of the *Anson's* exploit came from the pen of Thomas Crofton Croker, an Irish antiquarian and long-serving clerk in the Admiralty. He remarked later that when the *Anson's* 'crippled state, and the great exhaustion of her crew is considered', her sharp action with the *Loire* 'must stand amongst the most extraordinary instances of courage and perseverance upon record'.[52]

This adulation was by no means ubiquitous. In such a competitive profession as the officer corps of the Royal Navy, where too many people were chasing too few commands, and employment depended upon reputation and patronage, jealousies abounded and egos could be remarkably fragile. Captain Newman would, fittingly, be given command of the *Loire*, which was taken into the service. But Durham's official account of her capture, published in the *London Gazette*, angered Newman and the ex-officers of the *Mermaid*. They felt that their own part in her defeat had been purposely concealed by Durham in his determination to claim all the glory for himself. Their resentment surfaced in a letter, published under the pseudonym 'A British Seaman's Friend', which appeared early in 1800 in the *Naval Chronicle*, a recently-founded periodical for sea-officers and others interested in matters nautical:

I remember to have heard much, during last winter [1798–99], of the action between the squadron, off the coast of Ireland, and particularly of the engagement which afterwards ensued between his Majesty's ship *Mermaid*, then commanded by Captain Newman, and the French frigate *la Loire*.... I always heard this action mentioned with the highest praise, on account of the great superiority of the French ships, in number of guns and weight of metal, with the addition of having a great many disciplined troops on board. The rules of the service not permitting that any Gazette account should be published respecting the engagement of a single ship, when no capture took place, the public were never officially made acquainted with all the particulars of this engagement...

There followed a brief account of the *Mermaid's* action with the *Loire*, and Newman's despatch to Kingsmill was appended. The letter stressed the *Mermaid's* 'inferior force' compared to that of her opponent, and continued: 'The silence of an Officer with such reputation as Captain Durham possesses, respecting the previous drubbing which *la Loire* had received from the *Mermaid*, had always surprised me; and I have heard many naval men express their astonishment at it'. Quite possibly, Newman's brother-in-law, Captain Brace of the *Kangaroo*, had a hand in drafting this letter, for it mentioned that he 'fortunately repaired the damages, sustained in the first attack of the ship, in sufficient time to come up with her [the *Loire*] again after her action with the Mermaid, and materially to assist Captain Durham in the capture of her'.[53]

Durham, it seems, being away at sea, did not read this letter immediately; it appears to have come to his attention when, later in the year, it was referred to in a footnote to a biographical article about Sir John Warren in an issue of the same periodical. Under the pseudonym 'Nauticus' a rejoinder (of sorts) appeared. No allusion was made to Durham's alleged failure to give Newman the credit he deserved: with an egotism not untypical of Durham, its probable author, the letter consisted entirely of a glowing summation of his own role. It was headed Portsmouth and dated 1 May 1800. He was returning from a cruise on that day and put into Plymouth the following week, but there seems little doubt, from both content and style, that the wording was his; to disguise this he may have persuaded a friend to pen it for him. The *Anson*, it related, sailed from Plymouth in September 1798 and not long afterwards took the *Flore*. Afterwards Durham, responding to orders from Captain Countess, 'cheerfully joined' the latter's little squadron and kept in company for three weeks, despite all hardships, until the enemy appeared. There was the vexation of losing her mizenmast, main and topsail yards in chase, just as she was about to close with the *Loire*, and the ensuing encounter with the five fleeting frigates. In that attack she 'had four officers and fifteen seamen badly wounded; four of the latter since dead; and the rest lost to the service; not a sail left to the yards, standing and running rigging cut to pieces, fore and main masts, fore yard, topmast, and bowsprit, shot through in several places and close on a lee shore'. This was either a deliberate or inadvertent inflation of the *Anson's* casualty figures, or Durham had – which is most unlikely – been in error when he reported to Bridport a few days after her brush with the frigates that there were eight wounded, whom he named, including one commissioned, one warrant, and one petty officer; no fatalities were listed. While this letter to the *Naval Chronicle* neglected to mention Newman or the *Mermaid*, it did concede that the *Kangaroo* 'is entitled to every applause, having carried a press of sail, and greatly assisted to exchange prisoners in a heavy sea, but did not come up till eight minutes after *La Loire* struck'. This was hardly the confirmation that the sloop had been 'close under' the French frigate's stern, as Brace insisted she had been, nor of the apparent fact that she had shot away the *Loire's* mizenmast, which had immediately preluded that ship's surrender.[54]

This letter, by its sins of omission, inflamed the wrath of Newman, Brace, and their associates. A communication, therefore, duly appeared in print above the signature 'Veritas':

> I have lately seen... a letter which respects the capture of *La Loire*, which grossly misrepresents the circumstances. The writer (amongst other things,) takes upon himself to say, as of his own knowledge, that the *Kangaroo* 'did not come up till eight minutes after *La Loire* had struck.' In this he tells an infamous, wilful, and malicious falsehood.[55]

Since Brace became a post-captain a mere six months after this activity off Ireland, Durham's failure to give him what he saw as his due obviously had no deleterious effect upon his career. But his resentment festered, and was ventilated in an obituary for Captain Newman (probably with input from Brace's pen) which appeared in the *Naval Chronicle* during 1813. 'Captain Durham, in his public letter, mentioned his obligations to Captain Brace *"for his services in taking possession of La Loire,"* but without referring to the previous action of the latter with the *Mermaid*. As to the *Kangaroo*, also, the fact was that Captain Durham was much more indebted to Captain Brace than he stated'. To prove it, the periodical carried the relevant extract from Brace's shipboard journal:

> At half past 8, A.M. on the 18th, we discovered a ship to leeward, disabled, standing to the southward; got up top-gallant masts, and made all sail in chase: discovered her to be an enemy. The *Anson*, being far to leeward, came up with her head in a line with the other's stern. The frigate fired a shot at us, and several volleys of musquetry, which the *Anson*, from her position, did not return. We fired our broadside. Immediately afterward, the Frenchman's mizen mast went, and with it the colours, which he did not attempt to hoist again. We

then hoisted out our boats, sent one to the *Anson* for orders, and the other
boarded and took possession of the frigate, three quarters of an hour before
any other came on board. Next morning we took the prize in tow, the *Anson*
being unable to do it.

The obituary went on to describe the letter by 'Nauticus' as 'very inefficient
as an explanation of Captain Durham's silence respecting the *Mermaid*, and
slight notice of the *Kangaroo*'. That letter's assertion that the sloop 'did not
come up till 8 minutes after *La Loire* had struck' was, it pointed out, at
obvious variance with Brace's journal, and 'Nauticus' had at the time in the
Naval Chronicle received from 'Veritas' 'the most pointed and unqualified
contradiction, which stands unrepelled'.[56]

Following the war, Brace and Newman would find in the naval historian
William James someone who would champion them with a fairly mighty
pen, to Durham's detriment. James not only gave credence to Brace's
avowed instrumentality in the *Loire*'s surrender; he downplayed the *Anson*'s
achievement by emphasising the *Mermaid*'s, and commented dismissively
that the duel on 18 October was hardly an equal one: 'whatever chance of
succeeding... the *Loire* may have had with the *Mermaid*, she had very little
with the *Anson*, and none whatever with the *Anson* and *Kangaroo* united'.
Yet Durham's log for the day of action related that 'at 13 Mins past 12, shot
away the Enemy's Mizen Mast, at 15 mins past 12 she struck', saying nothing
about any intervention in the action by the *Kangaroo*. He was evidently
convinced that his ship had delivered the final blow, but it is strange that
if the *Kangaroo*'s intervention did indeed take place as her captain insisted,
'Veritas' failed to mention it in his letter to the *Naval Chronicle*.[57]

That he made enemies was probably not something that worried Durham
inordinately, so long as they were not in a position to do him harm: every
successful officer must have attracted his share of detractors. There was always
something of the buccaneer about Durham. He was ever the adventurer,
sailing close to the wind in quest of self-aggrandisement. His unabashed
opportunism and acquisitiveness – of money, though not, it seems, of the
fripperies, as distinct from the basic comforts, which money can buy – took
on the appearance of an inherent character trait which was perhaps moulded,
and certainly accentuated, by his stark awareness of being a younger son.

Around this time he became involved with a young woman close to the
royal court whom he wanted to marry. Lady Charlotte Matilda Bruce, born
on 28 March 1771, had since 1796 been lady of the bedchamber to the
younger daughters of George III. Her widowed mother, Martha, Countess

of Elgin, was governess to the Prince of Wales's only child, Princess Charlotte. Martha had been appointed to that responsible position – it was certainly no sinecure – shortly after the princess's birth in January 1796 and was to hold it until 1804.

Known to close friends (as well as to Queen Charlotte) as 'Chasse', Lady Charlotte was the only surviving daughter of Charles Bruce, fifth Earl of Elgin. Her mother, born Martha Whyte, was the daughter of a Scottish banker in London of Fife background. Martha had been left motherless as a new-born babe and brought up by her paternal uncle, a Kirkaldy merchant, and his wife. She had married the fifth earl in 1759 and borne eight children, but only four had reached adulthood. The earl had died aged thirty-nine, a fortnight before Lady Charlotte's birth. His sickly six-year-old son William Robert had succeeded him, but passed away within a few weeks, when the family earldoms of Elgin and Kincardine had devolved upon the second son, Thomas, born in 1766, destined to be ever linked in the public mind with the Parthenon marbles. Between Thomas and Charlotte were two brothers: Charles Andrew, who was employed by the East India Company, and James, member of Parliament for Marlborough, who drowned while crossing the river Don at Barnbydown, Yorkshire, in July 1798.

Lady Charlotte's father and Durham's (exact contemporaries) had friends and connections in common, and at least one Fife gentry family, the Prestons of Valleyfield, featured in both their lineages. The earl owned incidental acreage in Largo, where James Durham was by far the largest of several landed proprietors, but his main estate centred on Broomhall, his seat in west Fife overlooking the Forth above the village of Limekilns, a few miles from Dunfermline. A keen improver bent on exploiting the limestone of the area to full capacity, the earl had installed new extracting machinery shortly before his untimely death. As a paternalistic employer he was looking forward to the development of a model workers' village (a venture brought to fruition by the seventh earl, Lady Charlotte's brother, and named Charlestown).[58]

Despite the potential of its lime quarries and coalworks, the estate that the seventh earl inherited, in trust until he came of age in 1787, was heavily encumbered by debt. Consequently his widowed mother impressed the virtue of economy on her children, and would have strictly practised what she preached had she not felt she had a certain status to maintain. An eminently sensible, very religious woman, who was on personal terms with the evangelical tract writer Hannah More and with Beilby Porteus, the evangelical-inclining Bishop of London, she received constant moral support during her widowhood from Thomas Brudenell Bruce, first

Earl of Ailesbury, whose seat was at Tottenham Park, Wiltshire. A cousin of her late husband, and a relatively pious man who regretted many of the characteristics of what he called 'this degenerate age', Lord Ailesbury became very close to the countess's children, acting virtually as a surrogate father to them.[59]

Although born in Scotland, Lady Charlotte was brought up mainly in London, spending her childhood at her mother's small house in Dean's Yard, close to the Abbey and to Westminster School, which her brothers attended. She had lived briefly in St Andrews when her brother Thomas was at university there, but otherwise had seen very little of her ancestral country. She must have spoken in the English tones that her mother considered 'much prettier' than the Scottish accent,[60] and as lady of the bedchamber spent her time with the royal household chiefly in London or Windsor. When the French Revolution broke out she, then eighteen, had been staying in Paris, where Thomas was. When Durham got to know her she was living with her mother and a youthful companion, Louisa Dillon. Although the post of governess took the countess to Princess Charlotte's home at Carlton House, she had her own residence, and had moved from Dean's Yard to Downing Street. Lady Charlotte's education, typifying that of young ladies of her time and class, emphasised social and cultural accomplishments at the expense of academic subjects. She played the pianoforte, loved music and dancing, and read the sort of works deemed suitable for her sex.

Lady Charlotte's letters reflect a sparkling personality and a lively mind, and portraits of her show a rather enchanting brunette with deep chestnut tresses – fashionably powdered at this stage – and a beguiling expression in her lustrous dark eyes. She bore a distinct physical resemblance to her clever and handsome brother, the earl. But a decided obstacle to the sort of marriage her mother would have liked for her, as the daughter of an ancient noble house, was undoubtedly her family's straitened financial circumstances. 'My effects are small having lived far beyond my income in hopes of serving Charlotte Bruce my Daughter and appearing according to the Rank your Mother and Fathers Widow ought to live in', wrote the countess, in morbid mood at Bath, to Thomas in 1796. 'As I did that from Duty I have no remorse being conscious that in my own Person or expence I never indulged in any article since your Fathers Death. I wish I had more to leave but Alas my Blessing is the most I have to bequeath to my Children.' She exaggerated, of course. Still, it was true that Charlotte was no heiress. Martha asked Thomas to make over after her death £1,000 to each of her siblings, and to let Charlotte have the pick of the furniture, which regrettably 'is not much', from the house in Downing Street – should she require it.[61]

By the time Charlotte reached her mid-twenties Martha had begun to despair of her finding a suitable husband. She thought fate had conspired against her, but Lord Ailesbury disagreed. 'I cannot allow you to call your daughter unfortunate as she has almost every advantage it is possible for a young woman of fashion to have, and the things most wanted depend on herself entirely', he observed. The problem was, he believed, that Lady Charlotte's innate vivacity and sense of humour occasionally took an inappropriate turn, scandalising the straitlaced, and frightening off potential suitors of a desirable kind. 'Her spirits at times carry her beyond the bounds of propriety and puts [*sic*] her in the power of her enemies, which nobody is without, to speak against her manners as not suited to her station about the Princess in particular: that Jollity, which the young men call it & like... should be a pattern of good rather than a pattern of bad manners.'[62]

Indeed, Martha herself, in June 1798, confided to Thomas, who was on the continent:

> I am sorry... there is no prospect for Charlotte tho' she has gone thro' a Winter of much Dissipation – much against my wishes and judgment her Conduct is – for after twenty-five tis respectability not Giddy Idle Dissipation that makes a Woman esteemed. I pity her, poor Soul – for she is not comfortable... For her Sake I have wished you Over – as I am sure you would have prevented her doing many things which my Speaking only encourages.[63]

Ironically, not many months had passed since Martha had written: 'Oh that she were well-married. She is now in a Frame of Mind that would make her a Blessing – abundantly prudent and every way a charming companion'. But at the time Charlotte had been unwell. Her mother had explained that the 'Languor she complains of is returned a good deal' and that 'She is thin and don't eat'. Sir William Farquhar, Martha's physician, pronounced Charlotte 'nervous'. Gradually her health had picked up: 'her Asses Milk has done wonders, and her spirits are better'[64] – too much improved it would seem.

'I never write anything I do not think, or that I wish to conceal, yet I should be sorry that my letters went to a snuff shop', Durham's late mother had once remarked to Aunt Betty: she insisted on burning the intimate meanderings that the old lady had received. It is probable that Durham had a similar attitude, for few if any personal papers concerning his courtship appear to have survived, and certainly no *billets-doux*. By the end of 1798, when he was being fêted in high places as the captor of the *Loire*, the couple had reached an understanding. Lady Charlotte's acquaintances realised that Durham had become her beau, and when, on 25 October, Byam Martin's mother, flush with pride over her son's capture of the *Immortalité*, met Lady Charlotte at a 'drawing room' reception at St James's Palace, she playfully referred to their mutual fondness for naval officers. From Lady Charlotte's perspective Durham, though not an aristocrat, was an acceptable marriage partner. He came of good family, with baronets and an earl or two in his genealogy. He was proving more successful than the run of post-captains, and owing primarily to prize money he was already worth £17,503 in Bank of England consols (government stocks) – nearly £1,000,000 in today's money![65] Their mutual Scottishness was an obvious bond, and Durham had the added bonuses of being brave, good-looking and personable, his physical attractiveness enhanced by the blue and gold uniform of the senior service.

Despite her lack of money Lady Charlotte was a prize catch for a laird's younger son dependent for his livelihood upon his own sword. Winsome and animated, she offered him an *entrée* into royal and English aristocratic circles, and to influential connections useful to his career. Her relatives such as Lord Ailesbury (a personal friend of George III) would surely be obliged to act as his patron, for her sake. Her brother, Lord Elgin, was on the threshold of a diplomatic career under the aegis of Pitt and Dundas, and thus Durham would acquire yet another tie with the powerful fellow Scot who had already taken a benevolent interest in his career: on 18 December 1798, Durham's former brother-in-law James Strange, back from India with a fortune, married Dundas's daughter, Anne Drummond, widow of a London banker. This, incidentally, gave Durham a personal connection, albeit slight, to the great Admiral Adam Duncan, created a viscount following his decisive victory over the Dutch at Camperdown on 11 October 1797 – an inadequate reward, many felt, for preventing the Dutch and French fleets combining, and thereby averting a likely invasion. In 1777, when a post-captain, Duncan had married one of Dundas's nieces, whose father, a former solicitor-general for Scotland, had become lord president of the court of session, following in his father's footsteps. 'It would seem', a naval historian has written, 'that his [Duncan's] alliance with this influential family obtained him the employment which he had been vainly seeking during fifteen years.'[66] There can be little doubt that Durham's personal links with the Dundases had a beneficial impact on his career as well.

Eager though she was to see her daughter married, Lady Elgin had reservations about Durham, for she knew so little of him first-hand. If

she had heard that he had fathered an illegitimate child she can hardly
have been shocked, given the prevalence of openly acknowledged 'natural'
offspring among sections of the nobility and gentry. But as a puritanically
minded evangelical she would probably have been disappointed, and
inclined to wonder what other skeletons might be lurking in his cupboard.
She endeavoured to learn more about his disposition. Knowing of his
kinship with the Anstruthers she asked the elderly widow of Sir John
Anstruther of that ilk what sort of husband he was likely to make. Lady
Anstruther, born Janet Fall or Fa', was the daughter of a prominent Dunbar
merchant and provost who descended, it was said, from a prolific family
of gypsies encamped in Roxburghshire. She proved, frustratingly, to be the
soul of discretion. Reported Queen Charlotte, in whom Martha confided,
to 'Chasse' herself: 'the good old lady would never say a word more than
that C.D. was a very agreeable companion and that She had never seen
Him long enough to Judge of His Character'.[67]

To Martha this must have looked as if Durham was being damned with
faint praise. Nevertheless, after consulting the king and queen, and relying
on Sir James Steuart of Coltness as an intermediary, she became more or
less reconciled to the fact that the marriage was likely to go ahead. She
wished, the queen observed to Lady Charlotte, to dispel reports that were
circulating, which had her 'flatly Contradicting an intended match between
You and C.D.'. At the same time, Martha had pointed out that since
Durham was at sea 'Nothing could be determined on until his return. Out
of delicacy to You [her daughter], she thought it right to deny anything
being settled, and that He Himself must be sensible it could not be any
objection to Himself or Family.' The queen, aware of Lady Charlotte's
tendency towards uninhibited high jinks, suggested that after marriage she
model herself on a friend turning forty, the Countess of Radnor, daughter
of the first Lord Feversham.

> Lady Radnor is perfectably able to guide You and Her great Propriety of
> Conduct may serve You for the best example in this Life. She was very young
> when She married, but very Steady, never flirting nor Giddy, and always made
> an exemplary Wife and Mother. Suppose you took her for your Pattern? It
> will ensure You both Comfort and Happiness and the Esteem of the World.[68]

Having won Lady Charlotte's heart, Durham, with characteristic impatience,
wanted to make sure of her hand. On 19 January 1799 he wrote to the
Admiralty from the *Anson* in the Hamoaze, the broad tidal estuary of the

Tamar near Plymouth Dock, asking them to replace him with an acting captain for the duration of the forthcoming cruise. The ship was 'in every respect ready for sea, and only waits for a fair wind to go out of the Harbour'. He urgently required leave of absence: 'the situation of my private affairs are such, that it is indispensably necessary for my present attendance'. But the Admiralty was unmoved; in those dangerous times an officer of his proven ability could not be lightly spared. Still under his command, the *Anson* sailed from Plymouth on 26 January, and on 2 February, in company with Captain Countess's *Ethalion*, captured the Dunkirk-based *Boulonnais*, a French cutter-privateer of 14 guns and seventy men. She was 'a remarkably fine vessel, copper bottomed, the capture of her gives me great satisfaction as she has greatly annoyed the Trade in the North Sea', wrote Durham to Bridport. On his arrival at Cawsand Bay with the prisoners of war he was informed by Plymouth's port-admiral that there was no room for them, so the *Anson*, on 25 February, anchored at Spithead.[69]

He was glad of the venue, for it was closer to London, and securing Lady Charlotte was uppermost in his mind. On 7 March he asked the Admiralty 'to indulge me with a few weeks leave of absence, my private business being of the greatest importance, and absolutely requires my personal attendance'. It was to no avail. However, since the *Anson* was undergoing maintenance work at Portsmouth Dockyard for what appeared to be an indefinite period, he decided that he may have time to marry before sailing again. Martha was somewhat dismayed by what was, of necessity, his urgent rush. On 11 March, in Scotland, Lady Charlotte's brother, the Earl of Elgin, married Mary Hamilton Nisbet, only child and heiress of a wealthy East Lothian landowner, William Hamilton Nisbet of Dirleton, whose wife was a cousin of the Duke of Rutland. The bride brought to the marriage the interest from £10,000, settled on her by her father in the form of a non-negotiable bond. The earl was about to take up the post of ambassador extraordinary and minister plenipotentiary to Turkey. Martha anxiously awaited her son's arrival in London, for both Durham and Lady Charlotte had been pressing her to consent to an immediate wedding. 'Charlotte has been with me today at Nunn and Barbers [haberdashers at York Street, Covent Garden], to order some of her little matters, as Captain Durham's hurry is beyond everything I ever met with', she wrote to her new daughter-in-law on 14 March.

> He has too good an excuse, for he cannot get leave of Absence and were it
> not my declaring that I will not let her go away without Elgin giving her She

would have been of[f] this week. I now apply to you... to beg you will hurry your Husband up.... I am sure if he knew the situation I am in – Very uncomfortable indeed – He would not lose time.[70]

Durham was compelled to cool his heels for a fortnight. On 26 March he appeared in person at the Faculty Office in Doctors Commons to obtain a special licence to enable him, a member of the Church of Scotland, to be married according to the rites of the Church of England, and to dispense with the need for banns. The following day a contract of marriage was drawn up, overseen by Lord Elgin, Sir James Steuart, and James Strange. This document showed that in contrast to the groom's £17,503 in government stocks Lady Charlotte was worth £5,214, consisting of £4,000 in two equal amounts from each of her brothers, £691 in government stocks, and £523 due by a promissory note made out by Martha that same day. The wedding took place, without further delay, on 28 March at Martha's home in Downing Street, conducted by her friend the Bishop of London. No less than six witnesses, instead of the usual two, signed the register (of St Margaret's, Westminster) below the names of the nuptial pair. These included Lady Charlotte's two bridesmaids, Lady Frances Bruce (Ailesbury's daughter) and Lady Charlotte Bellasyse, as well as Durham's proud father James, Lord Ailesbury, and Sir James Steuart's wife, Alicia. A silver teapot from Queen Charlotte took pride of place among the wedding presents.[71]

So began a marriage in which husband and wife, like countless naval couples, were destined to spend comparatively little time together. Lady Charlotte, who, as protocol demanded, relinquished her paid role as lady of the bedchamber upon marriage, seems to have spent the early years in lodgings close to her husband's English ports of call, for the couple as yet took no settled residence. The fact that Durham's middle name was Charles pleased her. Being her father's name, and that of one of her brothers, she had a sentimental attachment to it. Furthermore, she herself, owing to her mother's grief at the loss of the fifth earl so close to Charlotte's birth, had been christened 'Charles Martha', and as such she was recorded in the family Bible. The impetuously bestowed male name easily metamorphosed into the fashionable feminine form. Martha, redolent of the industrious housewife in the New Testament, underwent a transformation into the more aristocratic Matilda (although 'Martha' appeared on the marriage contract). Being thus no stranger to name changes, Lady Charlotte, or 'Chasse', preferred Charles, or 'Chas', for Durham, and in her hands his initials P.C.D. (as he habitually signed himself in personal correspondence) became C.P.D.[72]

and Durham hosted a dinner and ball aboard, at which the king and queen were guests of honour. Before festivities began, his majesty was locked in discussion about the issue of Catholic emancipation with two ministers who had come aboard for that purpose. They were William Windham and the lord chancellor, Alexander Wedderburn, Lord Loughborough (afterwards first Earl of Rosslyn). Keeping a respectful distance as they paced the quarterdeck, Durham and Harry Neale caught hardly a word of what was being said. But they could not help noticing that the king appeared 'much agitated', and they were intrigued to hear him exclaim, 'Never! I would rather lose my crown!' while raising his hat with both hands.[1]

At dinner Windham sat at the head of one table, Loughborough at that of another, while the king presided over a third. It was the procedure on such occasions for the captain to present the king with the first plate, and etiquette demanded that the approach was made from the left. Being unused to the role of waiter, Durham made a *faux pas* by serving the dish on the king's right, which appeared to disconcert his majesty, 'What, what, not much accustomed to this I see!', he snapped. 'Go and get your dinner.'[2]

On 15 October the *Anson*, with Lady Charlotte aboard, arrived at Portsmouth in company with the *Cormorant*, 20 (Captain the Hon. Courtenay Boyle), which had also been on duty at Weymouth. A few days later Durham sat on the court martial of a marine corporal who was sentenced to 150 lashes for desertion, in a procedure known as 'whipping round the fleet'. The privilege of attending the king and queen had been all very well, but it robbed Durham quite literally of a golden opportunity to line his pockets. Lord Bridport had put him in charge of a small frigate squadron, so that the *Alcmene*, 32 (Captain John Gore) and the *Triton*, 32 (Captain Henry Digby) came under his orders. On the very morning that instructions had come to take the *Anson* round to Weymouth this squadron had been due to sail. Captain William Pierrepoint of the 38-gun *Naiad* was put in charge of it in Durham's stead. On 16 October, while cruising, Pierrepoint sighted a Spanish frigate, the *Thetis*, 34, and was joined by the *Ethalion* (Captain James Young) who helped to capture her. The following day the *Alcmene* and *Triton* took her consort, the *Santa Brigida*, also a 34. Both Spaniards had been returning from Vera Cruz in Mexico with immensely valuable cargoes. The *Thetis* carried, in specie, 1,385,292 Spanish dollars, the equivalent of £311,690 sterling (about £18,711,400 in today's currency). The *Santa Brigida* also contained a treasure trove, which included 3,000 dollars in each of 446 boxes (totalling 1,338,000 dollars), and a cargo of indigo, cochineal and sugar with an estimated value of £5,000. When all this booty reached Plymouth it was loaded onto no less than sixty-three artillery wagons before scores of onlookers and hauled to safety accompanied by armed guards and musical bands. Pierrepoint and his fellow captains received in prize money what a rueful and envious Durham described as 'something very considerable', thus becoming rich men overnight: in consideration of the cargo alone, irrespective of what the vessels might bring, each captain's share was worth about £40,731, which would be £2,442,000 today.[3] Had Durham commanded that squadron as planned, he might, therefore, have instantly almost trebled his personal fortune.

The *Anson* was at Plymouth preparing to escort as far as Madeira a convoy of East Indiamen and a 12-gun brig bound for Botany Bay when, on the evening of 15 March 1800, a mutiny of uncertain cause broke out aboard the 20-gun French-built British frigate *Danaë* which was cruising off Brest. Most of the officers and crew of this prize of war, captured by Sir Edward Pellew in 1798, were asleep when a party of seamen armed with cutlasses rushed onto the quarterdeck. They included, it would seem, a high proportion of resentful recently pressed men, and they made a beeline for the master, wounding him badly in the head. His anguished cries for help were heard by the lieutenant of marines, who alerted the captain. Twenty-year-old Lord Proby, son of an Irish peer, the Earl of Carysfort, was by objective accounts a kind, considerate captain. He now attempted to reach the quarterdeck by the after hatchway, but when he was nearly at the top of the ladder, hatless, a blow from a cutlass to his head sent him reeling. To prevent the officers and the majority of the men, who remained loyal, from coming up on deck and overpowering them, the mutineers wasted no time in battening down the gratings, and placing boats on them which they loaded with shot. Next morning they anchored at Camaret Bay and sent the jollyboat to the French corvette *Colombe* lying nearby, requesting her to send troops aboard.

When the two vessels were steering for Brest the following day, they fell in with the *Anson*, which had set sail which her convoy, as well as with Captain Keats's *Boadicea*. Supposing the *Danaë* and *Colombe*, from their appearance, both to be French, Durham and Keats gave chase. The mutineers had been deprived of Bridport's private signals, which Proby had thrown overboard in a weighted canvas bag, but by hoisting horary and numerical ones they satisfied their pursuers that they were a British vessel and her prize, and the chase was called off. The former *Vaillante*, taken into Brest, was now reclaimed by her country of origin, and her officers and loyal crew became prisoners of war. But not for long, for the French authorities repatriated them the following month.[4]

On 27 April the *Anson* captured the French brig-privateer *Vainqueur*, pierced for 16 guns with a crew of seventy-five. She was sailing from Bordeaux to St Domingo with a diverse cargo. From her crew Durham learned that several privateers were about to sail from her port of origin on raiding missions against British trade. He promptly stationed the *Anson* some way off the mouth of the Gironde and as soon as they were sighted, two days later, sent home his prize. They were the *Brave*, 36, and the *Druide*, *Guepe*, and *Hardi*, all of 18 guns. When they saw the *Anson* they 'dispersed in different directions' and he steered in chase of the largest. Having crossed upon opposite tacks with her he poured in a broadside, which he assumed must have done a great deal of damage to her hull. But finding that she kept the wind and outsailed him he bore up and pursued the *Hardi* instead. She struck, proving to be 'a very fine new ship just off the stocks', with 194 men. About the same time he captured 'a very valuable ship' from the Dutch colony of Batavia in the East Indies, bound for Hamburg with the governor of Batavia on board.[5]

From men on his French prizes and on fishing boats he received information about the privateers which he felt was reliable. He learned that the *Hardi* and her consorts intended to cruise in the eastern Atlantic between the Channel mouth and the Azores in search of British prey, while the 18-gun *Messina*, which had left Bordeaux at the same time as the *Vainqueur*, was to station herself near the Cape Verde islands off the west coast of Africa with the same aim. 'Being in possession of the above intelligence I should have followed the Enemy, had I not been afraid of encroaching upon their Lordships' indulgence' he explained to the Admiralty, to whom he circulated a description of the *Brave*. He arrived at Plymouth Sound with his prisoners on 9 May and waited there for further orders.[6]

On 6 June he sailed for Minorca (wrested from Spain in 1798) with a convoy of twenty store ships and victualling vessels for the troops there under General Sir Ralph Abercromby. He sailed in company with the 24-gun armed transport *Calcutta*, which was taking the Banffshire fencibles to the garrison at Gibraltar. At daylight on 27 June, four days after his arrival at the Rock (where he was detained by contrary winds), he discovered a large convoy of between forty and fifty vessels of various types in the Straits. He immediately gave chase, but they sought refuge under the guns of the batteries between Algeciras and Tarifa. These, along with twenty-five heavy Spanish gunboats, which had been harrying British merchantmen in the area for some time, subjected the *Anson* to a sustained fire. Despite that, as well as rough winds, he succeeded in capturing eight of the convoy, assisted by two 'row boats' from Gibraltar, and believed that in more favourable conditions he could have captured more with the aid of boats made available by the 24-gun *Constance* (Captain John Baker Hay). One of his prizes was retaken, but Durham returned to his anchorage with the rest. He was 'sorry to find they are not very valuable'.

Almost invariably, the gunboats managed to elude capture by retreating into creeks where they could not be followed. But on the night of 29 June Durham came up with two of them and cut them off from the shore, precluding their usual means of escape. They fled across the Straits, making for the Spanish enclave of Ceuta. But the *Anson*, in close pursuit, forced them onto rocks on the Moroccan coast. There they were captured by the ship's boats, commanded by a fifteen-year-old midshipman, Joseph Needham Tayler, who had started his career aboard a flagship and had not been with Durham very long. He 'boarded them in the most gallant style'. Named the *Gibraltar* and *Salvador*, they were 'fine vessels commanded by King's officers'. Each had a crew of sixty and mounted two long 18-pounders in addition to eight smaller guns. Having 'defended themselves very gallantly', they had suffered a number of casualties. As for Midshipman Tayler, in admiration for the pluck and promise he displayed, Durham presented him with a sword; this spontaneous gesture told the boy, who normally carried only a dirk, that he had proved himself a man.[7]

Hampered almost all along by the direction of the winds, the *Anson* reached Minorca on 18 July, anchoring at Port Mahon. On returning to Spithead Durham had some explaining to do to the Admiralty. When escorting the Minorca convoy he had been furious to find, on reaching the rendezvous at Lisbon, that the *Calcutta* had parted company, and had dashed off letters recording his amazement both to her commander, Lieutenant John Anderson, and the Admiralty. On reaching Gibraltar he found that she had arrived ahead of him, but his letters had already been sent. In now informing the Admiralty that during the voyage Anderson had mistaken another British frigate for the *Anson* and followed her instead, he took the opportunity of reminding their lordships that all the convoys he had escorted had reached their destinations safely. He also told them of the circumstances surrounding an encounter (reported in the press) that had taken place on 26 July with a small Danish frigate which had under convoy nine merchantmen flying Danish colours. He had brought these vessels to, and sent his first lieutenant on board the frigate to inform her captain that he intended to inspect the convoy for war contraband. The captain proved belligerent, declaring that he would fire upon the *Anson*'s boats despite the consequences. Having been satisfied that the merchantmen's papers were in order, Durham allowed them to set sail: 'I did not feel myself authorized to proceed to extremities.'[8]

On 2 September 1800, along with seven other post-captains and four flag-officers, including Vice-Admiral Sir Henry Harvey, presiding, he sat on a court martial aboard the *Cambridge* at the Hamaoze to try one of the ringleaders of the *Danaë* mutiny. The man, John Marret, a bilingual native of Jersey who had been pressed into service on Proby's ship, had since the mutiny been a crew member on a French privateer, the *Vengeur*. She had been captured by the British, and as he stood with other prisoners of war in an inspection parade at Plymouth held specifically to find any former mutineers, he was recognised by the former first lieutenant of the *Danaë*. The court martial sentenced Marret to be hanged at the yardarm of whichever ship the Admiralty directed. A week later this sentence was carried out aboard the *Pique*, 38, on which he had been held during his trial: the grim spectacle was 'a dreadful example to all mutineers'.[9]

In November the *Anson* was ordered off Le Havre to ascertain the French naval presence there. It was paltry, he subsequently reported to Admiral Mark Milbanke, commanding at Portsmouth: 'There appears to be only one small ship ready for sea; the rest are in a dismantled state and [gave] no appearance, that I could discover, of preparing for sea; nor could I learn from the fishermen who were in great numbers in the Bay, that they were making any preparation for sea.' He remained off Le Havre 'until the tides could no longer admit of the enemys ships sailing from that port', and returned to Portsmouth with a number of complaints about his ship. She was making 'a considerable quantity of water through the bows' and appeared to have a defective stern; he was unable to stow enough drinking water for her designated 330 men because too much room in the hold was occupied by shingle, which should be replaced by iron ballast; her gun carriages needed repainting. Having noticed throughout his command of her that she was 'the first ship in any Roadstead to start her Anchors' he had now – after six years! – reached the conclusion that those anchors, being meant for a 50-gun ship, not a 64-gun one, were too light and that heavier anchors should be substituted.[10]

She underwent repairs, though apparently not the modifications that Durham hoped for, and then cruised off Brest. On 15 February off Ushant he chased a French privateer, which successfully evaded him. The following day he fell in with seven British merchantmen which during the night had parted from their escort, the 38-gun *Topaze* (Captain Stephen

Church). With the privateer at large and a fierce wind blowing from the east Durham took them under his protection. Using what he termed his 'utmost endeavour' he succeeded in reuniting them with the *Topaze* and the rest of her convoy, and then hauled his wind. Thwarted for several days by the state of the weather, he eventually managed on 20 February to anchor at St Helens.[11]

His command of the *Anson* was now at an end. On 1 January, to mark the opening of the nineteenth century and the Union with Ireland, a large promotion took place in the Royal Navy, mainly of flag-officers, and this was accompanied by a change in the command of about thirty post-ships. Although remarkably junior when appointed to the *Anson*, Durham had over the past six years established himself as one of the navy's most outstanding captains, and he was now rewarded with the command of the frigate *Endymion*. That superb vessel, based in certain design features upon the *Pomone* and built at Randall's Yard, Rotherhithe, was launched in 1797. Pierced for 40 guns, she carried twenty-six 24-pounders on her maindeck, fourteen 32-pounder carronades on her quarterdeck, and two 9-pounders plus four 32-pounder carronades on her forecastle. She had a complement of 320 men (later increased to 340). 'She was very fast, handled well, and was an excellent sea-boat, and could if required carry 24 pdrs without serious damage to the hull', writes a modern authority, who describes her as the 'star' of the crack or 'super' frigates produced during the 1790s. 'Indeed she was so highly regarded that she was still the benchmark for sailing qualities as late as the Experimental Squadrons of the 1830s', for only two frigates 'more powerful' had seen service in the Royal Navy.[12]

Durham's appointment to the *Endymion* had been recommended by the outgoing first lord, Earl Spencer, and his board. It was warmly confirmed by Earl St Vincent, who succeeded Spencer on 19 February 1801. He sent Durham 'a very flattering letter' telling of his 'great pleasure' in seeing him in command of that ship. It was however no 'rubber stamp' appointment: the crusty and acerbic St Vincent, known for his crusade against corruption in the administration of naval dockyards, was very much his own man, and would not have appointed Durham had he not also been convinced of his excellence.

Nineteen years earlier, when St Vincent, or Captain Jervis of the *Foudroyant*, as he then was, had been in Kempenfelt's squadron, he had been wounded during the action with de Guichen while engaging and capturing an enemy ship. On hearing of Jervis's injury, Kempenfelt, who fully appreciated that officer's merits, had sent for Midshipman Durham and told him to go aboard the *Foudroyant* to find out how he was. 'Young gentleman,' the admiral added, 'take a good look at that officer – he is not a common captain of a man of war.' At some stage Captain Durham acquainted St Vincent with that compliment from one of the navy's greatest flag-officers. His lordship was so pleased that he proved very friendly to Durham 'ever afterwards'. But soft soap alone did not wash with St Vincent: to gain appointment an officer had to prove himself by his deeds. His correspondence as first lord is full of letters from the often aristocratic champions of hopefuls seeking promotion and commands. He would not be wheedled, and his mastery of the politely terse, definitive put-down in replying to solicitations from those whom he had no intention of obliging makes fascinating reading. Among those whom he disappointed was the disgraced Captain Molloy, who was bluntly told that the sentence of his court martial was 'completely justifiable', and whose plea for flag-rank was accordingly rejected.[13]

Durham formally took command of the *Endymion* on 26 February, when he went aboard and, as customary, read out his commission. A cluster of his followers went with him. Among the young officers already aboard was Charles Austen, a protégé of Durham's predecessor, Captain Thomas Williams, and younger brother of the novelist Jane. She hoped that Charles might be lucky enough to be made first lieutenant of the *Endymion*, but was realistic enough to add: 'I suppose Captain Durham is too likely to bring a villain with him under that denomination'.[14]

Sailing under Admiralty orders – which meant that he had no admiral over him and consequently would be entitled to all three-eighths of any prize money ensuing on each capture – he arrived at Lisbon, where three of his crew deserted, on 8 April as the senior British naval officer at that port. He had orders to take charge of a convoy of merchantmen, and found that these would not be ready to depart for several weeks. There was talk of evacuating the British residents of Lisbon, who included the Duke of Sussex, in the wake of an expected invasion of Portugal by French troops under General Andoche Junot. But the invasion did not eventuate. While he waited for the convoy Durham put to sea 'for the protection of the trade for a few days', since a number of enemy privateers were reportedly cruising in the vicinity of the Straits. He immediately discovered about sixteen 'totally unprotected' vessels belonging to a Portuguese convoy returning from Brazil, and took them under his protection. Two Spaniards that were sailing with them, which he regarded as fair game, escaped during heavy gales which lasted for five days and prevented him from hoisting out his boats. He remained with this convoy for eight days, and on 13 April captured the *Furie*, a 14-gun French cutter-privateer with a crew of sixty-four. She had been in sight of ships belonging to the convoy which had separated in the fierce weather.[15]

It was not until 4 May that Durham sailed from Lisbon with his convoy, the *Lapwing*, 28 (Captain Edward Rotheram) keeping company. To the south of Cape Finisterre they fell in with the *Anson*, now commanded by former prisoner of war Captain William Cracraft. She was escorting merchantmen from Oporto to Ireland, Bristol, and Liverpool. For further security the two convoys sailed together, under Durham's orders, until they approached the Channel, when Cracraft and his vessels steered an independent course. In the prevalent thick weather, and with a southerly wind, Durham was in no mood to risk all his ships on a lee shore. Accordingly, he took under his protection the vessels that were bound for ports on the south coast of England and ordered Rotheram to sail for the Downs with the remainder. He arrived at Spithead on 25 May.[16]

Towards the end of September, after further successful cruising, he was one of six post-captains who were on hand to flank the coffin of Vice-Admiral Lord Hugh Seymour as it was conveyed in solemn procession at Portsmouth on a pall-covered hearse drawn by horses with black plumes. Seymour, who had captained the *Leviathan*, 74, at the Glorious First of June, and in 1796 had been chosen as member of Parliament for Portsmouth along with Durham's second cousin Thomas Erskine; he was commander-in-chief on the Jamaica station, dying of 'the fatal fever of that clime' on 11 September, aged forty-two. His body was shipped to England on a schooner and disembarked at Portsmouth Dockyard. The procession made its way from the Dockyard along Queen Street to the Lion Gate at the town ramparts, with Admiral Milbanke, the port-admiral, and Major-General Whitelocke, the lieutenant-governor of the garrison, as chief mourners, and troops of dragoons leading and bringing up the rear. In full dress uniform with black crape round his arm, Durham walked at the left of the coffin, behind Robert Stopford and Charles Stirling; on the right, in corresponding order, were Frank Sotheron, Joseph Yorke, and Samuel Hood. Their positioning, as in all things naval, was determined by seniority.[17]

That autumn, having cruised fruitlessly off Madeira for eight days, he escorted ten East Indiamen, along with some South Atlantic whalers glad of a convoy, home from the island of St Helena, owned by the East India Company, the established rendezvous for the Company's ships awaiting a naval escort back to British waters. It was the first and last time he would sail so far south, below the Equator. He was accompanied for part of the homeward voyage by the brig *Star*, 16, from the Cape of Good Hope. Her captain, John Gardner, was facing a court martial at Portsmouth on what would turn out to be spurious charges. Durham reached the Downs safely with all but one of the Indiamen, a vessel laden on the East India Company's account. She belonged to 'some private individuals of Bengal' and seemed to have 'intentionally parted company' off the Azores. In gratitude for his 'care and attention' the Company's directors voted him £400 'for the purchase of a piece of plate'.[18]

Durham arrived at Portsmouth from the Downs on 8 November. A few days later he was reunited with the five captains who had walked beside Seymour's coffin with him, when they assembled aboard the *Gladiator* in Portsmouth Harbour as members of the court martial on Vice-Admiral Sir William Parker. It sat on 13 and 14 November under the presidency of Admiral Sir Thomas Pasley. Also among the eight captains who, with five flag-officers, composed the court was Captain James Newman, whose unacknowledged duel with the *Loire* had sparked ill feeling against Durham earlier and would continue to do so. Vice-Admiral Parker had been recalled from his post as commander-in-chief on the Halifax station at his own request to explain why, in technical contravention of Admiralty orders, he had sent the *America*, 64, and the *Cleopatra*, 32, from his station to the West Indies. He 'made a defence so forcible, convincing, and exculpatory, as impressed the whole Court, not only with a complete conviction of his innocence, but also of his having acted upon principles dictated by an ardent desire to serve the country', reported an eyewitness. Durham and the other judges found that his conduct, though 'indiscreet', was 'justified' and that he had no other goal than 'the good' of the service. After the verdict Pasley expressed much pleasure in returning to him the sword that he had worn 'with so much honour'. (Parker had participated memorably in Lord Howe's action of 29 May 1794 and had been third in command at the battle of Cape St Vincent, for which he had received a baronetcy.) When his acquittal became known church bells in Portsmouth pealed in celebration and he was besieged by rejoicing wellwishers.[19]

Noting that Lady Charlotte sped to Durham's side during his brief snatches of shore leave, the initially dubious Queen Charlotte had no doubt that their love would endure. 'You can never be in better Company than that of your Captain', she told 'Chasse' in the autumn of 1800, 'and you seem to feel that so thoroughly that *I foresee it will be lasting.*' Lady Charlotte took rooms at inns at the home ports where her husband's ship was due, and she got to know many of his colleagues. Her natural effervescence made her popular. A lieutenant on a vessel in Aboukir Bay, formerly a midshipman aboard the *Anson*, gladly tried to obtain for her preserved ginger, attar of roses, and other goods from the Levant. Prince William's friend William Dyott, who 'got very intimately acquainted' with her at Weymouth not long after her marriage, considered her 'one of the most delightful women in the world'. He therefore found it 'a cruel disappointment' when his military duties prevented him from accepting an invitation to Lord and Lady Radnor's country house near Salisbury 'whilst Lady Charlotte was there'. Nelson's flag-captain, Thomas Masterman Hardy, liked her. On 6 November 1801, when Hardy, then of the *Isis*, disembarked at Deal, he was invited to dine with the Durhams '& of course I could not refuse, her Ladyship was very pleasant and we had a long talk about Weymouth'. Lady Charlotte left the following day for Portsmouth where the *Endymion* was bound 'as soon as the Weather will permit'. In March 1802, a few days before the coming of peace, Hardy attended a ball at the Assembly Rooms in Portsmouth. This large, unpretentious native of Dorset afterwards joked that his sister would 'be astonished to hear that Lady Charlotte Durham was my partner last but you know that Captains at Portsmouth are Nobbs'.[20]

The war had been going in favour of Britain, which had got possession of Malta, and had taken Ceylon and the Cape of Good Hope from Holland and Trinidad from Spain. The Royal Navy had command of the seas, and British commerce had increased by sixty per cent over the past decade. Napoleon's ambitions in the Baltic and in Egypt had been checked by British arms, and his hopes of invading England had received a setback. There was discontent in regions of Europe occupied by French troops. However, Britain's national debt had doubled, the price of wheat had soared, and the poor were short of bread. Therefore, when in the autumn of 1801 Bonaparte proposed peace to Henry Addington, who had replaced Pitt as prime minister, the British government, as glad as the French were of a respite, proved amenable. The ensuing treaty was signed at Amiens on 25 March 1802 between Britain on the one side and France, Holland and Spain on the other. France ceased occupying Naples and the Papal States, and possession of Egypt reverted to Turkey. Britain retained Ceylon and Trinidad, but ceded to their former masters other colonies acquired. While peace freed Britain from the burden of heavy taxation necessary to maintain large forces to resist a possible invasion, it had not, therefore, left her with a great deal to show for nine years of costly warfare. Britain had not formally recognised the republics that France had established in

Holland, Switzerland and Lombardy, but the impression of tacit British connivance strengthened French influence in those places. Richard Brinsley Sheridan remarked that it was 'a peace which all men are glad of, but no man can be proud of'.[21]

Not 'all men', actually; certainly not those who lived by their swords. A verse doing the rounds summed up the situation:

> Oh! Says the admiral, The wars are all over;
> Says the captain, My heart will break;
> Oh! Says the bloody first lieutenant,
> What course of life shall I take?

Durham now had the unaccustomed experience of being on land and on half-pay of eight shillings a day for an indefinite period. Throughout his life he displayed restless energy, and during this enforced shore leave he moved at a pace which made the Dowager Countess of Elgin fear would wear her daughter out as he flitted with Lady Charlotte from one Scottish locality to another. Martha, who was now living with her charge, the Princess Charlotte, at Shooter's Hill south of London, was alarmed by the hectic schedule that he had set. 'From the want of Children and he having no time for anything, they have not chose a Residence and the Flying about is too much', wrote Martha to Lady Charlotte's brother, the earl. 'But tho' she never said it to me I know she sacrifices herself... her great Weakness makes it painfull to her tho' she would convince you tis to her Taste.' Martha, who was in poor health herself, and for several days during the late summer of 1802 lingered at death's door, was especially perturbed to learn that her daughter had suffered 'a dreadfull Fall' out of a phaeton which might have 'been her Death'. It had made Lady Charlotte 'very ill', although she was described as 'well but weak' by Lady Robert Manners who saw her some time later. 'That she is all ways poor thing' was Martha's written comment. The Earl and Countess of Elgin, in Constantinople, were by this time the parents of two-year-old George and baby Mary, and Martha fervently wished a child upon Lady Charlotte. 'Would to God she would follow Lady Elgin's recent example and give us a little Girl', she wrote. 'This is all I want... I am sure she would be an excellent Mother – and with much Gratitude to God I can assure you she is an excellent Wife.'[22]

On 14 September 1802 Durham's father gave a ball at Largo House for Lady Charlotte, attended by family and friends from across the district. It was perhaps to mark this merry occasion that a strathspey by Nathaniel

Gow which bears her name was composed. Jamie and Tom had returned from their postings in Ireland at the peace, and the three Durham brothers and their wives spent the autumn at Largo. There was thus a very welcome full house for the widowed, convivial-natured James Calderwood Durham. Only Tom's wife, Elizabeth Young, thin and delicate, had been blessed with children. The elder of her two boys, James Steuart Durham, had come into the world in October 1794, before the move to Ireland; his middle name was a fond tribute to his father's great-uncle, Sir James Steuart of Coltness, who played a not insignificant part in the lives of the laird of Largo and his family. Tom and Elizabeth's younger children had been born in Londonderry: Thomas in February 1796 and Lillias in March 1799.

Jamie's wife Elizabeth had a compensation for her childlessness in her lifelong devotion to dogs. She was never without at least two pampered pugs or spaniels. One of the latter, a particularly beautiful animal given to her by Lady Charlotte, was called 'Chasse' after its donor. 'Little Mrs Durham', who had been orphaned early in life and brought up by her uncle, an Anglican prelate, was a devout woman who had inherited his collection of books on divinity. Of more interest to her husband was the acreage at Rush Mead in Bethnal Green that had come to her from her father. The site contained extensive brickfields, but Jamie had bought back the lease, and advertised the land for development. By 1789 construction had begun on Durham Place, fronting Hackney Road, and within a few years the equally commemorative Elizabeth, Lausanne and Sheldon Streets had been built. His profits enabled Jamie to repay the several thousand pounds that his brother Philip had lent him at the start of the war. But he paid the money into a bank which failed, so that Durham lost the lot. Whether Jamie made good that debt a second time is not recorded.[23]

Around this time the Durhams moved, at last, and no doubt to Martha's relief, into a permanent residence. They chose 5 Gloucester Place, near Portman Square. While not as exclusive as addresses south of Oxford Street in Mayfair it was, nevertheless, in a desirable neighbourhood, where Admiral Sir James Wallace, a former governor of Newfoundland, lived until his death in 1803. The Durhams' neighbours included several titled persons and senior naval and military figures such as Vice-Admiral Sir John Orde and Major-General Sir Eyre Coote.[24]

It was probably during these months of peace that the portrait of Durham by the fashionable artist James Northcote was painted. Depicting him in dress uniform wearing the epaulette on each shoulder that proclaimed him to be a post-captain of more than three years' seniority, and with what appears to be the gold medal awarded following Warren's action off Tory Island in 1798, it is, despite the name of the sitter painted at the bottom, barely credible as a likeness of him. There are the familiar nut-brown eyes, firm broad shoulders and nicely shaped hands with long fingers, and there is the characteristic fair complexion with pink cheeks. But, perhaps owing to the fall of the light or to a token sprinkling of hair powder – officers were directed to wear such powder when in uniform, except at sea or in bad weather – the hair is mousy rather than its usual richer hue. Loose curls frame his face but the hair on the crown has been grown long, and pulled back into the queue which, tied with black ribbon, had become *de rigueur* for naval officers since the mid-1780s and would continue so for about another decade. The thinnish lips, with their peaked Cupid's bow redolent of his maternal grandmother and his uncle, William Calderwood, have in the picture been plumped and softened. And the deep, resolute, dimpled chin has been entirely remodelled, presumably to suit the artist's aesthetic preferences, into a rounded cherubic one of abbreviated proportions. As in all his portraits Durham looks younger than what must have been his chronological age: here he seems to be only in his early thirties.[25]

For such a man, energetic, impatient, still avidly seeking the rewards of prize money, and home, as it were, in the surf of the sea, the novelty of this unavoidable leisure-time on half his normal salary must swiftly have palled. He was not yet forty, and as the months dragged by he undoubtedly asked himself with some anxiety what he was to do with the remainder of his life should hostilities not be renewed.

But there were too many flaws in the treaty of Amiens, too many causes of dispute left unsettled, for the peace to be anything more than a truce. Britain viewed with abhorrence Napoleon's election in August 1802 as first consul for life, his continuing overseas adventurism, and his confrontational attitude. He sent spies into British ports, attempted to kindle unrest in Ireland, refused to make a commercial treaty with Britain, and launched intemperate verbal attacks on British statesmen that were printed in the official French newspaper. He was angered by the sanctuary Britain gave to outspoken opponents of his regime, by Britain's failure to surrender Alexandria as demanded by the peace of Amiens, and by the retention of Malta, to which Britain clung as a strategic counter to his schemes in the Levant and Egypt and as compensation for recent French territorial acquisitions. On 18 May 1803 Britain declared war, Napoleon having refused an ultimatum demanding that France should withdraw troops from Holland and Switzerland, and allow Britain to hold Malta for ten years.

The peace of Amiens, then, had lasted thirteen months. Hitherto, the wars that Britain had waged against France since 1793 had as their central object the restoration of the monarchy. This new war was fought against a megalomaniac dictator who had aggressively exported republican principles and was determined to subjugate an entire continent to his will. However, Britain stood alone, without active continental allies. Holland was in thrall to Napoleon; Spain, while resentful that despite her right of pre-emption he had sold Louisiana to the United States, was attached to him by agreement; Russia, though dependent on trade with Britain, was courting his friendship; Austria was weary of war; Prussia stayed grimly neutral. In these circumstances, the British concentrated their efforts on defending England, seizing colonies, and blockading enemy ports. Well might the *Naval Chronicle* comment: 'If at any time the British Navy was an object of more peculiar concern to the country than at another, it is at the present, when an implacable enemy threatens us with invasion.'[26]

Durham, destined to go to sea again, was creeping up the post-captains' ladder. On the top rung, somewhat anomalously, stood a gallant commander of a bygone period, who had first set foot on the ladder nine years before Durham was born. Next came thirty-seven men posted in the year of the *Royal George* tragedy. Durham was number 191 on the list of 684, only a fraction of whom had any realistic prospect of obtaining a ship. With his record and contacts, there was no conceivable danger of him being stranded 'on the beach'. But as a captain of almost ten years' standing he was too senior, in the Admiralty's view, for another frigate command. He was, therefore, appointed in mid-April amid rumours of war to the 98-gun, three-deck *Windsor Castle*, and hastened to Portsmouth to join her.[27]

She was one of four ships of the line which, along with six frigates also lying at Portsmouth, had been prepared for commissioning several weeks previously, and there were officers aboard before he was named as captain. With the resumption of war came the urgent need for crews, and around noon on 7 May 1803, with hostilities imminently expected, a despatch sent express was received at Portsmouth. Durham, assisted by Captains Willoughby Lake and Henry Hill, oversaw the enterprise with alacrity and determination. Troops from the garrison guarded the escape routes from Portsea and Gosport, and 700 men were caught in what was effectively a dragnet. The emergency was such that the companies of two naval vessels which returned to Portsmouth on 16 May from foreign stations were immediately discharged into the *Windsor Castle* and another second-rate fitting out in the harbour without getting a chance to step ashore.[28]

Durham's tenure on the *Windsor Castle* was very short. On 29 May, a week after the declaration of war, he was appointed to the *Defiance*, and took command on 2 June. The latest in a succession of vessels of that name, she had participated in Nelson's victory at Copenhagen in 1801 as the flagship of Rear-Admiral Thomas Graves. Of 74 guns and 1,645 tons, she was launched in 1783 and had the distinction of being the fastest-sailing third-rate in the Royal Navy. A nineteenth-century commentator, who seems to have consulted Durham directly, wrote that in the initial cruise under his command she had 'four months' bread and provisions on board, and 304 tons of water and beer, besides 107 tons of iron, and 160 tons of shingle ballast. Notwithstanding her lading, she was a fast and lively ship, and remarkably healthy. Indeed, while Durham captained her, 'She never met with any damage, such as losing masts or springing yards, except that which the shot of the enemy effected.'[29]

On 10 July 1803 Durham took the ship across Spithead to St Helens. He was having trouble filling her complement of 515 men, and he complained that the Admiralty had not issued press warrants for her. This did not deter him from pressing a seaman out of a merchantman returning from the Mediterranean. That vessel, however, was suspected of having disease aboard, so that on 12 July the *Defiance* was put under quarantine. A fortnight later she was ordered to Plymouth, where the press-gangs had been unprecedently active, 'to be manned and paid'. By 7 August, when the *Defiance* lay in Cawsand Bay, twenty-one men from Fife who had volunteered at Leith eleven days earlier on the understanding that they would be joining him had still not arrived. He requested the Admiralty to ensure that they were sent to him, as the men had in good faith envisaged, and to no other captain. Despite what he had told his mother shortly after commissioning the *Anson* he was only too happy to have his countrymen aboard. He also awaited with impatience men from three homecoming vessels who had volunteered for the *Defiance*. One of these vessels was the 38-gun *Diana* (Captain Thomas Maling), which had arrived at Portsmouth on 4 June from Naples with the family of Lord Elgin, who was himself returning overland.[30]

Following the breakdown of the peace Admiral William Cornwallis had resumed the command of the Channel Fleet which he had assumed in 1801 in succession to St Vincent. With Ushant as their rendezvous, and Torbay their refuge in disruptive heavy gales, his ships, numbering about seventeen, kept close watch on Brest, Lorient and Rochefort. Meanwhile, a squadron under Nelson, who had been given the Mediterranean command, was similarly vigilant at Toulon, and another under Pellew cruised off the north-west Spanish ports of Ferrol and Corunna between the Bay of Biscay and the Atlantic. At the beginning of June 1803 Cornwallis instituted an inshore squadron, based at the entrance of Brest Harbour, with instructions, in time of westerly gales, to shelter in Douarnanez Bay. The inshore squadron was commanded from the end of June by Rear-Admiral Cuthbert Collingwood, who was soon reporting to Cornwallis that 'The general conversation at Brest was the invasion of England'.[31]

Cornwallis's idea was not that the enemy should be sealed into harbour but that the inshore squadron should observe, pursue and harry any French force that should put to sea until he arrived to bring it to action. Although the French naval presence at Brest, as at Lorient and Rochefort, was comparatively weak during 1803, it increased at the beginning of 1804, when he urged extra vigilance on the part of his captains. Napoleon, who proclaimed himself emperor of France in May that year, established an army of about 15,000 men at Boulogne. He is reported to have observed that the Channel was a mere ditch, and that if he could have command of it for twelve hours, England's fate would be sealed. Along with 200,000 regular soldiers and militia, some 347,000 volunteers stood under arms to repel a French invasion. But it was, as usual, Britain's 'wooden walls' that provided the country's first line of defence. The vital role of her blockading squadrons in the war against Napoleon has been summed up in the unrivalled and oft-quoted words of the American naval expert Alfred Thayer Mahan: 'Those far distant, storm-beaten ships, upon which the Grand Army never looked, stood between it and the dominion of the world.'[32]

On 17 August 1803 the *Defiance* sailed to join Collingwood off Brest, taking fresh vegetables and live cattle for the use of the squadron. She was seventy-six men short of complement, and Durham regretted that a number of her crew were 'raw Irishmen'. (Such prejudice against the Catholic Irish was widespread, since they were often perceived to be feckless and lazy, and many of them in the fleet had been implicated in the Great Mutiny and similar occurrences, including a plot on the *Defiance* herself in 1798 to murder the officers and hand her over to the French.) Durham, always quick to be riled by what he perceived to be the incompetence or stupidity of others, was angered by the knowledge that several men from the *Puissant*, who had been dispatched from the Nore to Portsmouth by Admiral Lord Keith for the *Defiance*, had been sent aboard the *Majestic* instead. He asked the Admiralty to transfer them to him, including one whom he named, 'who had sailed with me ever since I was first appointed a Captain and

Volunteer'd for me at my desire and was forwarded to the Nore at my particular request from Dunbar'. However, Rear-Admiral Bartholomew Samuel Rowley, who investigated, assured the Admiralty that the man in question had not been intended for the *Defiance*. This prompted Durham to protest that, on the contrary, the man had 'left a very comfortable situation for the express purpose' of serving with him, and that Rowley must have the wrong person in mind. 'I am extremely hurt their Lordships would suppose I should make any representations contrary to what I was thoroughly convinced in my own mind was perfectly right; their Lordships may not be aware that the Relations and Friends of the said Men are in the constant habit of writing me respecting them, and that my Family feel themselves oblig'd to supply them, from time to time, with any necessaries they may require, in consequence of the said Men having Volunteer'd for me, tho' not one of them ever join'd me.' Whether this had any effect is unclear.[33]

Three months later, on 20 November, following a refit, the *Defiance* again sailed from Plymouth for Brest, taking livestock, vegetables and provisions for the squadron. This time Durham carried sealed instructions from the Admiralty directing him to take the *Goliath* (Captain Charles Brisbane) under his orders and watch enemy preparations at the port of Rochefort. He was to report, as appropriate, to Cornwallis or to Pellew regarding the strength and probable intention of the French force there, and on the likely destination of any enemy squadron he might fall in with, which was accompanied by transports and troops.[34]

On 9 December he assured Cornwallis by letter – for without orders to the contrary he was not to leave his station unless the enemy should actually put to sea – that he had 'no reason to believe anything has escaped since I have been here and trust that nothing will escape during the time I have the charge'. The previous day he ordered the *Goliath* inshore to reconnoitre, and, having discovered a French convoy standing along the coast, Brisbane sent two six-oared cutters to intercept them, one commanded by a naval lieutenant and the other by a lieutenant of marines, each assisted by a midshipman. In the face of heavy fire from the batteries of *Les Sables d'Olonne* and a gunboat, they successfully drove part of the convoy on shore, and despite the forty French soldiers aboard her they took possession of a British brig, pierced for 14 guns and mounting six, captured some days earlier by an enemy privateer. A British marine was injured, and the two lieutenants who commanded the cutters and had both volunteered for that duty later died from the wounds they, too, had received in boarding the brig. There were about fifteen French casualties.[35]

The *Flying Fish*, 'a valuable ship' bound for London from Africa with a cargo that included ivory and gold dust, was recaptured by Durham on 11 December. She had been taken six days earlier by the *Brave*, a 16-gun St Malo-based privateer. On examining the French prize-master's log Durham found that a 36-gun privateer out of Bordeaux was cruising with the *Brave*, both ships 'committing great depredations on our own commerce'. Since he was unable to leave his station to cruise to the westward as far as the exact latitude and longitude where he knew the privateers to be, he could do no more than pass the information to Cornwallis.[36]

Several days later he learned from the master of a vessel under Swedish colours that a French three-decker at the Île d'Aix outside Rochefort had very recently been on the point of sailing with a complement of at least 1,500 men but re-anchored owing to the British presence nearby. He shortly afterwards learned from Captain George Wolfe of the *Aigle*, 36, that as well as the three-decker there were at Île d'Aix a two-decker, two frigates and a corvette, all seemingly 'quite ready for sea'. From his anchorage in the Pertuis (passage) d'Antioche south of the Île de Ré, Durham sent the news to the admiral.[37]

Meanwhile, at daylight on 11 December close off Baleines, Captain Brisbane discovered a convey of 200 sail steering northward and proceeded with the *Goliath* up the Pertuis Breton north of the Île de Ré to intercept and destroy as many as he could. Several were subsequently driven on shore and the rest turned back. They sheltered under the batteries of St Martin, off which Brisbane anchored and ordered his boats ashore. He was convinced that they would have been driven out and destroyed had not 'the wind suddenly shifted, and blown a strong gale from an opposite quarter, which prevented the boats from rowing ahead'. He continued at anchor until the convoy had 'completely dispersed, some returning to Rochefort, others getting into various creeks in shallow water, which meant the *Goliath* was unable to follow them'. Accordingly he weighed, intending to rejoin Durham off Chassiron, when early that evening a gale developed suddenly from the westward, placing the ship in danger.

The night was pitch black, for in an apparently deliberate attempt to disorient the ship the glow from the nearby lighthouse had been extinguished. In order to work off the lee shore that threatened her, the *Goliath* maintained 'a very heavy press of sail'. But it proved unavailing. Owing to the 'very heavy swell' she lost ground on both tacks, and the sea crashed over her forecastle. She spent the early hours of 12 December riding by two anchors and two cables, but at daylight Brisbane realised that this could not long continue 'in a gale blowing directly on shore, with the sea breaking over her, and nearly within gun-shot of the enemy's batteries'. He therefore ordered the cables to be cut. The tiller 'was broken by a heavy sea striking under the quarter' impeding his progress, and fierce westerly gales prevented him from reaching Chassiron for a fortnight. The broken tiller would soon be followed by a damaged rudder, the latest in a string of mishaps to befall her: Durham therefore doubted her fitness 'to be constantly engaged when there is western in the wind, with a lee shore, and of course under a press of sail'. She had experienced 'the loss of sails, anchors and top masts'; had 'only one tiller, and that sprung', her master had been declared 'unfit for duty' owing to an accident, and she was several officers and 134 men short of complement. By contrast the *Defiance*, which had sheltered in Quiberon Bay during the gales, had suffered no damage and was 'in a perfect state for service'.[38]

On the morning of 20 January 1804, during a gale from the west, Durham observed a ship standing in for the French coast, and from her appearance guessed she was a French vessel called the *Brutus*, whose description had been circulated. He sent the *Goliath* to examine her, but since the sea was heavy he doubted that she could be boarded. However, 'that judicious officer Captain Brisbane succeeded in taking possession of her'. She was indeed the *Brutus*, 'with a number of suspicious passengers on board'. Durham ordered Brisbane to send her into port, and to take all her officers aboard the *Goliath* and proceed with that ship to Cornwallis to obtain further orders. Meanwhile, Durham learned from the master of an American vessel bound to Bordeaux from Boston, which had just come from the Île de Ré, that 'A day or two previous to his sailing a convoy of gun-brigs and boats, and *chasse-marées* with their guns on board, had sailed to the eastward, and 250 gun-boats were ready to sail'. Troops awaiting embarkation were believed to be at Rochefort.[39]

Cornwallis evidently shared Durham's reservations regarding the *Goliath*, for early in February he sent the *Impétueux*, 74 (Captain Byam Martin) to relieve her. During that month the *Defiance* was blown off course by 'a violent gale' from the north-west, and owing to a sudden change of wind 'could not regain our station, notwithstanding every exertion in my power,' wrote Durham to Cornwallis. On 23 February he learned from the master of an American schooner, which had sailed from Bordeaux, that thirty gunboats carrying 'a number of troops' and twelve merchantmen 'with about 6,000 troops on board' had left that port for Rochefort. 'The troops were marched down the south-west side of the river, and embarked a considerable distance from the town.' About 300 gunboats had been built at Bordeaux. Similar information was given to Durham by the master of a Danish vessel he boarded three days later. 'Great exertions are making in every department to forward the vessels for the invasion [of England]' Durham told Cornwallis. A large guardship, three frigates and two brigs lay in the entrance to the Gironde, and four transports 'at the bottom of the river, waiting for a southerly wind to sail for Rochefort'.[40]

However, it was the increased French force at Brest that was of more immediate concern to Cornwallis. On 20 February Captain William Prowse of the frigate *Sirius* had reconnoitred Brest Roads and reported that there were eighteen line of battleships, four frigates and three corvettes there along with smaller craft. Three of the frigates and one of the three-deckers were clearly ready for sea. Cornwallis stationed a squadron of fast-sailing two-deckers under Sir Thomas Graves off Brest and kept the remainder of the Channel Fleet with him off Ushant, ready to pursue the enemy should it put to sea. On 22 February he wrote letters recalling the *Defiance* and *Impétieux* to his station, leaving Captain John Maitland of the frigate *Boadicea* in command off Rochefort.[41]

The *Defiance* spent most of the following month refitting at Cawsand Bay. Court martials were held, at Durham's request, on a seaman who had deserted from one of the ship's boats off the French coast and on another who had taken the opportunity to abscond from the ship's launch at Plymouth Dock. The *Defiance* regained Brest on 24 March 1804, and was assigned to the squadron commanded by Vice-Admiral Sir Robert Calder. The son of a Scottish baronet who had obtained, through Lord Bute, a sinecural post at Court, and grandson on his English mother's side of a rear-admiral, Calder was Jervis's captain of the fleet at the battle of Cape St Vincent. Now fifty-nine, he had been cruising off Cape Clear when he was called to Ushant in mid-March. Having as his flagship the 98-gun *Prince of Wales*, he was now instructed by Cornwallis to take under his orders the *Defiance, Boadicea, Goliath, Minotaur* (Captain Charles Mansfield) and *Téméraire*, 98 (Captain Eliab Harvey) and cruise off Rochefort. If the ships and transports of that port, which were reportedly 'ready to sail upon some expedition', were to put to sea, his squadron was to communicate regularly to Cornwallis any intelligence he might obtain regarding the enemy, 'and continue upon this service until further orders'. In the temporary absence of Rear-Admiral Graves, who had made for Cawsand Bay, Cornwallis on 31 March put Captain Byam Martin in charge of the inshore squadron off Brest. In view of the 'very considerable' enemy force there, 'said to be on the point of sailing', it was 'of the utmost national importance that the port should be as closely watched as possible', Cornwallis stressed.[42]

Calder had, of course, been captain of the *Barfleur* when Durham first went aboard her as second lieutenant, and their paths had crossed more recently when both were members of the court martial on the *Danaë* mutineer John Marret. Whether any personal animosity already existed between them is unknown; they would end their present association on the sourest of notes.

Despite having been so recently refitted, the *Defiance* gave Durham trouble almost as soon as she sailed. On 4 April the carpenter reported a leak, which made her admit 'a considerable deal of water' over the following weeks, until she was able to put into Quiberon Bay for repair. She worked into the bay on 25 April and remained for several days before anchoring off Houat. While she was at Quiberon 'not less than 200 sail of vessels of different descriptions arrived from the southward', passing through the bay or sheltering in the creeks surrounding it. There were 'Gun Brigs of very large dimensions and uncommon fine Vessels, carrying very heavy metal with a Number of Troops on board.' Despite the 'unremitting exertions' of Captain John Wesley Wright, commanding the *Vincejo* brig and of the boats of the *Defiance*, all these vessels 'pass'd in safety'. On 28 April the barge and pinnace, which had been sent in shore to reconnoitre two Spanish brigs, came under attack from the batteries. A shot shattered the pinnace, wounding three of Durham's men and killing two others, who were surreptitiously buried on French soil.[43]

Captain Wright was liaising with French royalists along the coast. Durham warned him 'of his danger of being cut off by the enemy', who were wise to his operations. He paid no heed, and took to repeating a line from a poem he had recently read: 'return victorious, or return no more'. At seven in the morning of 8 May the *Vincejo*, becalmed in Quiberon Bay, was spotted by a flotilla of seventeen enemy sail. In an effort to escape, her crew worked the oars until they were exhausted. She was armed with twenty 18-pounder carronades, but the enemy kept out of her range, and her shot fell short. The ship, already leaky from having recently lost most of her keel, was subjected to a merciless battering from the enemy's long 18- and 24-pounders. Captain Wright, early in the action, was wounded by grapeshot in the groin. At eleven o'clock, when most of her crew had fallen and her hull was so riddled that she was sinking, Wright struck. He was thrown into the Temple in Paris, where he had been confined years before with Sir Sidney Smith. He was repeatedly questioned under unspeakable torture but steadfastly refused to co-operate with his interrogators. Durham recalled that Wright 'was more hated by the republicans than any other Englishman, having distinguished himself at the memorable affair of Acre'. (On 27 October 1805, six days after Trafalgar, this brave officer was found dead in his cell with his throat cut, the victim of suicide according to the French and – more credibly – of murder on Napoleon's orders according to the British.)[44]

Unlike a stirring victorious action, which naturally seized the public's imagination, work like Cornwallis's blockade of Brest – 'which deserves to rank as one of the most wonderful operations of the kind in history', to quote an eminent naval historian – made little direct impact on men and women back home. It was an unseen and largely unsung slog. As one writer has eloquently observed: 'Week after week, month after month, year after year, watchers from the French coast could see the white sails of the British ships keeping station with dogged tenacity and unwearied vigilance. In fair weather and foul, through the bitter winter gales of the Channel and the scorching heat of Mediterranean summers, the weather-worn squadrons kept their ceaseless watch, never to leave their posts save when driven from them by storm and tempest.'[45]

Nobody appreciated the Royal Navy's role as the guarantor of Britain's liberty and commerce better than the merchants of the City of London, and on 26 March 1804 the mayor and corporation of the City unanimously passed a resolution thanking Cornwallis and his flag-officers for 'their very eminent services' and 'their great zeal and uncommon exertions' in keeping Britain's enemies 'in a constant state of alarm', not daring to put to sea. Included in this resolution were Nelson, blockading Toulon, and Rear-Admiral Thornbrough and Captain Sir Sidney Smith, blockading the Texel and Dutch ports. The captains, officers, seamen and marines belonging to the respective fleets were thanked 'for their exemplary conduct and their strict regard to discipline whilst blockading the ports of the enemy during a length of time, and with difficulties arising from bad weather, unparalleled'. A copy of the resolution reached Cornwallis in April. It was inspiring, he responded, to be thus noticed.[46]

Much information regarding movements on the French coast was provided by the captain of the 44-gun *Severn*, the intriguing, Jersey-born Philip d'Auvergne, Duc de Bouillon (adopted at the age of thirty-two owing to their common ancestry by the representative of the French ducal house to whose title he succeeded). Captain Prowse, in the *Sirius*, was ordered at the beginning of April to cruise for ten weeks off Cape

Finisterre, protecting British merchantmen and intercepting enemy cruisers, and warning Pellew, off Ferrol, of any ominous developments. On his way to that station Prowse carried stores and men to Calder at Rochefort.[47]

At the end of May Thomas Simons, Durham's second lieutenant, gained valuable intelligence regarding the enemy strength in that port from the master of an American vessel bound from Rochefort to New York. The master reported that five line-of-battle ships lay in the Roads, as well as a sloop of war and twelve gunbrigs newly arrived from Bordeaux. In addition, a new frigate had just been launched and with it in the harbour were a number of small gunboats. A frigate chased in and almost cut off by the *Goliath* and *Boadicea* on 22 May turned out to be from Bordeaux, where she had landed Napoleon's brother Jérôme Bonaparte, who had been in America. 'The enemy's vessels are in a perfect state of readiness to sail', wrote Durham on the basis of this intelligence, 'and the general opinion at Rochefort is that the expedition would certainly leave France the early part of June.'[48]

In July and August 1804 the *Defiance* underwent repairs in Portsmouth Harbour. While she was there several of her crew deserted, including a quartermaster who failed to return from ten days' leave. As usual in such cases, an irritated Durham promptly issued their descriptions and requested the Admiralty to direct the impress service around the country to look out for them. He also applied for the ship's sizeable deficit of marine privates to be filled. But he managed to escape some of these routine worries of command during a brief period away from port, during which the ship was in the care of William Hellard, her first lieutenant.[49]

Later that year Durham and Captain Wolfe of the *Aigle* quarrelled over the distribution of prize money for a Russian vessel which the *Aigle* had detained the previous winter while she was in company with the *Defiance*. Wolfe was obstinately resisting the claim of Durham and the *Defiance*'s crew to a share of the money that had become payable now that the ship had been condemned as a prize. 'I beg to know in what way you wish this business to be settled' wrote Durham acerbically. 'I am ready to submit my claim to any number of Brother Officers – Flag Officers – or meet you in a Court of Law, whichever is most agreeable to you.' Wolfe's reply does not appear to be on record. Neither does that of the man responsible for deciding such matters, King's Advocate Sir John Nicoll, whose opinion Durham sought.[50]

Meanwhile, apparently with his father's encouragement, Durham had his mind on a parliamentary seat in his home region. On 15 January 1805 he wrote to his patron and fellow Tory, Lord Melville, seeking his support for an attempt to become member for the Kinghorn boroughs of Fife. As a member of Parliament he would receive no salary, but he would wield a not insignificant amount of influence useful to himself, his family and his friends, and he would not need to relinquish his active naval career. 'I trust I shall have the honor of your Lordship's good wishes in the event of becoming a candidate – from being blown off with the fleet I have had no communication with England these three weeks', he informed Melville from aboard the *Defiance*, newly arrived at Plymouth.[51] He failed in his aim, but 1805 would unfold as one of the most momentous years of his life.

On 19 February 1805 Cornwallis ordered Vice-Admiral Calder in the *Prince of Wales* to succeed Rear-Admiral Alexander Cochrane in command of the squadron off Ferrol and watch the enemy's ships at that port and at Corunna, about twelve miles to the south-west. Calder's instructions were to use his 'best endeavours to intercept them should they attempt to put to sea', to gather all the information he could regarding their 'proceedings and designs', and to communicate such intelligence assiduously to the commander-in-chief. He reached his station on 2 March. The squadron consisted of the *Malta*, 80 (Captain Edward Buller), the *Montagu*, 74 (Captain Robert Waller Otway), the *Repulse*, 74 (Captain the Hon. Arthur Kaye Legge), the *Terrible*, 74 (Captain Lord Henry Paulet), Byam Martin's *Impétieux* and the big frigate *Indefatigable*, commanded by Graham Moore. Durham's *Defiance* and the 74-gun *Hero* (Captain the Hon. Alan Hyde Gardner) joined a little later.[52]

That part of the Spanish shoreline patrolled by the squadron was well known to Calder as being subject to 'very thick fogs... attended with a very heavy swell, which tumbles in on this coast with light winds, and makes it very unsafe for large ships to keep close in with the land'. But he provided his captains with detailed advice regarding its navigation, and was hopeful that the 'General Instructions' he issued to them would prevent the enemy slipping out of port unseen. His ships

are to keep as close in shore as the Wind and Weather will permit them in safety, and to endeavour daily to look into those Ports: it is advisable to do this as early and as late in the Day as they can, and to place themselves during the Night in the driftway of the Harbour mouth, so that the Enemy may not be able to come out without their being perceived. Upon such discovery you are to throw up Rockets, burn blue lights, and fire Guns until noticed and joined by me. On my approach you will make known their bearing, force, and how they are steering...

> As the Enemy may attempt to run Frigates and Corvettes with stores along
> shore into Ferrol and Corunna during the Night when the Wind is Easterly,
> I would particularly have you close in on the Weather shore always as the day
> breaks.[53]

Over the ensuing weeks there were various changes to enemy numbers in
the ports under surveillance. In mid-May the *Defiance* and the *Indefatigable*
reported that the ships at both Ferrol and Corunna were 'in perfect readiness
for sea'. About a month later Captain Moore found that the enemy force at
Ferrol consisted of '13 sail of the line, 3 frigates, a corvette and a brig', and
this information was confirmed by the commanders of two neutral vessels
which, on leaving Ferrol, were promptly detained by Captain Prowse.[54]

Napoleon had now decided that Vice-Admiral Pierre-Charles Silvestre
de Villeneuve would be in naval command of the invasionary expedition
to Britain. To secure that mastery of the Channel crucial to the invasion's
success, the French emperor devised a clever plan. Villeneuve would
sail from Toulon for Martinique, followed by Vice-Admiral Honoré-
Joseph-Antoine Ganteaume's Brest fleet, thereby luring away the British
blockading squadrons. If Ganteaume should fail to make the rendezvous
Villeneuve, having waited there for thirty-five days, would make for Ferrol
and break the British blockade. The French and Spanish ships thus liberated
from that port would sail with Villeneuve to Brest, joint with Ganteaume's
fleet, and sail to Boulogne to await final instructions from the emperor.

Managing to avoid Nelson's fleet, which had sailed for Sardinia,
Villeneuve slipped out of Toulon on 30 March and on 9 April reached
Cadiz, where he effected a junction with a Spanish squadron under the
Sicilian-born Admiral Don Federico Carlos Gravina, despite the presence
off that port of a British squadron commanded by Vice-Admiral Sir John
Orde. On 12 May Nelson set out for the West Indies. He missed his quarry,
who had put to sea again. But in the ensuing rush homewards Nelson
steered in the direction of Cape Spartel while Villeneuve followed a more
northerly course towards Ferrol and thus managed to evade his pursuer.[55]

Calder, meanwhile, was in dread of a drawn battle, which he suspected
would be interpreted by the public as a defeat. He believed that he had an
insufficient number of ships of the line with which properly to blockade
Ferrol, and asked in vain for more. Owing to several comings and goings
the strength of his squadron fluctuated, and he wished that some ships
which had been out for a long time, including the *Defiance*, would be
allowed home to refit. He fretted about dwindling supplies, and Admiral

Lord Gardner, temporarily commanding the Channel Fleet in Cornwallis's absence, observed that 'off Ferrol is by no means a place for victuallers to be sent, as there is always a heavy swell even in a calm, and, when there is any wind, so heavy a chopping sea as to prevent boats from clearing victuallers'. On 29 June water and provisions sent from Plymouth were unloaded after nearly a week's delay owing to bad weather, giving the squadron enough victuals for three months. Nearly a fortnight later Cornwallis sent a despatch vessel to Calder off Ferrol, and another to Rear-Admiral Charles Stirling off Rochefort, conveying the news that Nelson had advised that the combined Franco-Spanish squadrons under Villeneuve were on their way home from the West Indies.[56]

'I shall pay every attention in my power to prevent being surprised, or be caught by them embayed', wrote Calder to Cornwallis on receipt of this information on 15 July, 'and as far as the force placed under my directions will enable me, I shall endeavour to prevent the combined squadrons expected from the West Indies from making a junction now at Ferrol, which I have little doubt is their intention, and then to make the best of their way into Rochefort.' The number of enemy ships at Ferrol, he added, were 'increasing daily', and appeared to total '16 sail of the line, 5 frigates, and 3 corvettes'. That same day he was reinforced, on Cornwallis's orders, by Stirling's squadron. His battle force now consisted of his own flagship and that of Stirling, the 98-gun *Glory*, the *Barfleur*, 98 (Captain George Martin), the *Windsor Castle*, 98 (Captain Charles Boyles), and eleven other ships of the line: the 80-gun *Malta*, the *Defiance*, *Hero*, *Repulse*, *Ajax* (Captain William Brown), *Dragon* (Captain Edward Griffith), *Thunderer* (Captain William Lechmere), *Triumph* (Captain Henry Inman), *Warrior* (Captain Samuel Hood Linzee), all of 74 guns, and two 64s, the *Agamemnon* (Captain John Harvey) and the *Raisonable* (Captain Josias Rowley). He also had with him the *Sirius* and the *Frisk* as well as the 40-gun frigate *Egyptienne* (Captain the Hon. Charles Elphinstone Fleeming) and the *Nile* lugger (Lieutenant John Fennell), which had both been with Stirling.[57]

With this force Calder was ordered by Cornwallis 'to proceed 30 or 40 leagues to the westward, and to cruise six or eight days, for the purpose of intercepting the French and Spanish squadron... after which I was to return to my post off Ferrol, and Rear-Admiral Stirling off Rochefort'. These instructions were received in orders brought by the *Egyptienne* shortly before the rest of Stirling's squadron joined Calder.[58]

Since the *Defiance* was a fast-sailing vessel commanded by 'an officer of known skill and activity', as a contemporary of Durham put it, she was employed by Calder as 'one of the eyes' of the squadron. On arrival off Finisterre he sent for Durham and instructed him to perform that service again, telling him that in looking out for Villeneuve he could take up any position he chose, 'only don't lose sight of me.'[59]

While consequently ensuring that Calder's flagship was always visible from the masthead of the *Defiance*, Durham positioned himself a good way from the *Prince of Wales*. He was sometimes on her weather-bow and sometimes on her weather-quarter. On 21 July, towards half-past eleven in the morning, when the *Defiance* was upon Calder's weather-bow, her master, William Kirby, said to Durham: 'Sir Robert is standing too much to the north east to fall in with the enemy if they are making [for] Ferrol or Cape Finisterre.' Having consulted the chart Durham agreed, and the ship was put about to the west-south-west. The *Prince of Wales* still stood to the eastward.[60]

During the night the *Defiance* continued to work westward under easy sail. By the next morning, 22 July, she was about ten miles to windward of Calder, and 'barely in sight' from the flagship's masthead, as Ralph Randolph Wormeley, a former midshipman on the *Prince of Wales*, would recall. In latitude 44° 17' north by longitude 11° 52' west from Greenwich, most of the British squadron were in their prescribed order of sailing in two columns, steering south-west by west on the starboard tack. Some six or seven miles ahead of the vice-admiral was Captain Brown's *Ajax*, and Captain Griffith's *Dragon* was seven or eight miles to leeward. Calder was obliged to use these ships of the line as look-outs because he had only two frigates. Captain Fleeming's *Egyptienne* was two miles on Calder's weather-beam, and the *Sirius* was also to windward. A light breeze blew from the north-west, and there was much cloud. In the words of someone on the former frigate, written the following day, the sea was 'smooth and the weather hazy.' Durham's log noted 'moderate winds with thick hazy weather and rain'.[61]

At about twenty minutes before noon, in an apparent brightening of the skies, Durham sighted Villeneuve's Franco-Spanish fleet. It was steering a direct course for Ferrol, in three columns. Since the *Defiance* was too far from her squadron for the displayed signal – 'I have discovered a strange fleet' – to be seen, Durham attracted Calder's attention by the time-honoured method of letting fly top-gallant sheets, yawing the ship, and firing guns. Wrote Midshipman Wormeley many years later, when he was himself a post-captain: 'I well remember the confidence placed in the vigilance, management, and good fortune of the *Defiance*, and her distinguished captain... a burst of delight thrilled through the decks of the

Prince of Wales, while everyone exclaimed, "the *Defiance* has realised our hopes"'. Had it not been for Durham's discovery, Villeneuve 'must have passed in shore of us, and thereby secured their arrival off Ferrol without any contact with the British fleet'.[62]

Villeneuve had express orders from Napoleon to avoid conflict with the British until he had been reinforced by the squadrons at Ferrol and Brest and taken them up the Channel as far as Boulogne where an invasionary force was gathering. His supplies were low, and sickness, scurvy and dysentery had broken out among his crews. He was conscious of the 'bad masts, bad sails and bad cordage' of the ships in his squadron, and held a very low opinion of the fitness of those of Admiral Gravina. He had successfully escaped Nelson's unrelenting pursuit, only to find Calder blocking his way into port. Regardless of the emperor's wishes, he had no option but to fight.[63]

When his look-out vessels first signalled that they observed enemy sail in the north-north-east, Villeneuve determined to take advantage of the clearing of the haze by continuing on a course to the east-south-east. Once it became apparent that an entire British squadron was on the horizon, he instructed that the order of sailing in three columns be altered to the line of battle in designated order on the larboard tack, and that the ships be cleared for action. Gravina hauled to the wind, his squadron of six ships taking the van. Following his flagship, the *Argonauta*, 80, in a northerly direction were the *Terrible*, 70, *America*, 64, *Espana*, 64, *San Rafael*, 80, *Firme*, 74, *Pluton*, 74, *Mont Blanc*, 74, *Atlas*, 74, *Berwick*, 74, *Neptune*, 80, *Bucentaure*, 80 (Villeneuve's flagship), *Formidable*, 80 (bearing the flag of Admiral Pierre Dumanoir le Pelley), *Intrépide*, 74, *Scipion*, 74, *Swift-sure*, 74, *Indomptable*, 80, *Aigle*, 74, *Achille*, 74, and, finally, the 74-gun *Algésiras* (flagship of Rear-Admiral Charles-René Magon). This line looked 'very good' and 'in close order' wrote a lieutenant on Captain Rowley's *Raisonable*, 'their frigates to windward, seven in number and two [sic] brigs, all of them close to the wind on the larboard tack; wind about N.N.W., fine pleasant weather, smooth water'.[64]

In effecting an engagement Calder manifested 'great skill and intrepidity', Durham much later conceded. About twenty minutes to one, having got near enough to the enemy fleet to assess its strength, Durham signalled the information that Villeneuve had with him twenty sail of the line, five frigates and two brigs. (In fact, there were seven frigates.) There were, therefore, more line-of-battle ships than Calder had originally been led to expect, and he must have ruefully remembered his unmet requests for reinforcements. He now ordered his squadron to 'prepare for action' and to 'form line in close order'.

Remembered that lieutenant on the *Raisonable*: 'The most prompt obedience was observed, every ship having as much sail as she could make.'[65]

At about two o'clock Calder signalled the *Defiance* and the other detached ships of the line to rejoin him. The frigates were to keep sight of the Franco-Spanish and accordingly steered closer to them. Having approached within less than two miles of Villeneuve's fleet Durham made sail, and at three took his place in the line which had formed on the starboard tack, standing almost due south, bringing it to leeward of the enemy. Captain Gardner's *Hero*, 74, was the van ship, leading the *Ajax*, 74 (now also taking her place in the line), *Triumph*, 74, *Barfleur*, 98, *Agamemnon*, 64, *Windsor Castle*, 98, *Defiance*, 74, *Prince of Wales*, 98, *Repulse*, 74, *Raisonable*, 64, *Dragon*, 74 (when she arrived, tardily, from her far-flung position to leeward), *Glory*, 98, *Warrior*, 74, *Thunderer*, 74, and *Malta*, 80.[66]

Before battle was joined, shots from the *Sirène*, one of Villeneuve's frigates, rang out in warning through the fog that had descended. She was towing a Spanish galleon laden with specie and a valuable cargo. The galleon had recently been recovered from a British privateer. But now Captain Prowse's *Sirius*, intent on capturing such a rich prize, was endeavouring to cut her and the *Sirène* off from their fleet. Unluckily for Prowse, the three headmost Spanish ships, led by Gravina's flagship, fell out of line to protect the threatened vessels. Abandoning his designs on the galleon, Prowse, now in grave danger, put about. Which, if any, of the three Spaniards fired on his frigate as they loomed one by one out of the fog is a matter of dispute, and it may have been when the *Sirius* came abreast of the fourth ship in the enemy van as a result of her manoeuvre that she incurred casualties.[67]

Calder's intention was to attack Villeneuve's centre with his van, but his leading vessel, confused by the impaired visibility, got abreast of the enemy's rear. At about half-past four, therefore, Calder gave orders to tack in succession to the north so as to fetch the centre. Meanwhile, fearing trickery, Villeneuve directed his fleet to make the same manoeuvre. The leading British ship, the *Hero*, unaware of Calder's latest signal, tacked to starboard on coming up with the enemy rear. She received the fire of the larboard guns of the *Argonauta* – which, owing to Villeneuve's order, had shortly after five o'clock come abreast of the rearmost French ships and was steering south-west by west – and replied with her starboard guns. Repelled by two Spaniards, the *Ajax*, directly astern of the *Hero*, bore away towards the *Prince of Wales*, so that Captain Brown, through a speaking trumpet, could apprise Calder of the change of position in the respective vans. The *Ajax* then wore and fell into line astern of the *Glory*.

Meanwhile, making their way more or less sightlessly through the fog, the *Triumph*, *Barfleur*, *Agamemnon*, *Windsor Castle*, and *Defiance* successively tacked in the wake of the *Hero*. 'At 4 modt breezes with thick hazy wr answered the Signal to bring the Enemy to close action at 5.10 found by HM Ship *Windsor Castle* that the Enemy had tack'd, tack'd ship accordly at 5.30 commenced action being thick foggy wr' is the unpunctuated summary of occurrences in Durham's log. Little was visible, but by six o'clock the sustained cacophony of 'a tremendous carronade' assailed the ears as each ship engaged the first adversary she encountered in the fog, exchanging fire at close range. By seven the action had developed into a general *mêlée*, the smoke of the guns merging with the elements to create a dense grey mass billowing from the sky. 'It became so thick that it was impossible to see anything', wrote Villeneuve. 'We fired by the light of the enemy's fire, almost always without seeing them.' He could no longer tell whether the British were to starboard or larboard. The fact was that since Calder's ships had tacked in the wake of the *Hero* as she came up with the *Argonauta*, the two fleets were running parallel to each other on the same starboard tack.[68]

The *Defiance* received several shots in her hull, masts, yards and rigging. Amid the blindfold muddle several of Calder's ships – his flagship, Captain Lechmere's *Thunderer* and Buller's *Malta* – found themselves in combat with several opponents at once, and consequently received a battering. Durham appears to have left no detailed snippet concerning the action, and what is perhaps the only surviving description of the *Defiance*'s movements that day outside the sketchiness of his log came from the pen of somebody aboard Captain Fleeming's *Egyptienne*. At twenty-five minutes past seven this now anonymous person saw the *Windsor Castle* 'with her fore topmast cut away keeping up a most brilliant fire'. Fifteen minutes later he 'observed the *Defiance*, then ahead of the *Windsor Castle*, throw all aback, which prevented the latter from being raked by a French ship who bore up for that purpose, and who hauled her wind between the *Windsor Castle* and a Spanish ship, who at 7.45 stood out of the line with her main and mizenmasts gone; [the *Egyptienne*] tacked and stood towards her, but perceiving the *Defiance* did not fire at her, concluded she had struck, when we re-tacked to be ready to assist the *Windsor Castle*'.[69]

Reminiscing, Durham praised 'the most determined bravery' with which the enemy fought throughout the action. In twice coming to the aid of beleaguered Spanish vessels, imperilling herself, the French ship *Pluton* evinced outstanding gallantry. The *Mont Blanc* and *Atlas* also played a full part and suffered materially as a result. But Gravina's squadron bore the brunt of the contest, and was consequently very roughly handled. Reported the first lieutenant of the *Egyptienne*: 'The fog became less thick towards 7 o'clock, when we saw a two-deck ship with her topmasts gone, and immediately tacked to make a dash at her, as she was going to leeward, but finding she was observed she struck her colours, luffed to under the lee of our line, and away went her main and mizenmasts; another soon shared the same fate.' The ships he described were the 74-gun *Firme* and the 80-gun *San Rafael*, both Spaniards. Unlike the British, the enemy did not customarily heave their dead overboard as soon as they expired, and consequently the decks of both ships were strewn with corpses as well as with those barely clinging to life. Each prize had 'lost from 100 to 150 men, and as many wounded', added the lieutenant; the actual figures were higher.[70]

'At 7 saw that one of the Enemie's [*sic*] Ships had struck', reveals Durham's log. 'Made sail ahead still keeping a constant fire on the Enemy at 8 being thick foggy wr left of [*sic*] firing.' Most vessels on both sides of the conflict did the same. The fog now began to dissipate, and the ships of the respective squadrons displayed their distinguishing lights. With the enemy scarcely within range to windward and darkness descending, Calder at about half-past eight made the private night signal to cease action. Certain of his ships failed to notice it, and consequently intermittent firing continued for a further hour.[71]

Calder's squadron brought to on the starboard tack, facing approximately south-west by west. Some of his ships were scattered at a distance: the *Windsor Castle* (towed by the *Dragon*), the dismasted prizes, the *Malta*, and the frigates. Total British casualties were reported as forty-one killed and 158 wounded. (Villeneuve's were 476, most of them on board the captured *Firme* and *San Raphael*.) The *Windsor Castle*, with ten dead and thirty-five wounded, the *Prince of Wales*, with three dead and twenty wounded, and the *Malta*, aboard which the corresponding figures were five and forty, had suffered quite severely, while casualties aboard the *Ajax* and *Thunderer* were moderate. With one dead and seven wounded, the *Defiance* had fared comparatively well. There were no casualties aboard Captain Griffith's *Dragon*, which had got very late into battle, and none aboard Captain Linzee's *Warrior*.[72]

On Calder's instructions the *Nile* and the *Frisk* went around the squadron after the action gathering details of the damage sustained by each line-of-battle ship. Only the *Dragon* was structurally unscathed, and the *Windsor Castle* alone was disabled. The remaining thirteen had varying degrees of damage, and during the hours of darkness routine repairs were performed. Notes Durham's log: '11.40[p.m.] Cross'd a New Mizen topsail Yard the old one being shot away through the Slings.' His ship's mainmast, foreyard and driver-boom were hurt, and her lower rigging, stays and sails cut about. In precise circumstances not described in the sources, her cutter had been sunk by the enemy. And one of her maindeck guns was unserviceable.[73]

Dawn on 23 July revealed a day promising to be as foggy as its predecessor, the weather, in the words of one eyewitness, being 'thick and hazy'. 'People employed repairg the rigging and making every preparation to renew the action', ran Durham's log. Calder was examining the reports of damage aboard his ships which had been collected for him overnight. He was soon to learn that the *Barfleur* had since sprung a yard. Although, later that morning, only the *Windsor Castle* answered affirmatively his signal enquiring who wished to lie by to refit, he found the damage aboard his other ships 'much more considerable' than he had anticipated. He would later testify that while they were making good their defects during the night 'I did flatter myself that I should, the next morning, have been in a condition to renew the engagement; and with that view I did all I could, consistently with the attention necessary to prevent a separation between any parts of the squadron, to keep as near as possible to the enemy during the night.' But Villeneuve's ships at the start of 23 July stood 'about eight or nine miles to windward, collecting themselves into a body', and as far as Calder and the officers aboard the *Prince of Wales* could tell they 'had not suffered in their masts and yards, except one, which had lost her fore-topsail-yard, and was in the act of replacing it'. By contrast, not one of Calder's own ships seemed to be in a suitable state 'to carry sufficient sail to windward, particularly as there was a heavy swell, which would have endangered the crippled masts and yards of my squadron, had I been rash enough to have attempted it.'[74]

Between the two fleets at daybreak lay the advanced British squadron, consisting of the *Barfleur, Hero, Triumph*, and possibly the *Agamemnon*. To windward of them lay the enemy. About five miles to leeward of the main British force lay the *Windsor Castle*, towed by the *Dragon*, and at a comparable distance further to leeward, invisible to the vice-admiral, were the *Thunderer*, the *Malta*, the two frigates, and the crippled prizes. At about ten minutes to eight Calder sighted the *Thunderer*, which signalled the *Malta*'s bearings. Shortly afterwards the *Malta*, apparently towing the *Firme*, came into view, along with the *Sirius*, towing the *San Rafael*, and the *Egyptienne*. Calder signalled the *Malta* to join him, and the *Egyptienne* assumed responsibility for the *Firme*. 'Her rudder', Captain Fleeming discovered, was 'disabled, many of her ports [were] blown off, and she made so much water through the shot holes that we could just keep her free.' As for the *San Rafael*, 'all her masts were gone, except the fore-mast, which was not fit to carry sail'.[75]

'The prizes are now wrecks', Captain Buller of the *Malta* advised Calder by letter that day.

> I have on board the *Malta* all the principal officers of the [captured] Spanish ships, with 100 Spanish seamen. I have had the misfortune to have 5 men killed and 40 badly wounded, but the ship is in a perfect state for battle [this was despite the fact that her mizenmast had been damaged, her mizen topmast and topsail yard shot away, and her mainyard very badly hurt]. I am in love with all hands... God bless you, Sir!... wishing you every possible success...[76]

Calder's misgivings about recommencing battle that morning in view of the damage to his ships was compounded by his determination to safeguard his prizes, 'wrecks' though they were reported to be, and his awareness that he required more frigates. He was painfully aware that the enemy had 'three sail of the line and three or four frigates constantly advanced on their weather-bow', a detachment alert to capture any of his ships that might through some movement of his become isolated from the main body of his fleet. 'This I conceive it was my duty, on every occasion, to prevent. By doing so, I preserved the victory I had acquired, in spite of their very great superiority.'[77]

In addition he was fearful that in the continued absence of his vessels and those of Rear-Admiral Stirling from their respective stations, the enemy squadrons at Ferrol and Rochefort would put to sea. He knew that 'there were 16 sail of the line at Ferrol, within a few hours sail, who, if not already out, might, on receiving intelligence from the combined squadrons, have come out to their assistance, or, in the event of my not being in a situation to return to Ferrol, the continuance of which blockade was one main object of my instructions, there would be no force to oppose those squadrons, and that they would more than probably have pushed for England, to facilitate the invasion which was then every moment expected. I really felt that I should be running too great a hazard, and putting my fleet into a situation of danger which I could never have justified.' Moreover:

> I am far from encouraging the idea, that on no account is an engagement to be risked where the enemy is even greatly superior: I know too well the

spirit, the valour, and bravery of my countrymen, to entertain such a thought; my conduct in commencing the action is a decisive proof of it. But I do deprecate the idea, that, under all circumstances, an engagement must be continued as long as it is practicable to continue it, whatever may be the opinion of the officer commanding a squadron that he puts to hazard, by such continuance, the advantages he had gained by his original attack... I contend that every case of an engagement with a superior force must depend upon its own circumstances; and the propriety or impropriety of entering into, or renewing it, must depend upon the discretion of the commander, to be exercised according to the best of his judgment, and subject to that responsibility which attaches to all persons in situations of command.[78]

Calder felt it wise to keep his squadron together, making no attempt to renew the action unless the enemy offered it, or an opportunity of engaging in more favourable circumstances than prevailed on 23 July presented itself. And fearing that Villeneuve's aim was to join up with the ships at Ferrol, he considered it his duty to keep between the Franco-Spanish fleet and that port. He sought to try to draw the enemy northward, so that he could accompany the stricken *Windsor Castle*, *Firme*, and *San Rafael* out of the reach of the squadron at Rochefort, and perhaps have a chance of re-attacking Villeneuve before the latter could get safely into a French port. 'Having formed this conclusion, I acted upon it during the two days that the enemy remained in sight, keeping my squadron collected under an easy sail, certainly never offering, but as certainly never avoiding an engagement, had the enemy chosen to bring it on.'[79]

At nine o'clock in the morning of 23 July Calder stood on to the north-east, protecting the *Windsor Castle* and the prizes, while the cutter *Frisk* sailed with a despatch and enclosures for Cornwallis. 'Yesterday at noon I was favoured with the view of the combined squadrons of France and Spain', began Calder's triumphal account of the previous day's happenings for the commander-in-chief.

I have to observe the enemy had every advantage of wind and weather during the whole day. The weather had been foggy at times a great part of the morning, and very soon after we had brought them to action the fog was so thick at intervals that we could with great difficulty see the ships ahead or astern of us. This rendered it impossible to take the advantages of the enemy by signals, as I could have wished to have done. Had the weather been more favourable I am led to believe the victory would have been more complete.

I have very great pleasure in saying every ship exerted and was conducted in the most masterly style, and I beg leave here publicly to return to Rear-Admiral Charles Stirling, and every captain, officer and man whom I had the honour to command on that day my most grateful thanks for their very conspicuous, gallant, and very judicious good conduct.

The Honourable Captain Gardner, of the *Hero*, led the van squadron in a most masterly and officer-like manner, to whom I feel myself particularly indebted.

Churlishly, perhaps, there was no mention of Durham, whose vigilance had brought Calder in sight of Villeneuve. The dispatch continued:

The enemy must have suffered greatly. They are now in sight to windward, and when I have secured the captured ships, and put the squadron to rights I shall endeavour to avail myself of every opportunity that may offer to give you some further account of these combined squadrons.

At the same time it will behove me to be upon my guard against the combined squadrons at Ferrol, as I am led to believe they have sent off one or two of their crippled ships last night for that port. Therefore, possibly I may find it necessary to make a junction with you off Ushant with the whole squadron.

I am under the necessity of sending the *Windsor Castle* to you, in consequence of the damage she sustained in the action. Captain Buller has acquainted me that the prisoners on board the prizes assert Ferrol to be the port to which the enemy's squadrons are bound.[80]

Villeneuve, early on the morning of 23 July, was reforming his line on the starboard tack, still in a southerly course. The British, by concentrating to leeward and standing on the larboard tack, drew further away, giving Villeneuve – who had shifted his flag to the frigate *Hortense* – the impression that, although under topsails only, they were endeavouring to flee. At a quarter to ten he ordered his ships to tack in succession, retaining their order, and to go on the same tack as the British, who were then pursued. Not long afterwards one of Villeneuve's frigates, the *Didon*, which had been sent on ahead to reconnoitre, came so near that on Calder's orders she was chased away by Captain Inman's *Triumph*, which tacked to do so. The *Triumph*'s mainmast had been much injured in the previous day's action and her foremast was sprung; to Inman's intense relief they did not, now, go by the board. The enemy, he saw, 'were in Line of Battle to windward of this Frigate, about three or four miles farther I suppose on our Weather Beam under their topsails... apparently repairing their Damages'. He noticed that 'one of the ships in the Rear appeared to have the Head of her Bowsprit gone, and apparently in tow of another, a second with his foreyard down and fore top gallant mast, another with one of her topsail yards down', but he did not report this to Calder for 'four or five Days after the Business was over'. It is possible that the vice-admiral might have been induced to fight afresh had he been aware of such details, for the Spanish ships in particular had received very substantial damage. When Calder remarked in his despatch to Cornwallis that the enemy fleet 'must have suffered greatly' he was perhaps referring exclusively to casualties, for as far as the condition of their ships were concerned he was influenced by the impressions he had gained at first light.[81]

At noon, in cloudy weather and with a heavy swell, the moderate breeze remained in the north-west. An hour and a half later Villeneuve gave orders to bear up together to the north-east for a general chase, and let Gravina know that he was bent on a decisive engagement. A little after three o'clock the Franco-Spanish fleet in line abreast, steering north-east by east, was seen by the British, who immediately hoisted their colours and hauled closer to the wind in expectation of an attack. But at about four o'clock Villeneuve, having changed his mind, hauled to the wind on the same tack as Calder's vessels, signifying his disinclination to renew action after all. He would limply explain to his government that 'it was impossible to engage in the manner I wished'. Calder, who showed no intention of becoming the aggressor, resumed his course, steering north-east like the enemy.[82]

Villeneuve's decision not to strike at a fleet inferior in numbers exasperated his superiors. Rear-Admiral Magon, aboard the *Algésiras*, was reputedly so livid that 'he stomped and foamed at the mouth, and furiously pacing up and down his own ship, when he saw that of the Admiral passing him in retreat, cursed him, and flung at him in ungovernable rage whatever happened to be at hand'. Recriminations erupted in the combined fleet, the French accusing their allies of having 'thrown away two ships by gross incompetence and blundering', and the Spaniards countering that they had endured the heat of the conflict unaided, and that their two captured vessels had been 'deserted in action and sacrificed'.[83]

Between six and seven the following morning, 24 July, Durham was ordered to keep sight of the enemy, then some eighteen miles distant, and accordingly took up his station between the two fleets. Since midnight the light wind had gradually changed direction in favour of the British, and by eight o'clock was north-north-east, though north-west occasionally.

The Franco-Spanish fleet was thus brought nearly astern of Calder's. 'Fully expecting' that Calder, now having the wind, which increased in strength as the day went on, would renew the action, Durham made the signal 'You can weather the enemy'. He was perplexed when no movement ensued. With topsails, topgallants and foresails set, Villeneuve's fleet, bound for refuge at Vigo, edged away, steering south-east by south, while Calder's continued under easy sail south-east by east. Durham signalled Calder again: 'The enemy increase their distance'. As before, there was no reaction. At about five o'clock in the afternoon, frustrated and incredulous, he enquired by signal 'Am I to keep sight of the enemy?' This time Calder responded. He answered in the negative and recalled the *Defiance* to her station in the line. Within an hour the enemy had disappeared from view.[84]

Durham was infuriated with Calder, believing firmly that the vice-admiral's prime duty was to engage the enemy, and that the fate of the two tumbledown prizes was a secondary consideration. Possessing a sharp eye for value, Durham might have guessed that neither the *Firme* nor the *San Rafael* would be of use to the Royal Navy except in the role of prison hulks. Calder had possessed a golden opportunity, and in Durham's view a patriotic responsibility, to recommence action, and he had wilfully let it pass. No doubt it also occurred to Durham that a further action offered the prospect of richer prizes. As the ship resumed her place in the line, Durham summoned his officers and told them 'to be particular in their journals, as that was not the last they would hear of that affair'.[85]

He then went on board the *Prince of Wales*, to be mildly admonished by Calder. 'Captain, you made me some improper signals – you were over-zealous', the vice-admiral said. 'However, I will read you some of my despatch that is gone home.' Calder then produced a copy of the account of proceedings that he had written the day after the action to Lord Barham, who in May had replaced Melville as first lord of the Admiralty. 'I have had the good fortune to have fallen in with the combined squadrons of Toulon and Cadiz upon their return from the West Indies. The action has been unique, having been fought in a fog at night', were its opening sentences. Calder undoubtedly passed over the middle of the despatch, in which as a reward for what he considered a victory he none-too-subtly solicited favours from the Crown. But he perhaps read out the conclusion:

> I shall, as soon as I have secured the prizes and put my squadron to rights,
> do everything I shall judge prudent at these critical times; well knowing the

consequence of risking this squadron at this moment when the Ferrol and Rochefort squadrons are upon the move. If I find things are as I apprehend, I shall make the best of my way to Ushant. I shall look about me for a few days, in the hope of falling in with Lord Nelson, who may be close at the heels of these gentry. Let what will happen, rest assured, my lord, I shall be upon my guard, and at the same time do all in my power for his Majesty's service and the good of my country, as far as my abilities will enable me to act.[86]

Calder's assertion that 'good fortune' had allowed him to fall in with the enemy cut Durham like a lash. This most eager and prideful of captains had received several letters from colleagues in the squadron congratulating him on discovering Villeneuve's fleet on the morning of 22 July, including an especially complimentary one from Captain Legge. Yet here was his chief, with power to advance his reputation still further where it mattered, giving him no credit at all. Durham protested. 'Well,' replied Calder, after a pause, 'if I had thought it would have been a feather in your cap, I would have mentioned it.' An astonished Durham retorted 'that he thought bringing the fleet in sight of an enemy was a plumage in the cap of any officer', and quit the cabin in high dudgeon.[87]

of the fleet, praised by his admiral for 'his able assistance' which 'greatly contributed to the public service'. On personally bringing the glad tidings of that victory to his jubilant sovereign he had received a knighthood and, in common with the other senior officers present at the battle, the thanks of Parliament and a gold medal. The ministry had offered him an annuity of £1,200, but with commendable disinterest he had declined this strain on the public purse. Soon afterwards he had been created a baronet. He evidently expected that his behaviour on 22 July would also elicit reward. 'I hope your lordship and my royal master will think I have done all that was possible to have be [*sic*] done', he told Barham in the despatch of 23 July from which he had read extracts to Durham. 'If so, and you should think me deserving of any mark of his royal bounty, I beg leave to observe I have no children, but I have a nephew... to whom I hope his Majesty's royal bounty may extend, if my services should be thought worthy'.[1] (This was probably a veiled request not, as may be thought, for a peerage but for the baronetcy to be extended to his nephew by special remainder.)

In a letter to Calder, Cornwallis expressed 'his greatest satisfaction' at news of the action, and the Admiralty wrote in similar vein. With the disappearance of Villeneuve's fleet Calder had made for Ferrol, arriving there on 29 July. Two days later, finding things quiet, he sent Rear-Admiral Stirling and four sail of the line to Rochefort, from where a French squadron under Captain Zacharie Allemand (comprising five ships of the line, three frigates and two brigs) had put to sea in the interim. Calder's squadron off Ferrol now consisted of nine sail of the line, including the *Defiance*. In view of the prevailing north-easterly wind, Calder thought it likely that Villeneuve had steered for Cadiz, off which port a small British squadron under Vice-Admiral Cuthbert Collingwood had arrived on 8 June. It was some time before Collingwood learned that Villeneuve had put into Vigo, and by 7 August, when he asked Rear-Admiral Sir Richard Bickerton to carry that intelligence to Nelson, who was assumed to be in the vicinity of the Straits, it was too late. Nelson was bound for Britain.[2]

On 14 August Calder joined Cornwallis off Ushant, and the carpenter of the commander-in-chief's flagship, the *Ville de Paris*, immediately came on board the *Defiance* and the other vessels that had been in action to ascertain which, if any, should be sent to Britain to refit. The following afternoon Nelson arrived on his way home. On 16 August Cornwallis, understanding that Villeneuve had put into Ferrol, gave Calder command of eighteen sail of the line. These included six 74s and Rear-Admiral Thomas Louis's 80-gun flagship, the *Canopus*, each of which had been left with Cornwallis

Above: 1 Durham's birthplace, Largo House, Fife. Built in the 1750s, it is now a ruin.

Left: 2 Durham's remarkable grandmother, Margaret Calderwood. By Allan Ramsay.

3 Durham's father, James
Calderwood Durham. By
George Romney.

4 Durham's mother,
Anne Calderwood
Durham. By George
Romney.

5 The loss of the Royal George at Spithead on 29 August 1782.

6 A frigate near the entrance to Falmouth Harbour, where Durham's *Anson* was based.

7 The capture of the *Loire* by Durham's *Anson*, 18 October 1798, with the *Kangaroo* in company.

8 Calder's Action, 22 July 1805. The *Defiance* is firing at far left.

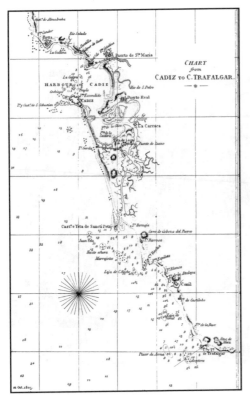

9 Chart of the Spanish coast from Cadiz to Cape Trafalgar.

10 Nelson explaining tactics to his commanders before Trafalgar. Durham is probably the booted figure on the extreme right.

11 A woman such as Jane Townshend aboard a man-of-war.

12 The battle of Trafalgar, 21 October 1805. Watercolour by W.L.Wyllie, R.A.

13 Nelson's funeral at St Paul's Cathedral, showing Durham, other banner-bearers, and clergy around the coffin immediately before it was lowered into the crypt.

14 Carlisle Bay, Barbados, where Durham's flagship was stationed when he was naval commander-in-chief at the Leeward Islands.

Left: 15 Sir Philip Durham as a vice-admiral about 1820. By Sir Henry Raeburn.

Below: 16 HMS *Victory*, in Portsmouth Harbour, flying Nelson's famous signal at Trafalgar on an anniversary of the battle. Watercolour by W.L. Wyllie, R.A.

by Nelson, and the 100-gun *Britannia*, flagship of Rear-Admiral the Earl of Northesk. Except for the *Prince of Wales*, the undamaged *Dragon* and the frigate *Sirius*, none of the ships in Calder's fleet had been with him on 22 July. His orders were 'to endeavour, as soon as possible, to get information of the enemy's force and situation, and use your utmost exertion to prevent their sailing, or intercept it should they attempt it'.[3]

Villeneuve had, however, put into Cadiz, where his fleet was watched, hawk-like, by Collingwood's squadron. The faint-hearted French admiral had steered northwards from Vigo, but to Napoleon's disgust and consternation his resolve had faltered, and he failed to effect a junction with Ganteaume's Brest fleet or with Allemand's marauding squadron. Had Villeneuve continued on his voyage to Brest and received the reinforcements awaiting him there, he would have had under his command a presumably invincible force.

When Napoleon, at Boulogne overseeing final preparations for the invasion of Britain, learned on 22 August of Villeneuve's flight southwards, he flew into a paroxysm of rage. The admiral was 'a coward and a traitor' who 'has no plan, no courage, and no insight'. His behaviour disrupted his emperor's plans, diverting the latter's attention from the assault upon British soil that was imminent to a military campaign east of the Rhine. Lacking the grand fleet which was to convey them across the Channel, the troops with whom Napoleon had aimed to 'put an end to the destinies and existence of England' were left idle at Boulogne. Their camp was therefore broken up, and they commenced the march towards the Danube which was to culminate in the crushing French defeat of the Austrian and Russian armies at Austerlitz on 2 December. Unsatisfactory though Calder's meagre victory was, it had saved England from being overrun.[4]

Meanwhile, in the wake of 22 July, the number of floggings taking place aboard the *Defiance* seems to have escalated. Previously, they appear to have been sporadic, the last occurring on 1 July, when a seaman endured thirty-six lashes for striking the boatswain's mate. Now, there was a spate of them. On a single day shortly after the sea-fight one seaman received forty-eight lashes for being 'Dead Drunk' during action, another (a mere) twenty-four for striking the boatswain's mate, and a marine twelve for being 'Drunk at Quarters'. On subsequent occasions a dozen lashes each were inflicted on two quartermasters and five seamen for neglect of duty and on another for 'disobedience'; eighteen on a seaman for theft; and twenty-four each on two seamen for disobeying orders, on another for insulting the sentinel at his post, and on a marine for insolence to his sergeant, while an unrecorded number were given to a seaman for 'Insolence and disobedience of Orders'. These punishments were par for the course in the Georgian navy: Durham was no sadistic monster. But the fact that they had suddenly increased in frequency aboard his ship can perhaps be partially ascribed to his continuing fury with Calder. While he was surely too balanced an individual actually to vent this wrath upon his men, his mood probably did not incline him to err on the side of leniency when faced with a miscreant. It must have been a relief to him and his jaded crew alike when the *Defiance*, having parted company from Cornwallis on 18 August to have her masts changed and undergo 'extensive repairs' at Portsmouth, anchored at Spithead on 29 August.[5]

Encouraged by the 'approbation' with which Cornwallis and the Admiralty had greeted what he genuinely regarded as his creditable victory of 22 July, Calder wrote to Barham on 17 August, the day before he sailed from Ushant with his new fleet, urging 'some mark of royal favour' for his flag-captain, William Cuming, and for Rear-Admiral Stirling. He also hoped that lieutenants and midshipmen who had been aboard the ships of his squadron during the action would be promoted. He noted that the Admiralty had 'not judged it advisable' to reproduce the whole of his report of 23 July to Cornwallis in the *London Gazette*. (As published it was shorn of its conclusion, in which Calder explained his imperative need to keep watch upon Ferrol, which Captain Buller had learned from the Spanish prisoners was the combined fleet's destination.) This omission 'has led I perceive the papers and the world to bestow on me many remarks, and to publish a great deal of nonsense', Calder observed, adding stoically: 'but this I must put up with.'[6]

Had the conclusion to his despatch appeared in the *Gazette*, Calder might have been spared the intemperate outcry against his performance that had arisen at home: 'The clamour against poor Sir Robert Calder is gaining ground daily, and there is a general cry against him from all quarters', wrote Admiral Lord Radstock, who had been third-in-command at the battle of Cape St Vincent. Speaking up for Calder were, pre-eminently, his elderly brother-in-law, Admiral Robert Roddam, and, in the Lords, his childhood friend, the Earl of Romney, as well as the Duke of Norfolk. But the conviction that Calder had neglectfully allowed the combined fleet to escape was reinforced by printed translations from French accounts – some inspired if not actually composed by Napoleon – which misrepresented the encounter as a triumph for Villeneuve, and alleged that Calder's fleet had cravenly fled despite the French admiral's efforts to re-engage. 'I was busy all night keeping the Fleet in order, that I might be ready to renew the Engagement at daybreak', ran Villeneuve's reproduced despatch of 27 July.

> At the first peep of dawn, I made Signal to bear down upon the Enemy, who had taken their position at a great distance; and endeavoured, by every possible press of sail to avoid renewing the Action.
>
> ...this affair has been honourable to the arms of both Powers [France and Spain]; and had it not been for the thick fog which continued to favour the movements and retreat of the Enemy, he would not have escaped our efforts, nor a decisive Action.[7]

Commented the *Naval Chronicle*, which published this despatch:

> Sir Robert Calder has not yet, even to the Admiralty, as we have reason to believe, given that explanation of his conduct, which his Country expects, and his character demands. With his character, and its failings, we are well acquainted, but we now wish only to regard his talents. The French Fleet certainly did not run away; but on the contrary they may be said even to have pursued us: and this may, perhaps, have been occasioned by some feint of our Admiral, in order to attack the French to greater advantage. But the whole is at present merely conjecture, until some further explanation of this Action has taken place. The account which the French have published in the *Moniteur*, allowing for their usual boasting, and vanity, contains a greater portion of truth than usual.[8]

The depiction of flight, of course, reflected ignominiously on Calder and his captains. Hardly wishing to be associated with failure, possibly fearing that it might ring the death knell of his career, Durham on reaching London almost certainly made it clear that on 22 July Calder could have done no better. Perhaps he spoke similarly of events on the following day. 'None of his [Calder's] captains say he could have done more on the 23rd,' Captain Codrington wrote, 'and, I believe, he is only blamed for giving unfounded hopes of his doing more afterwards.' Durham left his contacts in high places with the unmistakable impression that he considered Calder's conduct on 24 July to be deplorable.[9]

News that Calder and his subsequent force of eighteen ships had caught Villeneuve and struck the decisive blow against the combined fleet was daily hoped for. The knowledge that Villeneuve was still at large, wrote

Lord Minto, caused the 'greatest alarm ever known in the City of London', and it was being said that if the combined fleet should capture 'some valuable merchant fleets of ours' that were on their way home, the East India Company and 'half the City' would go bankrupt. But many people had lost faith in Calder. For example, Lady Malmesbury, wife of the former ambassador extraordinary to the French republic, scoffed that he 'will never catch anything but crabs'. A feeling that only the hero of the Nile and Copenhagen was equal to the task of destroying the Franco-Spanish naval threat had been steadily gaining ground. 'There is again a great bustle on account of the invasion, but there is a general hope in the possibility of Nelson's getting a knock at the combined fleets', remarked Minto on 8 August. Three weeks later he met Nelson in Piccadilly, surrounded by an adulatory crowd of all classes. 'It is really quite affecting to see the wonder and admiration, and love and respect, of the whole world, and the genuine expression of all these sentiments at once, from gentle and simple the moment he is seen.'[10]

Having left the greater part of his squadron with Cornwallis, Nelson had reached Spithead aboard the *Victory* on 18 August. Basing himself at his Surrey home, Merton Place, he had talks in London with war secretary Lord Castlereagh, with Barham and, on 1 September, with Prime Minister Pitt, who, brushing aside Nelson's suggestion that Collingwood should take command of the fleet deemed necessary to defeat Villeneuve, insisted that he must do so. When Pitt asked him to be ready to sail in three days, Nelson answered that he was 'ready now'. Early the following morning Captain Henry Blackwood of the frigate *Euryalus* arrived at Merton with the information that the enemy had put into Cadiz. Nelson immediately left for London, and requested permission to take command of the British naval force off Cadiz, comprising the ships under Collingwood and Calder. The Admiralty acceded at once, and since he was held by Lord Barham to have been on leave from his post in the Mediterranean, his commission as commander-in-chief did not need to be renewed.

'Lord Nelson's new appointment is very extensive and in some degrees unlimited', reported the press on 6 September, explaining that it comprised not only the Mediterranean but included Cadiz. 'His Lordship has the selection of his own favourite officers.' Lord Barham had told him to name the officers he wanted with him, and to select the ships he required in addition to those already on the station. There can have been few officers who would have rejected the opportunity to serve with the eminent, gifted and charismatic hero. To be put under Nelson's orders, wrote Byam Martin, to be thereby 'pushed into the stream of Nelson's glorious career', was 'an order which no man ever received but with a feeling of pride and delight; it was as good as the best prize in the lottery to be placed under such a man'.[11]

Nelson 'had a most happy way of gaining the affectionate respect of all who had the happiness to serve under his command', this associate of Durham went on. 'I never conversed with any officer who served under Nelson without hearing the most hearty expressions of attachment and admiration for his frank and conciliatory manner to all who showed themselves zealous in the execution of their duties.' The extraordinary affection and loyalty evoked by Nelson in his officers can be seen in a remark of Durham's former shipmate Captain Stopford, in a letter written home that summer during the exhausting chase of Villeneuve to the West Indies and back: 'We are all half-starved, and otherwise inconvenienced by being so long away from a port, but our full recompense is that we are with Nelson.'[12]

Durham, whom the fates so favoured, was extremely lucky now. During a visit to the Admiralty he had a fortuitous meeting with Nelson in the waiting room. Whether they had ever before come face to face is unknown. But with the empty right sleeve he jokingly called his 'fin', and perhaps also with the green shade he often wore over one eye, the spare, sunken-cheeked Nelson must have been instantly recognisable, while Durham's reputation as an outstanding captain had seemingly reached the great man. 'I am just appointed to the Mediterranean command and sail immediately', said Nelson. 'I am sorry your ship is not ready; I should have been very glad to have you.' 'Ask Lord Barham to place me under your Lordship's orders and I will soon be ready' was Durham's instantaneous reply.[13]

Having been in the right place at the right time, Durham, thirsting for a clash with Villeneuve that would remove the tarnish of the first, received orders signed by Nelson and dated 11 September, forwarded to him at the George Inn, the hostelry in Portsmouth's High Street favoured by officers of rank and substance, and where Nelson would on 14 September spend his final night ashore. 'You are hereby required and directed to put yourself under my command, and follow and obey all such orders and directions as you shall from time to time receive from me for his Majesty's service' ran one, in the predictable wording of such documents. 'You are hereby required and directed, the moment his Majesty's ship under your command is in all respects ready for sea, to repair with her to St Helens, and join the *Victory*, holding yourself in constant readiness to proceed in company with her to sea', instructed the other. 'But should the *Victory* sail previously to your joining her you are to apply to the Lords Commissioners of the Admiralty, who will furnish you with my rendezvous, where I desire you will join me with the utmost possible expedition.' The rendezvous, it would transpire, was between Cape St Mary and Cadiz and should Nelson not be found there, having already left in pursuit of Villeneuve, directions would be left either at Cape Spartel or Tangiers.[14]

Durham, who was too impatient and too much the warrior to relish the routine of mandatory paperwork – his slapdash ways occasionally earned him a rebuke from naval bureaucrats and superiors – had long since acquired the habit of delegating the chore of writing up his log in neat to somebody else. But from 6 September he maintained it himself, in a careful hand. He was on a portentous mission, under the foremost sea commander of the age; the circumstances were special. It was as if he sensed that the log would become a document of lasting historical significance, and wanted his personal imprint on it. He would continue to fill it in himself until the end of the year.[15]

Owing to repair work the *Defiance* (with a new master, John Osman) was unable to leave Spithead until 24 September. Having learned from Durham, as well as from the captains of the *Agamemnon* and the *Royal Sovereign* (which was to be the new flagship of Collingwood, Nelson's intended second-in-command) that their ships were not yet ready for sea, Nelson set sail in the *Victory* on 15 September, accompanied by the *Euryalus*. A great crush of wildly cheering well-wishers had seen him off at Portsmouth when he arrived to be rowed out to his ship, lying at St Helens. 'I had their huzzas before', he remarked to his flag-captain, Thomas Hardy, as the barge pulled away from the shingly beach. 'I have their hearts now.' Three days later, when passing the Lizard, he was joined by the *Ajax* and the *Thunderer*, which, following Calder's action, had put into Plymouth to refit.[16]

One morning, several weeks earlier, Nelson had been walking in the grounds of Merton with his friend Captain Keats, Durham's former colleague in Warren's squadron. As they strolled, Nelson outlined the plan of attack which he had in mind:

No day can be long enough to arrange a couple of fleets and fight a decisive battle according to the old system... I shall form the fleet into three divisions in three lines; one division shall be composed of twelve or fourteen of the fastest two-decked ships, which I shall keep always to windward or in a situation of advantage, and I shall put them under an officer who, I am sure, will employ them in the manner I wish, if possible. I consider it will always be in my power to throw them into battle in any part I choose; but if circumstances prevent their being carried against the enemy where I desire, I shall feel certain he will employ them effectually and perhaps in a more advantageous manner than if he could have followed my orders. With the remaining part of the fleet, formed in two lines, I shall go at them at once if I can, about one third of their line from their leading ship... I think it will surprise and confound the enemy. They won't know what I am about. It will bring forward a pell-mell battle, and that is what I want.[17]

Nelson may or may not have realised that this hearkened back to bygone methods. The idea of the reserve squadron to windward was advocated by a Spanish naval tactician who flourished in the first half of the sixteenth century and whose writings influenced Henry VIII's admiral, Lord Lisle. The projected use of three squadrons, and a headlong charge to bring on a *mêlée*, revive memories of the first Dutch war, fought during the Cromwellian period. Nelson's prime concern appears to have been

the breaking up of the established order in single line, leading by surprise and concealment to a decisive *mêlée*. He seems to insist not so much upon defeating the enemy by concentration as by throwing him into confusion, upsetting his mental equilibrium in accordance with the primitive idea. The notion of concentration is at any rate secondary, while the subtle scheme for 'containing'... is not yet developed. As he explained his plan to Keats, he meant to attack at once with both his main divisions, using the reserve squadron as a general support. There is no clear statement that he meant it as a 'containing' force, though possibly it was in his mind.[18]

There was some way to go between this plan and that put into practice at Trafalgar.

Hampered initially by a fierce gale from the west-south-west and subsequently by a persistent light and contrary southerly wind, Nelson arrived off Cadiz a fortnight after he set sail from St Helens. His haunting fear was that Villeneuve would deprive him of a battle by remaining in port, as Ganteaume had done at Brest, thereby confounding Cornwallis. Nelson had accordingly sent the *Euryalus* ahead to Collingwood with orders that upon arrival he was not to be greeted with the customary firing of salutes and hoisting of colours, since this would be likely to alert the enemy to his resumption of the Mediterranean command and convince the already timorous Villeneuve not to put to sea. His reception was, nonetheless, rapturous – 'the sweetest sensation of my life'. The battle plan that he had revealed to Keats was expounded at a dinner party attended by fifteen of his commanding officers on 29 September, his forty-seventh birthday, and at an identical function the next day attended by another fifteen. 'The Officers who came on board to welcome my return, forgot my rank as Commander-in-Chief in the enthusiasm with which they greeted me', he wrote. 'As soon as those emotions were past, I laid before them the Plan I had previously arranged for attacking the Enemy; and it was not only my pleasure to find it generally approved, but clearly perceived and understood.' This plan was unveiled at a specially convened meeting in his great-cabin on 4 October. His tactics were hailed as the inspiration of a genius. As he reported delightedly to Lady Hamilton: 'when I came to explain to them the "*Nelson touch*", it was like an electric shock. Some shed tears, all approved – "It was new – it was singular – it was simple!" and from Admirals downwards, it was repeated – "It must succeed, if ever they will allow us to get at them!"'[19]

Nelson added, however, that despite this chorus of approval, there might be 'Judases' among them. He might well have been thinking of Calder, whom he had once suspected of being his professional enemy. During the battle of Cape St Vincent, the then Rear-Admiral Nelson, with his flag aboard the *Captain*, wore out of the line to attack the Spanish van. It was a stunning manoeuvre, though as Calder had reputedly been quick to point out to Jervis it constituted 'an unauthorised departure from the prescribed mode of attack'. Jervis apparently retorted: 'If ever you commit such a breach of orders I will forgive you too.' He wrote an encomium to Nelson in his despatch, which Calder persuaded him to dispense with, since 'any eulogy on his conduct would encourage other officers to do the same, whilst the exclusive praise of one individual would act as a discouragement of the rest'. Jervis was won over by Calder's reminder of the lingering bitterness shown by those of Howe's captains who, following the Glorious First of June, were left out of the despatch in which he lauded some of their colleagues. But while Calder may genuinely have had only the best interests of the service in mind, Nelson and his friends believed that he had been motivated by jealousy. Reinforcing that assumption was the tactlessness of Calder's garrulous spouse, described by another naval wife as 'a clever pleasant woman but a bore [who] talks of nothing but ships and sea service'. After a dinner at her Hampshire home held in the autumn following Jervis's victory, Lady Calder, made 'still more talkative than usual' by 'half a dozen glasses of wine', decried the knighthood of the Bath given to Nelson for his conduct, insisting that the 'red ribbon' of that most prestigious and coveted of orders should have gone not to him but to her husband.[20]

However, Nelson could not help but sympathise with Calder in his present distress. No longer stoic, the latter had on 22 September written as follows to Lord Barham:

> Your lordship knows I have been absent from England on service ever since the account of the victory I obtained over a very superior enemy arrived in England; consequently I know little or nothing of what is passing there, further than I perceived by the newspapers that John Bull thought I might have done more; but I never dreamt that any prejudices could have gone forth so as to have in any manner affected my character as an officer or as a man, in not having brought the enemy to action on the succeeding day, after the victory I had obtained over them. Having now obtained this information from a quarter not to be doubted, I must request of your lordship and the board to cause an enquiry to be made into my conduct upon that or any other day, by the officers of the Channel fleet where I was serving, or in any other manner your lordship and the board may judge best for his Majesty's service...
>
> ...I have most seriously considered and weighed all this matter... I feel myself very much flattered by your lordship's good opinion, and I have no doubts of my removing the many illiberal charges that have been made against my character. At the same time I am fully aware that courts martial never did any officer any good in the public opinion, and that it is only a necessary evil that we are obliged to have recourse to. Having had the honour of being known to you ever since you commanded a frigate in the West Indies, since which I have frequently received from you marks of attention, and I have ever considered your lordship as my oldest and best friend I now therefore crave leave to put myself into your hands as such, and under your lordship's kind protection.[21]

Not unnaturally, this matter obsessed Calder and on 30 September he wrote an anguished letter to William Marsden, first secretary to the Admiralty:

> Having learnt with astonishment, yesterday, by the ships just arrived, and by letters from my friends in London, that there has been a most unjust and wicked endeavour to prejudice the public mind against me as an officer, and that my conduct on the 23d of last July, in particular, has been animadverted

on, in the most unjust and illiberal manner, for such it must be deemed, having been done at a time when I was silent abroad, employed in the service of my King and Country.

I must therefore request you will be pleased to move the Lords Commissioners of the Admiralty to grant an inquiry into my conduct on the 23d of July last, or upon the whole, or such part of it (when in the presence of the enemy) as shall appear to their Lordships, for the good of His Majesty's service, and for the purpose of enabling me to give my reasons, publicly, for my conduct at that time, and to refute such unjust, illiberal and unfounded assertions, when I trust I shall make it appear to the satisfaction of my King, Country, and Friends, that no part of my conduct and character, as an officer, will be found deserving of those unfavourable impressions, which, at present, occupy the public mind; being conscious that everything in my power, as an officer, was done for the honour and welfare of my King and Country, after a very mature investigation of all the existing circumstances, and the very critical situation I was placed in, with the squadron I had the honour to command.

Calder enclosed this letter with one to Lord Barham, repeating his plea for an enquiry, and bemoaning the omission of his full despatch from the pages of the *Gazette*.[22]

It now fell to Nelson to break the news to Calder that, in view of the controversy surrounding his conduct in July, Lord Barham had come independently to the conclusion that he should go home and explain himself. In his letter of 22 September Calder had requested

> that the *Prince of Wales* and *Sirius*, now here [off Cadiz], may be ordered back to Ushant, or England, to attend the same, with as many of the ships as were under my orders in the action, that the nature of our service will admit of; in particular I would wish to have the *Windsor Castle*, *Thunderer*, *Ajax*, *Agamemnon*, *Hero*, *Repulse*, *Defiance* and *Triumph*. But if the exigencies of the service will not permit all of these ships to be present, I must submit to have only those that can be assembled without prejudice to the service.

And in his letter to Barham eight days later Calder stated: 'If the enquiry is granted, I shall be compelled to call upon most of the captains who were with me in the action, in order to refute the malicious reports and to clear my character from all and every suspicion.' The Admiralty instructions conveyed to him by Nelson were that any captains that he selected as witnesses were to leave their ships and accompany him home for the court martial only if they chose to do so.[23]

On 2 October Nelson wrote to inform the Admiralty that Captains Brown of the *Ajax* and Lechmere of the *Thunderer* had agreed to return with Calder and that acting captains would be appointed in their stead. When the *Defiance* joined the fleet Durham would also be permitted to return, if he wanted to, and his ship put under the command of an acting captain 'but I do not feel authorised to order him, or any others, who may not wish to go home on this service, without their Lordships' direction, although I am at the same time satisfied that they would not deprive Sir Robert Calder of any evidence he might think necessary to have'. He added that when the *Sirius* joined from Gibraltar 'I shall determine upon sending Captain Prowse home with the others.'[24]

Although Calder was wary of Durham, he perhaps did not yet appreciate the full extent of that officer's contempt for him, nor how strong was Durham's desire to see action under Nelson. At this stage Calder was busily refuting remarks attributed to Lieutenant Nicholson of the *Frisk* cutter, whom he had sent to Ushant and to Britain with despatches following the engagement with Villeneuve. Nicholson had allegedly said that Calder had told him on parting: 'I have written to the Lords Commissioners of the Admiralty that I shall bring the enemy to action again, but you may assure them afresh, that I have it in my power to do so, and that I am determined upon it; this you may also say to Admiral Cornwallis.' In his letter of 30 September to Barham, Calder poured scorn on the allegation. 'With respect to what I have seen in the papers as to what Lieut. Nicholson... said, I can only say it is erroneous... and false that I ever said I would or that I could bring the enemy to action', he wrote. 'Believe me, my lord, I am not in the habit of telling officers what are my private intentions in service; and much less to a lieutenant of a cutter, who was so little known to me.'[25] If Calder had learned from his friends at home that Durham had been vociferously criticising him he made no mention of it now.

The *Defiance* joined the fleet off Cadiz on the morning of 7 October, bringing 750,000 Spanish dollars for the garrison at Malta. Captain Thomas Francis Fremantle of the 98-gun *Neptune*, to whom Durham paid his respects, found that 'if I am not very much mistaken he has been speaking his mind *rather freely* of Sir Robert Calder in England.' Like many officers in Nelson's fleet, Fremantle sympathised with Calder in his plight. He 'has no idea of the misery that waits him, I pity him most truly'.[26]

One of the first things that Durham did on arriving off Cadiz was to go aboard the *Victory*. In his memoir he described the disheartening news awaiting him, for Nelson, he claimed, said:

> Durham, I am glad to see you, but your stay will be very short, for Sir Robert Calder sails tomorrow, and takes with him all the captains who were in his action, to give evidence on his court-martial. I am very sorry to part with you, but you will have to leave your ship under the command of your first lieutenant; but go on board the *Prince of Wales* and settle that with Sir Robert. The wind is at N.E.; the enemy will be out.[27]

Put like that, the impression is that Durham would definitely have to accompany Calder and all that remained were the arrangements. These alleged words of Nelson's have appeared in several books about Trafalgar. One historian has observed that by drawing Durham's attention to the fact that Villeneuve would soon be coming out of port, Nelson was inadvertently 'turning a knife in the wound'. Another, overlooking the salient point that Durham ostensibly had no option but to return with Calder, interprets Nelson's prediction regarding the imminence of battle as a 'hint' that Durham should stay.[28]

Had Nelson presented the situation to Durham in the stark terms described, the latter's dreams of glory and of that most welcome concomitant of victory, prize money, would have vanished in a trice. Yet it is doubtful that Nelson gave Durham the idea that he had no choice. For that would have contradicted both what Nelson had told the Admiralty on 2 October, and what Nelson told Durham in a letter. Written and received on 7 October, it drew an immediate, emphatic dictated response:

> I have the Honour to acknowledge the receipt of your Lordship's Letter of this Day's Date, allowing me if willing the Liberty of returning to England in order to answer such questions as may be found necessary to put to me by the Court appointed to enquire into the conduct of Vice-Admiral Sir Robt. Calder Bart. between the 22d and 25 of July last when in sight of the Combined French and Spanish Squadrons.
>
> After an attentive perusal of your Lordship's Letter and the Consideration that the Enemy in great force are on the Eve of sailing, I cannot volunteer quitting the Command of a Line of Battle Ship entrusted to me at so critical and momentous a period. Added to this, my Lord, it is now only fourteen Days since I was within the Jurisdiction of the Lords Commissioners of the

Admiralty who would doubtless have detained me in England, had they
deemed it necessary or even proper.

I am therefore bound to say, in compliance with the request made in
your Lordship's Letter, that I cannot voluntarily incur so great a Risque and
Responsibility as might attach to me in thus returning to England.[29]

The following day Captain Fremantle gave 'a tolerable enough' dinner
aboard the *Neptune* for Durham and the colourful Captain Eliab Harvey of
the 98-gun *Téméraire*, an inveterate gambler who had once reputedly lost
£100,000 in a single evening playing hazard. Like Durham, Harvey had
seen service under Howe during the American War of Independence. He
had been a midshipman aboard Howe's flagship, the *Eagle*, when Durham
was an able seaman aboard the *Edgar*. Posted in 1783, aged twenty-four,
he had commanded a frigate at Jervis's reduction of Martinique and
Guadeloupe in 1794 and off the French coast for a time as part of Warren's
squadron. His subsequent sea-going career had been disrupted by ill health,
and he represented his native Essex in Parliament.[30]

A few places senior to Durham on the list of post-captains, Fremantle
had as a young frigate captain served under Nelson in 1794 at the reduction
of Bastia in Corsica. As captain of the *Seahorse* in 1797 he had distinguished
himself at Santa Cruz, and his ship had taken Nelson, whose right arm had
been shattered in the action, back home. Having commanded the 74-gun
Ganges at the battle of Copenhagen, Fremantle was one of the handful
of captains in this, Nelson's final and greatest campaign, who had already
captained a ship-of-the-line in a major fleet action. He, Collingwood
and Hardy were the only members of that celebrated group of Nelson's
intimates, dubbed by him the 'Band of Brothers', currently on the station.
Another member, Canadian-born Captain Benjamin Hallowell of the
Tigre, celebrated for having in 1799 had a coffin made for Nelson out of
the mainmast of the wrecked Nile prize *L'Orient* ('so that when you are
tired of this life you may be buried in one of your own trophies') had been
with Nelson off Toulon and during the chase of Villeneuve to and from the
West Indies. But the *Tigre* had been detached from Cadiz to Gibraltar on
2 October with the rest of Rear-Admiral Louis's squadron. And another of
the select band, Sir Edward Berry, Nelson's flag-captain aboard the *Vanguard*
at the battle of the Nile, who following Calder's action had replaced John
Harvey as captain of the *Agamemnon*, had not yet arrived from England.

As Durham, Fremantle and Harvey ate, their central topic of conversation
must have been the anticipated forthcoming showdown with Villeneuve.

They no doubt touched upon the Calder affair, but it was surely Nelson's proposed tactics that dominated their thoughts. Durham had, of course, missed the dinner parties aboard the *Victory* a fortnight earlier as well as the meeting on 4 October at which Nelson had briefed his commanding officers. But the battle plan had undergone refinements since then, and a 'Secret Memo' setting out Nelson's ideas was in Durham's hands within a day or two of his dinner aboard the *Neptune*. This was the finalised explication of the 'Nelson touch' reproduced below in the original, idiosyncratically punctuated form in which it appears among Durham's papers:

Thinking it almost impossible to bring a Fleet of Forty Sail of the line into Line of Battle in variable winds, thick weather and other circumstances, which must occur without such loss of time that the opportunity would probably be lost of bringing the Enemy to battle in such a manner as to make the business decisive, I have therefore made up my mind to keep the Fleet in that position of sailing (with the exception of the First and Second in command), that the order of sailing is to be the Order of battle; placing the Fleet in two lines of sixteen Ships each, with an advanced Squadron of eight of the fastest sailing, two-decked Ships, which will always make if wanted a line of twenty-four sail, on whichever line the Commander-in-Chief may direct.

The Second in Command [Collingwood] will after my intentions are made known to him have the entire direction of his line to make the attack upon the Enemy, and to follow up the blow until they are captured or destroyed.

If the Enemy's Fleet should be seen to windward in Line of Battle, and that the two Lines and the advanced squadron can fetch [i.e. reach] them, they will probably be so extended that their Van could not succour their Rear.

I should therefore probably make the Second in Command's Signal to lead through about the Twelfth Ship from their Rear (or wherever he could fetch if not able to get as far advanced). My line would lead through about their Centre and the advanced squadron to cut two or three or four Ships ahead of their Centre, so far as to ensure getting at their Commander in Chief, on [*sic*] whom every effort must be made to capture.

The whole impression of the British fleet must be to overpower from two or three Ships ahead of their Commander in Chief supposed to be in the Centre to the Rear of their fleet. I will suppose twenty sail of the Enemy's Line to be untouched, it must be some time before they could perform a Manoeuvre to bring their force compact to attack any part of the British Fleet engaged, or to succour their own Ships which indeed would be impossible, without mixing with the Ships Engaged.

The Enemy's Fleet is supposed to consist of forty six Sail of the Line, British Fleet of Forty. If either is less a proportionate Number of Enemy's Ships are to be cut off. British to be one fourth superior to the Enemy cut off.

Something must be left to chance, nothing is sure in a Sea fight beyond all others, Shot will carry away the Masts and Yards of friends as well as Foes; but I look with confidence to a Victory before the Van of the Enemy could succour their Rear, and then the British Fleet would most of them be ready to receive their twenty Sail of the Line, or to pursue them, should they endeavour to make Off.

If the Van of the Enemy tacks the Captured Ships must run to leeward of the British Fleet, if the Enemy wears the British must place themselves between the Enemy and the captured, and disabled British Ships; and should the Enemy close, I have no fears as to the result.

The Second in Command will in all possible things direct the movements of his line, by keeping them as compact as the nature of the circumstances will admit. Captains are to look to their particular line as their rallying point, but in case Signals can neither be seen nor perfectly understood, No Captain can do very wrong if he places his Ship alongside that of an Enemy.

There followed a diagram to illustrate 'the intended attack from to-windward; the enemy in the line of battle ready to attack'. The memorandum concluded:

The divisions of the British Fleet [i.e. presumably the two main divisions as distinct from the 'advanced squadron'] will be brought nearly within Gun Shot of the Enemy's Centre. The Signal will most probably be made for the lee line [led by Collingwood, and including the *Defiance*] to bear up together. to set all their sails, even steering [i.e. studding] sails in order to get as quickly as possible to the Enemy's Line and to cut through, their exact place beginning from the twelfth Ship from the Enemy's Rear, some Ships may not get through but they will always be at Hand to assist their friends, and if any are thrown round the Rear of the Enemy, they will effectually complete the business of Twelve Sail of the Enemy.

Should the Enemy wear together, or bear up and sail large still the twelve ships, composing in the first position the Enemy's Rear are to be the object of attack of the lee line unless otherwise directed by the Commander in Chief, which is scarcely to be expected as the entire management of the lee line after the intention of the Commander-in-Chief is signified, is intended to be left to the judgment of the Admiral commanding that line.

The remainder of the Enemy's Fleet thirty-four Sail are to be left to the management of the Commander in Chief, who will endeavor [*sic*] to take care that
the movements of the Second in Command are as little interrupted as is possible.
   (signed) Nelson & Bronte.[31]

Across the bottom of Durham's copy of what has become an extremely
rare document was a postscript: 'NB. When the *Defiance* quits the Fleet for
England you are to return this secret Memo to the *Victory*'. At first glance
this might have disconcerted Durham, leading him to assume either that
Nelson had not yet received his letter of 7 October in which he refused
to return with Calder, or had decided to compel him to do so after all.
Yet he must have realised that Nelson was unlikely to part with the ship
as well. It would seem, indeed, that the postscript had nothing to do with
Calder's court martial, since an identical message was written on the copy
of the memorandum sent to Captain George Hope of the *Defence*. 'The
injunction to return the memorandum may well have been added to all
copies issued, and this may account for their general disappearance', one
historian has suggested in view of the instruction to Hope.[32]

   Nelson certainly knew of Durham's decision by 10 October, when
he informed Collingwood by letter: 'I am not a little troubled about Sir
Robert Calder. Durham has refused voluntarily to go home.' Collingwood
replied at once: 'I think Sir Robert Calder had better not urge Durham,
if he declares that he cannot be useful to him. It makes my heart ache.'
Perhaps the inwardly warm but outwardly frosty second-in-command
realised just how recalcitrant Durham could be: the name of the latter's
ship was an apt one. Indeed, shortly before Calder's action Durham had
(unlike one of his fellow captains) spurned a request from no less a naval
personage than Lord St Vincent to leave his ship and return to London to
give evidence on his lordship's behalf at a trial in Westminster Hall.[33]

   Calder himself seems to have been unaware of Durham's refusal, for on
10 October he told Nelson:

in conformity to your Lordship's opinion, as well as that of Vice-Admiral
Collingwood's, and my own, I have summoned Captain Durham to attend on
my inquiry, as I mean to do Rear-Admiral Stirling, and all the Captains who
were under my orders, when in presence of the Enemy, between the 22nd
and 24th of last July – conceiving it proper, for the satisfaction of the Public
Service, as well as to clear my character as an Officer. I am sorry to put any
Officer to any difficulties, but the Service must not suffer.'[34]

He was in for what seems to have bordered literally on a rude awakening. There was a short, strained meeting between him and Durham aboard the *Prince of Wales*, in the presence of Brown and Lechmere. Having assured himself that the Admiralty order said that prospective witnesses were to go home only 'if willing', Durham behaved in a disdainful manner. In the words of 'the gallant Captain himself':

> I went on board Sir Robert Calder's flag-ship, and found there the Captains who were going home. Sir Robert presented me with a public letter, addressed to Lord Nelson, signed by the Captains, requesting permission to go home. I said, 'Sir Robert, I will neither sign the letter nor go home.' I then *ran* out of the cabin, got into my boat, and returned to my ship.[35]

This incident apparently took place on 11 October. Calder, though doubtless taken aback, put a brave face on things. He wrote to Nelson that same day:

> Captain Durham having declined to attend me in England... unless he has a positive order to do so, I beg your Lordship will not give yourself any further trouble upon the occasion, as his evidence can be of no moment to the Public Service; and, as to myself, I am willing to relinquish any private consideration on my own account. My reasons for having summoned him in the first instance were, that I might not have been suspected to have collected only such as were my supposed friends, and thereby occasioned the inquiry to be called a *packed* business. This matter now being settled respecting Captain Durham, permit me to repeat to your Lordship my strong wishes to return to England, without further loss of time, in the *Prince of Wales*, that my mind may be put at ease, and for the re-establishing of my health, which has suffered so very seriously from my severe and long services.[36]

Despite the prospect of battle, Calder assumed that his flagship could be spared since the three-decker *Royal Sovereign* had joined the fleet. Nelson, however, told him that he would have to make the homeward voyage in another vessel, possibly Collingwood's relinquished flagship, the *Dreadnought*. This to Calder was a humiliation severely felt. 'I am this instant honoured with your Lordship's letter: I own I was not prepared for its contents', he wrote on 12 October. 'Believe me, they have cut me to the soul.' He begged at least to be allowed to take his flag-captain, William Cuming, with him, as well as such officers from his flagship as 'I find necessary for the justification of my conduct', adding: 'My heart is broken'.[37]

Calder's piteous tone made Nelson relent, preferring to sacrifice the *Prince of Wales* than to see his already hapless colleague distressed. 'Sir Robert felt so much even at the idea of being removed from his ship, which he had commanded in the face of the fleet', he explained to Barham.

> I may be thought wrong as an officer to disobey the orders of the Admiralty by not insisting on Sir Robert Calder quitting the *Prince of Wales* for the *Dreadnought*, and for parting with a 90-gun ship... but I trust I shall be considered to have done right as a man and to a brother officer in affliction. My heart could not stand it, and so the thing must rest.

And to Lady Hamilton he wrote that Calder had 'a right to be treated with respect'; Calder's 'misery' had melted his heart. 'He is in adversity, and if ever he has been my enemy, he now feels the pang of it, and finds me one of his best friends.'[38] Durham's thoughts when he realised that a powerful three-decker was being withdrawn from a fleet which was far short of the forty ships envisaged by Nelson in his 'Secret Memo', were, if voiced, probably unprintable.

Having earlier thanked Nelson 'for all your kindnesses to me since I have been under your command' and wished him 'every possible success', Calder departed on 14 October in the *Prince of Wales*, taking Brown and Lechmere with him. 'I am glad Sir Robert Calder is gone; and from my heart I hope he will get home safe, and end his inquiry well' wrote Nelson, aware that the Rochefort squadron was on the loose, and that it had almost captured the newly arrived *Agamemnon*. 'I endeavoured to give him all the caution in my power respecting the cry against him; but he seemed *too wise*.'[39]

Fremantle felt that Durham was 'justified in not volunteering to quit his Ship under the present circumstances'. But not everybody applauded Durham's resolve to remain with the fleet. As we have seen, Nelson and Collingwood had reservations about it. Captain Codrington of the *Orion* wrote disapprovingly that of the captains on the station who had been in Calder's action Durham was '*the only man amongst them under obligations to Sir Robert*' yet 'begged to decline leaving his ship *at so important* a moment!'[40] What those 'obligations' – if indeed they existed – might have been is unknown.

If ever an officer was lucky to be under Nelson now it was the courtly Codrington, who had never shared Durham's dedication to an active sea-life year in and year out. In January 1797, 'the most active period of the war', he resigned the command of a 32-gun frigate 'and went to enjoy the sports of the field and the luxury of home'. He spent so much time in land-locked comfort that when, in 1801, an aristocratic friend of his suggested that he be given a new command, Lord St Vincent had not unreasonably asked: 'Are you quite sure that Captain Codrington wishes to be employed?' It was not until May 1805 that he had gone afloat again, when he took command of the ship that would a few months later participate in history's most celebrated sea-battle. (Well might Byam Martin comment that Codrington's career 'affords as striking an instance as can be produced of the ease with which a pet child of good fortune may almost sit still and find the golden ball fall into his lap, while others have exhausted a long life in looking for it'.)[41]

'The last Fleet was lost to me for want of Frigates', wrote Nelson regarding his pursuit of Villeneuve that summer. 'God forbid this should.' Perhaps that lack of 'eyes' was the reason that Prowse, the experienced captain of the *Sirius*, did not return home for Calder's court martial; certainly his ship could not be spared. With the *Naïad* (Captain Thomas Dundas) and the *Phoebe* (Captain the Hon. Thomas Bladen Capel) she formed the frigate squadron commanded by Captain Blackwood of the *Euryalus*, scanning the approaches to Cadiz for any sign that Villeneuve's fleet was on the move.[42]

'Painters employed Painting Ship', records Durham's log for 9 October, and, a week later, 'Painters Painting Ship's Sides'. They were still at it on 19 October, their efforts in the meantime probably having been disrupted by rain. Nelson had directed that his ships be given fresh coats of paint in order to acquire the 'checkerboard' look of the *Victory* – yellow at the outer sides of the gundecks, with horizontal black bands in between, black ports, and yellow lower masts encircled in black. Concerned for the safety of the 750,000 dollars aboard the *Defiance* in the event of battle, Durham enquired what should be done with it. 'If the Spaniards come out, fire the dollars at them, and pay them off in their own coin', Nelson replied light-heartedly. But on 14 October the 150 casks containing the money (5,000 dollars in each) were transferred to the frigate *Aimable* (Captain the Hon. Duncombe Pleydell Bouverie), which had arrived the previous day, and carried by her to Malta. Another frigate accompanied her, taking an equal amount of dollars to the garrison.[43]

By mid-October Nelson had with him twenty-seven sail of the line, the rest having gone to Gibraltar to rewater. There were the three flagships, each of 100 guns: his own *Victory*, captained by the large, stalwart Hardy, who had commanded a brig at the Nile; Collingwood's *Royal Sovereign*, captained by Edward Rotheram, first lieutenant of the *Culloden* at the Glorious First of June, who was felt to have been promoted beyond his deserts by Collingwood, his fellow Northumbrian; and the *Britannia*, bearing the flag of the third-in-command, the Earl of Northesk, who was married to Earl St Vincent's niece, and captained by Charles Bullen, first lieutenant of the *Monmouth* at Camperdown. There were four 98s: Captain Eliab Harvey's *Téméraire* and Captain Fremantle's *Neptune*; the *Dreadnought*, captained by John Conn, who had commanded a bomb vessel at Copenhagen and was, it seems, married to one of Nelson's cousins; and the *Prince*, captained by Richard Grindall, a comparative veteran at fifty-five years of age, who in 1794 had become separated from the huge convoy that Durham had proceeded to bring singlehandedly into the Downs. The following year Grindall had been wounded in Bridport's victory over the French off the Île de Groix. Nelson noted that the *Britannia* and the *Prince* 'sail most wretchedly', and that he longed 'for faster sailing ships'.[44]

There was one 80, the *Tonnant*, whose captain, Charles Tyler, had served under Sir Hyde Parker in the Baltic. In addition to Durham's *Defiance* and Codrington's *Orion* there were fourteen 74s. These were the *Achille*, captained by Richard King, son and namesake of the former port-admiral at Plymouth and at a few weeks shy of his thirty-first birthday conspicuously younger than his peers; the *Ajax*, commanded in Captain Brown's absence by her first lieutenant, John Pilford, who had been master's mate on one of Howe's 74s at the Glorious First of June and was a lieutenant on one of Bridport's 74s in his action off the Île de Groix; the *Belleisle*, captained by William Hargood who had seen action under Rodney, had been Prince William Henry's first lieutenant on a frigate and become his closest naval friend; the *Bellerophon*, captained by John Cooke who had served under Rodney, Bridport and Warren, and had commanded a fireship at the Glorious First of June; the *Colossus*, captained by James Nicoll Morris, who when in command of a frigate in 1799 had conveyed Lord Elgin to Constantinople; the *Conqueror*, captained by Sir Edward Pellew's younger brother Israel; the *Defence*, captained by the first Earl of Hopetoun's grandson George Johnstone Hope, who had commanded a frigate during Sir William Hotham's action with the French off Genoa in 1795 and possibly shared a common Hope ancestor with Durham; the *Leviathan*, captained by Henry William Bayntun who had reached commissioned rank when only sixteen; the *Mars*, captained by a grandson of the first Earl of Fife, big and hearty George Duff who had seen service with Rodney; the *Minotaur*, captained by Charles John Moore Mansfield;

the *Revenge*, captained by Robert Moorsom who in his youth had served under Keppel, Darby and Kempenfelt; the *Spartiate*, captained by Anthony Molloy's brother-in-law Sir Francis Laforey, who had inherited his admiral father's baronetcy; the *Swiftsure*, captained by American-born William Gordon Rutherford, who was quite possibly another of Durham's distant relatives and had served with distinction under Jervis in the West Indies; and the *Thunderer*, commanded in Captain Lechmere's absence by her first lieutenant, John Stockham.

Three 64s completed the sail of the line destined to fight at Trafalgar: the *Polyphemus*, captained by Robert Redmill, who had commanded a fireship in Hotham's action in 1795; the *Africa*, captained by Commodore Duckworth's flag-captain at the reduction of Minorca in 1798, Henry Digby; and the *Agamemnon*, captained by Sir Edward Berry, who had served at the Glorious First of June, St Vincent, and the Nile, and was considered to attract such good fortune that when his ship hove into view on 13 October Nelson exclaimed: 'Here comes Berry! Now we shall have a battle!'

There were, as well, Captain Blackwood's squadron of four frigates (three of 36 guns, the other of 38) commanded by himself and Captains Prowse, Capel and Dundas respectively. And there was the 10-gun schooner *Pickle*, commanded by Lieutenant John Richards Laponotière, and the 8-gun cutter *Entreprenante*, commanded by Lieutenant Robert Benjamin Young.[45]

Though few of these men had sailed with Nelson before, his charisma and vision had formed them into a new 'Band of Brothers', bound together by ties of pride, duty, honour and service, and with a steely determination to carry their leader's electrifying plan into devastating effect. The *esprit de corps* which coalesced largely owing to the 'Secret Memo' of 9 October and its verbal preludes, found succinct expression in a letter Nelson wrote to Collingwood on that same day: 'We can, my dear Coll, have no little jealousies. We have only one great object in view, that of annihilating our enemies.'[46]

At daylight on 19 October amid clear and fairly calm conditions, Prowse's reconnoitring *Sirius* noticed that the enemy were making preparations to leave Cadiz Harbour (probably bound for Italy) and informed Blackwood's *Euryalus* by signal. By eight o'clock, nineteen of Villeneuve's ships were under way. At nine Blackwood ordered the *Pickle* 'to proceed with all possible despatch' to the main British fleet, some fifty miles to the south-west off Cape Spartel, to alert them to developments. 'The signal was instantly made to chase', reported Colin Campbell, an eighteen-year-old midshipman aboard the *Defiance* and relative of the Marquis of Lothian, to his father, a Lanarkshire laird. 'We were then a long way off Cadiz and made all sail for it. We did not however expect they were coming out as they had often before got under weigh [*sic*] for a few hours.'[47]

Determined to prevent the enemy from entering the Straits of Gibraltar, the British made all sail to the west towards Cape Trafalgar. The wind was light and variable. By four o'clock nine of Villeneuve's ships had come out of port, and the *Naiad* and the *Phoebe* were repeating Blackwood's signals to Nelson via Hope's *Defence*, Morris's *Colossus*, and Duff's *Mars*, positioned between the frigates and the other ships of the line. Early that evening Blackwood counted twelve enemy sail, about three miles off Trafalgar. With the *Sirius* in company he bore up and stood towards them to watch their movements; they were standing to the northward on the larboard tack.[48]

Next day at dawn Blackwood saw nine more enemy ships emerging from Cadiz. From his masthead twenty-two of Nelson's were visible. At twenty past eight he spotted Berry's *Agamemnon* with a prize in tow, a heavy French brig. Unaware of the danger, she was steering a course straight for the enemy in the north-east. It took several warning shots from the *Euryalus* before she noticed Blackwood's signal and, still towing her prize, she hauled off to the wind on the starboard tack. By ten to nine nearly all Villeneuve's ships were visible. About an hour later Blackwood observed a number of them wearing and standing towards Cadiz. At ten a squall came on, and conditions grew hazy with increasingly heavy rain. Blackwood accordingly lost sight of the enemy. But when the weather cleared at thirty minutes past noon he rediscovered them, lying to leeward under light canvas on the larboard tack, and at two he noticed his own fleet in the south-south-west, standing to the westward. As the *Victory*'s assistant flag lieutenant wrote, Nelson had 'kept the fleet from the enemy's sight until they should be a sufficient distance from the land; judging that, if they saw our force (though so much inferior), they might be induced to avoid us'.[49]

The frigates maintained their vigil throughout the night. 'His Lordship's instructions were strictly observed, and every movement of the enemy was indicated to us by our chain of communication, and as the enemy tacked or wore we had immediate intelligence of it, and regulated our conduct accordingly, tacking occasionally to preserve a relative situation with the enemy and ensure a meeting in the morning.'[50]

On the morning of 21 October, Villeneuve's thirty-three sail of the line could be seen ten or twelve miles away. They were 'in two irregular divisions' forming an uneven line of battle curving gently from north-north-east to south-south-west. There were two French 80s: Villeneuve's flagship, the *Bucentaure* and Dumanoir-le-Pelley's *Formidable*, as well as the *Neptune*, and the *Indomptable*, bearing 84 each. There were fourteen French 74s: the *Achille, Aigle, Algésiras* (Magon's flagship), *Argonaute, Berwick, Duguay-Trouin, Fougueux, Héros, Intrépide, Mont Blanc, Pluton, Redoubtable, Scipion* and *Swift-sure*. There was a Spaniard carrying 140 guns, the *Santissima Trinidad*, the biggest man-of-war in the world and flagship of Rear-Admiral Don Baltazar Hidalgo Cisneros, and two of 112 guns: Gravina's flagship the *Principe de Asturias* and the *Santa Ana* with Vice-Admiral Don Ignacio Maria de Alava on board. There was the Spanish 100-gun *Rayo*, the 84-gun *Neptuno* and the 80-gun *Argonauta*, and eight Spanish 74s: the *Bahama, Monarca, Montanes, San Augustin, San Francisco de Asis, San Ildefonso, San Juan Nepomuceno*, and *San Justo*. And there was one Spanish 64, the *San Leandro*. Also in the combined fleet were five 40-gun French frigates and two French brigs of 18 and 16 guns respectively.[51]

Remembered a marine lieutenant on Captain Hargood's *Belleisle*: 'I was awakened by the cheers of the crew and by their rushing up the hatchways to get a glimpse of the hostile fleet. The delight manifested exceeded anything I ever witnessed, surpassing even those gratulations when our native cliffs are descried after a period of distant service.' It was no doubt a scene replicated on the *Defiance* and every other ship in Nelson's fleet on that fateful Monday morning. Rocky Cape Trafalgar stood east by south, five leagues, and Cadiz north by east, nine leagues. The wind was light and variable during the morning blowing from north-north-west and later from south-west, and at noon from west-south-west, with a long swell to the sea.[52]

Shortly before seven the *Victory* made the signals to form the order of sailing in two columns and to prepare for battle; she followed these closely with the signal to bear up. By eight o'clock the two columns were formed and bearing eastward, their headmost ships about eight or nine miles from the enemy's centre. 'All our ships were carrying studding sails, and many bad sailers a long way astern, but little or no stop was made for them', Captain Moorsom of the *Revenge* would write.[53]

The *Victory* led the weather column, followed by the *Téméraire, Neptune, Conqueror, Leviathan, Ajax, Orion, Agamemnon, Minotaur, Spartiate*, the slow-sailing *Britannia*, and *Africa*. The lee column, led by Collingwood in the *Royal Sovereign*, consisted of the *Mars*, the *Belleisle, Tonnant, Bellerophon, Colossus, Achille, Polyphemus, Revenge, Swiftsure, Defence, Thunderer, Defiance*,

Prince, and *Dreadnought*. About half-past nine, in response to a signal from Collingwood, the *Belleisle* and *Tonnant* had changed places in view of the former's superior sailing. His own ship, having been newly coppered, sailed well, and he did not want too large a gap between her and the vessels immediately astern. As the *Belleisle* overtook the heavy-sailing *Tonnant*, Captain Tyler raised his voice above the familiar strains of 'Britons Strike Home', played by his ship's band, and yelled to Captain Hargood: 'A glorious day for old England! We shall have one apiece before night!'[54] The remark reflected the confidence of most who sailed that day with Nelson.

Since it was contained in Collingwood's despatch, the order of sailing described above has been widely accepted, and was probably at least broadly accurate. That the *Bellerophon* was the fifth ship in the lee line is confirmed by a letter written by a midshipman on board her, while Captain Moorsom appears to contradict his chief's positioning of the *Revenge*: 'My station was the sixth ship in the rear of the lee column; but as the *Revenge* sailed well, Admiral Collingwood made my signal to keep a line of bearing from him, which made me one of the leading ships through the enemy's line.' The order of sailing given in Lord Northesk's despatch agreed with Collingwood's only on the relative positions of the *Victory*, *Téméraire*, *Neptune*, *Conqueror*, and *Africa* in the weather column and of the *Royal Sovereign*, *Bellerophon*, *Colossus*, *Achille* and *Swiftsure* in the lee. He placed his own flagship sixth in the weather column and the *Defiance* ninth in the lee, as apparently originally envisaged. A contemporary print, based on information received from officers aboard the *Euryalus*, shows the *Defiance* last in her column, and seems to have influenced Sir Henry Newbolt and Sir Julian Corbett in their accounts of Trafalgar. However, another contemporary print places her eleventh, followed by the *Thunderer*, *Defence*, *Swiftsure*, *Polyphemus*, *Dreadnought*, and *Prince*, which according to a lieutenant on the *Tonnant* moved like a 'haystack'. Durham himself is silent on the matter. His memoir reflects egocentrism, not a broader sense of history. Regarding the battle, it is of limited value, infuriatingly stating: 'The details of this glorious action are so well known that it would be useless to insert much of them here.'[55]

Contradictions in the various logs concerning the times of occurrences can be explained largely by discrepancies in the timepieces aboard the different ships. In consequence, times given by historians tend to be approximations. The progress of the British columns, as they drifted swanlike under the pallid grey sky towards the shallow crescent of the enemy line, was agonisingly slow owing to the mildness of the breeze, which at intervals inclined to calm. Its lightness prevented the enemy 'from forming with any precision', wrote an eyewitness, so that they 'presented the appearance of a double line convexing to leeward'.[56]

This bunched formation of the combined fleet was hardly the orderly single line that Nelson had anticipated when he drew up his plan for a clean penetrating thrust through their centre. Since the enemy did not hoist their colours until the very last minute before firing began, Nelson, who was determined to pit his ship against Villeneuve's, did not know where in the line the French admiral's flagship was located. Being a small three-decker, the *Bucentaure* was not easily distinguished from a distance. Indeed, at around twenty to eleven Collingwood signalled that Villeneuve seemed to be aboard a frigate. It looked to Nelson as if the enemy intended to escape back to Cadiz, and so, sometime around eleven, he signalled Collingwood with the disconcerting message: 'I intend to push or go through the end of the enemy's line to prevent them from getting into Cadiz'. He soon realised that he had misread their intention, and made another signal, instructing his fleet to anchor when the battle was over.[57]

Although Collingwood was a vice-admiral of the Blue, he flew a white ensign, for Nelson had decided that to avoid confusion the entire fleet should wear the same colour. Each British ship had a Union Jack at her foretopgallant stay and another at her main topmast-stay. Their bands played rousing tunes, ranging from 'Rule Britannia' to 'The Fall of Paris'. In the light wind the fastest-sailing ships managed about three knots and the slowest two, but when the wind was at its gentlest the average rate of sailing fell to one and a half knots, and that of the very slow *Prince* to only one. As Nelson, obviously impatient for battle, neared the enemy line, he remarked to his flag-captain: 'Hardy, what would poor Sir Robert Calder give to be with us now? Tell your friend Durham he was the most sensible man of the party to stick to his ship.'[58]

Aboard the *Defiance*, as aboard every ship in the opposing fleets, preparations were being made for battle. While the decks were being cleared for action under the supervision of Lieutenants Hellard, Simons, Hargrave, Pidgley and Purches, the carpenter, William Caught, was noting whatever was being jettisoned to create space. A sheep pen and four hen coops, several tables, eight wardroom berths, a barrel of pitch and a large quantity of oakum were among the items he subsequently neatly listed as 'Thrown Overboard'. The young Scottish surgeon, William Burnett, destined for eminence later in life and a knighthood for his contribution to medicine, was in the cockpit laying out his saws, knives, tourniquets, basins, sponges and bandages – none of them sterilised, since the connection between germs and infection was not yet understood. He had on hand pails of water, and flagons of spirits to dull the senses of amputees.[59]

Unlike some admirals and captains, Durham approved of having 'a few women' in a fleet, to, as he explained to a startled landlubber, 'wash and mend, &c'. And so, also preparing for battle was Jane Townshend, the only woman identified by name as having been aboard a British ship at Trafalgar. She won written praise from him for her 'useful services' that day. What those were is a mystery. Jane may have assisted one or more of the gun crews by keeping them supplied with powder cartridges, or she may have helped Burnett to tend the wounded.[60]

'Standing in for the Enemy's Fleet', is the entry in Durham's log under the heading 'Bearings &c at Noon'. The parallel column, headed 'Remarks &c', tells that at twelve precisely the *Defiance* acknowledged the telegraphed general signal 'England Expects That Every Man Will Do His Duty'. Blackwood considered that signal 'such a one as would immortalize any man', but it was regarded as unnecessary by Collingwood. 'What is Nelson signalling about?' he grumbled, 'We know what we have to do.' There were numerous foreigners among Nelson's crews, but the signal seems to have thrilled most British hearts if not a few non-British ones. As news of the signal spread through the decks of the *Belleisle*, for instance, 'it was received with enthusiastic cheers, and each bosom glowed with ardour at this appeal to individual valour'. Aboard the *Britannia* the signal 'was *joyfully welcomed* by the ship's company.' These examples probably typified the reaction through the fleet.[61]

The signal having been acknowledged by the *Defiance*, wrote Midshipman Campbell, 'Captain Durham then turned the hands up and made a short, but very expressive speech to the ship's company which was answered by three cheers. Everything being then ready – Matches lit – guns double shotted with grape and rounds and decks clear – we piped to dinner and had a good glass of grog.'[62]

In view of the 'dead stark calm' it would be about an hour before the *Defiance*, towards the rear of her column, joined the battle which was beginning far up ahead as Durham gave his pep talk. With 'less angle to make towards the enemy's line' than the van of the weather column, Collingwood's *Royal Sovereign* was the first British ship into action. When Nelson had agreed to relinquish the lead of the weather column, he decided that Collingwood should no longer lead the lee. Seeing the widening gap between the second-in-command's flagship and the ships directly astern of her, and unaware that the *Belleisle* had just been instructed to overtake the *Tonnant*, he signalled the *Mars* to take second place in the column.

But Collingwood guessed Nelson's real intention. He knew that the commander-in-chief was giving him the hint to shorten sail and allow Duff to pass him. This, without a direct order from Nelson, Collingwood was determined not to do. He pressed on ahead of his column. Even when the *Victory* signalled the *Mars* to lead the lee column Collingwood paid no heed. The *Royal Sovereign* 'dashed directly down' towards the enemy's centre while her exhilarated admiral munched an apple. At about twenty to twelve the first shots boomed out at her, but she did not answer them until fifteen minutes later, when she opened fire on the twelfth, thirteenth, fourteenth and fifteenth ships from the enemy's rear, and stood on under full canvas to break their line. About noon, with her starboard and larboard guns blazing, she slowly cut through between Alava's flagship the *Santa Ana*, and the *Fougueux*. 'Look at that noble fellow!' exclaimed Nelson, who had evidently forgiven Collingwood's failure to fall astern of Duff. 'Observe the style in which he carries his ship into action!' And at the same time Collingwood was remarking 'What would Nelson give to be in our situation!'[63]

'I thought it a long time after I got through their line before I found my friends about me', Collingwood would reflect. 'Duff, worthy Duff, was next me but found a difficulty getting through for we had to make a kind of S to pass them in the manner they were formed.' Hauling up under the stern of the *Santa Ana*, the *Royal Sovereign* poured in a vicious raking broadside which sent lethal metal tearing through the Spaniard's hull from stern to stem. She then sheered up on the *Santa Ana's* starboard bow to begin a ferocious contest at very close range.[64]

Before the belching black smoke of cannon-fire completely engulfed the scene, Collingwood saw that the *Belleisle*, *Mars* and *Tonnant* had pushed through the enemy line and had begun to 'engage warmly'. Several enemy ships came to his adversary's aid, but finding that from where they stood they were doing almost as much damage to each other as to the *Royal Sovereign*, they desisted, after some fifteen minutes. At twenty past one the *Santa Ana* lost her mizenmast. An hour later, in trying to get to leeward of the British flagship, she had the misfortune to broach to and her remaining masts fell over the side. She then struck to the *Royal Sovereign*, which had taken such a battering that she was 'scarcely manageable'.[65]

'Nobly done, Hargood!' exclaimed Nelson on seeing the *Belleisle*, still ahead of the *Mars*, follow Collingwood's flagship into action. As she did so she came under heavy fire from ships that had pressed up from the enemy's rear and which left her 'masts and yards and sails hanging in the utmost confusion'. Having reserved her shot until she was in a position to fire simultaneous broadsides from larboard and starboard, she steered for the stern of the *Indomptable*, which subjected her to 'the most galling raking fire'. Towards one o'clock the *Fougueux*, with her larboard bow, ran on board the *Belleisle* nearly amidships on the starboard side. A brisk exchange ceased when the French vessel dropped astern.

But other ships took the *Fougueux*'s place, and on more than one occasion the *Belleisle* had three of them attacking her at the same time. With her main topmast and mizenmast gone, her 'gallant little' captain fought bravely on. His ship proved a target for every enemy vessel that passed her, and at ten past two her mainmast fell, followed shortly afterwards by the foremast. She was now completely dismasted, and her hull was smashed to pieces. Luckily, other British ships came up and deflected her opponents' attention. The *Belleisle*, her captain 'severely bruised', remained unvanquished with an ensign fixed to the stump of her mainmast and a Union Jack held up defiantly from the end of a pike.[66]

Coming up rapidly in the wake of the *Belleisle*, the *Mars* as she sought an opening in the enemy line had the misfortune to be raked by several of the enemy, including the *Pluton* and Magon's flagship the *Algésiras*. To avoid running into the *Santa Ana* she was obliged to turn head to wind, exposing her stern to enemy fire until the *Tonnant* arrived and diverted her tormentors, the *Monarca* and *Algésiras*. At about a quarter past one a cannon ball from the *Pluton* struck Captain Duff in the upper chest carrying off his head and killing two seamen standing behind him at the break of the quarterdeck. Command now devolved upon the *Mars*'s popular first lieutenant, William Hennah. In the words of her master, she was 'entirely ungovernable', with 'every one of our braces and rigging shot away'.[67]

Meanwhile the *Tonnant* had penetrated the enemy line by passing between the *Monarca* and the *San Juan Nepocumeno*, 'so close that a biscuit might have been thrown on the decks of either of them', as the British ship's third lieutenant put it. She came under a punishing raking fire from a Spanish three-decker which crossed her bows bringing down her fore and main topmasts and inflicting casualties. The *Tonnant* did not respond, concentrating her fire on the *Monarca* and the *San Juan Nepocumeno*. Shortly after one o'clock the former struck her colours, but rehoisted them on finding that the *Tonnant* could not immediately take possession owing to a raking by the *Algésiras*, which locked her bowsprit in the *Tonnant*'s main shrouds. The British ship's main topmast was shot away and her opponent 'attempted to board us with the greater part of her officers and ship's company'. A sharpshooter in the tops hit Captain Tyler in the left thigh, and he was taken below, the first lieutenant, John Bedford, assuming command. The marines valiantly repelled the boarders, only one of whom set foot on the *Tonnant*, while cannon shot from her main and lowerdeck starboard guns and grape from those on her forecastle smashed into her adversary. At about two the dismasted *Algésiras* struck; her captain had been mortally wounded and Magon lay dead at the base of the poop ladder. The *Tonnant's* second lieutenant with a marine officer and up to sixty men took possession of her.[68]

The *San Juan Nepocumeno* now drifted nearly on board of the *Tonnant*. The Spaniard fired, shooting away the British ship's gaff. Retaliating at once, the *Tonnant* wrecked the Spaniard's foremast. 'We cheered and gave her another broadside, and down came her colours.' The fourth lieutenant and a small number of seamen got into the jollyboat to take possession of their second prize. But the boat swamped and overturned, and four of the *Tonnant's* crew jumped overboard to rescue the non-swimmers. The incident proved fortunate for a black seaman who saved the life of the trapped fourth lieutenant, who was to leave him 'a handsome legacy' in his will; it proved more immediately fortunate for the *San Juan Nepocumeno*, which took advantage of the mishap by rehoisting her colours.[69]

While Collingwood was gliding into action, Nelson, reneging on his undertaking to allow the *Téméraire* to overtake the *Victory*, ordered his flag-captain to put on more sail in a determined bid to outrace Captain Harvey. At around noon, as the two vessels steered keenly towards the gigantic *Santissima Trinidad* and Villeneuve's flagship *Bucentaure* in the enemy's centre, the *Victory* signalled the *Téméraire* to drop astern. Instead, she ranged up on the flagship's quarter, and Nelson called out: 'I'll thank you, Captain Harvey, to keep in your proper station, which is astern of the *Victory*!' Harvey obeyed. At twenty past twelve, with hardly any wind to help Nelson into battle, the *Bucentaure* aimed her first shot at the *Victory*. It fell short, but as the *Victory* came slowly up others found their target, and a well-directed fire from several ships in Villeneuve's van did considerable mischief. All her sails were shredded and her foremast studding sail booms shot away. As she got close to the *Bucentaure* her mizen topmast was mauled and her wheel destroyed, so that her first lieutenant and her master had to take turns steering her in the gunroom. Upon the *Bucentaure's* lee quarter stood the French *Neptune*, and the *Redoubtable* ranged up between them, to prevent the *Victory* cutting through.[70]

Captain Hardy observed that if she attempted to do so she would run on board one or another of these vessels. 'I cannot help it', Nelson replied. Hardy then headed as if to run on board the *Redoubtable*, and at a minute or two before one o'clock the *Victory* began to pass under the *Bucentaure*'s stern. Every one of her larboard guns, double- and in some cases treble-shotted, fired successively into the French flagship's cabin windows, killing or wounding nearly 400 men. The *Victory* was herself, almost simultaneously, raked from ahead by the French *Neptune* with terrible effect. The *Victory* continued for a short time to fire her larboard guns at the *Bucentaure*, before devoting her full attention to the *Redoubtable*, alongside which she had arrived at about ten past one. With the *Victory*'s starboard fore topmast studding sail boom-iron hooking into the leech of the *Redoubtable*'s foretopsail, the two vessels enacted a ferocious contest. At about twenty-five past one Nelson, walking the quarterdeck with Hardy, was struck in the left shoulder by the musket ball which mortally wounded him. According to a contemporary account, Hardy took his hand and said: 'I hope, my Lord, you are not badly wounded?' 'Yes — my back is broke, Hardy, they have caught me at last', was the reply. As a couple of seamen carried Nelson down to the cockpit he said: 'Put something over my face; don't say a word about *me*.' The seamen complied, with a cloth that also partially obscured his decorations. Meanwhile, armed with a musket, an eighteen-year-old midshipman on the *Victory* systematically picked off every soldier in the *Redoubtable*'s mizen-top, and satisfied himself that he had avenged his admiral.[71]

With scarcely a breeze to puff out her sails, Durham's *Defiance* at last drew within range of Villeneuve's fleet at around the time that Nelson was shot. As she approached she was met by the blasting cannon of the third ship from the enemy's rear, identified by Durham as Gravina's 112-gun flagship the *Principe de Asturias*. Aching though Durham was for action, he restrained himself from responding prematurely to the provocation, loathe to see ammunition go astray. At twenty past two he gave the order to open fire, 'and not before a great Number of Shot went over us and much of our running rigging shot away', he noted in his log.[72]

Within minutes of pushing his way through the rearmost cluster of enemy vessels Durham took his first prize, without firing a shot. The ship that he came alongside was not Gravina's flagship, which was preoccupied with Captain Moorsom's *Revenge*, but the 74-gun *San Juan Nepocumeno*, fresh from her aborted surrender to the *Tonnant*. Although she was within pistol shot, the enveloping smoke of surrounding engagements now became so dense that the Spaniard could hardly be seen from the *Defiance*. The Spanish captain, Commodore Cosma Damian de Churruca, and his second-in-command had apparently already lost their lives, but as the *Defiance*'s guns were about to begin firing Durham glimpsed, through a dissipating drift of smoke, an officer whom he assumed to be the captain desperately gesturing at him with his hat. This was probably Joaquin Nunez Falcon, to whom command had fallen; his officers also seemed keen to attract Durham's eye.

Consequently, Durham ordered his gun crews to 'stand fast', and within a minute or two of this suspension of fire the *San Juan Nepocumeno* hauled down her colours. She was already in what Nunez termed 'a lamentable state' and had no stomach for another fight. She had three officers killed and one wounded; the comparable figures for her men were 100 and 150 respectively. Durham sent his boats to her to bring off some of her officers, but on noticing the *Dreadnought* nearby, in the heat of battle he left possession of the prize to that ship. His precipitate action left Captain Conn with the impression that the Spaniard had struck not to Durham but to himself.[73]

At ten past two, according to Durham's log, the massive menacing form of Gravina's flagship loomed out of the billowing smoke and bellowing din of battle and came close alongside the *Defiance*. Durham and his men would need all their coolness and courage now. The *Principe de Asturias* had emerged from a brief skirmish with the *Revenge*, whose topsail yards she had completely carried away when a British three-decker (possibly the *Dreadnought*) pushed up to Captain Moorsom's aid and the big Spaniard bore away. Now she concentrated her formidable power upon the *Defiance*, 'Keeping a Constant Fire we doing the same'. It was fortunate for Durham that whereas he aimed shot into her hull with murderous effect, the shot she fired from her lofty decks did no comparable damage to his ship or crew.[74] There were disadvantages to towering over an opponent; the great vessel's shot fell wide of her opponent's hull.

This David and Goliath struggle is best told by Midshipman Campbell:

[We] hammered away upon her within pistol shot for ¾ of an hour when not being able to stand the *little* Defiance any longer she bore up before the wind and ran to leeward. When we got her stern to us we raked her hotly with plenty of grape and canister. The slaughter on board of her must have been very great. She ran to leeward and never re-entered the action again. She only killed one man on board of us; the whole of her shot went through our rigging and mastheads. They fired so high that they shot away our main-top-gallant-truck. Every one of our shot told upon her and made the splinters fly.[75]

Campbell may have overestimated the time taken for the *Principe de Asturias* to flee, for Durham wrote in his log that she hauled off at twenty to three. He was unable to follow his chastened tormentor since his sails and rigging were badly cut. It seems that Gravina's flagship subsequently suffered rough treatment from the *Dreadnought* and a two-decker, possibly the *Revenge* or the *Thunderer*, and that while so engaged she sustained a couple of broadsides from the slow-sailing *Prince*, which lumbered into action shortly after three o'clock. Losses on board the *Principe de Asturias* were certainly considerable – fifty-four dead and 109 injured, including Rear-Admiral Don Antonio Escano – for which the *Defiance* was partly responsible. Gravina himself was mortally wounded in the left arm; its amputation failed to save his life.[76]

The *Defiance* now stood on for a French 74, which had been 'playing away on our bow' and was thought by Durham to be carrying 80 guns. She was the *Aigle*, described by a midshipman aboard the *Bellerophon*, which had just done bloody conflict with her, as 'the best manned ship' in Villeneuve's fleet, 'full of picked grenadiers'. With 'Victory or Death' chalked on some of her lower-deck guns in response to Nelson's celebrated signal, Captain Cooke's ship had sailed into battle in the wake of the *Tonnant* and broken the line under the stern of the *Monarca*. As his vessel luffed up to leeward of the Spanish ship the *Aigle* crowded on sail and ran her aboard on her bow. The two ships fought each other with 'the utmost fury' while the *Bellerophon* simultaneously engaged with the *Monarca* (which ultimately struck to her), and while, for a time, three other enemy ships harassed her as well.[77]

About one o'clock the *Bellerophon*'s main and mizen topmasts collapsed over the starboard side towards the *Aigle*, and a hand grenade hurled from the French ship's tops or a cannon's flash, or both, set alight the gunner's store-room. The fire was quickly extinguished by the gunner and several men with buckets of water, so that the blaze itself and the threat it posed to the nearby magazine remained generally unknown. The men on the poop were being cut down with such ruthless efficiency by snipers stationed aloft in the tall *Aigle* that Cooke, frantically discharging his pistols at would-be boarders, called the survivors down to the quarterdeck. But decimation by musketry and grapeshot continued. Amid the hectic preparations for battle Cooke had forgotten to remove his epaulettes, those symbols of status that made him a prime target. When his first lieutenant, William Pryce Cumby, reminded him of this, he replied: 'It is now too late to take them off. I see my situation but I will die like a man.' Shortly after one o'clock the master was killed, his leg torn off. A few minutes later, as Cooke was reloading his pistols, he was hit in the chest by grapeshot. He preferred to die where he fell, rather than endure the discomfort of being carried below, his last words being 'Tell Lieutenant Cumby never to strike.'[78]

But things were not going well aboard the *Aigle* either. Early in the action her captain, Pierre-Paulin Gourrège, received five wounds, two of which proved fatal. Commander Jean-Pierre Tempié, who succeeded him in charge, was soon afterwards killed. The *Bellerophon* was bravely repelling boarders, and when, her fire slackening, a fresh attempt at boarding her was made, the two interlocked ships were providentially separated and the *Aigle* fell astern – 'under a raking fire from us as she dropped off', as one of the *Bellerophon*'s lieutenants noted in his journal.[79]

It was, therefore, a battered *Aigle* that faced the *Defiance*'s thunder. The damage that had prevented Durham's ship from pursuing the *Principe de Asturias* did not affect her ability to fight. She ran alongside the *Aigle* at ten past three, and 'made her fast' with rope. There was combat yet in the French ship's exhausted men, and 'we had it pretty hot', in Midshipman Campbell's phrase. The *Aigle*, wrote Lieutenant Classen, who assumed command when the acting captain fell, 'replied gallantly' to the *Defiance*'s 'vigorous fire in spite of our weakened crew'.[80]

After about twenty minutes the *Aigle*'s fire began to falter. Durham summoned his boarders to take possession. There now occurred one of the most dramatic and heroic incidents during that extraordinary day. In the belief that all of the *Defiance*'s boats had been shot through, one of the master's mates, James Spratt, a handsome and high-spirited thirty-four-year-old from Ireland, shoved an axe into his belt and proposed that a boarding party should swim to the *Aigle*. The instant Durham agreed, Spratt leapt onto the ship's side, calling on all who could swim to follow him. Amid the frightful noise of conflict no one seems to have heard him. Without a backward glance he placed his cutlass between his teeth and plunged into the sea alone.

Swimming the short distance to the *Aigle*'s stern he grabbed hold of the rudder chains and entered a gunroom port virtually unnoticed. In classic swashbuckling tradition, he cut down the few who saw him and tried to bar his way, and managed to run onto the poop deck. Before anyone realised that he was an intruder he had hauled down the French colours and was hoisting a British ensign and pennant in their stead. His swiftness and dexterity were astounding. Awestruck at his audacity, Durham yelled to the boarding party to hasten to Spratt's assistance. The *Defiance* managed to close with the *Aigle* and they got aboard.

As hand-to-hand fighting erupted on the quarterdeck, three grenadiers with fixed bayonets charged at Spratt on the poop. He nimbly evaded them by grasping at the signal halyards and jumping onto an arms chest. Before they had a chance to run him through he despatched two of them either with his axe or cutlass and seized the third and flung him onto the quarterdeck. As the man fell he dragged Spratt with him, and they landed together in a crumpled heap. The grenadier's neck was broken. But he had cushioned Spratt's fall and the latter escaped with bruising. Another grenadier now rushed at him, with a bayonet aiming for his chest. With his cutlass Spratt parried the thrust, and the weapon discharged into his right leg a little below the knee, shattering the bone. He managed to retreat between two of the quarterdeck guns, to prevent himself being stabbed from behind, holding off the grenadier and a couple of others until these assailants were overpowered by some of his shipmates.[81]

While these heroics were occurring on the *Aigle*'s quarterdeck, a sudden burst of musketry from her forecastle waist and tops took Durham by surprise. It was followed by renewed cannon fire, and jars filled with combustibles and foetid substances (known as 'stink pots') were hurled through the *Defiance*'s ports to overwhelm her gun-crews with their suffocating smell and hopefully cause a destructive explosion. Had Durham realised that the French ship had so much fighting spirit left he would not have given the order to board. The reason she had slackened fire was apparently fear that three British vessels which seemed to surround her would join the *Defiance* in the attack. When this did not happen she recovered her courage.[82]

At twenty-five to four Durham recalled his boarders. Most swam safely back to the ship but Spratt, with his mangled limb, was trapped. Leaning over the *Aigle*'s railing he indicated his leg and yelled: 'Captain, poor Jack Spratt is done up at last!' Rarely had Durham known an example of personal courage equal to Spratt's, and rescuing the brave officer was his immediate priority. His ship managed to warp alongside the *Aigle* and Spratt, catching hold of one of the latter's boat-tackle falls, swung himself to a lower-deck gunport of the *Defiance*. As he was pulled through to safety and carried down to the surgeon the ship cast off the lashings binding her to the *Aigle*. She then sheered off to pistol-shot distance from her obstinate foe and pounded her afresh, 'every shot of ours going through and through her', as Midshipman Campbell enthused.[83]

During this reinvigorated exchange Durham received a wound which would put him in the official list of casualties. A shaft of wood, splintering off from a mast or spar as it was hit, struck him in the 'leg and side'. But although he was to some extent bloodied, able only to hobble, and in much initial pain there is no indication that he left the deck to be treated, and he therefore must have witnessed the *Aigle* strike at eight minutes past four. 'We still held out for some time', wrote Lieutenant Classen, explaining the surrender,

> but the enemy's flaming sulphur-saturated wads having set the gun-room on fire close to the cable tier and to the taff-rail ['le couronnement' in the French original, which implies the stern galleries], the ship being stripped of her rigging, most of the guns dismounted, the captain and the commander killed, nearly all the naval officers wounded and two-thirds of the crew disabled, the ship – by what misfortune I know not – being isolated from the rest of the Fleet, we decided to haul down our colours in order to extinguish the flames and to preserve for the Emperor the scanty number of the gallant defenders who remained.[84]

The *Defiance*'s boats were got out and Durham appointed his fifth lieutenant, James Uzold Purches, as prize master of the *Aigle*. Purches took possession of her with twenty men, who were reportedly subsequently augmented by a number from other British ships. A doleful sight met their eyes, for the *Aigle*'s total casualties comprised a majority of her men in addition to seven officers killed and ten injured. 'The slaughter on board of her was horrid, the decks were covered with dead and wounded', wrote Midshipman Campbell of what he could see of her condition from aboard the *Defiance*. 'They never heave their dead overboard in time of action as we do.'[85]

Nelson died of his wounds at about half-past four, having been kept informed of the progress of the battle. 'His countenance brightened as the number of ships that had struck were related', wrote an officer who was with him, 'but when the number of nineteen sail was mentioned, an hectic flush of joy appeared on his wan face, and he seemed to revive a little.' 'My Lord, you die in the midst of triumph!' Hardy is said to have told him, 'Do I, Hardy,' he reportedly replied, smiling faintly. 'God be praised!' Then, 'convulsively' gripping Hardy's hand he 'expired calmly, and without a groan'. It was the first time a British flag-officer commanding in chief had been fatally wounded in action since Rear-Admiral Benbow in 1702.[86]

The battle had tailed off, its roar being largely confined to the ships in Collingwood's rear which had got late into action. At about the time that Nelson drew his final breath the French *Achille* was accidentally set alight during an encounter with Captain Grindall's *Prince* and was soon a blazing inferno. About five o'clock all firing ceased. British boats were making for the burning *Achille*, to try and save her crew. To the southward, four French ships under full sail belonging to Rear-Admiral Dumanoir's squadron could be seen growing ever smaller against the darkening sky, fugitives from the carnage. The British fleet was in no condition to give chase. For her part, the *Defiance* had several shot holes in the hull. Her bowsprit, fore and mainmasts had all been shot through, her mizenmast, three topmasts, jib, driver booms and gaff had extensive damage, and her rigging and sails were cut to pieces.[87]

All around, the sea's surface was strewn with what Campbell described as the 'wreck of masts and yards floating about and hundreds of dead bodies', the grim scene illuminated by the fierce glow of a blaze out of control. At about a quarter to six the *Achille* 'blew up with a terrible explosion' that sent a fireball hundreds of feet into the air. The 'sound, louder than any that had preceded it' and its attendant 'column of dark smoke' were heard and seen by throngs of worried Spaniards crowding the ramparts of Cadiz, home to numbers of Gravina's seamen. It killed most of the *Achille's* crew, those still trapped on board her. Wooden and iron debris and the mutilated remains of victims came crashing down on the already littered waters. It was the ghastly end to a harrowing, horrific, heroic day's work.[88]

The combined fleet had been devastated. It had failed to take a single British ship, but nineteen of its own were in enemy hands and another had blown up. The captures included the *Bucentaure* and the *Principe de Asturias*, flagships respectively of Villeneuve and Gravina, as well as the big *Santa Ana* and the even bigger *Santissima Trinidad*, on board of which Admiral Cisneros was severely wounded. The allied casualty list totalled almost 7,000, including several captains. Villeneuve was a captive, Gravina lay dying, and Magon was dead. The British had 1,663 casualties, including, of course, their legendary commander-in-chief, and two post-captains, the old friends Cooke and Duff, who had been killed and four post-captains who had been wounded: Durham, Tyler, Moorsom, and Morris of the *Colossus*. Morris had been severely wounded in the thigh. A tourniquet was applied, and he bravely remained on deck until the battle was over, when he fainted from loss of blood and was carried below.[89]

With 200 casualties, the *Colossus* had suffered heavily. Not far behind was Cooke's *Bellerophon*, with 150. The *Royal Sovereign* and *Belleisle* came next, with 141 and 126 respectively, followed by the *Victory* with 132, the *Téméraire* with 119 and Duff's *Mars* with 98. The *Defiance*, with seventy casualties, was in the upper-middle range. Several ships had very light casualties, not amounting to double figures, and the lumbering *Prince*, having come tardily into action, suffered none at all. However, as Collingwood was to reflect: 'People who cannot comprehend how complicated an affair a battle is at sea, and judge of an officer's conduct by the number of sufferers in his ship, often do him a wrong'. Killed aboard the *Defiance* were the second lieutenant, Thomas Simons, the boatswain, William Forster, a midshipman, James Williamson, eight seamen including a quartermaster, and six marines. Apart from Durham, whose injuries were reported to Collingwood as mild, the wounded were two master's mates, James Spratt and James (or Robert) Brown, two midshipmen, John Hodge and Edmund Andrew Chapman, thirty-nine seamen including a sailmaker, two quartermasters and a quartermaster's mate, and nine marines.[90]

While he rested on the sofa in his cabin nursing his wound, Durham received a visit from the slain commander-in-chief's flag-captain. 'I hope you are not badly wounded', began Hardy. 'I have a word of comfort for you'. He went on to tell him that 'one of the last things Nelson said before the action began' was to compliment Durham on his wisdom in remaining with the fleet.[91]

At about six o'clock on the evening of battle Collingwood, who had succeeded Nelson as commander-in-chief, shifted his flag to the frigate *Euryalus*. In conquering the *Santa Ana* his own ship, the *Royal Sovereign*, had suffered severely. Her main and mizenmasts and foretopsail yard were shot away, and her foremast left tottering, so that the *Euryalus*, being within hail, made Collingwood's signals during the remainder of the action and later took her in tow, to be succeeded in that task by the *Neptune*. Next day Collingwood sent Rear-Admiral Northesk and every captain and commander in the fleet a beautifully expressed and deeply moving memorandum which Durham would treasure among his papers.

The ever to be lamented death of the Vice Admiral Lord Nelson... who fell in the action of the 21st, in the Arms of Victory, cover'd with Glory, whose memory will be ever dear to the British Navy, and the British Nation, whose zeal for the honour of his King and the Interest of his Country will be ever held up as a shining example for British Seamen – leaves to me a duty to return my thanks to the Right Honourable Rear Admiral, the Captains, Officers and Seamen, and detachments of Royal Marines serving on board His Majesty's Squadron, now under my Command for their Conduct on that Day – but whence can I find language to express my sentiments of the Valour and Skill which was displayed by every Officer, every Seaman and every Marine in the Battle with the Enemy, where every individual appeared a Hero, upon whom the Glory of His Country depended: the attack was irresistible and the issue of it adds to the page of Naval Annals a brilliant instance of what Britons can do when their King and Country need their Service.

To the Right Honourable Rear Admiral the Earl of Northesk, the Captains, Officers, Seamen, and to the Officers, Noncommissioned Officers, and Privates of the Royal Marines, I beg leave to give my hearty and sincere thanks for their highly meritorious conduct both in the action and in their zeal and activity in bringing the captured Ships out from the perilous situation in which they were after their surrender, among the shoals of Trafalgar in boisterous weather.

And I desire the respective Captains will be pleased to communicate to the Officers, Seamen, and Royal Marines this public testimony of my high approbation of their conduct and my thanks for it.[92]

In the very early hours of 6 November, a tired Lieutenant Laponotière of the schooner *Pickle* arrived at the Admiralty in Whitehall, got the first secretary, William Marsden, out of bed, and handed him Collingwood's despatches concerning Trafalgar. Snatching up a candle, Marsden padded along the passage to the room where Lord Barham slept, drew aside the bed curtains and woke the elderly first lord 'from a sound slumber'. Following discussion about who should be immediately notified of events – the King, the Prince of Wales, the Duke of York, William Pitt, the Cabinet, and the Lord Mayor of London – Marsden spent the remainder of the night with as many Admiralty clerks as he could rouse, penning the necessary documents.

Next morning, when the second secretary, John Barrow, arrived for work, Marsden spoke for everybody who learned of the bittersweet triumph of 21 October. 'Never can I forget the shock I received', wrote Barrow, 'on opening the Board-room door, the morning after the arrival of the dispatches, when Marsden called out – "Glorious news! The most glorious victory our brave navy ever achieved – but Nelson is dead!"'[93]

That Trafalgar was no ordinary triumph was clear from the beginning. It was the most decisive sea-battle ever fought. True, Napoleon remained dictator of the continent, but his cross-Channel designs, to which he still clung, had been irrevocably checked. Saved from invasion, Britain had achieved a mastery of the seas that would, it transpired, remain unchallenged for one hundred years, and enable the nation to consolidate an empire unparalleled in modern times.

had already anchored off Cape Trafalgar, they obeyed, bringing their heads to the westward.[2]

Next morning at dawn there were light breezes blowing from the south-south-west. These gradually strengthened, accompanied by intermittent rain. Since she had lost all her masts during the previous evening, the *Aigle* had become an unwieldy hull drifting towards Cadiz. About eight o'clock in the morning, therefore, the *Defiance* stood inshore to take her in tow, and boats were lowered. But all attempts by the boats' crews to get a hawser on board the prize were foiled by the elements. The weather had turned squally with driving rain, and the *Aigle* was rolling helplessly in a heavy sea.[3]

Both ships were only two or three miles off San Sebastian's Point, where the 'bad coast' stretching north from Cape Trafalgar was rendered even more treacherous by sunken rocks. Much as it pained him to part with a capture, Durham, fearing that she would run ashore in the night and be wrecked, decided to curtail the vain efforts to secure her, and thus to evacuate the prize-crew. In connection with this, Lieutenant Classen of the *Aigle* would tell a dubious tale. He reported that 'an English captain' – who else but Durham? – 'came on board, inspected the ship, and decided that, the foul weather preventing her from being taken to her destination, she should be abandoned to the French after her cables had, by order of the admiral, been cut into fragments. Happily we prevailed upon the officer in command' – presumably the prize master, Lieutenant Purches – 'not to carry out this barbarous order.'[4]

Classen's assertions are scarcely credible. They are, first and foremost, unsubstantiated: there is no reference to such an order in any other source. Second, they contradict the humanity practised by the Royal Navy towards prisoners of war on captured vessels when danger struck or those ships were deliberately scuttled. Third, they are at variance with Collingwood's demonstrated character, as well as with Durham's. Classen went on to claim, accurately, that since the wind and the sea were rising inexorably it proved impossible to take off all of the prize crew. But his statement that '50 men with a lieutenant remained on board' is contradicted by Durham's log and two further knowledgeable British accounts, which show that Purches and twelve seamen were obliged, owing to the ferocity of the gale, to stay aboard the *Aigle*. Unwilling to risk the *Defiance* any longer on a leeshore, Durham recalled the boats, and she sailed to windward out of danger.[5]

As Collingwood wrote, the gale 'continued for three days, sometimes blowing with extreme fury', and played havoc with the dismasted British ships and their hulks of prizes. After the *Defiance* had given up efforts to tow her, the *Aigle*, under Classen's restored command, was thwarted by the weather in her aim of gaining Cadiz Harbour. Instead, she anchored for safety some miles off the islet of Sancti Petri. When two British vessels, one of them possibly the *Defiance*, appeared unexpectedly at daybreak on 23 October, Classen ordered the cable to be cut and stood closer inshore to escape them.[6]

That same day the senior French officer at Cadiz, the highly competent Captain Julien-Marie Cosmao-Kerjulien, decided to take advantage of the north-westerly wind by putting to sea to recover some of the drifting prizes. He set sail in the *Pluton*, along with the *Indomptable, Neptune, San Francisco de Asis, Rayo*, five frigates and two brigs. About noon he was spotted coming out of port, and this intelligence relayed to Collingwood. At three Cosmao's entire squadron was visible to leeward, 'apparently endeavouring to cut off and recapture some of the disabled prizes', noted Collingwood, who assumed that it was commanded by Gravina.[7]

The British commander-in-chief made the signal for his 'most perfect' ships, among which he counted the *Defiance*, 'to form the line ahead as most convenient'. Being on the look-out for the *Aigle*, with part of the prize-crew still on board, Durham's ship – to Collingwood's deep annoyance – got very tardily into line. Totalling ten ships, this line at four o'clock stood to the enemy in the east-north-east. Wisely, Cosmao did not press his luck. Having recovered the *Santa Ana* and the *Neptuno,* he returned to port.[8]

Owing to the prolonged gale following the battle of Trafalgar, the British were deprived of most of their prizes. One or two managed to get into Cadiz, several went aground or were wrecked, and some, proving more trouble than they were worth in the prevailing conditions, were destroyed by their British captors after their companies had been removed.[9]

The *Aigle* was one which grounded. She spent two nights anchored precariously in only eight fathoms off Sancti Petri, buffeted by high winds and the great swell, before running for the shore. She then, on 25 October, became stranded on the bar of sandy mud at the entrance to Puerto de Sancta Maria. That same day the *Defiance* attempted to take in tow the Spanish *Argonauta*, having received prisoners from her, but was unable to do so owing to the 'very heavy sea'. She had only her foremast standing and was in danger of running ashore. At half-past three Durham therefore sent his third lieutenant, Henry Hargrave, along with Colin Campbell, two other midshipmen and twenty men to bring her to anchor, 'which we did', related Campbell, after a great deal of difficulty, there being 600 Spaniards on board and most of them drunk and her decks full of wounded. It came on to blow a very heavy gale of wind that night and to blow harder and harder till the night of the 26th when it blew harder than I ever saw it. We did not expect she would ride the night out with us. The Spaniards were terribly frightened and all turned-to, to pray. She gained on us at the pumps fast and the sea broke clean over us. We hove all the main deck guns overboard and let go the sheet anchor under foot in case the best bow anchor should part; about 12 at night the iron littior broke in two and the rudder knocked about so much we thought it would knock her stern post in, but about 3 in the morning it broke adrift altogether which we were very glad of. At daybreak we found that our best bower anchor had parted in the night, but the sheet anchor still held on. We found that all the other hulks had gone ashore in the night... The two boats we came aboard in had both sunk astern.

Endeavouring to attract the *Defiance*'s attention, they hoisted a distress signal and fired guns, but she had disappeared from view.[10]

Next day the gale had abated somewhat (although there were still nasty squalls, rain and a heavy sea), and Captain Bayntun's *Leviathan* and the *Donegal*, commanded by Durham's good friend and fellow Scot Captain Pulteney Malcolm, sent their boats to the rescue. The *Donegal*, which took on board Midshipman Campbell and twelve of the *Defiance*'s party while Hargrave and the rest embarked on the *Leviathan*, had joined the fleet too late for battle, having earlier in the month been diverted by Nelson to Gibraltar. Formerly the *Hoche*, captured by Warren's squadron in 1798, she retook an escaped Spanish prize and performed 'heroic conduct' in saving enemy crews from wrecked vessels.[11]

The Spanish, meanwhile, behaved with conspicuous gallantry and humanity to the shipwrecked British seamen who fell into their hands owing to the gale, including Lieutenant Purches and his party. They risked their lives to save them, refused to consider them prisoners of war, and displayed remarkable generosity and hospitality. After being taken off the stranded *Aigle* by Spanish boats, Purches and his men were provided with lodgings in Cadiz, and were free to come and go as they pleased. Purches was supplied with 'plenty of mutton' and his men were treated with 'the greatest kindness'. They arranged to travel overland to Gibraltar on 'jack-asses'. But within a few days of their being saved two French frigates and a brig which went out to the *Donegal* to exchange prisoners took them on board her.[12]

Since the battle Collingwood had seen next to nothing of the *Defiance*, and knew none of the details concerning her part in the action or her activities since. He consequently rushed to an unjustifiably harsh judgment on her captain. 'But my lord', he wrote to Barham on 26 October,

> although the exertion on the 21st was very great, it was not equal by any means; some of the ships in the rear of my line, although good sailing ships, did not answer my expectation fully. The *Defiance*, I shall require some explanation from for giving me no assistance in the case of the disabled ships since the action; and when, with difficulty and signals flying for hours, I got her down to form a line when Gravina [*sic*, i.e. Cosmao] made his appearance on the 23rd, at daylight next morning he was again missing – a perfect ship – and I have seen nothing of him since. If he has found good employment it is unknown to me now, and I shall be glad to find he has.[13]

Whether the *Defiance* was included in the opening indictment is not clear, though it is likely. She was, after all, the swiftest sailing 74 in the navy, yet she had not got into action until some sixty minutes after the *Royal Sovereign* pushed through the enemy line. Her laggardly behaviour underlines just how weak the breeze was, as it was certainly not due to any slackness on her captain's part. Collingwood was ignorant of the strenuous efforts that Durham had made on 22 October to take the *Aigle* in tow. Surprisingly, he apparently remained unaware that two days later the *Defiance* had been among the vessels that responded to his general signal 'Prepare to quit and withdraw men from prizes after having destroyed or disabled them if time permits', by removing prisoners from the *Argonauta*, trying in vain to take that ship in tow, and finally sending a party aboard to anchor her, preventing her from becoming wrecked.[14]

Collingwood must accordingly have somewhat regretted his despatch to Barham when, almost as soon as it was sent, Durham, still in discomfort from his wound, went aboard the *Euryalus* to report. Collingwood, who was writing in his cabin, lay down his pen to listen to Durham, and was apparently impressed by what he heard. At one point, when Durham was praising the conduct of the frigates during the battle, Captain Blackwood interrupted, implying that one of the frigate captains – most probably Dundas of the *Naiad* – had not behaved as zealously as he might have done. 'Sir', snapped Collingwood, 'this has been a glorious victory for England and for Europe – don't let there be a reflection against a cabin-boy.'[15]

On 28 October, seemingly to make amends for his remarks to the first lord, Collingwood, in the course of a despatch to William Marsden, singled out Durham for praise: 'The *Defiance*, after having stuck to the *Aigle* as long as it was possible, in the hope of saving her from wreck, which separated her for some time from the Squadron, was obliged to abandon her to her fate, and she went on shore. Captain Durham's exertions have been very great.' To Durham's gratification, this encomium appeared in the *London Gazette* of 16 November.[16]

After leaving Collingwood's cabin to return to the *Defiance*, Durham fell into conversation with a French flag-officer standing beside the *Euryalus*'s capstan. As he might have suspected, it was Villeneuve. 'Sir, were you in Sir Robert Calder's action?', the defeated admiral asked. Durham replied that 'he was, and had commanded the ship that first discovered the fleet, and had remained with them for four or five hours till Sir Robert Calder came up'. Villeneuve sighed, and observed: 'I wish Sir Robert and I had fought it out that day. He would not be in his present situation, nor I in mine.'[17]

On 29 October ninety-four prisoners were sent by the *Defiance* to the *Téméraire*, which she also supplied with a main topsail and its corresponding yard. Captain Harvey's ship had played a distinguished part in the battle. 'Nothing could be finer', declared Collingwood of her performance. 'I have no words in which I can sufficiently express my admiration of it.' She had suffered heavy casualties, and as her captain wrote, her officers and men were 'in constant apprehension of our lives; every sail and yard having been destroyed, and nothing but the lower masts left standing; the rudder-head almost shot off and is since quite gone, and lower masts all shot through and through in many places'. The *Defiance*, which had joined her the day after the battle, signalling news of Nelson's death, took her in tow on 30 October, and they reached Gibraltar on 2 November.[18]

The terrible gale had, as Harvey observed, been '*shocking* for our poor wounded', and at Gibraltar the worst-off among these were transferred to hospital. They included James Spratt, whom Durham had failed to persuade to have his smashed limb amputated by surgeon Burnett. When Durham remonstrated with him Spratt held out his other leg, saying 'Never; if I lose my leg, where shall I find a match for this?' As a midshipman in the *Bellona*, 74, at Copenhagen, Spratt had attended Captain Sir Thomas Boulden Thompson in the cockpit when the surgeon sawed off that officer's injured and useless leg; perhaps, brave as Spratt was, the harrowing memory haunted him still.

At Gibraltar he contracted a fever, and in his writhings disturbed his bandages, so that his leg had to be encased in a special box to enable it to heal. His sufferings now intensified, owing to a sensation in his legs that mystified his doctors. When, after nine days, the box was removed an 'unparalleled sight' met their gaze. Hundreds of maggots an inch long were embedded in his calf. A panicked attempt to remove them with tweezers predictably failed, but they succumbed to poisonous liquid.[19]

In the meantime, on 10 November, the *Defiance* sailed to rejoin Collingwood, who ordered her home to repair. She arrived at Spithead on 1 December, and her defects were so heavy that she was directed into harbour, but not paid off. Durham departed for London on three weeks' leave of absence, and Lady Charlotte, who had apparently been staying with the Radnors, returned from Salisbury to be with her Trafalgar hero. She must have first learned of the battle in the newspapers, following publication on the evening of 6 November of an 'Extraordinary' edition of the *London Gazette,* which reproduced Collingwood's account.[20]

The vice-admiral's detailed list of casualties, which described Durham as 'slightly' wounded, had been published in the *Gazette* on 16 November. His relatives had, for some unfathomable reason, gained the impression that he had been wounded in the mouth. Such an injury, they must have realised, might well have entailed the loss of jaw and teeth, proving not merely disfiguring. In a sense, therefore, they must have been relieved to learn from the young Countess of Elgin, who was seemingly the first relative to see him following his return, that he had been wounded elsewhere. Nevertheless, despite Collingwood's official report, Mary found that the wound bothered Durham 'a good deal'. Indeed, his memoir states that it 'appeared slight at first, but it was many years before he completely recovered', though he was possibly gilding the lily when he continued: 'narrowly escaping the loss of his leg'.[21]

Durham was destined not to spend the height of Yuletide with his wife and intimates, for the court martial on Sir Robert Calder commenced on 23 December aboard the *Prince of Wales* in Portsmouth Harbour. Under the presidency of Admiral George Montagu, the local port-admiral, the court convened to enquire into Calder's 'conduct and proceedings... with His Majesty's squadron under his command, on the 23rd day of July last, and also into his subsequent conduct and proceedings, until he finally lost sight of the enemy's ships, and to try him for not having done his utmost to renew the said engagement, and to take or destroy every ship of the enemy, which it was his duty to engage accordingly'. Sitting in judgment with Montagu were Vice-Admirals John Holloway, Bartholomew Samuel Rowley and Edward Thornbrough, Rear-Admirals Sir Isaac Coffin and John Sutton, and Captains John Irwin, Robert Dudley Oliver, John Thomas Seater, James Athol Wood, John Larmour, Thomas Bladen Capel and James Bisset.[22]

Leading the prosecution was Moses Greetham, deputy judge advocate to the fleet, assisted by Charles Bicknell, solicitor to the Admiralty. Calder, advised by counsel Stephen Gazelee, conducted his own defence. He agreed that the court should proceed in the 'unavoidable absence' of Captain Prowse, who was still on active duty, and whose testimony he would have liked. Admirals Stirling and George Martin (the latter newly elevated to flag-rank), Captains Durham and Inman, and the master of Stirling's flagship, the *Glory*, were called as witnesses for the prosecution. Captains Legge, Boyles, Lechmere, Brown, John Harvey, Cuming, Griffith and Fleeming were summoned for the defence along with Calder's signal lieutenant and the chaplain to the *Phoenix*.

Brown and Lechmere must have cursed their decision to return with Calder where Durham had refused. The court martial had been delayed, they had missed Trafalgar needlessly, and they had the mortification of knowing that Durham, basking in a glory thereby denied to them, was present to give evidence after all. To add insult to injury, Brown was required to respond merely to a single question, which required a monosyllabic answer, for the court decided that further testimony from him was unnecessary.[23]

Durham's evidence was given on the first day of the court martial. 'Was you ordered to reconnoitre the enemy's fleet on Wednesday the twenty fourth of July and to observe their motions and at what time?' began the prosecutor. 'I was, between six and seven in the morning I believe', came the reply. 'Did you at any time on that day make a signal to the vice-admiral to ask if you should still keep the enemy's fleet in sight?' 'I did in the afternoon, about five o'clock.' 'What was the answer?' 'No.' 'Was you to windward of the enemy's fleet at that time?' 'Yes.'

Officers comprising the court then took up the questioning. 'When you last saw the enemy's fleet, under what sail were they standing, and what course were they steering?' 'They were under their topsails, topgallant sails and foretopsails, in general steering south-east and by south.' 'How did the British fleet then bear from the enemy?' 'The enemy bore about south-south-west of me, and the admiral I believe nearly north-east and by east of me eleven or twelve miles.' 'At the time you returned to the British fleet under what sail were they standing and what course were they steering?' 'They were steering by the wind on the larboard tack, I should suppose south-east by east, close by the wind; when I returned to the fleet they were under topsails and foresails. I believe we lay about south-east, and by east.' 'At what distance were you at that time from Ferrol by your reckoning?' 'When I made the signal shall I keep sight of the enemy, we were about one hundred and twenty-five miles from Ferrol as near as sea reckoning could bring it. I desired the master to work it, and bring it to me when he did.' 'Do you recollect the bearings of Ferrol at that time?' 'If I recollect right, about south-east by compass.' 'When you returned to the fleet, do you recollect what ships of the British fleet appeared to you to be in a disabled state?' 'The *Windsor Castle* had no fore topmast up. No other ship appeared to me to want anything.' 'What ships were towing the prizes at that time?' 'I think the *Egyptienne* and *Sirius* frigates.'[24]

That concluded Durham's evidence, for Calder declined the opportunity to cross-examine him as he had done with Stirling and Martin, and would do with Inman. Refusing the opportunity to cross-examine the master of the *Glory*, Calder had said: 'I never can ask that gentleman any questions.' With respect to Durham, whom he must by now have thoroughly loathed, his tone was perhaps somewhat more tart. 'I can ask Captain Durham no questions whatever', he explained. 'I beg leave to observe that to the court.' Later that day Durham was recalled by the court to clarify his evidence regarding bearings, and with that the Admiralty solicitor, Charles Bicknell, closed the case for the prosecution.[25]

Next day the trial was formally adjourned owing to an application by Calder for more time to prepare his defence, since he had expected that the prosecution's case would last longer. The court reassembled at ten o'clock on Christmas morning, with a full day of defence testimony ahead. Proceedings commenced with the reading out by Gazelee of the lengthy and impassioned statement which Calder handed him. The issue hinged, this declared, on two questions: 'whether I could have renewed the engagement, or if at all, with advantage', and whether 'it was prudent to have done so, or whether I did not wisely exercise the discretion necessarily reposed in me in the not doing it'. In a nutshell, on 23 July 'it was impossible for me to have done it, unless the enemy had chosen it', and on the following day 'although the wind was in a favourable quarter, I had no chance of doing it without separating my squadron, and that, from the lightness of the winds and other circumstances, it was a matter of great doubt, whether even if I had separated my squadron, I could have come up with them [the enemy], particularly if they had chosen to avoid me'.[26]

When reading the reports from his ships that reached him at dawn on 24 July, the statement explained, he realised that the damage they had sustained in the action was worse than he had anticipated, whereas the enemy appeared to have endured far less; not one of his fifteen ships was in a condition to carry enough sail to take them to windward and thus to come up with the enemy, particularly in view of the heavy swell; the fact that the *Barfleur* sprung her yards and the *Repulse* her bowsprit indicated what might have occurred had his other ships hoisted a big spread of canvas. If he had renewed the action, continued the statement, the disabled *Windsor Castle* and the prizes would have been captured by the enemy ships placed for that purpose on the weather bow.

By his procedure, Calder maintained, he

...preserved the victory I had acquired, in spite of their very great superiority, and in defiance of the many hostile squadrons I was surrounded by...

In endeavouring to compel a renewal of the action, I should also have sustained a very considerable inconvenience in the want of frigates...

Circumstanced as I thus was, it appeared to me impracticable to have forced the enemy to action, or, if at all, with such advantage as would have justified the attempt, even if I had had nothing to apprehend from any squadron but that which I was opposed to... but when I reflected that, in addition to that squadron and the Rochefort, which it appears were then actually at sea, there were 16 sail of the line at Ferrol, within a few hours sail, who, if not already out, might, on receiving intelligence from the combined squadrons, have come out to their assistance, or, in the event of my not being in a situation to return to Ferrol, the continuance of which blockade was one main object of my instructions, there would be no force to oppose those squadrons, and that they would more than probably have pushed for Ireland, or, perhaps, England, to facilitate the invasion which was then every moment expected, I really felt that I should be running too great a hazard, and putting my fleet into a situation of danger which I could never have justified.

I therefore judged it most prudent to keep my squadron together, and not to attempt to renew the engagement unless the enemy offered it, or an opportunity afforded itself of my doing so, under more favourable circumstances than at that time presented themselves.

At the same time conceiving that their object might be to effect a junction with the ships at Ferrol, I determined, if possible, to prevent their attaining that object, and to keep myself between them and that port, and, if possible, to draw them to the northward, that, by so doing, I might accompany the

Windsor Castle and the prizes out of the reach of the Rochefort squadron, and afterwards, perhaps, have an opportunity of re-attacking the enemy, before they could reach their own shores...

Having formed this conclusion, I acted upon it during the two days that the enemy remained in sight, keeping my squadron collected under an easy sail, certainly never offering, but as certainly never avoiding an engagement, had the enemy chosen to bring it on.

As for the second part of the issue at hand, 'the prudence of renewing the engagement', this statement asked the court to bear in mind that the combined fleet was numerically superior to his own, and did not lack frigates and other useful craft.

Against such a force I could not hope to succeed without considerable damage; I had no friendly port near me, and in that situation had the Ferrol and Rochefort squadrons fallen in with me, I must have become an easy prey for them. Had they taken a different course and sailed for Ireland, or even England, there was no squadron to arrest their progress. Had I been defeated, although many of the enemy's ships must have been disabled in the conflict, I should have lost the advantage I had before obtained, the enemy would have acquired spirit, their remaining squadrons would have been unmolested, and it is impossible to foresee what might, in that case, have been the consequence.

It would, Calder observed, be a grim state of affairs if officers placed in 'a situation of command' were 'to be censured for an honest exercise of the discretion necessarily arising from such a situation'. He believed that he had behaved 'wisely and beneficially', and suggested that events since the action bore this out. Owing to the 'line of conduct' he pursued 'I was enabled, after receiving a reinforcement, to pursue the combined squadrons into Cadiz, and thereby perhaps to have laid the foundation of that glorious victory which we have so recently celebrated'. He was deeply affected by the need to request the court martial, for missing 'the glories of Trafalgar' had augmented his 'sufferings'. But he trusted that the court would 'confirm me in that estimation with the profession and the public, which I have for so many years employed, and restore to me unsullied that fair name and reputation which has on this occasion been so cruelly and unjustly attacked'.

During this long rebuttal of the 'calumnies' which had been circulating against him, Calder courteously but unequivocally dismissed Durham's evidence.

With respect to the fact that Captain Durham was called to prove, I have to observe only, that, at the time he made the signal he speaks of, I had formed the plan which I meant to act upon – that night was coming on – and that the enemy were increasing their distance; the directing him to keep the enemy in sight would only have had the effect of separating him from me, and further weakening my force, which I could by no means afford to do.

I give Captain Durham every credit for his good intentions in making the signal, but he will forgive me for observing, that I was a little surprised at its being made. I best knew my own intentions, and had I thought it necessary for him to have kept sight of the enemy I should have made the signal for his doing so. He is a little mistaken in saying that he was ordered to reconnoitre the enemy's fleet on the 24th of July. The signal made to him was No.77 to bring to, and not No.19 to reconnoitre – of course this could be only a mistake.[27]

One of Calder's defence witnesses, Thomas Warrand, who had been his signal lieutenant, confirmed the vice-admiral's statement. 'What was the signal made to the *Defiance* between six and seven o'clock in the morning of the 24th [of July]?', Calder asked him. 'Number 77 to bring to.' 'What is the number of the signal to reconnoitre the enemy?' 'Number 19.' 'Was that the number made to the *Defiance* on that day?' 'No, it was not.'

The court then assumed the questioning. 'Was any signal made to the *Defiance* to look out between the British fleet and that of the enemy, or to watch their motions previous to that signal for her to bring to?', Warrand was asked.' No, none', he replied. 'Do you know by what accident the *Defiance* came into that situation?' 'Being the sternmost ship of the weather line, her signal was made to bring to as one of the enemy's frigates was come up astern to reconnoitre us, previous to which a signal was made to the *Dragon* to reconnoitre.' 'Was any signal made after that to call the *Defiance* to join the fleet before he made the signal to the vice-admiral to ask if he should any longer keep sight of the enemy?' 'None, except that of answering her signal.' 'Was the signal that was made by Captain Durham, to ask if he should still keep sight of the enemy, repeated by Rear-Admiral Stirling before it was answered by the vice-admiral?' 'I did not see it but on board the *Defiance*.'[28]

At this point the Admiralty solicitor proposed re-examining Durham. But Calder said that he 'conceived his mistaking the signal to be accidental', and consequently there was no further probing by the court into the discrepancies between Durham's memory and Warrand's. The respective logs of the *Defiance* and the *Prince of Wales* throw no light on the subject of the disputed signals.[29]

Obviously, either Durham or Calder and his lieutenant were in error, possibly owing to misty weather conditions – or one side was being deliberately untruthful. It is puzzling, and at this distance unfathomable.

With all the evidence completed, the court deliberated behind the locked and guarded great-cabin door from ten the following morning until just before four in the afternoon. When the door swung open and Calder was summoned, a crowd surged forward, Durham perhaps among them. 'The rush for admittance', wrote an eye witness, 'was similar to that which sometimes takes place in the gallery of the House of Commons. When everything was ready, there was the most profound silence, a sort of awful attention', as Moses Greetham intoned the verdict. The court found 'that the charge of not having done his utmost to renew the said engagement, and to take or destroy every ship of the enemy, has been proved against the said Vice-Admiral Calder; that it appears that his conduct has not been actuated either by cowardice or disaffection, but has arisen solely from error in judgment, and is highly censurable, and doth adjudge him to be severely reprimanded, and the said Vice-Admiral Calder is hereby severely reprimanded accordingly'.[30]

Calder was stunned and distraught. 'When my inquiry is finished', he had informed Barham, 'I trust I shall have every marked approbation conferred upon me that any officer before me has had, for obtaining a complete victory.' He now turned, and left the cabin without a word, accompanied by a group of friends and supporters, and got into his barge. There he sat slumped, 'scarcely lifting up his head, which was apparently bowed down by the weight of the sentence pronounced upon him'.[31]

There were many who believed with Captain Codrington that Calder had been 'wantonly ruined' by injustice. 'Had [Calder's] action not been', insisted Admiral Roddam, 'we should not have given so complete a blow off Cadiz.' A poetic contemporary reflected that

In antient [sic] times, the Roman's eagle eye
Was fix'd on conduct, not on victory:
And Fabius' [sic] shield its steady lustre pour'd
Midst all the lightnings of Marcellus' [sic] sword.
Unhappy Calder! We, like birds of night,
Are dazzled by an all-subduing light.
Tho' conquest-crowned, thy temperate valour weighed
Each doubtful point, then wisdom's voice obeyed
And then like Fabius didst prepare the way
For great Marcellus, and Trafalgar's day.[32]

With characteristic obstinacy, Durham had stuck to a principle, and he had been vindicated. He felt that Calder had been wrong, he had said so, and the court had agreed. Apart from Prowse, who was not actually in the fighting, he was the only one of Calder's captains on 22 July who had the glory of being at Trafalgar to recompense them for being in an action so little regarded by many of their countrymen. 'It is much to be regretted, that any opinion which might be entertained of [Calder's] conduct... should, in its consequences, have implicated the courage of the officers and seamen, who certainly never fought better, or under greater disadvantages, leaving out of the question their disparity of numbers', wrote Captain Inman's obituarist several years after Calder's court martial.

> To defeat the enemy, and to capture two sail of the line, were deserving of something like approbation; yet, what plaudits, what congratulations, what exultations for the successful efforts of their prowess on that day, were ever heard? None! Their merit was never acknowledged; the meed of applause was never bestowed; and both officers and seamen induced to believe, that they – the British fleet – had been defeated; that they had not behaved with the same firmness and resolution, which former times had so proudly witnessed![33]

The court's verdict ended Calder's career for the foreseeable future, and he retreated in dismay to his Hampshire home. His downcast mood was a far cry from the audacity he had displayed on hearing of Nelson's victory, for the first thing he had done was to write to Collingwood to press his entitlement to a share of the prize money, presumably on the grounds that ships of his squadron took part in the battle. Collingwood was shocked at his claim. 'There was a great indelicacy in it at all circumstances', he wrote from his new flagship, the *Queen*. 'He ought to have known he had no right. But it is a true Scotch principle to claim everything and get what they can, or Lord Keith would not have been so rich by many a good estate.'[34]

'What a contrast [Trafalgar is] with... Calder's puny, half-begotten victory!', Lord Minto had declared on hearing of Nelson's triumph. Unfortunately for Calder, the events of 21 October had influenced perceptions of those of 22–23 July. Observed naval historian Sir Julian Corbett incisively a century later:

> [Calder's] real defence was never raised. It was, that the situation, the real inner intent of Barham's orders, was never explained to him, and he did not

know that his one and only duty, whatever the result to his own fleet, was if he once got hold never to let go so long as he had a tooth left.

This principle – to fight to a finish when in doubt – has become an axiom in modern naval opinion, but it was scarcely so when Calder fought. The hardest part of his case is that he fought the action under one standard, and was tried for it under another. Between the action and the court-martial Nelson fought and won Trafalgar. Trafalgar set up an ideal of hot-pressed action and a sentiment of confident superiority which did not exist when Calder fought, anywhere but in Nelson and his band of brothers.[35]

Collingwood was rewarded for his part at Trafalgar with a barony, a pension of £2,000 a year for life, and a sword from the Duke of Clarence. On 3 December, two days before a national day of thanksgiving proclaimed by the king, the committee of the Patriotic Fund, meeting at Lloyd's Coffee House under the presidency of the Lord Mayor of London, voted to present Collingwood, Lady Nelson and Nelson's brother with suitably ornamented silver vases worth £500 each. Lord Northesk received a vase worth £300, as did Rear-Admiral Sir Richard Strachan, whose small squadron while he was a commodore had captured all four of Dumanoir's ships on 4 November off Cape Finisterre, thus rounding off Britain's victory. Appropriately inscribed swords worth £100 each were given to Durham and the other Trafalgar captains by the Patriotic Fund at Lloyd's. Generous sums were granted to officers, seamen and marines who had been wounded in action, and relief afforded to widows, orphans and other dependents; the money contributed on the day of thanksgiving – amounting to £100,000 – would be exclusively set aside for such purposes.[36]

In the meantime the *Victory* had arrived at the Nore with Nelson's body aboard, preserved in spirits. On 23 December the body, in a temporary coffin draped with an ensign, was taken to Greenwich Hospital for Seamen, to be received privately by the elderly governor, Admiral Lord Hood. The king insisted that St Paul's Cathedral should be the dead hero's final resting place, and on 27 December the date of the state funeral was fixed for Thursday, 9 January. Hitherto, all coffins buried in the crypt had been carried down a flight of stairs, but Nelson's was to be lowered by special machinery, and workmen needed time to prepare. Between 4 and 7 January an estimated 15,000 members of the public followed the Princess of Wales's lead in paying their respects at the bier during the official lying-in-state in the Painted Hall at Greenwich. So eager were they that when the doors were opened several people were trampled underfoot, and one man had his eye accidentally poked out.[37]

As a Trafalgar captain whose defective vessel had returned to Britain, Durham was in the right place at the right time. He was selected to play a prominent role at the obsequies, assisted by two young lieutenants. They were James Purches, who had not far to travel from his parental home in Stepney, and James Poate, who was not connected in any way with the battle. He was first lieutenant of a frigate that happened to be fitting out on the Thames, and thus he was at hand, though it might have been no coincidence that Poate was the nephew of a noted post-captain who had several times circumnavigated the globe.[38]

Durham was due to participate in the grand water procession which, on 8 January, accompanied Nelson's coffin along the Thames from Greenwich to the Whitehall stairs, whence it was conveyed to the great hall of the Admiralty known as the captains' room, where it lay overnight. But he was for some reason indisposed, and Captain Baynton of the *Leviathan* took his place, breakfasting at Lord Hood's apartments before embarking, bearing the official pennant known as the guidon, in the first barge. The day was one of biting gale-force winds, which impeded the black-draped barges in their progress towards the landing place opposite Somerset House, and which perhaps convinced the normally resilient Durham to remain at home for fear of becoming too ill to play his designated part in the funeral ceremony the following day.[39]

He rose very early on the morning of 9 January, and can be imagined shivering in the wintry chill as he put on the clothes that protocol demanded. His waistcoat, breeches and stockings were black, and he had black crape fabric around the arms of his full-dress uniform coat and in his captain's hat. Thousands of people were also up well before daylight, making their way to St Paul's, which was to open at seven, or to vantage points along the funeral procession's route. An hour before dawn the drums of the various volunteer corps in London began to beat, and soon the militia thus summoned lined the streets in double ranks, from the Admiralty to St Paul's. Groups of them were placed at each door of the cathedral to prevent a stampede by the milling multitude. By eight o'clock the first carriages of distinguished mourners, who included the Prince of Wales and dukes of the blood royal, were arriving at Hyde Park, where two hours later over 100 carriages were assembled. They were to proceed in orderly fashion across Piccadilly and onwards through St James's Park and the Horse Guards to the Admiralty, where Durham and the rest of the naval officers and men who were assigned ceremonial duties gathered. A taxing schedule awaited them all.

At half-past ten the regiments of cavalry and infantry quartered within a 100-mile radius of London who had served in Egypt following Nelson's triumph at the Nile began their slow march from St James's Park to St Paul's Cathedral, under the overall command of General Sir David Dundas. Accompanied by a number of field-pieces, they were led by a detachment of light dragoons, with four companies of grenadiers bringing up the rear. Martial bands with drums muffled played 'Rule Britannia', and military pipers performed Handel's 'Dead March in Saul'. The latter was repeated at intervals by military trumpeters, who also sounded a solemn dirge.[40]

As soon as these troops had passed the Admiralty the procession, preceded by six marshalmen on foot to clear the way, moved in behind them. Close on the heels of the leading figure, a messenger of the College of Arms in a mourning cloak and holding a silver-topped staff furled with sarsenet, came forty-eight pensioners of Greenwich Hospital and forty-eight seamen and marines of the *Victory*, walking in pairs. Towards the head of the procession were mourning coaches bearing, respectively, Captains Laforey of the *Spartiate* and Rotheram of the *Royal Sovereign* and the lieutenants assisting them. In front of Laforey's coach was carried the standard and in front of Rotheram's the guidon. Several coaches behind came that in which Durham, Purches and Poate sat, preceded by the banner of the deceased admiral as a Knight of the Bath which Durham was to carry into the cathedral in this great historic pageant of state.[41]

Still further back was the open four-wheeled 'funeral car', decorated with a carved replica of the head and stern of the *Victory*, and drawn by six black horses. Inside the 'transcendently beautiful and splendid' mahogany and gilt coffin, described as 'the most elegant and superb ever seen in Europe', was the narrow, thin-planked casket made from the mast of *L'Orient*. Hallowell's gift was now lined with padded white silk and enclosed in an oak-filled lead outer casing. In order to give the public a better view of the coffin the sumptuous black velvet pall adorned with six escutcheons of the arms of the dead hero, which had covered it during most of its lying-in-state, had been removed. Over the coffin, suspended atop foliage-entwined pillars covered with black velvet, was a canopy of the same material crowned by six sable ostrich plumes. It was edged with appropriate ornamental symbols in gold.[42]

At Temple Bar, situated at the junction of Fleet Street and the Strand, the procession was received by the Lord Mayor of London, Sir James Shaw, who subsequently joined it on horseback, holding the emblematic City sword, and by a delegation from the Corporation. Carriages bearing aldermen in scarlet gowns, sheriffs, and violet-robed representatives of the 'common council' fell at intervals into the procession. In front of them walked seven seamen from the *Victory*, who had shared the councilmen's barge. These handpicked sailors grasped the Union Jack and pennant flown by their ship at Trafalgar; the 'honourable tatters' of those relics 'attracted universal attention' from the spectators of all classes lining the route.[43]

When, towards one o'clock, the troops who had marched with the procession arrived at St Paul's, the respective regiments took their allotted positions in and outside the cathedral, the grenadiers filing in to stand on each side of the nave. The Greenwich pensioners and the seamen and marines of the *Victory* who had walked at the head of the procession ascended the steps to form a guard of honour at the great west door. Alighting from their coaches, Durham, Laforey and Rotheram, bearing their assigned banners and accompanied by the two lieutenants flanking each of them, entered the cathedral. They stood within the choir, along with officials of the College of Arms, as the first strains of organ music commenced.

On reaching the cathedral the coffin was again covered by its pall, and borne in by twelve men. It was preceded by a herald, behind whom walked Captain Moorsom of the *Revenge* with a lieutenant on either side. Moorsom was carrying the great banner, and immediately behind him were heralds bearing the gauntlet and spurs, the helm and crest, the target and sword, and the surcoat. Then came the Norroy King of Arms, Ralph Bigland, holding a black velvet cushion on which rested a viscount's coronet, and the cathedral's dean, senior clerics, and choristers. As it entered the coffin was received by Rear-Admiral Eliab Harvey, newly advanced to flag-rank, Vice-Admirals Thomas Taylor and James Hawkins Whitshed, and (surprisingly, in view of his perceived professional enmity to Nelson) Admiral Sir John Orde, Durham's neighbour in Gloucester Place. They were to carry the pall. Also on hand were Rear-Admirals John Aylmer, Sir Isaac Coffin, William Domett, Sir William Henry Douglas, Thomas Drury and Thomas Wells, who were to hold aloft the canopy. The ten admirals now got into position. On the outside of them, as they proceeded at a respectful pace with the coffin up the aisle through the nave to the choir, were six officers from the *Victory* carrying bannerolls depicting Nelson's family lineage. These officers (five lieutenants and the master) walked three a side, one behind the other.

At the rear of the coffin was the Garter King of Arms, Sir Isaac Heard, with his sceptre, and behind him was the chief mourner, the aged admiral of the fleet, Sir Peter Parker, flanked by Admirals Lord Radstock and Lord

Hood. Directly behind them were six so-called assistant mourners, filing in two by two: Admirals Sir Roger Curtis and Benjamin Caldwell, Admirals Sir Charles Morice Pole and Richard Rodney Bligh, and Vice-Admirals Charles Powell Hamilton and Charles Edmund Nugent. There followed Captains Hardy and Bayntun, both carrying the banner of emblems, with a lieutenant on either side. Nelson's sole surviving brother, a clergyman newly endowed with an earldom and a pension, came next with other male relatives of the deceased, and the remainder of the procession ensued.

When the coffin reached the choir it was placed on a bier covered with gold-fringed and tasselled black velvet. The pall was removed once more, and the Norroy King of Arms placed the cushion and coronet he had brought in on top of the coffin. Sir Peter Parker, his two supporters and his trainbearer took their allocated seats near the coffin. The assistant mourners, pallbearers and holders of the canopy sat on stools each side of it, the officers with the bannerolls stationing themselves close by.

All the unreserved seats in the cathedral had been filled almost as soon as the doors were opened at seven that morning, and 'not a symptom of impatience was discoverable' as these members of the public awaited the entry of the procession at one o'clock. Gradually the dignitaries were seated. On the south side of the choir, at the east end of the prebendial stalls, sat the Prince of Wales and his brothers. Facing them, on the north side, were London's Lord Mayor and civic officials. Nearby were the Duchess of York and Nelson's relatives. Naval and military officers, who had been in the procession, like Durham, sat near the altar. Altogether, a congregation estimated at not less than 10,000, and including women (Lady Charlotte quite possibly among them), were present to witness what was described as 'one of the most impressive and most splendid solemnities that ever took place in this country, or perhaps in Europe'.[44]

As dusk descended torches were lit in the choir, and the vast domed concourse was illuminated by lantern light. About five o'clock the procession, in inverted order and to the accompaniment of a dirge from the organ, made its solemn progress from the choir to the site of the grave in the floor beneath the dome, Durham holding his banner. The coffin was placed on a platform high enough to be visible from every part of the cathedral, and the viscount's coronet and its cushion were again laid on top. Sir Peter Parker and his supporters stood at the head of the grave, with the assistant mourners and the male members of Nelson's family nearby. The choristers sang anthems, concluding with an admired arrangement of 'His body is buried in peace; but his name liveth evermore.' Then, shortly after half-past five, the coffin was mechanically lowered into its hallowed resting place.

Heard, the Garter King of Arms, proclaimed Nelson's style and titles, concluding with the words: 'the Hero who, in the moment of victory, fell covered with immortal glory, let us humbly trust, that he is now raised to bliss ineffable, and to a glorious immortality!' The comptroller, treasurer and steward of Nelson's household then broke their staves and handed the pieces to Heard, who threw them into the grave. Then the seven seamen from the *Victory* stepped forward to deposit in the grave the Union Jack and pennant, furled. Spontaneously, and movingly, they first tore off pieces of the former, as revered keepsakes. And so, at six o'clock, the ceremony ended and Durham and the rest of the procession prepared to filter out into the cold dark night. Incredibly, the cathedral was not completely vacated until after nine.[45]

On that same day a print of Trafalgar was published by a well-known naval and military publisher who was official printseller to George III. Showing the purported position of the respective fleets at noon, it listed the names of the 'Gallant Heroes' who had commanded at the action. Above the depiction of the fleets on the verge of doing battle was a hand-coloured copperplate engraving showing the artist's impression of the scene in the *Victory*'s great-cabin as Nelson explained his tactics to his admirals and captains. Durham, of course, had not been present at that meeting, but the artist almost certainly did not know that or disregarded it if he did. If Durham is anywhere in the picture, he is probably the booted figure standing at the extreme right. It is not an obvious resemblance, yet something about the eyes, cheeks, demeanour and general cast of countenance suggests him in a way no other figure does. The artist, William Marshall Craig, was drawing-master to Princess Charlotte, and therefore an associate of the Dowager Lady Elgin.[46] In all likelihood he had an opportunity to glimpse her son-in-law and made an effort to include him.

As one of Trafalgar's 'Gallant Heroes' Durham had his share of adulation. His wound, which was 'getting much better', enhanced his reputation. In common with his escape from the *Royal George*, he would be able to dine out on the experience of fighting in the era's defining sea-battle for the rest of his life. It would always be a cause of regret on the part of his friends Malcolm, Moore and Stopford that they had narrowly missed the action. Once again, he had been very lucky.[47]

The day after Trafalgar, Collingwood, in whose gift the vacancy lay, had appointed the *Royal Sovereign*'s first lieutenant to the sloop *Weazle* with the rank of commander. On 24 December, the first lieutenants of the other British ships were rewarded for their part in the battle. The two who had been acting captains owing to the absence of their commanding officers were made post, along with the ostensible first lieutenant of the *Victory*. The rest were promoted to commander's rank, as was John Pasco, the actual first lieutenant of Nelson's flagship, who had on the admiral's orders been doing the duty of signal officer and was responsible for the substitution of the word 'expects' for 'confides' in the famous last signal; the enforced exchange of duties ensured him naval immortality but in terms of promotion it cost him heartbreakingly dear. The *Defiance*'s William Hellard, who had been commissioned a lieutenant only a few months after Durham, nearly a quarter of a century earlier, had got his step up at last. For his valiant conduct, and the disabling injury he suffered, James Spratt was, on Durham's recommendation, also made a commander. The first lieutenant of the *Mars*, who had been in command of that ship during most of the action, was posted on New Year's Day.[48]

Incredibly, and unwittingly cruelly, official notification of the promotions did not reach the bulk of the Trafalgar fleet, which remained at sea with Lord Collingwood, for months. Men and officers alike were feeling neglected and increasingly demoralised. There was jealousy of Durham and other captains who, owing to the condition of their ships, had got back to England in time to share in 'the *éclat* of victory', as Captain Codrington called it. 'Had we all gone home together it would have been highly gratifying', he wrote. 'Indeed, considering how little notice the Admiralty has taken of us... we are severely punished in our loss of Nelson, by this action of which the country is so proud. The suffering is ours, the joy has been confined to England.'[49]

It must have been galling for Collingwood, who had transferred to the *Queen*, that his former flag-captain, Rotheram, whom he regarded with disdain, had taken part in Nelson's funeral and had been lionised in the *Naval Chronicle*. And he was not happy with 'boasters', as Codrington dubbed Durham and Eliab Harvey. Collingwood had enthused to a brother admiral in December: 'The *Defiance* boarded *L'Aigle* and had the possession of her poop for some time when the Frenchmen rallied and drove them back and if I could tell you all the histories of all the ships you would find much to admire.' But, becoming increasingly frustrated and resentful at remaining behind with no news or instructions, he grew critical of Durham's not unjustifiable claim to have taken the *Aigle*. Perhaps he had been influenced by a letter from an officer aboard the *Bellerophon*, dated

2 December, and reprinted first in the Portsmouth press and then in the *Naval Chronicle*: the *Aigle* had been 'an easy conquest for the *Defiance*, a fresh ship'. Codrington wrote in February that Collingwood was 'quite indignant' at Durham's 'presumption', having seen the *Aigle* 'closely and singly engaged' with Cooke's 'very long before' Durham could have brought the *Defiance* into action.[50]

'Not a promotion of any officer in the fleet here except Adml Grindall, who was included in the promotion of flags [on 9 November], of which he was not informed till three months after, by the convoy, which is... like sending an express by the stage waggon', grumbled Collingwood privately in March. 'The consequence is that the Senior Officers are in extreme dejection with vexation and disappointment, and the younger ones all desirous of getting home, where they may have a chance of promotion.' To his knowledge nobody on the *Royal Sovereign* had been promoted, 'except those who were made angels in the Action, and my first Lieut't, who I put into a vacancy with which the Admiralty had nothing to do. But those who can make a good story out of *a very trifle* get whatever they please.'[51]

While promising to try to fulfil Collingwood's requests, Barham had reminded him of Admiralty regulations, 'by which they leave deaths and court martial vacancies to the commanding officers and reserve all others to themselves'. Learning that Durham and Hope had each obtained promotion for two of their officers further helped to sour Collingwood's mood. 'I cannot help thinking that there must have been something in my conduct of which your lordship did not approve and that you have marked your disapprobation by thus denying to my dependents and friends what was given so liberally to other ships of the fleet; for I have heard that the *Defence* and the *Defiance* had each of their two lieutenants promoted on the recommendation of their captains.'[52]

Meanwhile, following Nelson's funeral Durham and Lady Charlotte travelled to Scotland, since the *Defiance* was still refitting. One fellow countryman who took a more than ordinary interest in the battle of Trafalgar was an elderly merchant, John Clerk of Eldin near Penicuik, south of Edinburgh. Clerk had from his earliest youth been keenly interested in the sea and ships. He had for decades immersed himself in the theory and practice of naval tactics, staging mock encounters on his dining table using pieces of cork. He saw that the usual British plan of attacking an enemy fleet all at once, from van to rear, placed the advanced ships of the British line in unacceptable jeopardy. They were exposed to the full fury of their opponents, who disabled them and then bore away, repeating the tactic until the British were worn out and in no condition to continue the pursuit.

Clerk had sought to devise a way to enable British fleets effectively to engage their foes. The concept of breaking the line was central to him. He began to air his views in the late 1770s, and in 1780 had expounded his theories to Admiral Rodney, and thereafter to anyone else who would listen, including Henry Dundas (Lord Melville). In January 1782 the first part of his *Essay on Naval Tactics* was printed for circulation among about fifty of his friends, and he became convinced that his ideas had influenced the outcome of most of Britain's subsequent naval victories, including Rodney's of 12 April 1782, St Vincent's of 14 February 1797, and Duncan's of 11 October 1797.[53]

His pamphlet's suggestion for an attack from to-windward with the line broken up into divisions was echoed by Nelson's 'Secret Memo' of 9 October, and eight days after the battle Durham found time to dictate a letter to Clerk. Couched in the third person, it enclosed a copy of the 'Secret Memo': 'Captain Durham, sensible of the many advantages accrued to the British nation from the publication of Mr. Clerk's Naval Tactics, and particularly from that part of them which recommends breaking through the enemy's line, begs to offer him the enclosed form of battle, which was most punctiliously attended to in the very brilliant and glorious action of the 21st of October. Mr. Clerk will perceive with great pleasure, that the present form of battle is completely accordant with his own notions; and it is now sent as a token of respect from Captain Durham, to one who has merited so highly of his country.'[54]

Durham's letter thrilled Clerk, for although the elderly man's views had been praised by many naval officers, including Rodney, he had found it hard to prove a link between his published ideas and the naval victories for which he claimed credit. St Vincent, for instance, claimed that he had not heard of his *Essay*, and Clerk felt that he had never received his due. This clear statement from Durham was used by Clerk to claim a state pension. No remuneration appears to have been forthcoming, however, despite Captain Hardy's revelation in March 1806 that Nelson read Clerk's opinions 'with great attention, and frequently expressed his approbation of them in the fullest manner; he also recommended all the captains to read them with attention, and said that many good hints might be taken from them. He most approved of the attack from to-windward, and considered breaking through the enemy's line absolutely necessary to obtain a great victory.'[55]

A hero's welcome naturally awaited Durham from his father and other family members in Scotland, though not from his cousin Elizabeth (daughter of the lord advocate Henry Erskine) and her husband, Lieutenant-Colonel George Callander of Craigforth. Durham had, in his own words, been on 'Terms of great Intimacy' with both Elizabeth and her husband, 'previous to their marriage' in 1801. Since then, the couple had been an integral part of Sir James and Lady Steuart's circle at Coltness, where Elizabeth had been close to Aunt Betty until the latter's death in 1803. Since the elderly Sir James had no children, the Callanders aspired to inherit his estate.

They had reckoned without a vilifying rumour, started about 1804 and ascribed by Callander to a 'Villainous Combination' of Durham and his brothers, abetted by their mother's first cousin, James Wolfe Murray of Cringletie, a rising lawyer who was at the time sheriff of his native Peebleshire. The rumour, which reputedly originated with Durham, was allegedly designed to turn Sir James against Elizabeth so that she would not inherit the estate which Durham, so Callander believed, coveted for himself. The rumour was so defamatory that, wrote Elizabeth's outraged husband, such a 'large degree of malignant depravity' as it accused her of 'could only exist in a fiend in the human shape'.

Devastated by the rumour, the Callanders moved out of Coltness. Wolfe Murray (who in 1807 would marry Durham's niece Isabella Strange) advised Callander to drop his accusations against Durham and his brothers for everybody's sake, before a public scandal developed. But Callander persisted. When Durham arrived in Scotland Callander was all set to challenge him to a sword fight, and only by bluffing it out and denying in writing that he had maligned Elizabeth did Durham avert a duel. But ill feeling endured.[56]

8

Ruling the Waves

What a life of privation ours is…!
Admiral Lord Collingwood

'It was… a great day', Collingwood wrote a few months after Trafalgar, 'yet I feel we have much more to do; the French are venturing out with their squadrons and they must be crushed.' Since the *Defiance* was still undergoing repairs Durham was now appointed to the 74-gun *Renown*, destined for the Channel Fleet, which was once again under the command of St Vincent. That crusty old warrior hoisted his flag aboard the *Hibernia* in March 1806, and that same month the *Renown* joined him off Ushant. She was undermanned, with many foreigners among her crew, and three marines and five landsmen, described by Durham as 'all Irish Catholics of the worst description', took an early opportunity to desert. She was placed under the direct orders of Rear-Admiral Eliab Harvey, whose flag flew in the *Tonnant*, patrolling the familiar stretch between Brittany and Cape Finisterre.[1]

On 10 August Durham received his Trafalgar gold medal and an accompanying letter from Lord Howick, first lord of the Admiralty in the

Whig Grenville-Fox administration that had come to power following Pitt's death in January. 'Such a distinguished mark of approbation from a Sovereign who truly lives in the hearts of his people excites my warmest gratitude', commented Durham in acknowledging receipt of the medal, 'and I cannot refuse myself the pleasure of saying that pleasing as this communication must be, it is not a little enhanced by its coming through your Lordship.'[2]

His effusiveness is perhaps largely explained by the close working relationship that Howick had with Durham's cousin Thomas Erskine, newly elevated to a barony and to the Woolsack. Howick, who would in due course succeed his father as Earl Grey and sponsor the seminal Reform Bill of 1832, had long been associated with radical causes. In 1792 he had presented to the Commons a petition from the Society of Friends of the People, whose members included Erskine, pressing for parliamentary reform. Durham, of course, felt more comfortable with the Toryism of Lord Melville, who had been forced out of office early in 1805 and had been acquitted a year later of 'high crimes and misdemeanours'. But Howick's association with Erskine meant that the first lord and Durham were well acquainted.

Indeed, this personal connection made Durham, with confessed procedural 'Irregularity' since Harvey was in charge of the squadron, write to Howick on 31 August to acquaint him with an incident four days earlier when the squadron had chased 'a strange Squadron' but was unable to come up with it. 'Your Lordship will perceive that the *Renown* carried away all her sails in the Chace, and no wonder, as she has been out two and twenty weeks, without a supply.'[3]

Soon afterwards Durham was offered the opportunity to stand for the Admiralty borough of Dover. He declined, possibly owing to the expense involved, telling St Vincent, who had been ready if necessary to send him to Dover in a cutter, that he had no desire to enter Parliament. His decision proved wiser with hindsight than that of his friend Stopford, who was also with the Channel Fleet. Stopford was returned for Ipswich after laying out a substantial sum in election expenses and bribes, only to find, on returning from a cruise of duty, that Parliament had been dissolved before he had the chance 'of even franking a letter'.[4]

In October St Vincent, who always regarded Durham highly, rewarded his diligence and seniority with command of a detached squadron cruising off Lorient. This small force consisted of the 36-gun frigates *Tribune* (Captain Thomas Baker) and *Santa Margarita* (Captain Wilson Rathborne), Captain Robert Winthrop's 44-gun *Sybille*, the sloop *Surinam* (Captain

John Lake) and gunbrig *Contest* (Lieutenant John Gregory). In December the *Sibylle* was replaced by the *Emerald*, 36 (Captain Frederick Lewis Maitland), and in January the *Flora*, 36 (Captain Loftus Otway Bland) took over from the *Tribune*. Other ships joined and left this core group of vessels periodically.[5]

Patrolling between the Iles de Glénan and Belle-Île, with two frigates permanently stationed at strategic points along the coast, Durham's squadron kept a lookout for Napoleon's brother Jérôme Bonaparte, who was returning from across the Atlantic and would shortly be placed on the throne of Westphalia. The squadron watched and reported on enemy movements at Concarneau and Lorient and disrupted coastal trade, capturing many craft. A French ship of the line, *Veteran*, discovered fitting out at Concarneau, was of special concern; ever the active officer, and not always happy to delegate, Durham went close in-shore aboard the gunbrig to have a good look at her.[6]

His vigilance was unremitting, but when, in January 1807, he received a despatch with suggestions from St Vincent (who was spending the winter in London leaving the fleet in the charge of Vice-Admiral Sir Charles Cotton) he misinterpreted it as an implication that he had been lax, and wrote a pained reply. He was being over-sensitive, and the elderly admiral let him know it. 'Nothing was farther from any Intention than to impute any blame to you in my observation respecting the *Veteran*, but I think it due to Officers entrusted with particular Service, to point out whatever I imagine may conduce to their most effectual performance of it, and which it often happens that the Intelligence I receive, and cannot always communicate, may enable me to do without being an Eye witness of the immediate circumstances,' he explained. 'I have the greatest Reliance on your Vigilance, and wish you to understand my Suggestions as dictated for your Information, and not intended to convey Censure.'[7]

Durham was reassured by the compliment. 'I cannot refrain, my Lord', he replied on 28 February, 'from expressing my best Thanks for the particularly handsome manner in which your Lordship has been pleased in your letter of the 16th inst. to approve of my Conduct while on this station. Such praise my Lord I shall both court and glory in.'[8]

He had by that time been acquainted by the secretary for war, Windham, with the bare outline of 'an important and confidential mission' undertaken by a Monsieur Robert and two other French dissidents in their homeland to obtain information beneficial to the British war effort. Durham was sent 4,000 *louis d'ors* for the expenses of the three French spies, to be paid in instalments of no more than 1,000 to Robert as and when required. Windham's office cautioned Durham that 'it is by no means the intention or wish of His Majesty's Government to excite or encourage any insurrection or popular Tumult whatsoever, but on the contrary it is their decided opinion that these provinces should be kept in the utmost apparent state of tranquillity, and that whatever measures may tend to create the slightest public sensation should be studiously avoided'. Responsibility for conveying the spies to their coastal destination and directly liaising with them thereafter was given by Durham to Captain Lake of the *Surinam*, stationed for the purpose in Quiberon Bay.[9] No details of the enterprise survive in Durham's naval papers, and there is no mention of it at all in his memoir.

In March 1807 Durham was superseded in command of the squadron by Captain Henry Hotham, commanding the *Defiance*, and summarised his activities for the benefit of his successor. 'Our Boats have night and day been constantly employed in shore, when the weather would permit, and from the Declaration of the French themselves, have done more serious injury by the continual Interruption of their Trade, than it has ever before experienced', he reported *inter alia*.[10]

Durham had, in St Vincent's words, 'acquitted himself very well' while in charge of the squadron. The curmudgeonly admiral, not one to praise lightly, wrote that information he obtained from two passengers, friends of William Windham, 'confirmed the opinion I had formed of the obstruction of the coasting trade by the squadrons under the orders of Commodore Keats and Captain Durham carried on to an extent never known before'. Durham took the *Renown* into Plymouth, where for a short time the ship flew St Vincent's flag. Lady Charlotte, who was still in Scotland, was prepared to join her husband, but his mother-in-law argued that this was not a good idea. A letter from the dowager countess awaited him in response to one that he had written to her on 15 February. It gave Martha

the greatest Comfort to think you were safe and well at that time for the Dreadful Storms we have had has kept every one that has Friends at Sea in particular anxiety... I am glad you are to be in Port so soon tho' alass for so short a time that I fear it will not be worth Charlotte's while to come up to Portsmouth [*sic*]. Sir Harry Neale told Elgin you would not be detained ten days, & surely so long a journey for that short space is only meeting to part. You are however best judge, and she is ready to set out, but I must confess I have begged her to wait till she hears from you again – both on account of the Fatigue of the journey, & that it defeatts all her Plann of Oeconomy – for it will take more than her savings to bring her to Plymouth – I am persuaded [words missing] have not adverted to the difficulties she would be involved in by living at Plymouth in your Absence. She is comfortable & Creditable in Scotland & every one anxious to have her. By June (please God I live till then) I may have a Country House so she can be ready to fly to you but as yet I can say Nothing.[11]

On 27 March St Vincent's flag was struck aboard the *Renown*. He was in poor health, and never served at sea again. Durham described the ship as 'so extremely crank as frequently to have been in considerable Danger', and 'greatly injured by the very damp state of the magazine'. When these defects were remedied he returned in her to the coast of France, coming under Sir Richard Strachan's orders and reconnoitring French naval movements in the vicinity of Rochefort.[12]

In the late summer of 1807 another post-captain, Thomas Alexander, assumed acting command of the *Renown*. Durham had applied to be relieved temporarily for personal reasons. Voluntarily coming off active duty was conspicuously out of character, but there was an acute crisis in Lady Charlotte's immediate family, and Durham was, it would seem, needed for moral support.[13]

The crisis was triggered by the scandalous behaviour of his sister-in-law, the young Countess of Elgin. Following the birth of her fifth child in January 1806, she wrote from Scotland to her husband, who was being held effectively as a prisoner of war in France, announcing that his conjugal rights were at an end. She began a liaison with Robert Fergusson of Raith, a member of a prominent Fife family situated near Kirkaldy, who had fallen in love with her in Paris a couple of years earlier.

Lord Elgin was released on parole in July 1806. His wife offered to live with him, but made it clear that sexual relations were out of the question. She may well have found him physically repugnant, for a 'severe ague' – reputedly syphilis – had left him with an unfortunate facial disfigurement, the loss of his nose.

There was an heir to the earldom, Lord Bruce, born in April 1800, but a second son had died, and Elgin was anxious to secure the succession. Furthermore, he was prepared to endure neither celibacy nor the role of acquiescent cuckold. In December 1807 he sued Fergusson for criminal carnal knowledge of his wife and received £10,000 in damages, half of what he sought. A few months later he was divorced by the only means available in those days, an Act of Parliament, and his former countess soon married her lover.

Lurid and intriguing details which emerged at Fergusson's trial – risqué revelations of what the footman saw, and Lady Elgin's perceived coolness towards her husband following the erosion of his nose – titillated spectators and naturally did the rounds, making the divorce the talk of society. Queen Charlotte's thoughts were with the family: she regretted 'most Sincerely that all Prospects of Happiness and Comfort' expected from Elgin's marriage 'should be so frustrated'. All this, of course, must have mortified the Bruce family, especially Durham's mother-in-law, the God-fearing dowager countess, who had been ill. 'I have grieved for Her and indeed for all of you', wrote the queen. 'Thank God Yr Mother sees you happy with Yr Captain D.'[14]

The earl adamantly refused to allow his adulterous spouse access to her children, and there was as yet no substitute wife to supply her place. But Lady Charlotte, still without offspring of her own, stepped into the breach to oblige her beloved brother, becoming a surrogate mother to George, Mary, Matilda and Lucy, and receiving words of encouragement from the queen: 'You my dear Chasse I am sure will do justice to the dear and fine Children now under your Care both by inclination as also from Duty, and Yr own good Principles will supply you with what is Necessary to ingraft into their minds to avoid falling into the same Error of their lost Parent.' The queen was glad that Lady Charlotte had the companionship in Scotland of her elderly paternal aunt, Lady Christian Erskine (*née* Bruce), widow of John Erskine of Cardross and mother of three deceased sons.

> She bears so excellent a character and is so Respected by all ranks of People, that you judge right in saying that Her Presence gives you great Support in your new Occupation. Yr own good Conscience will justify You and the approbation of such an amiable Person will Support You in the world.
>
> I am sorry (that is selfish) that we shall not see You this year amongst us, but You judge it well I must say, for what you have now undertaken requires a constant attention which cannot be divided between the Hours of London and the School Hours for Children, neither as the enjoyment of the former nor the Progress of the latter could be obtained by coming amongst us.[15]

In the midst of all this turmoil Durham's father passed away at Largo on 5 April 1808 aged seventy-six, depriving the county of 'a most valuable and useful Magistrate and Country Gentleman'. Succeeded in possession of Largo by his eldest son, who coincidentally became a major-general that same month, he was buried in the family vault in the parish church, beneath 'his own aisle'. He died heavily in debt, owing a total of £32,700 (about £1,500,000 in today's money). Of this, £15,000 had been borrowed in relatively small amounts of between £100 and £2,000 from neighbours of the farmer and tradesman class, lending to local lairds on their bonds being one of the few forms of investment open to such people. In addition to the principal sum owed, plus interest, the estate was further encumbered by family annuities amounting to £1,118 a year which the new laird was obliged to continue paying out.[16]

Later in the year, in September, Durham's original captain, Admiral John Elliot, died at Mount Teviot, his country seat in Roxburghshire. Enjoying a £3,000-a-year sinecure as an official of the Scottish mint, he had not been to sea for years owing to poor health, but had of course lived to see his protégé achieve distinction. Although the Tory Dundases were Durham's main source of patronage, his ties with the influential Whig Elliots remained strong, giving him an enviable advantage during changes of ministry.[17]

During his extended period of leave, which dragged on into the summer of 1808, Durham learned that his old ship, the *Anson*, had been wrecked off the Lizard during a gale in December 1807, with the loss of sixty aboard, including her captain and first lieutenant. He also received the sad news that his countryman Basil Alves, who had captained the marines on board the *Defiance* at Trafalgar, had passed away aged only thirty. Meanwhile, as Durham could see for himself, work was proceeding in Edinburgh on the erection of a monument to Nelson on Calton Hill, paid for out of public subscriptions. The foundation stone was laid on 21 October 1807, and the monument, in the shape of a telescope, would be completed in 1815.[18]

Durham was tempted, in the first half of 1808, into trying to become a member of Parliament. According to his memoir, a friend (whom he does not name) had got into severe financial difficulties involving some sort of bank scandal, and expected to have to forfeit his seat in the Commons as a result. He talked Durham into agreeing to fill the vacancy. The constituency, also unspecified, was evidently one under government patronage, with particular ties to Lord Castlereagh. It seems to have had a large number of eligible voters, since Durham had to borrow no less than £3,000 from his bankers, Messrs Coutts of London's Strand, to expend in bribes.

Each day, an increasingly fretful Durham contacted one of the ministers, William Huskisson, asking when the writ for a by-election would be moved. He was constantly fobbed off with a non-committal reply, but at length learned that his friend had not had to quit his seat after all. 'Lord

Castlereagh does not like captains of men of war as members of parliament, because they are always off Cape Finisterre when they are wanted; and if they are sent for, they say they don't like being "whistled up to give a vote"', added Huskisson, suddenly frank. But at least Durham had the consolation of having the £3,000 refunded.[19]

In June 1808, without more ado, Durham went out to the Mediterranean to resume command of the *Renown*. With the rest of Strachan's squadron she had chased a French force which, in foggy weather, had slipped out of Rochefort, but the quarry managed to get into Toulon. Strachan had returned home and she was now part of Collingwood's squadron. Unhappily for Durham and other post-captains, new prize money regulations had just been introduced by the first lord of the Admiralty, Lord Mulgrave. These reduced the captains' share of prize money per vessel from three-eighths to two-eighths.[20]

Durham reached the Mediterranean as a passenger aboard the 32-gun frigate *Hyperion*, which was taking two high officials, Robert Adair and Sir Stratford Canning, to Constantinople for talks with the Turkish Sultan, who had been supporting Russian hostilities against Britain. The *Hyperion*'s captain, Thomas Charles Brodie, 'did not seem much at home in his profession', Durham noticed. Brodie became a laughing-stock among his lieutenants when he ludicrously ordered them to kill the geese they kept aboard as livestock, for fear the birds' cackling 'may discover us to the enemy'. He would confess to Durham that he had obtained command of the newly launched vessel through parliamentary influence, and that his previous employment in charge of sea fencibles in Ireland had been much more to his liking, since he had been able to hunt several times a week.[21]

Brodie's incompetence was apparent almost from the beginning of the voyage. While the *Hyperion* was running down the coast of Portugal on a hazy night the officer of the watch announced that she was 'close upon three or four large ships', and Brodie gave the order to clear for action. But Durham, rushing on deck, realised that what Brodie had taken for granted were enemy vessels were in fact the tall, shiplike, granite outlines of the Berlenga islets in Cape Carvoeiro, north of Lisbon, better known to British mariners as the 'Burling rocks'. He assured Brodie that if he hauled to the westward all would be well. The younger man did as he suggested, and he was proved right.

A day or two later, as Cape Trafalgar came into view, Durham advised Brodie to haul in and watch for Collingwood during the night. His lordship, he said, would probably be at anchor off the lighthouse at Cadiz.

Next day, Durham saved the ship from coming to grief on the flat shoaly foreshore of the small Spanish port of San Lucar, twenty-seven sea miles north of Cadiz. It was obvious to him at daybreak that she had passed Cadiz during the night, for he recognised a ruined Moorish citadel standing near San Lucar. He also observed angry breakers, and, sticking out above the water, the mast of a wrecked British schooner. The *Hyperion* was standing in to danger, and had Durham not yelled appropriate instructions to the helmsman she would have run aground.[22]

The *Hyperion* was put about, and took nearly two days to beat up to Collingwood's anchorage. The *Renown*, Durham learned, was at Minorca, where he consequently joined her. Unnerved by the close call off San Lucar, Adair and Canning had lost confidence in Brodie. They contrasted his ineptness with Durham's alertness, efficiency and skill, and vowed not to remain aboard the frigate following Durham's disembarkation. When she reached the Sicilian port of Palermo the two envoys hurried ashore, and persuaded Captain John Stewart of the frigate *Seahorse* to take them to their destination.[23]

'Old Cuddy', as Collingwood was known among his officers, was not the popular, charismatic leader that Nelson had been. His reserved, curt manner and unbending rigidity ensured that he was respected rather than loved. He had passed his sixtieth birthday, had wearied of the strain of command, and was conscious of every physical ache and pain. He longed for home and family, and his tranquil garden. Virtually his sole consolation as he languished, worn out in body and mind, was the company of his beloved dog, sadly to be washed overboard. That successive first lords ignored his requests to be replaced puzzled and vexed him. He had no inkling that Prince William Henry, Duke of Clarence, longed to succeed him, confronting the Admiralty with a delicate situation. Knowing that the prince was entirely unfit for such employment, yet wary of offending the royal personage by appointing somebody else, their lordships decided that the only solution was for Collingwood to remain on the station. He was destined never to set foot in Britain again.[24]

In September 1808 he instructed Durham to proceed to Gibraltar, and place himself under the orders of Rear-Admiral John Child Purvis. The following month Purvis ordered Durham to convey Prince Leopold of Naples to Sicily, where the exiled Neapolitan family had set up their court. Leopold, who was King Ferdinand's second son, had made an abortive bid for the Spanish throne. He was received aboard the *Renown* with an entourage of about a dozen noblemen.

The convoy, consisting of three Neapolitan frigates and several transports for baggage and horses, left Gibraltar on 1 November. Durham was prepared for an attack from a 'considerable force' of Algerine privateers which cruised nearby, making Leopold jittery. But the convoy was unmolested, arriving at Palermo on 10 November.[25]

Durham was graciously welcomed at court there, but insisted on remaining only a few days. He had been ordered by Purvis 'to proceed without a moment's delay to join Lord Collingwood off Toulon', and sailed from Palermo on 14 November. Four days later he fell in with Rear-Admiral George Martin, who in accordance with instructions from Collingwood took him under his command and ordered him to cruise between the gulfs of Palermo and Gaeta, keeping watch there and in the bay of Naples for the enemy. By the end of December the *Renown*, whose rendezvous was off Capri, had been joined in this work of reconnaissance by several smaller British vessels.[26]

Early in the New Year King Ferdinand's minister of foreign affairs, the Marquis di Circello, sent Durham a snuff box decorated with a portrait of the monarch set in diamonds. It was, the marquis explained, Ferdinand's reward to Durham for the 'kind attentions' he had shown to Prince Leopold, which the king would always remember. 'He entertains for your dignified Person the sentiments of an increased Esteem', Circello wrote.[27]

The gift, received aboard the *Renown* off Minorca in March, was valued, Durham would later happily ascertain, at one thousand guineas. It drew from him an immediate acknowledgement, outdoing Circello's flowery prose:

> Connected during a most eventful crisis as our two Countries have been, in friendly Intercourse cemented as well by the ties of common Interest, as by the paramount Feelings of long and mutual Regards, I consider this Token of His Majesty's Approbation as one of the most gratifying Events of my life.
>
> Added to which all the Acts of His Majesty towards me, have been conspicuously marked by a most friendly condescension and by an unbounded Hospitality.
>
> Contemplating with the purest Devotion in the dignified Person of His Majesty the firm and long approved Friend of my Country, and the inalienable Patron of the British Navy, I shall bear with me to the latest period of my Existence, the most grateful recollection of the Munificence of His Majesty the King of the Two Sicilies.
>
> Your Excellency has laid me under an indelible obligation by your Expressions of individual Regard; it will afford me the most lively Gratification to be again

in the Capital of Sicily, that I may personally give to your Excellency the reit-erated assurances of my most perfect Esteem and Friendship.[28]

At the end of March, in obeying Collingwood's signal to wear, the *Warrior* (Captain John William Spranger), collided with the *Renown*. Conditions were 'very hazy', and while hauling to the wind in an apparent endeavour to go astern of Durham's ship, the *Warrior* went on board of her before the main chains, injuring herself in the process. That Durham, unlike Spranger, failed to report an incident 'in which one of his Majesty's ships has received so much damage' irritated Collingwood.[29]

A month later, during a chase of several enemy ships which had emerged from Toulon, the *Renown* fell in with a French polacre. Despite blustery weather Durham sent a boat to take possession of her. His officer reported that she was 'a miserable vessel' crammed with invalided French soldiers being conveyed home from the coast of Spain. This was hardly the sort of cargo that Durham sought, and that evening he sent an officer to Collingwood's 110-gun flagship, the *Ville de Paris*, to ask what should be done with the polacre. No reply was received, and to Durham's consternation the *Renown* fell 'greatly astern' of the rest of Collingwood's squadron as a result of remaining by the inglorious capture during the night.

At daybreak Durham signalled for instructions. Obtaining no answer from the flagship, which was too far away for his signal to be read, he let the polacre go, and when the *Renown* drew nearer to the *Ville de Paris* he informed Collingwood by signal of what had transpired.

The commander-in-chief, cheated of an engagement with the French squadron, which escaped back into port, took a dim view of Durham's decision. In a stiffly-worded message dated 2 May he rebuked him for abandoning the polacre without authorisation, and in sight of the flag. A spirited rejoinder was at once forthcoming, regretting that Collingwood had 'thought it necessary to have animadverted on my conduct, and in terms so harsh':

My reasons for... abandoning the polacre were founded on the complete worthlessness of the vessel, the infirm and wretched state of upwards of sixty sick and wounded soldiers (immediately sent from a port in which a pesti-lential disease was raging) some of whom were reported to me actually in the agonies of death, and many others whose removal in an agitated sea would have been an outrage on humanity.

But however anxious I might have been to have kept possession of her, the state of the weather left me no choice. One of our cutters was lost alongside of her, and the crew, with the people who had been on board the vessel during the night, were with great difficulty saved. One alternative only was left, viz., my remaining in a line of battle ship by a polacre not at all sea-worthy, with a cargo of miserable and wounded soldiers, which would not only have further diminished the strength of your lordship's fleet in pursuit of the enemy, but would have justly subjected my name to obloquy, had an action taken place between the hostile fleets.[30]

Collingwood seemed to resent this heartfelt response, and ordered Durham to go in search of the abandoned polacre. The quest proved fruitless, but on 4 May, to the surprise of both men, Durham captured a similar ship off Marseilles. Three days out of Barcelona, she was the *Champenoise*, a French national armed vessel pierced for twelve guns but mounting only six. On board were a crew of thirty-one, plus fifty-two 'sick and wounded soldiers'. Collingwood arranged for the prize to be taken into Valletta by the *Leonidas*, onto which Durham was ordered to transfer most of the prisoners. Not proud of the capture, Durham observed sarcastically that he assumed that they were being sent to Malta 'for the benefit of the medical department'. Perhaps to his chagrin, his despatch announcing the capture appeared in both the *London Gazette* and the *Naval Chronicle*.[31]

In August 1809, after a cruise off Genoa, the *Renown* put into Port Mahon on the island of Minorca to obtain vegetables and bullocks for the flagship and stores for herself to last five months. That bustling seaport, with its fine harbour and sociable inhabitants, was a frequent, convenient resort for ships from Collingwood's squadron needing to refit, water and take aboard provisions. But Durham was appalled to find that the British agent responsible for naval victualling could not afford to pay the suppliers. The man 'had been for a considerable time in a state of insolvency, without Publick Money or any other except small sums which he procures from Individuals in Mahon who were hurt at the Disgrace brought on the English Nation in the Person of one of its Publick Agents who was incapable of paying for a few articles absolutely essential to the Preservation of the Seamen's Health and the wellbeing of the Publick'.

Feeling that this situation was untenable, Durham took it upon himself, at the risk of incurring Collingwood's displeasure, to sign bills for the amount of the debts in the name of the Victualling Board. 'I cannot however refrain from observing that although every captain in the Fleet has been here, the Responsibility of sanctioning these Bills has been thrown on me.'[32]

That autumn, while cruising off Genoa, Durham was ordered to join Collingwood off Toulon, where in the outer roads, fully equipped and ready for sea, lay a French fleet 'much superior to us in numbers'. It was commanded by Vice-Admiral Allemand aboard his 130-gun flagship *Austerlitz*, and comprised fourteen other ships of the line, two of them of 120-guns. A battle plan was drawn up by Collingwood with the *Ville de Paris* leading the van or starboard column and the *Royal Sovereign*, flagship of Vice-Admiral Edward Thornbrough, the rear. Collingwood entrusted Durham with command of the entire division of the van in which the *Renown* was stationed, 'and should the enemy come out, you will have a commodore's distinguishing pendant. If they do, this will give you the red ribbon, which is all your old friend can do for you.' But owing to foul weather the French did not set sail, and Durham's opportunity for further glory, culminating in the knighthood to which Collingwood had obliquely referred, evaporated.[33]

Taking advantage of a strong northerly gale, Collingwood's fleet rang for Mahon to replenish its stores. There, a French informant confirmed what Collingwood already knew, that a convoy of armed storeships and transports was preparing to leave Toulon with provisions for the garrison at Barcelona. The man brought intelligence that it would be ready to sail in about a fortnight, escorted by a strong and perhaps formidable naval force. Accordingly Collingwood, with fifteen or sixteen ships of the line, three frigates and a sloop, lay in wait off Cape San Sebastian on the Catalonian coast north of Barcelona, while two 38-gun frigates, the *Pomone* and *Alceste*, watched developments at Toulon.[34]

On the morning of 21 October, Rear-Admiral François-André Baudin, aboard the 80-gun *Robuste*, sailed from Toulon with two 74s, the *Borée* and the *Lion*, two 40-gun frigates and the convoy. Next evening the *Pomone* (Captain Robert Barrie) brought this news to Collingwood by firing guns and burning a blue light to indicate that the enemy was at sea. The *Renown* and the rest of the fleet were accordingly thrown into a mood of high anticipation.

Shortly before seven on the following morning, 23 October, Collingwood instructed his ships to prepare for battle. Less than two hours later the weathermost British frigate, Captain Charles Bullen's 38-gun *Volontaire*, made the signal for a strange fleet to the east-north-east. 'All eyes were instantly turned to that quarter, and we felt gratified with the sight of a numerous fleet of vessels, of various rigs and sizes, coming down before the wind, led and flanked by five larger ships, their sails swelled out by the favouring breeze', recalled a British officer. 'Down they continued to come, seemingly unconscious of any danger... with a convoy of seventeen or eighteen vessels of various descriptions'.[35]

While the French continued to come down towards the wind Collingwood advanced two swift-sailing 74s, Captain Hallowell's *Tigre* and Captain Fleeming's *Bulwark*. He made no further adjustments until the *Pomone* signalled, about ten o'clock, that the enemy had hauled to the wind. Collingwood now ordered other good sailers, including the *Renown* and Rear-Admiral George Martin's 80-gun flagship, *Canopus*, to join the chase and destroy the convoy.[36]

About noon the French naval ships stood on the larboard tack to the south-south-east while the convoy they were escorting steered north-north-west towards Cape Creux in disarray. By nightfall several of the convoy had fallen prey to the *Pomone* and *Volontaire*; the remainder escaped into Rosas Bay.[37]

Since Collingwood's signal detaching the *Renown* and other vessels had been made separately to each of them in turn, Durham and his fellow-captains were free to act according to their individual judgments. In the afternoon, when the French ships of the line and frigates tacked northwards, the *Renown*, *Tigre* and three other 74s – Captain Edward Griffith's *Sultan*, Captain John Harvey's *Leviathan* and Captain the Hon. Philip Wodehouse's *Cumberland* – did likewise and during the night fell in with Rear-Admiral Martin's flagship, the *Canopus*. Despite the maxim that in chasing to windward ships should always preserve the tack which drew them nearest to their quarry, the *Bulwark* and *Terrible* for some inexplicable reason continued to stand to the south-south-east, and became separated from the rest of the detachment, now effectively a squadron under Martin's command.[38]

Freshening winds whipped up a heavy swell, and the enemy was lost sight of among thickening haze. But on the assumption that the French would make for their own coast, Martin's squadron continued standing to the northward. Next morning, 24 October, the thick weather persisted, ensuring that the quarry remained elusive. Nevertheless, Martin's ships, 'all compact together', pressed onwards, their crews as expectant as huntsmen when 'the scent lies well'.[39]

However, towards noon, when his flagship had the misfortune to spring her mainmast, Martin signalled Durham, as the senior of his captains, advising that he felt that further pursuit would prove futile. Durham, however, was made of resolute stuff. Not easily dissuaded from an activity which promised to be lucrative, he begged to differ with his commanding officer. As the wind had not changed since the start of the chase, the quarry could not have gained safe haven in a port, Durham observed by signal. It was, moreover, unlikely that they had decided to tack to the southward, for that would lead them from their coast. In all probability they had been unable to weather the Bouches du Rhône, which the squadron, given its present course, would sight early that evening. Captain Hallowell of the *Tigre* signalled Martin along similar lines.

'This opinion of the two senior Captains in the squadron, officers, too, of such established name and reputation, as Captains Durham and Hallowell, I suppose decided the Admiral', wrote an officer aboard the *Tigre*, 'for we made no alteration in the course, but continued to stand in for the land'. The hazy conditions meant that objects 'at any considerable distance' from the squadron could not be distinguished. About four o'clock that afternoon, in diminishing light, the muddied appearance of the sea indicated that the ships were swiftly approaching the mouths of the Rhône, and Martin made the signal to sound, followed immediately by that to wear in succession. No sooner had he done so than the *Renown* signalled that there was a strange sail ahead, and she and her consorts continued to stand on.[40]

Aboard every other ship in the squadron eyes were strained in vain to glimpse what the *Renown* had seen, leading afterwards to rumours that the signal was a ruse by Durham to convince Martin to stand on for as long as the depth of the water and the remaining daylight permitted. Whatever the truth, it was as well that the signal was hoisted, for less than ten minutes later the *Tigre* made the signal for four sail to the north-north-east.

These would prove to be Baudin's flagship, the *Robuste*, the *Borée* and *Lion*, and the frigate *Pauline*. They were under topsails, feeling their way towards the mist-shrouded coast. Hoping for an action before dark, Martin signalled the *Renown* and his other ships 'to take suitable stations for mutual support and engage the enemy as they get up'. The British bore up under every stitch of canvas, their studding-sails newly set, and rapidly gained on the French. But the latter anchored, and Martin chose caution. Owing to the approach of nightfall, to the shoaly water, to the direction of the wind, blowing straight towards the land, as well as to his squadron's inexperience of that part of the coast, he decided to haul off. At seven, therefore, his ships shortened sail and came to the wind, keeping as close to the shore as was compatible with safety, in order to prevent the French slipping away in the dark.[41]

Around eight o'clock on the following morning, 15 October, the French, under top and foresails, were observed running along shore to the north-north-west, with a fresh breeze from the south-east. Hoping to close with them before they found shelter behind a sandbank, the British instantly made all sail in pursuit, and prepared for anchoring with springs. But at half-past eleven the *Robuste* and the *Lion* clewed up their sails, put their helms up, and with no more than a couple of cables' lengths between them ran themselves aground on shoals between two sandbanks near the village of Frontignan, about five miles east-north-east of Cette. Since the *Tigre* and *Leviathan*, which gave chase, had been warned off by fire from the batteries there, and by the shallowness of the water, the two other French ships succeeded in reaching Cette's harbour.[42]

The hazards posed by shoaly conditions along that unfamiliar shore convinced Martin's squadron to haul to the wind and stand off. Durham and the other captains were summoned aboard the *Canopus* for a council of war, after which a boat from the *Tigre*, commanded by a lieutenant, was sent towards the grounded French vessels, making soundings as she approached the shore. Pluckily, she continued in the face of their gunfire, and turned back only when pursued by four of the enemy's boats. She had ascertained that it would be impossible for her squadron to get within long gunshot of the *Robuste* and *Lion*.

About half-past two Durham and the rest of the squadron noticed that those ships were being dismantled and that their crews were quitting them. An hour or so later, amid fresh breezes and marked haze, the mizenmasts of both vessels went by the board. That evening the British stood to the southward, and about three in the morning tacked, with the intention of being close in with the wrecks by dawn.

Thick haze prevented the British glimpsing the two doomed ships until nearly noon on 26 October; the latter's main as well as their mizenmasts were gone. At half-past twelve the squadron bore up, and two hours later sent out boats to sound. These were fired upon, but returned safely at half-past five. In the meantime the wind had begun to drop, and by evening the squadron became virtually becalmed some six or seven miles from shore. About half-past seven, first one and then another brilliant burst of flame followed by billowing smoke showed the British that Rear-Admiral Baudin had ordered his crews to set their stricken vessels alight. In less than ten minutes both were blazing furnace-like fore and aft, and about half-past ten they exploded in quick succession with 'the blast and roar of thunder, filling the air with fragments of blazing wreck, that flamed and sparkled a moment in the sky, and then fell, like shooting stars of fearful omen'.[43]

Martin's squadron remained standing away to the southward until the following morning when, looking into Cette, it found that the *Pauline*, with masts and yards taunt, was afloat though precariously, and the *Borée*, with topmast struck and heeling sharply, appeared to be aground. The squadron then set sail for San Sebastian, rejoining Collingwood on the morning of 30 October, to acquaint him with the satisfactory news that through energy and persistence it had achieved the loss to France of a new 80 and a fine 74, and left a new 74 and a powerful frigate in jeopardy. Durham, miffed that Martin, and not he, had been in charge of the squadron during this episode, described falling in with the *Canopus* as 'an unfortunate circumstance' since 'it prevented him from being commanding officer at the destruction of the ships, the admiral being senior'. Knowing that he stood on the top rungs of the post-captains' ladder, and with hopes of an active flag career, Durham wanted to end his time in that rank on a high note. Martin would also be entitled to a third of Durham's share of any prize money, another result of Lord Mulgrave's regulations.[44]

On 31 October Collingwood sent several ships, excluding the *Renown*, to take or destroy those vessels of the enemy convoy that were sheltering in Rosas Bay. Under the general direction of the first lieutenant of the *Tigre*, who received an almost fatal head wound in the process, this task was accomplished by boats' crews during the night. All eleven vessels were either burnt or captured, frustrating French plans for revictualling the troops at Barcelona.

Although none of the *Renown*'s boats had participated in this enterprise, her captain and ship's company were entitled to a share of the prize money due. But since the sum paid out 'would be extremely insignificant if distributed among the whole fleet' Durham and his officers and men decided, in his words, 'to relinquish our respective Share to the officers and men *actually employed in the Boats* – to testify our admiration of their most gallant conduct, and in some manner to remunerate them for the same'. This concession extended only to those who had been in the boats, and not to their ships' companies generally, he reiterated.[45]

In carrying a great press of sail in chase off Cette the *Renown* had received much damage, and Durham was soon afterwards ordered to Cadiz, to take command of all the British naval vessels there in the temporary absence of Vice-Admiral Purvis. On 15 February 1810, in compliance with Purvis's orders, he arrived in the Downs with a convoy of merchant ships and transports from Cadiz, and a number of French prisoners of war destined for custody in England who had been put aboard the *Renown*. That ship was paid off in May, bringing to a close Durham's twenty-year period as a post-captain, for flag-rank was imminent. 'Very few captains in the navy had seen so much active service afloat, or had been so successful', he was to note with justified pride.[46]

During an audience with the newly-installed first lord of the Admiralty, Charles Yorke, Durham learned that a general naval promotion was about to be announced and that he was to be named a colonel of marines. This was a sinecure awarded to very senior and distinguished post-captains on the verge of receiving their flag, enabling them to enjoy an increased salary in the meantime. But Durham was unimpressed. Since he considered Yorke 'one of his oldest friends', he told him bluntly that he wished to be raised to flag-rank straight away, since 'it would be of more service to him if employed'. Yorke, whose brother Joseph was one of the lords commissioners of the Admiralty, pondered the point. Both brothers had apparently revised a derisive opinion of Durham that they had once held, and were happy to try to oblige him. Accordingly, the first lord persuaded the chancellor of the exchequer, Spencer Perceval, to add a few more flag-officers to the estimates. This enabled Yorke to include Durham (and Israel Pellew too) in the promotion gazetted on 31 July 1810. He was now a rear-admiral, on half-pay.[47]

He was soon reunited with Lady Charlotte, whose mother had died in June, and who continued to look after her brother's children and was especially close to the youngest girl, 'her little pet'. On a sunny morning in August following a dinner the previous day at Broomhall, Durham accompanied Lord Elgin and a young Fife neighbour, Elizabeth, daughter of James Townsend Oswald of Dunnikier, on horseback as far as Aberdour, where she was to meet her mother. Miss Oswald was clearly besotted with Elgin, and Durham did not spare her blushes. 'We cantered through all the beautiful places that lay in the way, Fordel, Otterstone... the grey and black horses found their paces suited precisely', she recalled many years later. 'On getting into my mother's carriage I found my cloak was missing. I said to Sir Philip "I have left my cloak at Broomhall, pray send it by the first opportunity." He looked at me with his quizzing turn of the eye and said "Are you quite sure you have left nothing else?".' He meant her heart.

Romance proceeded swiftly after that, and Elgin and 'Eliza' were married at Broomhall on 21 September with the Durhams among the wedding party.

Dressed in white satin and carrying a bouquet of orange blossom, the bride wore Lady Charlotte's own veil, since one that her ladyship had ordered as a gift for her had not arrived.[48] It now fell to the new Lady Elgin to look after the children for whom Lady Charlotte had cared. As one of their trustees, Durham had a certain involvement with them in the years ahead.

9

Sailor of Fortune

Already the sound of Durham's guns
came plainly down the drifting mist.
Trafalgar Refought (1905)

The esteem that his outstanding abilities enjoyed at the Admiralty ensured that unlike the vast majority of admirals, who were given no opportunity to fly their flags, Durham was repeatedly employed. Thus in April 1811, having been considered for the command of a sqadron off Cadiz, he joined the Baltic fleet of Vice-Admiral James Saumarez – a depressive whom Durham once claimed to have rescued from 'a madhouse'! – as junior flag-officer with his flag in the *Ardent*, 64. In September, having transferred to the *Hannibal*, 74, he joined Admiral Young's North Sea fleet, and was put in command of a squadron watching developments at the Texel. Young recognised his abilities by announcing that if the enemy came out Durham would lead the North Sea fleet into battle.[1]

Navigation in the North Sea was always hazardous, and in dark and blowy conditions a small error in reckoning could doom a ship. During tempestuous weather late in 1811 every British man-of-war that arrived home across that sea was far out of her reckoning. On Christmas Eve the Trafalgar ship *Defence* and a consort, returning from the Baltic, went down off Jutland; there were few survivors. That same evening the *Hero*, 74, commanded by Durham's foe Captain Newman, struck a sandbank off the Texel with the loss of all aboard. It was the very spot where, a year earlier, the Trafalgar ship *Minotaur* met her end. But Durham's squadron, obeying his dictum always to anchor during fierce North Sea storms, came to no harm.[2]

In March 1812 Durham, in London again, was unexpectedly summoned to the Admiralty and offered the command of four 74s lying at St Helens; his orders were to intercept a French squadron that had put out of Lorient. He impressed the Admiralty by leaving at once to hoist his flag in the *Venerable,* 74, and get his squadron to sea immediately. However, the enemy had returned to port.

A few weeks later he was given command of a sizeable squadron in Basque Roads (between the islands of Ré and Oléron), over the heads of more senior flag-officers who had also lobbied for it. With orders to prevent the enemy's ships in the Charente and Gironde from putting to sea and to be careful not to come under surprise attack from the Brest fleet, it formed part of Lord Keith's Channel Fleet. Durham arrived on his station in the *Hannibal,* shifting almost at once to the *Bulwark,* 74.

In July Durham ordered Captain John Carden's *Macedonian,* 38, inshore with a 4-gun brig to scrutinise French operations at La Rochelle while the flagship and the rest of the squadron stood within sight in the offing. On 7 August, having fired 'very severely' at a number of enemy vessels, Carden saw a large lugger run aground under one of the batteries. Hopeful of bringing her off after dark, he assembled volunteers to man the boats, led by his second lieutenant, George Pechell, nephew of Durham's former chief, Warren. At seven o'clock, therefore, the boats, including two cutters, set out for the lugger. Anticipating their approach, the enemy had moored her to the shore by chains. But neither this, nor constant musket-shot from the battery, nor the blaze of field pieces trained on them from the beach nearby, deterred Pechell and his men. One of these, the armourer's mate, managed to saw through the chains with his steel chisel, and the lugger was triumphantly brought off. Relinquishing their chance of monetary reward was not something which officers and men did lightly, Durham least of all. As flag-officer in command he was entitled to one-third of each captain's share of prize money. But he and the squadron decided to waive their claim, so that the crew of the *Macedonian* would be fully recompensed for conspicuous bravery.[3]

In the autumn of 1812, owing to the second Lord Melville's machinations, Durham stood while at sea as Tory parliamentary candidate for the Fife constituency of Kirkaldy Burghs. 'I do not believe I have any chance', he wrote on hearing the news. The campaign conducted on his behalf was characterised by the kind of chicanery which had been practised nearly fifty years earlier by his late relative Anstruther of Elie, who had in effect kidnapped a number of electors inimical to his political interests to prevent them from voting. Similar dirty tricks by Durham's friends were foiled; the electors of Kinghorn alone declared for him, those of the other burghs for his rival, coincidentally the brother of the man who had cuckolded Elgin.[4]

Needing a break from tedious blockade duty, and aware that the *Bulwark* needed caulking and disinfesting of rats at Plymouth, Durham went on leave in December. He first concocted a pact with his good friends Commodore Malcolm, who would substitute for him at Basque Roads, and Rear-Admiral Neale, commanding in Douarnenez Bay, binding each other to 'share equally, whether on leave of absence or on duty' all prize money to which they might be entitled while under Keith's orders. At this juncture lucrative captures proved elusive – 'I am in the way of so little Prize Money', Durham lamented – and he decided that the pact might at least bring him something.[5]

A poison pen letter sent to Lord Melville (the first lord) accused Malcolm and Durham, who resumed his station in March 1813, of following 'the present system of Lord Keith's for filling his pockets' by keeping 'the frigates and brigs as much at sea as possible' in the hope of taking prizes and denying them regular opportunities to put into Plymouth for fresh water and stores. Owing to this 'avarice', which negated 'the great and honourable aim of the service', the Basque Roads squadron had fallen into an inefficient state. Keith briskly dismissed these allegations, and it is unlikely that Melville seriously heeded them. Nevertheless, Durham, who had begun to station himself in the Breton passage with the aim of picking off the enemy's coastal craft more effectively, and sent sloops cruising for that purpose, was reminded of his primary task and ordered back to his former anchorage.[6]

With the outbreak of the war of 1812, the Admiralty had instructed Keith to apprehend 'all such American vessels... as you may fall in with', except those with British trading licences. 'The Americans are running in and out like rabbits; our ships have no chance with them or are unfortunate', Durham had grumbled. But ill luck never dogged him for long. By mid-1813 his squadron had captured American cargo vessels with a combined estimated value of over £800,000 (about £50 million today), and he chortled that he hoped the war would last indefinitely.[7]

Durham's tenure off Basque Roads ended in August 1813, and in November he was appointed commander-in-chief at the Leeward Islands. With a rapidity that again impressed the Admiralty, he dashed down to Portsmouth to cajole artificers into hastening repairs to the *Venerable,* and on Christmas morning he impatiently put to sea although her bulkheads were still down. Always interested in technological innovations, he had aboard six packing cases crammed with sealed tin canisters, containing roast beef, mutton, veal, and soup, from the Bermondsey pioneers of the canning industry.

Off Madeira six days later the *Venerable* captured the New York-bound brig *Jason,* a fine, brand-new, copper-bottomed French letter of marque out of Bordeaux. Pierced for 22 guns but mounting 14 until she jettisoned 12 during the chase, she bore a cargo that included silks and wines. She sailed so well that he decided to take her to Barbados for adjudication by the Vice-Admiralty prize court there, and installed a prize crew under the command of a lieutenant.

On 11 January 1814, off Tenerife, Thomas Forrest, commander of the *Cyane,* 22, went aboard the *Venerable* to report that four days previously two large French frigates had given chase near Palma. Uncharacteristically, given his innate wilfulness and lust for prizes, a tired Durham allowed his flag-captain, James Worth, to dissuade him from searching for them. Worth pointed out that in the face of contrary winds it would take two or three days for the *Venerable* to weather the Cape of Tenerife again, and by that time the frigates could be anywhere. But, retiring to his cabin for the night, Durham had second thoughts. He guessed that since Palma lay in the direction of the West Indies, the frigates remained nearby, awaiting British merchantmen bound to and from the Caribbean.

For four days the *Venerable,* disguised on Durham's initiative, beat against the wind accompanied by the *Cyane* and *Jason.* On the morning of 16 January the *Cyane* made the signal for two strange sail in the north-east. The *Venerable* immediately gave chase, leaving her companions far astern. The chivalrous convention that a line-of-battle ship did not attack a frigate without provocation had collapsed, and as daylight faded the flagship, already cleared for action, fired a few shot at the weathermost frigate, which hauled away 'dead on a wind'. Fifteen minutes later the leewardmost frigate, the *Alcmène,* 44, came under fire, and Durham hailed to her to surrender. She responded with a broadside, put her helm up, and, under full sail at the rate of nine knots, laid the *Venerable* on board. The blow was so forceful that Durham and most of the marines on the poop fell down. Durham believed that her captain intended to board; rather, he probably sought to disable the flagship's bowsprit and foremast to prevent her giving chase.[8]

Having secured the *Alcmène* to their ship fore and aft, boarders from the *Venerable* fought their way onto her and hauled down her ensign, three master's mates and a midshipman displaying particular gallantry. The flagship had two killed and nine wounded, four severely. Her adversary suffered thirty-two deaths, and among the fifty injured was her captain, Alexandre Ducrest de Villeneuve. In the rainy darkness the other frigate had made off, and when the consequently indignant Ducrest came aboard the flagship to surrender his sword and have his wounds dressed he willingly told Durham that her captain, his senior, had earlier shouted: 'If we part company, I shall change my course every two hours, two points west, and my rendezvous will be in the north-west'.

Durham calculated that the consort would therefore be about 200 miles away in the west-north-west. He sent the *Cyane* and *Jason* ahead to reconnoitre, while repairs were made to the flagship, prisoners brought aboard, and a prize crew under the *Venerable's* first lieutenant, an old follower of his, put in charge of the *Alcmène*. On 18 January he ordered a puzzled Worth to steer to the north-west, and shortly after noon the following day, when the flagship had run some 155 miles, a strange sail was sighted on the weather bow. The look-out hollered that she seemed to be a small British merchantman heading southward. But having climbed aloft to see for himself, Durham was convinced that she was the frigate.

He ordered his sceptical flag-captain to disguise the *Venerable* and steer straight for the stranger, which, mistaking the flagship for her consort, came down under full canvas before realising her error and hauling around. Durham spent the night huddled on the poop while three midshipmen watched the quarry. When dawn broke on 20 January she was two miles away after a nineteen-hour chase. The *Alcmène* was visible in the north-east but the *Cyane* and *Jason* were out of sight.

Soon the *Venerable* had drawn close enough to fire bow guns, and the enemy retorted with stern-chasers and quarter-guns. She attempted to escape by cutting away her anchors and throwing her boats overboard, but the flagship sailed too well. As the two vessels closed, the frigate sheered to larboard to give the *Venerable* a broadside. Worth ordered his helmsman to bring her larboard broadside to bear on the frigate. Durham countermanded this order, so that the frigate's broadside would pass obliquely. The enemy then sheered to starboard to give the flagship the other broadside, upon which, on Durham's instructions, the *Venerable* sheered to larboard and the frigate, her starboard guns having fired in vain, struck her colours.

Owing to Durham's 'judicious manoeuvres' his flagship had sustained no casualties and only a few shot through her sails. Her prize proved to be the *Iphigénie*, 44, (Captain Jacques-Leon Emeric), 'perfectly new' like the *Alcmène*. She carried 150 prisoners seized from a British convoy near the Canary Islands. Durham renamed her the *Palma* and her consort the *Dunira* after Lord Melville's Perthshire estate.[9]

The sight of these two prizes being led into Carlisle Bay gladdened the Barbados merchants, who considered it a 'singularly auspicious commencement' to Durham's tenure. They were deeply dissatisfied with his predecessor, the Trafalgar veteran Laforey, who had habitually broken appointments and had let the Leeward Islands squadron slide into 'a most deplorable state of inactivity', taken advantage of by marauding American privateers. Durham, to the colonists' delight, was very different. He told them that he would be available to them 'From daylight to dusk, and as many times in the night as you think proper to call on me', and assured them that his prime duty was 'the protection of commerce', which constituted 'the Sheet Anchor of our country; without it, we can have no Navy'. He was as good as his word. Under him the squadron became known for brisk efficiency, capturing, despite its inadequate numbers, many American privateers. He was furious when Captain Anthony Maitland of the *Pique*, 38, decided not to engage a comparable American ship that had been cruising menacingly near St Thomas's, despite having two brigs with him.[10]

By the time peace with the United States was declared in 1814 Durham's ships had captured eighty-four American vessels. 'Local circumstances have rendered these seas a scene of unexampled activity; and whenever opportunities have offered by falling in with American Cruizers [*sic*] our ships of war have been uniformly distinguished for their spirited intrepidity', observed the Barbados press. 'Although the Caribbean Sea has literally swarmed during the past season with multitudes of privateers, such has been the unremitting vigilance of the Commander-in-Chief in the very judicious distribution of the squadron under his orders, that the losses of the commercial community have been comparatively trifling. In many instances when fleets were known to have lost their convoy, the neighbouring seas have been completely scoured by our ships of war, to ensure their safe arrival.'[11]

Captured or detained vessels were sent for adjudication to the Vice-Admiralty courts in the region, whose judges determined their status and value if condemned as prize. But at the end of 1814 Durham ordered his captains and commanders 'in your own Interests as well as mine and that of all Officers and Men employed and belonging to the Squadron' to cease sending ships to Antigua for adjudication since his investigations confirmed that the court there, unlike its counterpart at Barbados, charged exorbitant fees. To reinforce this order he stationed a sloop off Antigua to redirect potential prizes to Barbados. This naturally incensed Edward Byam, the adjudicator at Antigua, who protested his innocence and complained to the Admiralty about Durham's high-handed action. 'I took it upon myself as the Guardian of the Sailors in the Squadron... not to suffer them to be any longer wronged, and, like a Merchant sending his vessel to the best Market, I have directed that all Vessels should proceed, for adjudication, to that Port [Bridgetown], where their condemnation will be attended with least Expense', was Durham's retort.

The Admiralty asked Durham for an explanation, but conceded that the squadron was within its rights to deal with any Vice-Admiralty court that it chose. Their lordships did, however, refer the matter to Sir William Scott , head of the Admiralty's High Court. He found that while Byam's fees did seem 'enormous', Durham's behaviour had been 'extremely unadvised'. Durham should have merely refused to pay the fee charged in the case of a small American schooner, which had precipitated his investigations, and referred any other excessive fees to the Admiralty. Proscribing the entire court at Antigua was 'not very consistent with natural justice'. Durham seems to have taken this to heart. Several months after Scott's finding he complained to the Admiralty of the 'enormous charges' made by the court at Tortola, which admitted that it contravened the scale of fees laid down by Scott.[12]

In the summer of 1814, as a result of a general promotion of flag-officers, Durham became a rear-admiral of the Red, and at the beginning of 1815 learned that he had been created 'a Knight Commander of the Most Honourable Military Order of the Bath'. This reward for his long and distinguished service during the wars led to confusion over his name, for in accordance with Lady Charlotte's preference he styled himself by his middle one. 'I am Sir Charles not Sir Philip' he had to explain to Sir Alexander Cochrane, commanding on the North American station – and to many others.[13]

For all its economic and strategic importance to Britain, and its lush beauty, the Leeward Islands station was a mosquito-infested, hurricane-swept colonial backwater. Durham found it a 'Dull place', and less than twelve months into his tenure, learning that peace had been declared in Europe and that Napoleon had been exiled to Elba, he applied to be relieved. At length he learned that Rear-Admiral John Harvey would be sent out to replace him, with the result that at Largo his brother, Lieutenant-General James Durham recorded in his diary: 'My brother... arrived on the 18th [June 1815] at Falmouth from the West Indies'. But he was misinformed. In view of the threat posed by Napoleon's escape from Elba and his landing in March 1815 on the south coast of France to begin a march on Paris, Melville informed Durham that he must remain where he was, since his 'conduct... has given such great satisfaction to the merchants and inhabitants of the Leeward Island, and to the Board of Admiralty'.[14]

Some time later Durham received an Admiralty despatch dated 26 March. It informed him that the ship which brought it also bore orders from the restored Bourbon monarch, Louis XIII, to the governor of Martinique, Comte de Vaugiraud, and the governor of Guadeloupe, Comte de Linois (both vice-admirals), to hold their respective islands in the royal name. If either or both declared for Napoleon, it would, nevertheless, be Durham's 'duty... to abstain from any hostile acts' against the tricolour 'unless the vessels which carry it should commit any act of aggression against British ships, or until you learn hostilities between France and this country have actually commenced. If Martinique and Guadeloupe continue faithful to Louis XVIII, and their vessels carry his flag, they must of course be treated as friends.'[15]

The governor of the Leeward Islands was Sir James Leith, British military commander-in-chief at Barbados, a fellow-Scot whose arrival in mid-1814 had been warmly welcomed by the bored Durham. But relations between them deteriorated following Leith's receipt of a despatch from Lord Bathurst, secretary of state for war and the colonies, dated 10 April 1815. Bathurst wrote that in view of events in France there was likely to be an attempt by Napoleon's adherents on Martinique and Guadeloupe to gain control of those islands, whose governors might consequently need aid in upholding Louis's authority. Accordingly, the Prince Regent directed that if the governors asked Leith for assistance he should 'without delay' give them all possible help from the force under his command.[16]

Vaugiraud was the very officer who, while piloting off Nourmoutier twenty years early, had been instrumental in running Durham's *Anson* aground. Still staunchly royalist, he found that following Napoleon's escape from Elba inhabitants of Martinique had again unfurled the revolutionary flag, and that most of the island's 1,200-strong garrison displayed Bonapartist sympathies. In response Vaugiraud assembled the garrison, relieved of their commands any officer who wished it (on condition they leave the island) and warned that any attempt to raise the tricolour would be punished as an act of rebellion. He also requested support from Leith, who in view of Bathurst's despatch agreed to provide it.

Durham made the necessary transport available. On 1 June he took a squadron into Gros Inlet Bay, St Lucia, where 2,000 troops under that island's governor, Major-General Edward Stehelin, embarked. While these preparations for a landing on Martinique were proceeding Durham, sensing that the war – and thus his active career – would soon be over, dictated aboard the *Venerable* (now captained by George Pringle), a brief synopsis of his naval career. 'During a service of Thirty-eight years', it concluded proudly, 'I have scarcely been on half-pay, but in constant employment, in which period I have been honour'd with the thanks of the House of Commons three times – and repeatedly received the marked approbation of the Admiralty.'

Acutely conscious of the Admiralty despatch of 26 March which told him to refrain from hostile action against the tricolour, Durham had in the meantime sent an officer incognito to Martinique to ascertain whether Vaugiraud was still in control. He was, though very precariously. Therefore, at sunset on 5 June, Durham and his ships sailed into Martinique's chief town, Fort Royal (since renamed Fort-de-France) and landed the troops. Led by Leith, they swiftly took possession of the military installations in the royalist cause. Their appearance was timely, for only 450 members of the garrison remained faithful to the Bourbon flag, and only half the island's 6,000-strong loyalist militia had weapons. Durham then went ashore to pay his respects to Vaugiraud, who demonstrated his gratitude for the assistance by publishing a decree 'by which British Vessels are received on the same footing as French'.[17]

But another crisis loomed. Apparently swayed by his second-in-command, General Boyer de Peyreleau, Guadeloupe's governor, Linois, with whom Durham had enjoyed a close friendship, declared for Napoleon. To Leith's disgust, Durham, who considered the despatch of 26 March his warrant, informed Linois that no hostile action would be forthcoming. This undertaking was trumpeted in Bonapartist circles throughout the French Antilles, and Durham allowed a French frigate from America with soldiers, ammunition and stores aboard to reach Guadeloupe unchallenged. Encouraged, Linois sent a detachment of troops to occupy Les Saintes, two small islands south of Guadeloupe. When an outraged Leith demanded that Durham now provide ships for a British military invasion of Les Saintes, aimed at restoring Bourbon authority, the admiral steadfastly refused, and a brisk exchange of letters between him and the general explaining their relative positions ensued. This was the only noteworthy instance during the conflict of 1793–1815 in which commanders of British land and sea forces were at odds with each other.

The cause of this dispute was Leith's belief that his letter from Bathurst clearly obligated him to restore by force of arms the usurped royal authority on the island, and Durham's insistence that his instructions dated 26 March prevented him from co-operating. Repeatedly, he rejected Leith's argument that since he would be defending France's lawful sovereign he would be committing no hostile act, and with characteristic obstinacy he remained inflexible even in the face of Leith's contention that by permitting vessels flying the tricolour to sail unhindered to and from Guadeloupe he was conceivably enabling Linois 'by force of Reinforcements and Stores to assume a defensive posture which may require a large force, and great expense to Government to reduce'.[18]

On 2 July, the Bonapartist occupiers having withdrawn from Les Saintes, Leith informed Durham that he planned to send troops to Guadeloupe and requested transport for them. Durham, who had already ordered his squadron to hamper any attempt by the Guadeloupe garrison to retake Les Saintes, replied that now that Les Saintes was back under Bourbon control he would convey the troops to those islands and keep all French men of war, whether they flew the tricolour or not, 'at a respectful distance'. He could not, however, assist Leith in a military strike at Guadeloupe, for in addition to the despatch of 26 March he had subsequent communications from the Admiralty recommending 'a cautious line of Conduct', including one dated as late as 18 May: 'I must have the positive Orders of my Board, or satisfactory proof of War having commenced in France... before I consent to join in Offensive Operations'. As soon as such orders arrived, Leith would find him fully ready to assist 'against the Common Enemy to the Civilized World'.[19]

Durham had told the Admiralty of Leith's proposed expedition to Guadeloupe, and while awaiting their reply he notified them on 25 July that he had warned Leith of the danger of attempting one at that period of the year, in view of 'the tremendous surf' and 'heavy rains' on Guadeloupe. Two days later a despatch vessel brought news of Waterloo, fought on 18 June, and in celebration the *Venerable* fired a 21-gun royal salute and hoisted the Union Jack. The despatch vessel also brought 'circular instructions' from the Admiralty, dated 21 June, directing the seizure and destruction of French ships, which Durham took as his authorisation to co-operate with Leith.[20]

The two commanders-in-chief, holding councils of war in Durham's cabin, hoped that when the people of Guadeloupe learned of Waterloo and of other setbacks for Napoleon the rebel regime would collapse without a fight. On 3 August they addressed a curt letter to Linois enclosing the text of a proclamation in French which they intended to distribute on the island as soon as they landed there, telling of Waterloo and of the futility of further resistance. Provided the inhabitants surrendered immediately, and swore an oath of fidelity to George III for the duration of the island's remaining under British protection, they, their property, commerce and way of life would come to no harm. But those who resisted, and their possessions, would be treated 'according to the laws of war and the right of conquest'.[21]

Perhaps suspecting a bluff, the authorities on Guadeloupe scornfully rejected these overtures. 'I have taken up my position, and I shall maintain it', Linois, pointing to the tricolour cockade in his hat, informed Durham's messenger. With Leith, and the governor of Grenada, Major-General Sir Charles Shipley (father-in-law of Durham's second cousin, the Earl of Buchan's heir), aboard the *Venerable*, Durham reconnoitred the coast of Guadeloupe looking for the ideal spot to disembark troops. By 7 August all of the 6,000 troops collected by the squadron from the British islands in the region had arrived at the rendezvous off Les Saintes, and at dawn the following morning an impressive force set sail for Guadeloupe.

Commanded by Durham in the *Venerable* (aboard which were Leith, his staff officers, and the 15th Regiment, supplied with three days' worth of provisions), it consisted of the 18-gun sloops *Dasher* (Captain William Henderson), *Barbadoes* (Captain John Fleming), and *Muros* (Captain George Gosling), the 16-gun sloops *Fairy* (Captain Henry Baker), *Espiègle* (Captain Charles Mitchell) and *Columbia* (Captain Henry Chads), and the brig *Chanticleer*, 10 (Lieutenant George Tupman). The frigates *Fox,* 32 (Captain Francis Willock) and *Niobe,* 38 (Captain Henry Deacon) acted as troopships. There were also a total of fifty-three transports and hired vessels, and two small ships, the *Badger* and the *Flying Fish*, would join at Guadeloupe. The enterprise was 'very much indebted' to Vaugiraud for sending two corvettes and a schooner carrying reinforcements from Martinique.[22]

In the morning a brigade of York Rangers led by Shipley was put ashore at Saint Sauveur under the protective guns of the *Fairy, Espiègle* and

Chanticleer. The latter's commander had selected an 'admirable position' and she 'swept the beach of the few [French] troops that made their appearance'. In the afternoon, at Grand Ance Bay, Leith disembarked with 2,000 men from the 15th and 25th regiments, 'well directed fire' from the *Fairy, Columbia* and *Barbadoes* having soon silenced an enemy battery and made Linois and Boyer with a 'large body of troops' retreat to an appreciable distance. Early the following day, 9 August, more troops were landed at Bailif, where, menaced by the guns of the *Columbia, Muros* and *Chanticleer,* a 'very large' enemy force withdrew to high ground.

Next morning, after a resistance lasting several hours, Linois and Boyer surrendered to Leith, and articles of capitulation were signed. At half-past ten a fort near the town of Basseterre had opened fire on the *Venerable,* which had taken several nearby French ships and a floating battery. Since Leith, in contravention of established precedent during conjoint British naval and military expeditions, failed to involve Durham in the peace negotiations, or apprise him of the cessation of hostilities, the flagship continued to pour broadsides into the fort. Eventually, a flag of truce was observed flying in Basseterre, and, with ships of his squadron in sight, Durham sent a boat ashore to receive the town's surrender. The fort hauled down the revolutionary flag, and at half-past three that afternoon Durham, through his telescope, saw British troops enter the fort and hoist the Union Jack. Shortly after this he learned to his astonishment that Linois and Boyer had already capitulated and that, in accordance with the terms agreed upon, they and other prisoners of war would be sent to France and put into Wellington's custody.

Durham was livid. The fort's had been the final tricolour flying in the Caribbean, and so, by a remarkable coincidence which he would always trumpet, he had achieved the surrenders of the first – in 1793 – and last tricolours of the French wars. But Leith's 'marked disrespect' in excluding him from the treaty's terms meant that placements in the acting government of Guadeloupe – even naval ones, which Durham not unreasonably considered within his gift – consisted of Leith's nominees. Durham protested to Bathurst, getting Leith's appointments overruled and himself a say in the new ones, and although in his despatch to the Admiralty describing the reduction of Guadeloupe he paid generous tribute to Leith, the general's behaviour gnawed at him for years.[23]

His had been an outstanding chief naval command, during which the celebrated liberator of Venezuela, Simon Bolivar, had attempted to enlist his help against Spain. Durham's zealous protection of British trade in the Caribbean, despite his inadequate number of ships, earned him encomiums in the Barbados press and from groups of merchants throughout the British Lesser Antilles. The merchants of Trinidad presented him with a 'beautiful' sword valued at 100 guineas (Durham is depicted holding it in a portrait by Sir Francis Grant.) Those of St Thomas in the Virgin Islands, especially grateful to him for restoring their island's status as 'the last Port of Rendezvous for homeward bound Fleets', gave him a star appropriate to his order of knighthood.[24]

In October 1815 Durham's brother Tom died and was succeeded as laird of Polton by his eldest son, James; his second son, Thomas Durham Calderwood – Tom had taken his mother's maiden surname on inheriting her family property – was acting as Durham's flag-lieutenant and would obtain his lieutenant's commission the following July. However, the hot and humid fever zone had disagreed with him and he never went to sea again. Early in 1816, while the *Venerable* was beginning her homeward voyage, Lady Charlotte, who had been staying with Sir James and Lady Steuart at Coltness, set out for Edinburgh. During the journey she was suddenly taken ill, and on 21 February she died shortly after arrival at George Square. She too was buried at Lasswade, and soon after his arrival at Spithead on 16 April Edinburgh society was agog with reports that her widower, with a cavalier disregard for mourning etiquette and with breathtaking bragger, was hot in pursuit of a wealthy heiress, Anne Isabella Henderson.[25]

Born on 28 January 1782, Anne was the only legitimate child of Sir John Henderson of Fordel, a trained lawyer and shrewd political operator who had sat in the House of Commons as a Whig. Sir John and Durham were second cousins. Now ailing, Sir John spent most of his time in self-imposed seclusion on the Fordel estate between Aberdour and Inverkeithing, attended by three illegitimate offspring, and seeing little of Anne. She was living in Paris with her inseparable cousin, Isabella Lockhart, daughter of a deceased 'yellow admiral'. Anne's mother, Loudoun, had been the only legitimate child of Lieutenant-General James Robertson, an avaricious self-made Scot who had been governor of New York. Loudoun had died a few days after Anne's birth; Sir John had never remarried but had taken, over the years, several teenage mistresses. Anne's maternal grandmother came from a prominent Portsmouth family named White, from whom, following the death of a 'lunatic' spinster cousin, Anne was set to inherit valuable lands at Fareham and on Portsea Island.[26]

Durham's tangible assets amounted to £42,956. These consisted of £21,000 in savings, his house in Gloucester Place (which he said was valued at £6,000), bank stocks worth £3,750, East India stock worth £2,400, and bonds totalling £9,206, comprising mainly bequests. Taking into account his 'Guadeloupe Prize Money' of some £5,000 and his outstanding debts, his total net worth was estimated at £52,749. This was an impressive sum – over £3 million in today's money – and highlights just how successful his career had been. But Anne's potential worth was considerably larger: about £80,000 sterling in Scotland (the equivalent of £5 million today) and £50,000 in England.[27]

Since the end of hostilities curtailed his employment prospects, the enterprising and energetic Durham was determined to become laird of Fordel. He was also aware of Anne's Hampshire inheritance, for when he was captain of the *Windsor Castle* at Portsmouth in 1803 he had obliged her father by inquiring about its current farm rentals and about Miss White's personal details: she was, Durham reported, 'about 37 silly and harmless'. In August 1816, unbeknown to Sir John inside the mansion, he paid a visit to Fordel, wandering about the grounds to ascertain its condition and value. He assured himself that, though neglected in recent years and encumbered by debt, he would be able to restore its prosperity just as his grandmother, Margaret Calderwood, had restored Polton's. He had her mathematical mind and astute business sense, and Fordel boasted prime arable land, quarries, collieries and saltworks, and a wooden railway built by Sir John which transported coal from the estate to the sea.

Anne had rejected at least two previous suitors, the infelicitously surnamed Major John Pine-Coffin and a fortune-hunting Irish Catholic baronet, Sir John Burke. Enlisting the aid of her relative Vice-Admiral Cochrane (uncle of the controversial and legendary 'sea wolf' Captain Lord Cochrane), and knowing that he had a rival suitor in a younger brother of Elizabeth Oswald, Durham courted Anne ardently, pursuing her to Paris and waxing irresistibly romantic: 'I... Strick [sic] my Red Flag not to the enemy but to an Angel I love with all my heart and soul'. While in Paris he pressed, successfully, for the Croix de Commandeur de l'Ordre du Mérite Militaire, which had been awarded by Louis XVIII to Sir James Leith following the reduction of Martinique and Guadeloupe, his role having been overlooked. He was the only British naval officer thus decorated.[28]

Having won Anne, he persisted in demanding that her lands not be entailed. This would have meant that, in the event of the marriage proving childless, Anne would be at liberty to nominate any heirs she chose, not necessarily her nearest blood relatives. But her father, her paternal uncle, and her chief trustee, the Earl of Lauderdale, regarded Durham as duplicitous and venal, intent on grabbing those lands for his family. Sir John bellowed about challenging him to a duel, and Lauderdale threatened to tell Anne that from the beginning Durham had been crowing indiscreetly to all his friends how rich marriage to her would make him. Despite railing at their 'Humbug' and vowing to cut off his right hand rather than agree to their terms, Durham capitulated, and had to agree, too, to pay off Sir John's debts, compensate him for moving out of his mansion into an Edinburgh townhouse, and give £7,000 towards the support of the three illegitimate children. Durham and Anne were married in London on 15 October 1817. 'This is the most valuable prize the gallant Admiral has yet obtained', the press had already reported. Sir John gave his daughter away and wished the couple well, but privately he was scathing about his son-in-law, and indignant that he was now calling himself Sir Philip Henderson Durham without seeking Sir John's approval.[29]

The childless marriage proved very close. Having taken a continental honeymoon, the couple went abroad again in 1819. Durham visited La Rochelle, Quiberon, and Rochefort, which he knew so well from the sea. He hoped to meet his valiant adversary, Captain Ségond of the *Loire,* and was sad to learn that he had recently died. At Toulon he had a chance encounter with a French captain who, as a young officer on the *Aigle*, had been sent aboard the *Defiance* at the close of the battle of Trafalgar. He had been given a meal in Durham's cabin, and Durham had slipped him two guineas as he was disembarking at Portsmouth as a prisoner of war. Despite Durham's protests he now insisted on reimbursing him.[30]

Durham enthusiastically welcomed the introduction of steam vessels, and, as laird of Fordel, frequently took one from Leith to London on business at the Coal Exchange and elsewhere. He proved a shrewd landlord and a hard-driving merchant, finding markets for Fordel's coal and salt, installing an iron railway to transport coal to Dalgety Bay, improving St David's Harbour there, and purchasing three sloops to carry the exports out to the Forth. He named one of Fordel's pits after his wife and others after vessels he had commanded and his flagships. From 1835–45 the collieries yielded an average annual return of £4,700. At Fordel he and Anne entertained so much that when they were alone they felt like 'Hermits'. Guests included the exiled Charles X (the former Comte d'Artois). The Durhams celebrated each anniversary of Trafalgar with a dinner party, at which, after a song, 'Toasts were given, healths drunk, all of which under the semblance of hilarity awakened a melancholy train of thought'. However, on one occasion French aristocrats sat among

Melville and other British invitees, so the cook endeavoured 'to make as *French* a dinner as possible' and reference to Trafalgar was 'of course carefully avoided'.[31]

Durham had become a full admiral of the Blue on 22 July 1830, the day his brother, the laird of Largo, became a full general. On 1 December he was invested by William IV as a GCB (Knight Grand Cross of the military division of the Bath), and around that time he was appointed equerry to the king's brother, the Duke of Cambridge. He held that post until his death as an admiral of the Red, by which time, having succeeded his brother as laird of Largo in 1840 and his nephew Tom as laird of Polton in 1842, he had added Calderwood to his middle names. In 1830 he served, briefly, as Tory MP for the Admiralty borough of Queenborough, Kent. In 1832, his former midshipman Captain Joseph Needham Tayler, who wielded political influence in the seat of Devizes, persuaded him to stand for Parliament in the Conservative interest. He lost humiliatingly, but in 1834 was returned owing to a deal with the resigning Liberal member. Vowing initially to sit as an Independent, he soon accepted the Conservative whip. His first act was to introduce a petition to the Lords in support of his brother's claim to the Rutherford peerage; unfortunately, a genealogist discovered that far from being the daughter of the first Lord Rutherford, the great-grandmother of the admiral and the general was almost certainly his sister, and so the claim collapsed. Beyond a debate on manning the navy – he perhaps perversely declared that he had always preferred pressed men to volunteers – and another on the distribution of liquor among seamen, Durham seldom attended the Commons and gladly accepted the Chiltern Hundreds in the autumn of 1835 in order to become commander-in-chief (port-admiral) at Portsmouth, the most prestigious of the home commands, living with Anne at Admiralty House in the Dockyard and keeping a bountiful table.[32]

In 1836 divers retrieved several articles from the wreck of the *Royal George* and Durham's brother, the general, mounted one of the cannon, an iron 32-pounder, on a plinth in front of Largo House. With his Trafalgar background, Durham was chosen, in 1838, to be the first naval president of the Army and Navy Club in London, founded in 1837 on the initiative, partly, of Wellington. In October 1837 he commanded a squadron of small ships off Brighton during Queen Victoria's visit there, and lent the private band that he had aboard his normal flagship, the 120-gun *Britannia,* for the town's official celebrations. He attended Victoria's Coronation in June 1838. To mark the striking of his flag on 19 April 1839 a song was composed in honour of:

The vet'ran who shared in Great Nelson's last fight
When their thunders rolled over proud Spain

and in 1841, but for ill health, he would have assumed command of Britain's Mediterranean fleet in succession to Stopford. During Colonel Charles Pasley's operations (1840–43) to clear the submerged *Royal George* with the use of gunpowder, a small telescope was recovered and presented to Durham, and a stamp with which he had marked his books and linen was brought up.[33]

Troublesome relatives, including two illegitimate children whom her father had failed to reveal, vexed Durham and Anne. Particularly exasperating were Anne's cousin Isabella and her husband, the Marquis de Riario Sforza, nephew of the Neapolitan minister Circello. This extravagant, impoverished, freeloading pair were constantly demanding handouts; Durham, who financed their children's education, once refused to return to his Mayfair townhouse at 9 Hill Street until Anne sent them packing, and added that at sea with only 'one shilling' in his pocket he had at least been carefree. Following Anne's sudden death on 18 December 1844 he left for Rome, to emphasise to Riario's brother, a cardinal, the necessity of keeping funds for the three Riario daughters out of Isabella's clutches. He took a French war steamer from Marseilles to Livorno. Her captain relinquished his cabin to Durham, who was 'in his element', remaining on deck during a gale which sent his companions scuttling below. But he caught bronchitis, and on 2 April 1845, having been to Rome, he died at a Naples hotel.

As the Neapolitan steamer conveying his body as far as Malta entered Valletta Harbour, boats of the British squadron were sent with a guard of marines to land the body, flags were lowered to half-mast and minute guns boomed from the flagship. After three weeks in quarantine the body was taken to Portsmouth by the naval steam sloop *Hecate* and put aboard the *Comet* for the final voyage to Largo Bay. The Admiralty had ordered naval honours for Durham, and accordingly the steamer's officers, in full-dress uniform, and their crew, were in the funeral procession on 28 May when he was buried in the family vault at Largo. 'The gallant admiral... a hero of Trafalgar', commented a London newspaper, 'unlike many of his companions in arms survived for years to see his country enjoying the fruits of those naval achievements which have made her what she is. Still there arises a melancholy feeling as we thus contemplate another of the mighty and victorious spirits of the war passing away'.[34]

Notes

CHAPTER 1: SEABORNE

1   NRAS 3215, Durham of Largo Papers, Bundle 72, Appendix, vol. 1, p.84; Oliver Warner, *Trafalgar*, London, 1959, p.60.

2   William Laird Clowes and Alan H. Burgoyne, *Trafalgar Refought*, London, 1905; George Dingwall, *The Vicinity of Largo Bay*, Kirkaldy, 1946, p.55.

3   NRAS 3246, Dundas of Arniston Papers, Bundle 157, nos 1 and 24; memorial tablet to Durham, Largo parish church; NRAS 3215, Durham of Largo Papers, Bundle 72, Appendix, vol. 1, pp.14 *et seq.*; cf. John Marshall, *Royal Naval Biography*, vol. 1, part 2, London, 1823, pp.450-4, and William Laird Clowes, *The Royal Navy: A History*, London, 1900, vol. 5, p.41; David Stevenson, *The Beggar's Benison*, East Linton, 2001; James Denniston, ed., *The Coltness Collections*, pp.337-407; Alexander Fergusson, ed., *Letters and Journals of Mrs. Calderwood of Polton*, Edinburgh, 1884; see also NRAS 3246, Dundas of Arniston Papers, Bundles 150, 153, 160.

4   Eric Eunson and John Band, *Largo: An Illustrated History*, Ochiltree, 2000; Walter Wood, *The East Neuk of Fife*, 2nd ed., 1887; Ae.J.G. Mackay, *A History of Fife and Kinross*, Edinburgh, 1895; Loretta A. Timperley, *A Dictionary of Landownership in Scotland c. 1770*, Edinburgh, 1976, pp.149, 152; NRAS 3215, Durham of Largo Papers, Bundle 72, Appendix, vol. 1, pp.104-8, and Bundle 45; Anne Calderwood Durham to Henrietta Cumming, n.d., University of Edinburgh Special Collections, La.II.81/16.

5   See James Anthony Gardner, *Recollections of James Anthony Gardner Commander R.N. (1775–1814)*, ed. Sir R. Vesey Fitzgerald and John Knox Laughton, London, 1906 (Navy Records Society Publications, vol. 31), p.16.

6   For details see A.T. Mahan, *The Major Operations of the Navies in the War of American Independence*, London, 1913, pp.68-75. Piers Mackesy, *The War for America, 1775–1783*, Lincoln, Nebraska, 1992; and also Charles R. Ritcheson, *British Politics and the American Revolution*, Norman, Oklahoma, 1954, pp.254-70, which contains minor inaccuracies.

7   Log, HMS *Trident*, PRO ADM 51/1011; *Scots Magazine*, vol.40, 1778, p.366; Alexander Murray, *Memoir of the Naval Life and Services of Admiral Sir P.C.H.C. Durham*, London, 1846, p.3. This memoir was in fact penned by Durham; his great-nephew Alick, son

of James Wolfe Murray of Cringletie and Durham's niece Isabella Strange, hurriedly completed it following Durham's death.

8   *Ibid.*, p.4.

9   *Ibid.*, p.5; Tom Wareham, *Frigate Commander,* Barnsley, 2004, p.xv.

10 Log, HMS *Edgar,* PRO ADM 51/301; George Rodney to Philip Stephens, 28 January 1780, *New Annual Register... 1780*, pp.18-19; 'History 1780', *Scots Magazine*, vol.44, 1782, p.178; 'Extract', *ibid.*, vol.46, 1784, p.614; J. Ralfe, *The Naval Chronology of Great Britain,* London, 1820, vol.3, pp.38-9.

11 John Knox Laughton, ed., *Letters of Lord Barham,* vol.1, London (NRS Publications, vol.32), pp.xxxii-xxxiii, 340; memoir of Hector MacNeill, in A.I.B. Stewart, 'Harping On', *Kintyre Magazine,* no.30, Autumn 1991, p.6; Julian Corbett, ed., *Signals and Instructions 1776–1794,* London, 1908 (NRS Publications, vol.35), pp.1-8, 40; Murray, *op.cit.,* p.11.

12 *Barham Letters,* vol.1, pp.xxxiv-xxxv, 356-60; G.R. Barnes and J.H. Owen, eds., *The Private Papers of John Earl of Sandwich,* vol.4, London, 1938 (NRS Publications, vol.78), pp.16, 77-8, 286; Murray, *op.cit.,* pp.12-14

13 J.S. [Julian Slight?], A *Narrative of the Loss of the Royal George at Spithead in August 1782,* 2nd ed., Portsea, 1840, pp.16-17 and 8th ed., Portsea, 1847; *Notice of the Royal George, 108 Guns, which was lost at Spithead, 20 August 1782,* Portsmouth, 1782; *Nautical Magazine,* vol.4, p.436; Wood, *op.cit.,* p.18; Murray, *op.cit.,* p.18; *Naval Chronicle,* vol.7, 1802, p.71; PRO ADM 1/5321, Part 1. Regarding Durham's rescue, Sarah Tytler, *Three Generations,* London, 1911, pp.64-5, is incorrect.

14 *Ibid.*

15 R.F. Johnson, *The Royal George,* London, 1971, Appendix III, pp.179-86.

16 *Ibid.*, pp.81-3, 125-6; Geoffrey Regan, *Geoffrey Regan's Book of Naval Blunders,* London, 2001, p.126; Scarritt Adams, 'The Loss of the Royal George 1782', *History Today,* vol.9, pp.837-40.

17 Murray, *op.cit.,* pp.20-1, does not volunteer the family connection.

18 *Scots Magazine,* vol.44, 1782, pp.605-7.

19 Murray, *op.cit.,* pp. 21-2.

20 PRO ADM 1/5322 and ADM 12/24; Murray, *op.cit.,* p.22; *Scots Magazine,* vol.46, 1784, pp.181-83.

21 Murray, *op.cit.,* pp.22-4

22 Muster rolls, HMS *Salisbury,* PRO ADM 36/10721; J.S. Yorke to Charles Yorke, 8 October [1786], British Library Add. MSS 35392, Hardwicke Papers, fo.47; Philip Ziegler, *King William IV,* London, 1971, pp.60-3; Johnson, *op.cit.,* p.88; Thomas Byam Martin, *Letters and Papers,* ed. R. Vesey Hamilton, vol.1, London, 1903 (NRS Publications, vol.12), pp.29-30; H. Dillon, *A Narrative of My Professional Adventures,* vol.2, London, 1956 (NRS Publications, vol.93), p.435.

CHAPTER 2: EARNING A REPUTATION

1   Anne Calderwood to Elizabeth Steuart of Coltness, 18 February 1788, NRAS 3215, Durham of Largo Papers, Bundle 72, Appendix, vol.1, pp.129-34; same to Henry Dundas, 28 March 1790, NLS MS 1046, Meville Papers, fo.62.

2   James Calderwood Durham to Henry Dundas, 27 March 1789, *loc.cit.,* fo.57 (enclosure).

3   NAS SC 20/50/16, Durham's Last Will and Testament; NAS CH 2/960/5, Largo Kirk Session Records.

4   Philip Durham to Anne Calderwood Durham, 1 July 1790, NAS GD 172 Henderson of Fordel Papers, 1068/5; same to same, 23 June 1790, GD 172/1068/3.

5   *Scots Magazine*, vol.52, 1790, pp.649, 650.

6   Philip Durham to Anne Calderwood Durham, n.d. [ca. July 1790], NAS GD 172/1068/5; same to same, 'Saturday' [ca. July 1790], GD 172/1068/6.

7   Thomas Erskine to Henry Erskine, 25 December 1791, Fergusson, *Henry Erskine*, p.391; Philip Durham to Anne Calderwood Durham, 23 June [1790], NAS GD 172/1068/3; same to same, 'August. Friday' [1790], GD 172/1068/4; same to same, 1 July [1790], GD 172/1068/5; James Calderwood Durham, n.d. [August 1790], GD 172/1068/1; NRAS MS 3215, Durham of Largo Papers, Bundle 72, Appendix, vol.1, p.140. When his wife acquired Polton Mr Durham adopted her maiden surname as his middle name.

8   Margaret Calderwood to Anne Calderwood Durham, n.d. [1756], quoted in Fergusson, *Henry Erskine*, p.54; Philip Durham to Anne Calderwood Durham, 1 July [1790], NAS GD 172/1068/5; same to same, 'August. Friday' [1790], GD 172/1068/4.

9   *Scots Magazine*, vol.52, 1790. pp.645-4.

10 Philip Durham to James Calderwood Durham, n.d. [ca. 15 August 1790], NAS GD 172/1068/1; same to same, GD 172/1068/2, which obviously predates it. See also Philip Durham to Anne Calderwood Durham, 23 June 17909, GD 172/1068/3.

11 Philip Durham to James Calderwood Durham, NAS GD 172/1068/1.

12 Philip Durham to Anne Calderwood Durham, 4 August 1790, NAS GD 172/1068/7.

13 *Scots Magazine*, vol.52, 1790, p.650. This fleet is emphatically not to be confused with the so-called Russian Armament ordered by the prime minister, Pitt, the following year, when Hood had his flag in the *Victory*. See Omond, *op.cit.*, pp.128-30; Dillon, *op.cit.*, vol.1, p.29.

14 Philip Durham to Anne Calderwood Durham, 4 August 1790, NAS GD 172/1068/7.

15 Same to same, 13 August, 7 September 1790, NAS GD 172/1068/8-9. Hew Elliot cannot be precisely identified.

16 Same to same, 13 August, 7 September 1790, NAS GD 172/1068/8-9.

17 Muster-roll, HMS *Barfleur*, PRO ADM 36/10795; James Anthony Gardner, *op.cit.*, pp.112, 114. The article by Sir John Knox Laughton on Calder in the *Dictionary of National Biography* entirely omits this phase in his career.

18 *Scots Magazine*, vol.52, 1790, pp.467-68, which lists those promoted.

19 Philip Durham to Anne Calderwood Durham, 23 October [1790], NAS GD 172/1068/10.

20 John Elliot to Sir Gilbert Elliot, n.d. [October 1790], NLS MS 12865, Minto Papers, fos.16-17.

21 For this episode see NLS MS 12866, Minto Papers, fos.35-46 inclusive.

22 *Steel's Original and Correct List of the Royal Navy... April, 1791* (London, 1791), p.25.

23 John Elliot to Sir Gilbert Elliot of Minto, 8 November 1790, NLS MS 12865, Minto Papers, fo.18. Muster-roll, HMS *Barfleur*, PRO ADM 36/10795. Philip Charles Anstruther entered the ship on 30 September. He received his lieutenant's commission in 1796 and died, still a lieutenant, in 1814. His cousin Philip Anstruther, third son of Sir Robert Anstruther of Balcaskie and Lady Janet Erskine, who entered the *Barfleur* as a volunteer on 1 October and discharged on 10 November 1790, died a lieutenant in 1796. See Wood, *op.cit.*, p.277; *Times*, 23 July 1796.

24 Philip Durham to Anne Calderwood Durham, 24 [November 1790], NAS GD 172/1068/12; cf. same to same, n.d. [ca. November 1790], GD 172/1068/11; Anne Calderwood Durham to Elizabeth Steuart of Coltness, 6 December 1790, NRAS 3215, Largo Papers, Bundle 72, Appendix, vol.1, p.141. The *Daphne* was a small frigate, and therefore a post-ship. See

Robert Gardiner, *Warships of the Napoleonic Era*, London, 1999, p.39.

25 Murray, *op.cit.*, p.25; O'Byrne, *op.cit.*, p.319.

26 Richard Woodman, *The Sea Warriors: Frigate Warfare in the Age of Nelson*, London, 2001, pp.4-10. The Channel Fleet was still sometimes known as 'the Grand Fleet'. Dillon, *op.cit.*, vol.1, p.217.

27 *Steel's Original and Correct List of the Royal Navy... February, 1793*, pp.11,15; Log, HMS *Spitfire*, PRO ADM 51/829. Woodley had, of course, been made a master and commander on the same day as Durham. Murray, *op.cit.*, p.26, states that the *Spitfire* had 20 guns.

28 *Caledonian Mercury*, 18 May 1793.

29 *Ibid.*, Philip Durham to Philip Stephens, secretary to the Admiralty, 15 February 1793, NAS GD 172/634; Stephens to Durham, 16 February 1793, GD 172/634. Murray, *op.cit.*, p.26, mistakenly gives the date of *L'Afrique*'s capture as 13 February; cf. PRO ADM 51/829, Log, HMS *Spitfire*. According to Durham's first letter to Stephens, he anchored at St Helens on 15 February. On 16 February, the *Childers* took her prize into Dover, and the *Iphigenia* captured *L'Elizabeth*. On 17 February the *Juno* took *L'Entreprenant*. See PRO ADM 51/189, ADM 51/476; Byam Martin, *op.cit.*, p.172n. In those days logs ran from noon on one day to noon the next, and can therefore cause confusion.

30 Pellew captured his prize on 19 June 1793. Gates, *op.cit.*, p.527, misdates Pellew's action and is clearly wrong in asserting that the *Cléopatre* 'was the first prize brought into Spithead since the commencement of the war'.

31 Durham to Stephens, 19 February 1793, NAS GD 172/634. In one chase he lost a seaman, 'who drowned by falling overboard from the Fore Topgallant Yardarm'. Durham to William Devoynes, chairman of the Committee for the Relief of the Relations of those killed in Battle, n.d. *ibid.* [ca.23 May 1793].

32 Same to same, 15, 19, 26, 28 February 1793; Durham to Sir Hyde Parker, 28 February 1793; Stephens to Durham, 9 March 1793; Beeston Long to Durham, 15 March 1793, with enclosure, 14 March 1793, NAS GD 172/634.

33 Durham to Long, 26 March 1793, NAS GD 172/634.

34 Durham to Stephens, 15 April 1793; Durham to the Master of Lloyd's Coffee House, 15 April 1793; Sir Hyde Parker to Durham, 9 April 1793. See also T.N.R. Wareham, 'The Frigate Captains of the Royal Navy, 1793–1815', unpublished PhD thesis, University of Exeter, 1999, p.268.

35 Durham to Stephens, 26 April 1793 (two letters); Durham to Sir Peter Parker, 26 April 1793, NAS GD 172/634. (Sir Peter Parker was commander-in-chief, Portsmouth.)

36 Same to same, 28 April 1793, NAS GD 172/634.

37 Same to same, 4 May 1793; Durham to Andrew Lindegren, 4 May 1793; Durham to the Master of Lloyd's Coffee House, 4 May 1793; NAS GD 172/634. He also escorted into Guernsey a South Atlantic whaler ignorant of the war with France. For details of prize money regulations see Dillon, *op.cit.*, vol.2, p.111. At this period captains were entitled to three-eighths of prize money paid out per vessel.

38 Durham to Stephens, 23 May 1793 (two letters); same to same, 21 June 1793; Stephens to Durham, 21 June 1793; NAS GD 172/634; Murray, *op.cit.*, p.27; Burney, *op.cit.*, vol.4, p.109.

39 Anne Calderwood Durham to James (Jamie) Durham, 1 January 1792, NRAS MS 3215, Durham of Largo Papers, Appendix 72, vol.1, p.144.

40 Philip Durham to Elizabeth Steuart of Coltness, 11 February 1794, Fergusson, *Henry Erskine*, p.372; NRAS 3246, Bundle 161, Autographs, Receipt, 23 October 1793, signed by Durham.

CHAPTER 3: FRIGATE STAR

1   For a full discussion of this see Gardiner, *Frigates of the Napoleonic Wars*, especially pp.152–84, and his *Warships of the Napoleonic Era,* London, 1999, pp.39–60. Also useful are Brian Lavery, *Nelson's Navy: The Ships, Men and Organisation 1793–1815,* London, 1989, pp.49–52; Wareham, *op.cit.*, pp.115 *et passim.*

2   Byam Martin, undated memorandum, quoted in Wareham, *op.cit.*, pp.118–9; see also Dillon, *op.cit.*, vol.1, p.75n; Gardiner, *Frigates of the Napoleonic Wars*, p.158.

3   *Ibid.*

4   Tom Wareham, *The Star Captains: Frigate Command in the Napoleonic Wars*, London, 2001, pp.8–9, 78–9. This excellent book is based on the author's thesis, cited above.

5   University of Cambridge MS Add 9303/14, Sir Graham Moore Diaries, vol.14. I am grateful to Dr Tom Wareham for this reference.

6   James Dennistoun to George Mercer, 6 April 1845, NAS GD 172/1135/11; Robert Henderson of Earlshall to Peter [Henderson?], 10 October 1816, NAS GD 172/1082/35; Marry Murray to Anne Henderson, 3 October 1817, NAS GD 172/1077/3; Durham to Philip Stephens, 4 December 1793, NAS GD 172/634; same to same, n.d. [ca. 4 December 1793], *ibid.*; Stephens to Durham, 14 December 1793, *ibid.*; Durham to Nepean, 22, 23 January 1797, *ibid.*

7   James, *op.cit.*, vol.3, pp.65–6.

8   Durham to Stephens, 10, 14, 28 January 1794; NAS GD 172/634 Durham to Vice-Admiral Joseph Peyton, 23 January 1794, *ibid.*; Durham to Sir Peter Parker, 28 January 1794, *ibid.*; *Naval Chronicle*, vol.3, 1800, pp.337–8, cites five frigates, a brig and a cutter. It names the frigates as the *Carmagnole*, 50, *Pomone*, 44, *Engagéante*, 36, *Résolue*, 36, and *Babet*, 72.

9   Durham to Peyton, 23 January 1793, NAS GD 172/634.

10 Durham to Navy Board of Ordnance, 30 January 1794, *ibid.*; Durham to Commissioners of the Navy, 12 February 1794, *ibid.*

11 Durham to Elizabeth Steuart of Coltness, 11 February 1794; Fergusson, *Henry Erskine*, p.372. See also *ibid.*, pp.376, 386.

12 Durham to James Duff, H.M. Consul, Cadiz, ca. 20 May 1794; NAS GD 172/634; Durham to Thomas Drury, 29 May 1794, *ibid.*; same to same, 3 June, 1794, *ibid.*; Murray, *op.cit.*, pp.29–30.

13 Durham to James Calderwood Durham, 14 August 1794, NRAS MS 3215, Durham of Largo Papers, vol.2, p.273; Durham to Anne Calderwood Durham, August 1794, *ibid.*

14 See Gardiner, *Frigates of the Napoleonic Wars*, pp.41–2; Warren to Stephens, 24 April 1794, quoted *ibid.*, p.42; *Naval Chronicle*, vol.3, 1800, pp.337–8.

15 Durham to Peyton, 6 October 1794, NAS GD 172/634.

16 Amanda Foreman, *Georgiana Duchess of Devonshire*, London, 1999, p.90; Gardiner, *Frigates of the Napoleonic Wars*, pp.41–2; Durham to Anne Calderwood Durham, NRAS MS 3215, Durham Largo Papers, Bundle 72, Appendix, vol.2, pp.275–6.

17 Gardiner, *Frigates of the Napoleonic Wars*, p.30.

18 NRAS MS 3215, Bundle 72, Appendix, Durham of Largo Papers, vol.1, p.38; Sir John Knox Laughton, ed., *Letters and Papers of Charles, Lord Barham*, London, 1907 (NRS Publications, vol.32), pp.viii–ix.

19 Durham to Anne Calderwood Durham, October 1794, NRAS 3215, Durham of Largo Papers, Bundle 72, vol.2, pp.273–4; same to same, December 1794 [mistranscribed 1784 by the nineteenth-century copier], *ibid*; *Gentleman's Magazine*, August 1845, p.193.

20 William Hotham, *Pages and Portraits of the Past*, London, 1919, p.113; St Vincent to

Spencer, 5 August 1800. H.W. Richmond, ed., *Private Papers of George, second Earl Spencer*, vol.4 (NRS Publications, vol.54), London, 1924, p.8.

21 Walter Vernon Anson, *The Life of Admiral Sir John Borlase Warren*, n.p., 1914, p.44n; *Naval Chronicle*, vol.3, 1800, pp.452-54.

22 Pellew to Philip Stephens, 23 January 1795, PRO ADM 1/102.

23 Durham to Philip Stephens, 18 February 1795, PRO ADM 1/1717; Byam Martin to [?Lady Martin], 9 March 1795, Sir Richard Vesey Fitzgerald, ed., *Letters and Papers of Admiral of the Fleet Sir Thomas Byam Martin*, vol.1, London, 1903 (NRS Publications, vol.24), pp.258-9.

24 PRO ADM 1/5332, Proceedings of the Court Martial on Thomas Worth, 31 March 1795; Durham to Commissioners of the Navy, 9 March 1795; NAS GD 172/634; Durham to Navy Office, 26 May 1797, *ibid.*

25 Gardiner, *Frigates of the Napoleonic Wars*, p.42.

26 Anson, *op.cit.*, pp.48-55; Arthur Bryant, *The Years of Endurance 1793–1802*, London, 1975 [first published 1942], pp.146-7; Julian S. Corbett, ed., *Private Papers of George, second Earl Spencer, First Lord of the Admiralty 1794–1801*, vol.1, London, 1913 (NRS Publications, vol.46), pp.65-66; Warren to Spencer, 22 July 1795, *ibid.*, p.90.

27 Murray, *op.cit.*, p.31; cf. *Spencer Papers*, vol.1, p.67.

28 *Naval Chronicle*, vol.3, 1800, pp.338-45; Murray, *op.cit.*, p.31; *Spencer Papers*, vol.1, p.67. Thornbrough's name appears in some sources as Thornborough.

29 Anson, *op.cit.*, p.57; Murray, *op.cit.*, pp.30-31.

30 *Ibid.*, p.32; *Spencer Papers*, vol.1, pp.67-68; *Naval Chronicles*, vol.3, 1800, p.343.

31 James, *op.cit.*, vol.1, pp.146 *et seq.*, 181-2; Michael Duffy and Roger Morriss, eds., *The Glorious First of June 1794: A Naval Battle and its Aftermath*, Exeter, 2001, especially pp.37, 58, 60, 68, 71, 78, 94.

32 Log, HMS *Anson*, PRO ADM 1/117; *Spencer Papers*, vol.1, p.67-8; *Naval Chronicle*, vol.3, 1800, p.343.

33 Log, HMS *Anson*, PRO ADM 1 /117; Warren to Spencer, 29 June 1795, *Spencer Papers*, vol.1, p.78.

34 Log, HMS *Anson*, PRO ADM 1/117; Warren to Spencer, 24, 29 June 1795, *Spencer Papers*, vol.1, pp.74-5, 75n., 78; Murray, *op.cit.*, p.32; for details see James, *op.cit.*, vol.1., pp.244-50.

35 *Ibid.*, p.250; Log, HMS *Anson*, PRO ADM 1/117; Warren to Spencer, 29, 30 June 1795, *Spencer Papers*, vol.1, pp.76, 79, 86.

36 Warren to Bridport, 27 June 1795, *Spencer Papers*, vol.1, p.76; Warren to Spencer, 29 June 1795, *ibid.*, 86.

37 Same to same, 29 June, 3 July 1795, *ibid.*, pp.79, 81.

38 Same to same, 27 June 1795, *ibid.*, p.79.

39 Same to same, 3 July 1795, *ibid.*, p.80.

40 Same to same, 3, 10 July 1795, *ibid.*, pp.81, 82-83.

41 Bryant, *op.cit.*, p.148; *Naval Chronicle*, vol.3, 1800, pp.345-6; Warren to Spencer, 12, 22 July 1795, *Spencer Papers*, vol.1, pp.84-85, 90-91.

42 *Naval Chronicle*, vol.3, 1800, pp.346-7; *Spencer Papers*, vol.1, pp.65-66.

43 Murray, *op.cit.*, pp.34-5; Warren to Spencer, 22 July 1795, *Spencer Papers*, vol.1, p.88.

44 *Ibid.*, p.89.

45 Murray, *op.cit.*, p.35; Warren to Spencer, 22 July 1795, pp.90-91.

46 *Ibid.*, p.90; James, *op.cit.*, vol.1, pp.251-2; Bryant, *The Years of Endurance 1793–1802*, p.148; *Naval Chronicles*, vol.3, 1800, p.348.

47 Benjamin Bower to Durham, 26 June 1795, NAS GD 172/634; Nepean to Durham

27 July 1795, *ibid.*
48 Murray, *op.cit.*, p.36.
49 Spencer to Warren, 31 July 1795, *Spencer Papers*, vol.1, p.96.
50 Warren to Spencer, 31 July 1795, *ibid.*, p.94; James, *op.cit.*, vol.1, p.252.
51 Spencer to Warren, 31 July 1795, *Spencer Papers*, vol.1, pp.96-7; Murray, *ibid.*, p.37.
52 Warren to Spencer, 28 August 1795, *Spencer Papers*, vol.1, p.101.
53 Same to same, 11 September 1795, *ibid.*, pp.102-6.
54 *Ibid.*; Nepean to Durham, 6 September 1795, NAS GD 172/634; Log, HMS *Jason*, PRO ADM 51/164; Alexander M. Delavoye, *Life of Thomas Graham, Lord Lynedoch*, London, 1880, pp.93-4. Graham evidently erred when he recalled that the count sailed 'on board the *Artois* with General Doyle'. *Ibid.*, p.94.
55 *Ibid.*, pp.94-5; Warren to Spencer, 11 September 1795, *Spencer Papers*, vol.1, p.106.
56 Antony Brett-James, *General Graham: Lord Lynedoch*, London, 1959, p.59; Warren to Spencer, 3, 16 October 1795, *Spencer Papers*, vol.1, p.109.
57 Murray, *op.cit.*, pp.37-8.
58 *Ibid.*, pp.38-9.
59 *Ibid.*, pp.39-40, which seems to amalgamate this with Wright's later incarceration in the Temple; for Wright see Tom Pocock, *A Thirst for Glory: the Life of Admiral Sir Sidney Smith*, London, 1996, pp.40 *et seq.*
60 Murray, *op.cit.*, p.41; Durham to Nepean, 14 December 1795, NRAS GD 172/634.
61 Warren to Durham, 14 December 1795, NAS GD 172/683; Durham to Nepean, PRO ADM 1/1717.

CHAPTER 4: PRIZES ON SEA AND LAND

1 Durham to Nepean, 26 December 1795, 25 January 1796, NAS GD 172/634; Nepean to Durham, 3 February 1796, *ibid.*
2 Bryant, *op.cit.*, p.182.
3 Nepean to Durham, 28 December 1795, NAS GD 172/634; Durham to Nepean, 6 February 1796, *ibid.*
4 *Naval Chronicle*, vol.3, January-July 1800, p.350; Warren to the Admiralty, 24 March 1796, Roger Morris, ed., *The Channel Fleet and the Blockade of Brest, 1793–1801*, London, pp.148-9; James, *op.cit.*, vol.1, pp.320-21, which accuses Warren of exaggerating the strength of the French squadron in his report to the Admiralty.
5 Durham to Warren, 24 March 1796, NAS GD 172/634.
6 Durham to Navy Board, 10 June 1796, *ibid.*; Navy Board to Durham, 13 June 1796; Admiralty to Durham, 13 June 1796, *ibid.*; Durham to Navy Board, 7 August 1796, *ibid.*
7 Charles Hope *et al.* to Durham, 16 August 1796, *ibid.*
8 *Scots Magazine*, vol.58, 1796, p.362; cf. the memorial tablet in Largo parish church, erected by Durham in 1845, which misdates her death to 1797.
9 James, *op.cit.*, vol.1, pp.344-5. Had Keats written the despatch, his first lieutenant, Henry Lloyd, might have been promoted, instead of remaining in that rank throughout his career, dying a 'retired commander' (of 1830 vintage) in 1841. Syrett and DiNardo, *op.cit.*, p.279.
10 James, *op.cit.*, vol.2, pp.22-8; Gates, *op.cit.*, pp.415-23; Bonamy Dobree and G.E. Manwaring, *The Floating Republic*, London, 1935, repr. 1987; James Dugan, *The Great Mutiny*, London, 1966.
11 Anson, *op.cit.*, pp.82-3.

12 Log HMS *Anson*, PRO ADM 51/1205; Durham to Sir Richard King, 6 December 1797, PRO ADM 1/1719. See also Minto to Lady Minto, 24 May 1797, Minto, *op.cit.*, vol.2, p.396.

13 *Ibid.*; Warren to Bridport, 18, 24 July 1797, Morriss, ed., *op.cit.*, pp.256, 257-8; James, *op.cit.*, vol.2, pp.84-5, which describes the *Calliope* as a '28-gun frigate mounting, like others of her class, 32 or 34 guns'. Marshall, *op.cit.*, vol.2, p.230, misdates this incident.

14 Nagle to Warren, 31 July 1797, Morriss, ed., *op.cit.*, pp.261-2; Durham to Bridport, 20 July, 8 August 1797, NAS GD 172/634.

15 Duckworth to Bridport, 3 September 1797, Morriss, ed., *op.cit.*, pp.267-8.

16 *Ibid.*, pp.240, 270.

17 Warren to Spencer, 24 March 1797, *ibid.*, p.187; cf. Pellew to Spencer, 10 arch 1797, *ibid.*, pp.184-5.

18 Spencer to Pellew, 14 March 1797, *ibid.*, pp.185-6.

19 Durham to Bridport, 27 November 1797, NAS GD 172/634.

20 Same to same, 27 November 1797 (a second letter), NAS GD 172/634.

21 Keats to King, 3 December 1797, quoted in Durham to Evan Nepean, 6 December 1797, PRO ADM 1/1719.

22 Keats to Durham, 6 December 1797, *loc.cit.*

23 *Naval Chronicle*, vol.30, 1813, p.367; Durham to Stopford, 4 January 1798, NAS GD 172/634.

24 *Ibid.*

25 Stopford to Bridport, 11 January 1798, NAS GD 172/634.

26 Durham to Bridport, 8, 19, 27 February 1798, NAS GD 172/634. The word he used was 'retaken'. See also *Naval Chronicle*, vol.30, 1813, p.368.

27 Nepean to Durham, 9, 23 May 1798, NAS GD 172/634.

28 Log, *Anson*, PRO ADM 51/1245; Murray, *op.cit.*, pp.42-3; O'Byrne, *op.cit.*, p.319; Marshall, *op.cit.*, vol.2, p.432, gives her number of guns as 36.

29 Murray, *op.cit.*, p.27; 'Autobiography of General Durham', NRAS 3246, Dundas of Arniston Papers. Thomson's sister became the general's second wife.

30 James, *op.cit.*, vol.2, pp.122-3; 'Autobiography of General Durham', NRAS 3246, Dundas of Arniston Papers; Bryant, *op.cit.*, pp.259-60.

31 James, *op.cit.*, vol.2, p.124; Durham to Collector of Customs, Ireland, 2 October 1798, NAS GD 172/634.

32 Durham to Bridport, 16 October 1798, NA GD 172/634; James, *op.cit.*, p.125.

33 *Ibid.*, pp.126-7; Durham to Collector of Customs or any of His Britannic Majesty's Officers in Ireland, 2 October 1798.

34 *Naval Chronicle*, vol.3, 1800, pp.351-2; James, *op.cit.*, vol.2, p.126.

35 *Ibid.*, p.127; Warren to Kingsmill, 16 October 1798, George Countess to Evan Nepean, 8 November 1798, *Naval Chronicle*, vol.3, 1800, pp.355-6; Durham to Bridport, 16 October 1798, NAS GD 172/634; Log, HMS *Anson*, PRO ADM 51/1245; Murray, *op.cit.*, p.43.

36 Letter from 'Nauticus' (very probably Durham himself), *Naval Chronicle*, vol.3, 1800, pp.397-99.

37 Durham to Bridport, 16 October 1798, NAS GD 172/634.

38 James, *op.cit.*, vol.2, pp.128-8; Letter from 'Nauticus', *Naval Chronicle*, vol.3, 1800, p.396; Log, HMS *Anson*, PRO ADM 51/1245.

39 Warren to Kingsmill, 16 October 1798, *Naval Chronicle*, vol.3, 1800, pp.352-3; Sir Robert Gardiner, *Memoir of Admiral Sir Graham Moore*, London, 1844, pp.18-22; James, *op.cit.*, vol.2, pp.128-9. As James observes (p.133), this action off Tory Island is very difficult to reprise: 'The official letter contains no particulars, and the entries in the different ships'

logs are confused, and, in some instances, contradictory.' The account of the French ships' number of guns given by James, p.124 (but see also p.132), differs from that in the *Naval Chronicle*, vol.3, p.396, which, being in accordance with despatches by Warren and his captains, I have preferred. There is a diagram, and brief description, of this action in *Steel's Original and Correct List of the Royal Navy... 1799*, London, 1799.

40 Countess to Nepean, 8 November 1798, *Naval Chronicle*, vol.3, 1800, pp.355-56; James, *op.cit.*, pp.130-31.

41 James, *op.cit.*, vol.2, p.131; Moore, quoted in Sir Robert Gardiner, *op.cit.*, pp.22-23.

42 Log, HMS *Anson*, PRO ADM 51/1245; Durham to Bridport, 16, 27 October 1798, NAS GD 172/634; letter from 'Nauticus', *Naval Chronicle*, vol.3, 1800, p.396; Warren to Nepean, 20 October 1798, NAS GD 172/634; cf. Murray, *op.cit.*, p.44, which quotes Warren as saying 'in the most gallant manner'; Warren to Admiralty, 18 November 1798, *Naval Chronicle*, vol.3, 1800, p.357.

43 Durham to Bridport, 16, 27 October 1798, NAS GD 172/634; Moore to Warren, 16 October 1798, *Naval Chronicle*, vol.3, 1800, pp.354-55; Byam Martin to Bridport, 22 October 1798, Hamilton, ed., *Letters and Papers of Sir Thomas Byam Martin*, vol.1, pp.276-79, 282-84; James, *op.cit.*, pp.136-7, 143-55.

44 Log, HMS *Anson*, PRO ADM 51/1245; Newman to Kingsmill, 19 October 1798, *Naval Chronicle*, vol.3, 1800, pp.43-5; cf. James, *op.cit.*, vol.2, pp.137-8.

45 *Ibid.*, pp.139-40; Newmark to Kingsmill, 19 October 1798, *Naval Chronicle*, vol.3, 1800, p.45; Log, HMS *Anson*, PRO ADM 51/1245.

46 Log, HMS *Kangaroo*, PRO ADM 51/1255; Durham to Bridport, 27 October 1798. NAS GD 172/534, in which he spells the French captain's name Segone; Letter from 'Nautilus', *Naval Chronicle*, vol.3, 1800, pp.396-7; Log, HMS *Anson*, PRO ADM 51/1245; Nelson to William Marsden, 21 July 1805, Sir Nicholas Harris Nicolas, *The Dispatches and Letters of Vice Admiral Lord Viscount Nelson*, London, 1846, vol.6, p.483. *Steel's Original and Correct List of the Royal Navy... 1799*, p.41, was mistaken surely in stating that this action took place off Cape Clear. Durham's log indicates that the *Anson* did not arrive off that cape until 25 October.

47 Durham to Bridport, 27 October 1798, NAS GD 172/634; James, *op.cit.*, vol.2, p.141; Murray, *op.cit.*, pp.46, 100.

48 Durham to Bridport, 27 October 1798, NAS GD 172/634; Dowager Lady Martin to Sarah Martin, 26 October 1798, Hamilton, ed., *Letters and Papers of Sir Thos. Byam Martin*, vol.1, p.282; James, *op.cit.*, vol.2, pp.144, 145; Syrett & DiNardo, eds., *op.cit.*, p.221; Hinton died in 1816, still a lieutenant.

49 Log, HMS *Anson*, PRO ADM 51/1245; Durham to Bridport, 27 October 1798, NAS GD 172/634; Edward Brace to Evan Nepean, 27 October 1798, PRO ADM 1/1519; Brace's shipboard Journal, quoted in *Naval Chronicle*, vol.30, 1813, p.371. See also *ibid.*, p.372 for an allusion to Durham's treatment of Newman.

50 Bridport to Durham, 30 October, 2 November 1798, NAS GD 172/634: see Dillon, *op.cit.*, vol.1, p.343; T. Crofton Croker, ed., *Popular Songs Illustrative of the French Invasion of Ireland: Parts III and IV: The Bantry Bay and Killala Invasions*, London, 1857, pp.114-18.

51 Murray, *op.cit.*, p.48.

52 Warren to Durham, with enclosures, 5 December 1798, NAS GD 172/634; Crofton Croker, ed., *ibid.*, p.108. Thomas Crofton Croker is not to be confused with Admiralty official John Wilson Croker, his patron.

53 *Naval Chronicle*, vol.3, 1800, pp.42-45; the editor believed that the writer was incorrect in stating that naval rules precluded single actions being described in the *London Gazette* if they did not result in capture (*ibid.*, p.42n).

54 *Ibid.*, pp.395-7; cf. Durham to Bridport, 16 October 1798, NAS GD 172/634.

55 *Naval Chronic*le, vol.3, 1800, p.516.

56 *Ibid.*, vol.30, 1813, pp.371-2; Log, HMS *Anson*, PRO ADM 51/1245.

57 James, *op.cit.*, vol.2, pp.141-2; Log, HMS *Anson*, PRO ADM 51/1245.

58 Charles E. Pearce, *The Beloved Princesss: Princess Charlottte of Wales*, London, 1911; Timperley, *op.cit.*, p.157; Sydney Checkland, *The Elgins, 1766-1917: A tale of aristocracts, proconsults and their wives*, Aberdeen, 1988, pp.2-3.

59 *Ibid.*, p.9.

60 *Ibid.*, p.5.

61 Martha, Countess of Elgin to Thomas, Earl of Elgin, 23 December 1796, NRAS Broomhall MSS 20/1/141.

62 Earl of Ailesbury to Martha, Countess of Elgin, undated [c.1797], *ibid.*

63 Martha, Countess of Elgin to Thomas, Earl of Elgin, 22 June 1798, *ibid.*, 20/1/25.

64 Same to same, 30 January, 9, 23 February 1798, *ibid.*

65 Anne Calderwood Durham to Elizabeth Steuart of Coltness, 9 October 1788, NRAS MS 3215, Durham of Largo Papers, Bundle 72, Appendix, vol.1, p.137; Dowager Lady Martin to Sarah Martin, n.d. [26 October 1798], Hamilton, ed., *Letters and Papers of Sir Thos. Byam Martin*, vol.1, p.281; 'Articles on the Marriage of Philip Charles Durham Esq. and Lady Charlotte Matilda Bruce. Dated 27 March 1799', Broomhall MSS 20/7.

66 Sir John Knox Laughton, entry on Duncan, *Dictionary of National Biography*, vol.6, p.159. In May 1800 Admiral Duncan's daughter married Sir Hugh Dalrymple Bt, providing another link with Durham. *Naval Chronicle*, vol.3, 1800, p.420.

67 Queen Charlotte to Lady Charlotte Bruce, n.d. [ca. December 1798], NAS GD 172/1082/7.

68 Same to same, *ibid.*

69 Durham to Nepean, 19 January 1799, NAS GD 172/634; Durham to Bridport, 2 February 1799, *ibid.*; Durham to Nepean, 3 March 1799, *ibid.*

70 Same to same, 6 March 1799, *ibid.*; Martha, Dowager Countess of Elgin to Mary, Countess of Elgin, 14 March 1799, Broomhall MSS, Box 24. For Mary Nisbet see Checkland, *op.cit.*, pp.28-30; William St Clair, *Lord Elgin and the Marbles*, London, 1967, pp.4-6; Nisbet Hamilton Grant, ed., *The Letters of Mary Nisbet of Dirleton, Countess of Elgin*, London, 1926; see also J.L. Morison, *The Eighth Earl of Elgin: A Chapter in Nineteenth-Century Imperial History*, London, 1928.

71 'Articles on the Marriage... 27 March 1799', Broomhall MSS, 20/7; Register of St Margaret's Westminster, 1799, p.111; *Naval Chronicle*, vol.1, 1799, p.347; NAS SC 20/50/16, Durham's Last Will and Testament, 24 February 1844.

72 Bruce of Elgin family Bible, Broomhall; Queen Charlotte to Lady Charlotte Durham, October 1800, NAS GD 172/1072/3.

CHAPTER 5: TRAFALGAR'S PRELUDE

1 Durham to Nepean, 26 December 1795, 25 January 1796, NAS GD 172/634; Nepean to Durham, 3 February 1796, *ibid.*; Murray, *op.cit.*, p.48.

2 Brooke, *op.cit.*, pp.343, 344; Murray, *op.cit.*, pp.48-9; *Naval Chronicle*, vol.4, 1801, pp.165, 251, describes the San Fiorenzo as having 44 guns: modern sources give 36, 38, or 42. I have followed Gardiner, *Frigates of the Napoleonic Wars*, pp.186, 187.

3 *Naval Chronicle*, vol.2, p.446; Pierrepoint to Bridport, 19 October 1799, *ibid.*, vol.3, 1800, p.144; James, *op.cit.*, vol.2, pp.356-9.

4 *Naval Chronicle*, vol.3, 1800, pp.293-4; James, *op.cit.*, vol.3, pp.34-5, 232, 323; for further

details see Dudley Pope, *The Devil Himself: The Mutiny of 1800*, London, 1987. 'Lieutenant Grant's Journal of the Lady Nelson's Voyage to Australia', www.tased.edu/au/tasonline/ladynel/journal.htm describes being part of Durham's convoy.

5   Durham to Nepean, 30 April, 9 May 1800, NAS GD 172/635; *Naval Chronicle*, vol.3, 1800, pp.416 (where two of the ships' names are misspelled), 498n. In an obituary for Durham in the *Annual Register, 1845*, part 1, p.266, the governor of Batavia is described as 'late' in the sense of 'former'.

6   Durham to Nepean, 9 May 1800 (three letters), NAS GD 172/635.

7   Same to same, 21, 27, 30 June 1800, *ibid.*; Durham to Lieutenant J. Anderson, 21 June 1800, *ibid.*; Murray, *op.cit.*, p.50; cf. O'Byrne, *op.cit.*, pp.1161-62, where we are told that Tayler 'assisted in taking possession of one of them – the crew having previously jumped overboard'.

8   Durham to Nepean, 11, 13 September 1800, NAS GD 172/635.

9   Pope, *The Devil Himself*, pp.134-40; cf. *Naval Chronicle*, vol.1, 1801, p.242, which mistakes the names of Marret and Lake.

10   Durham to Milbanke, 8 November, 9 December 1800, NAS GD 172/635; Durham to Nepean, 23 November 1800, *ibid.*; Durham to Principal Officers and Commissioners of the Navy, 9, 15, 16, 24 December 1800, *ibid.*; *Naval Chronicle*, vol.6, 1801, p.439. The number of men aboard at the time was apparently 327.

11   Durham to Nepean, 20 February 1801, NAS GD 172/635.

12   *Naval Chronicle*, vol.5, 1801, pp.78-9; Murray, *op.cit.*, p.50; James, *op.cit.*, p.104; Gardiner, *Frigates of the Napoleonic Wars*, pp.43, 46. The *Naval Chronicle*, vol.3, 1800, Appendix, gives her number of guns as 44. The two more powerful frigates were the *Egyptienne* and the *Forte*.

13   Murray, *op.cit.*, pp.15, 50; see also Edward Pelham Brenton, *Life and Correspondence of John, Earl St Vincent*, vol.2, London, 1838, pp.52-3, 106-7, 108-9, 116-7, 122-3, 142, 145; *Letters of Admiral of the Fleet the Earl of St Vincent... 1801–1804*, ed. David Bonner Smith, vol.1, London, (NRS Publications, vol.55) pp.313 *et seq.* Molloy died in 1814, a superannuated captain, and father-in-law to Rear-Admiral Sir John Poor Beresford, who had married Mary Ann Molloy in 1809. *Naval Chronicle*, vol.21, 1809, p.519; vol.32, 1814, p.264.

14   J.H. Hubbock and Edith C. Hubbock, *Jane Austen's Sailor Brothers*, London, 1906, p.109.

15   Durham to Nepean, 26 February 1801, 8, 9, 13, 17 April 1801, NAS GD 172/635; Durham to Charles Arbuthnot, British Consul-General in Lisbon, 8 April 1801, *ibid.* Murray, *op.cit.*, p.51, gives 24 February as the date he took command of the *Endymion*. By an Admiralty Order in Council (superseded on 15 June 1808) captains were entitled to three-eighths of prize money awarded per vessel; if a flag-officer was present he took one of the captain's eighths. See Richard Hill, *The Prizes of War: The Naval Prize System in the Napoleonic Wars*, Stroud, Gloucs., 1998, pp.202 *et seq.*

16   Durham to Nepean, 24 May 1801, NAS GD 172/635; cf. *Naval Chronicle*, vol.5, 1801, p.537.

17   *Ibid.*, vol.6, 1801, pp.435, 462-65.

18   Durham to Nepean, 31 October 1801, NAS GD 172/635; Durham to Secret Committee, India House, 31 October 1801, *ibid.*; *Naval Chronicle*, vol.6, 1801, p.420; William Ramsay to Durham, 19 February 1802, Murray, *op.cit.*, pp.51-2.

19   *Naval Chronicle*, vol.6, 1801, p.420.

20   Queen Charlotte to Lady Charlotte Durham, 7 October 1800, NAS GD 172/1072/3; William Robilliard to the Earl of Elgin, 25 April 1801, Broomhall Papers, 20/1/59; Reginald W. Jeffery, ed., *Dyott's Diary 1781–1845*, vol.1, London, 1907, p.134; Thomas

Hardy to Mr Manfield, 7 November 1801, in A.M. Broadley and R.G. Bartelot, eds., *Nelson's Hardy: His Life, Letters and Friends*, London, 1909, p.77; same to same, 28 March 1802, *ibid.*, p.88.

21 See Arthur Bryant, *Years of Victory, 1802-1812*, London, 1945, pp.1 *et seq.*

22 Gardner, *Recollections*, p.235; Israel Schomberg, *Naval Chronology*, 5 vols., London, 1802, vol.5, p.394; Sir William Erskine of Torry to Alexander Scrymgeour-Wedderburn, 20 February 1802, NRAS 783, Bundle 91/20; Dowager Countess of Elgin to the Earl of Elgin, 29 September 1802, Broomhall Papers, 20/1/61; for Martha's illness see Queen Charlotte to Lady Charlotte Durham, 4 October 1802, NAS GD 172/1072/4.

23 'Autobiography of General Durham', *loc.sit.*; NRAS 3215, Durham of Largo Papers, Bundle 72, Appendix, vol.1, p.345, 355-6; Currie, ed., *op.cit.*, p.110; Murray, *op.cit.*, p.27. I am not sure whether the bank in question was one run by James Strange. See Durham to Messrs. Walwyn and Strange, 29 December 1798, British Library Add. MS. 35155, fo.101.

24 See the various editions of *Boyle's London Directory*, and similar works.

25 I viewed this portrait in March 2002 at the Scottish National Portrait Gallery; it was kept in storage and in need of cleaning. For hair powder see *Keith Papers*, vol.2, p.412. The medal commemorating Warren's action is depicted in Clowes, *op.cit.*, vol.6, p.347.

26 *Naval Chronicle*, vol.10, 1803, p.1.

27 *Ibid.*, vol.9, 1803, Appendix 1, and vol.11, 1804, Appendices 1 and 2.

28 *Ibid.*, vol.9, 1803, pp.410, 421.

29 *Ibid.*, p.422; Joseph Allen, 'England's Wooden Walls: The Defiance'. II, *United Service Journal*, May 1844, pp.98-102.

30 Durham to Nepean, 17 July, 7 August 1803, NAS GD 172/635; Durham to Admiral George Montagu, n.d. [ca. 21 July 1803], *ibid.*; *Naval Chronicle*, vol.9, 1803, pp.420, 494 and vol.10, pp.172, 173.

31 Collingwood to Cornwallis, 4 July 1803, *Blockade of Brest*, vol.1, p.62.

32 See Bryant, *Years of Victory*, p.52 *et seq.*; A.T. Mahan, *The Influence of Sea Power upon the French Revolution and Empire, 1793-1812*, Boston, Mass., 1892, vol.2, p.118.

33 Durham to Collingwood, 19 September 1803, NAS GD 172/635; Durham to Colpoys, 24 September 1803, *ibid.*; Durham to Nepean, 27, 29 September, 22 October 1803, *ibid.*

34 *Naval Chronicle*, vol.10, 1803, p.511; *Blockade of Brest*, vol.1, p.203.

35 Durham to Cornwallis, 9 December 1893, *ibid.*, p.213; Brisbane to Durham, 9 December 1803, *ibid.*, p.214. See also *ibid.*, p.215n.

36 Durham, to Cornwallis, 11 December 1803, NAS GD 172/635; same to same, 12 December 1803, *Blockade of Brest*, vol.1, p.215.

37 Same to same, 7, 8 January 1804, *ibid.*, pp.240-41.

38 Brisbane to Durham, 7 January 1804, *ibid.*, pp.241-3; Durham to Cornwallis, 10 February 1804, NAS GD 172/635.

39 Durham to Cornwallis, 20 January 1804, *Blockade of Brest*, vol.1, pp.254-55; same to same, 10 February 1804, NAS GD 172/635.

40 Same to same, 26 February 1804, *ibid.*; 'Intelligence gained by Captain Durham', 23-24 February 1804, *Blockade of Brest*, vol.1, pp.285-6.

41 Cornwallis to William Marsden, 22 February 1804, *ibid.*, pp.281-2; Cornwallis to Durham, 22 February 1894, *ibid.*, pp.280-1.

42 Cornwallis to Calder, 25 March 1804, *ibid.*, pp.297-8; Cornwallis to Byam Martin, 31 March 1804, *ibid.*, pp.299-300.

43 PRO ADM 51/1441, Log, HMS *Defiance*; Durham to Calder, 4, 23, 24 April and n.d. [ca. 1 May 1804], NAS GD 172/635; Murray, *op.cit.*, pp.52-3.

44 *Ibid.*, p.40; *Naval Chronicle*, vol.15, 1806, pp.190-93; vol.34, 1815, pp.375-6, 441 *et seq.*, *ibid.*, vol.36, 1816, pp.1 *et seq.*, 90 *et seq.*

45 'Sir Robert Calder', *Blackwood's Magazine*, vol.187, 1910, pp.326-7. Regrettably, this sensitively written article bears no attribution.

46 Clowes, *op.cit.*, vol.5, p.122; Sir John Perring to Cornwallis, 9 April 1804, *Blockade of Brest*, vol.1, pp.301-3.

47 See *Ibid.*, pp.35n-36n, 300-1. For Auvergne, sometimes styled the 'Prince de Bouillon', see *Naval Chronicle*, vol.13, 1805, pp.169-91.

48 Intelligence gained from the American ship *Little John... on the 28th May, 1804*', *ibid.*, p.333.

49 Durham to the Impress Service, North Shields, 29 July 1804, NAS GD 172/635; Durham to Montagu, 29 July 1804, *ibid.*; Durham to Marsden, 3 August 1804, *ibid.*

50 Durham to Wolfe, 1 October 1804, *ibid.*, Durham to Nicholl, 1 November 1804, *ibid.* The name of the Russian vessel was not given.

51 Durham to Melville, 15 January 1805, NAS MS 1053.

52 Cornwallis to Marsden, 19 February 1805, *Dispatches and Letters relating to the Blockade of Brest*, ed. John Leyland, vol.2, London 1902 (NRS Publications, no.21), p.185; Calder to Marsden, 2 March 1805, *ibid.*, pp.194-5.

53 *Ibid.*, p.195; 'General Instructions to the Ships of the Squadron placed to watch the Enemy's motions at Corunna and Ferrol', dated 2 March 1805, *ibid.*, pp.196, and 10 March 1805 in NAS GD 172/637. See also Calder to Durham, 10 March 1805, *ibid.*

54 Lord Gardner to Marsden, 27 May 1805, *Blockade of Brest*, vol.2, pp.278-9; Calder to Gardner, 3 June 1805, *ibid.*, pp.284-5; Gardner to Marsden, 15 June, 6 July 1805, *ibid.*, pp.289-90, 299-300.

55 Alan Schom, *Trafalgar: Countdown to Battle 1803-1805*, London, 1992, pp.206, 210 *et seq.*

56 'Biographical Memoir of Sir Robert Calder, Bart.', *Naval Chronicle*, vol.17, 1807, p.111; Cornwallis to Marsden, 6, 9 July 1805, *Blockade of Brest*, vol.2, pp.299, 301; Calder to Marsden, 11 July 1805, *ibid.*, pp.301-2; Calder to Cornwallis, 15 July 1805, *ibid.*, pp.303-4.

57 *Ibid.*; Nicholson to Calder, 12 July 1805, *ibid.*, p.305; James. *op.cit.*, vol.4, p.2.

58 Proceedings of the Court Martial on Vice-Admiral Sir Robert Calder, PRO ADM 1/5371; Calder to Cornwallis, 15 July 1805, *Blockade of Brest*, vol.2, pp.304-5.

59 Allen, *op.cit.*, p.102; Murray, *op.cit.*, p.53.

60 Allen, *op.cit.*, p.102; PRO ADM 51/1640, Log, HMS *Defiance*. Murray, *op.cit.*, p.54, mistakes the name of the master as 'Mr Osmond', leading to confusion. The muster book of the *Defiance*, PRO ADM 36/16344, shows that John Osman joined the ship on 1 August 1804 and discharged on 2 November of the same year. Kirby became master on 6 April 1805 and discharged on 16 September that year, and Osman replaced him the following day.

61 'Letter from an Unknown Correspondent', 23 July 1805, *Blockade of Brest*, vol.2, p.320; Edouard Desbrière, *The Naval Campaign of 1805: Trafalgar*, trans. and ed. by Constance Eastwick, Oxford, 1933, vol.1, p.78.

62 Stephen Popham to Sir Home Popham, 3 August 1805, *Letters and Papers of Charles, Lord Barham*, ed. J.K. Laughton, vol.3, London, 1911 (NRS Publications, vol.39, p.263); Murray, *op.cit.*, p.57; for the American-born Wormeley see *Recollections of R.R. Wormeley, rear-admiral, R.N., written down by his three daughters*, New York, 1879.

63 'Sir Robert Calder', *op.cit.*, pp.329-30.

64 Desbrière, *op.cit.*, p.76; James, *op.cit.*, vol.4, p.3; 'Private Letter from the Senior Lieutenant of the Egyptienne', 29 July 1805, *Blockade of Brest*, vol.2, p.316; C. Northcote Parkinson, ed., *Samuel Walters, Lieutenant, R.N.: His Memoirs*, Liverpool, 1949, pp.32, 33. Walters gives a different order for the enemy line.

65 Murray, *op.cit.*, p.55; 'Letter from an Unknown Correspondent', *op.cit.*, pp.320-1; Parkinson, *op.cit.*, p.32.

66 James, *op.cit.*, vol.4, p.3; cf. Parkinson, *op.cit.*, p.32.

67 James, *op.cit.*, vol.4, p.4; cf. 'Sir Robert Calder', *op.cit.*, p.330 and 'Letter from an Unknown Correspondent', *op.cit.*, pp.321-22.

68 Desbrière, *op.cit.*, pp.79-80; Parkinson, *op.cit.*, pp.32-33; James, *op.cit.*, vol.4, p.5; PRO ADM 51/1640, Log, HMS *Defiance*; Villeneuve, quoted in 'Sir Robert Calder', *op.cit.*, pp.330-31.

69 PRO ADM 51/1640, Log, HMS *Defiance*; James, vol.4, pp.6, 358; 'Letter from an Unknown Correspondent', *op.cit.*, pp.322-23. There is an account of Calder's action, with diagram, in Julian S. Corbett, *The Campaign of Trafalgar*, London, 1910, pp.193 et seq.

70 Murray, *op.cit.*, p.55; 'Sir Robert Calder', *op.cit.*, pp.317-18; Parkinson, *op.cit.*, p.33. The discrepancy in times given is probably explained by the inexact nature of timepieces aboard the various ships.

71 PRO ADM 51/1640, Log, HMS *Defiance*; Desbrière, *op.cit.*, p.81; 'Private Letter', *op.cit.*, p.318; James, *op.cit.*, vol.4, p.6.

72 PRO ADM 1/5371, Calder Court Martial; Desbrière, *op.cit.*, p.81; *New Annual Register... 1805*, London, 1806, p.79; O'Byrne, *op.cit.*, p.1344 (cf. James, *op.cit.*, vol.4, p.6, which gives the total British casualties as 39 killed and 159 wounded); 'Letter from an Unknown Correspondent', *op.cit.*, p.323. Four men aboard the *Dragon* had been wounded in an explosion; Corbett, *op.cit.*, p.202.

73 PRO ADM 1/5371, Calder Court Martial; *Naval Chronicle*, vol.17, 1807, pp.100n-101n; PRO ADM 51/1640, Log, HMS *Defiance*; cf. Murray, p.57, which in an apparent misprint gives the number wounded as eleven.

74 'Letter from an Unknown Correspondent', *op.cit.*, p.323; PRO ADM 51/1640, Log, HMS *Defiance*; James, *op.cit.*, vol.4, pp.7-8; *Annual Register... 1805*, p.570.

75 PRO ADM 1/5371, Calder Court Martial.

76 Buller to Calder, 23 July 1805, *Blockade of Brest*, vol.2, pp.324-5.

77 *Annual Register... 1805*, p.571.

78 *Ibid.*, pp.571, 572.

79 *Ibid.*, p.572.

80 Calder to Cornwallis, 23 July 1805, *Blockade of Brest*, vol.2, pp.311-13.

81 Desbrière, *op.cit.*, vol.1, p.83; 'Sir Robert Calder', *op.cit.*, p.332; James, *op.cit.*, vol.4, p.8; *Naval Chronicle*, vol.17, 1807, p.100n; Nicholas Tracy, 'Sir Robert Calder's Action', *Mariner's Mirror*, vol.77, 1991, p.266; Calder to Cornwallis, 23 July 1805, *Blockade of Brest*, vol.2, pp.312-13.

82 James, *op.cit.*, vol.4, pp.8-9; 'Sir Robert Calder', *op.cit.*, p.332.

83 Quoted *ibid.*

84 James, *op.cit.*, vol.4, p.9; PRO ADM 1/5371, Calder Court Martial.

85 Murray, *op.cit.*, p.56.

86 Calder to Barham, 23 July 1805, *Barham Papers*, vol.3, pp.259-60.

87 Murray, *op.cit.*, p.56.

CHAPTER 6: TRAFALGAR: GLORIOUS VICTORY

1 'Sir Robert Calder', *op.cit.*, p.325; Calder to Barham, 23 July 1805, *Barham Papers*, vol.3, pp.259-60.

2 'Sir Robert Calder', *op.cit.*, p.333-5; Desbrière, *op.cit.*, vol.1, pp.92-3; *Naval Chronicle*, vol.17, 1807, p.101.

3 PRO ADM 51/1640, Log, HMS *Defiance*; Cornwallis to Calder, 16 August 1805, *Blockade of Brest*, vol.2, pp.344-5; cf. Cornwallis to Marsden, 19 August 1805, *ibid.*, pp.346-7; James, *op.cit.*, vol.3, p.302. Durham's log records seventeen sail and one brig.

4 'Sir Robert Calder', *op.cit.*, pp.334-5; Alan Schom, *Trafalgar: Countdown to Battle 1803-1805*, London, 1992, pp.237-42; Oliver Warner, *A Portrait of Lord Nelson*, London, 1958, p.279.

5 PRO ADM 51/1640, Log, HMS *Defiance*; Murray, *op.cit.*, p.58; Allen, 'The Defiance', *op.cit.*, p.103.

6 Calder to Barham, 17 August 1805, *Barham Papers*, vol.3, p.267; see also Calder to Cornwallis, 23 July 1805, *Blockade of Brest*, vol.2, pp.312-3.

7 'Sir Robert Calder', *op.cit.*, pp.334-5, 340-41; Julian S. Corbett, *The Campaign of Trafalgar*, London, 1910, p.202; *Naval Chronicle*, vol.14, 1805, pp.170-1.

8 *Ibid.*, pp.157-8.

9 Edward Codrington to Jane Codrington, 30 September 1805, Lady Bourchier, ed., *Memoir of the Life of Admiral Sir Edward Codrington*, vol.1, London, 1873, p.51. Thomas Fremantle to Betsey Fremantle, October 1805, in Anne Fremantle, ed., *The Wynne Diaries 1798-1820*, vol.3, p.212.

10 Earl of Minto to Countess of Minto, 8, 16, 29 August, 3 September 1805, *Life and Letters of Sir Gilbert Elliot, First Earl of Minto from 1751 to 1806*, ed. Countess of Minto, vol.3, London, 1874, pp.356, 363, 366, 368; Lady Malmesbury to Lady Minto, 2 August 1805, *ibid.*, p.366n.

11 Carola Oman, *Nelson*, London, 1947, p.515; Desbrière, *op.cit.*, vol.1, pp.188-9; Nicolas, *op.cit.*, vol.7, London, 1846, p.27.

12 *Ibid.*, pp.307-8.

13 Murray, *op.cit.*, p.58.

14 *Ibid.*, pp.58-9; Desbrière, *op.cit.*, vol.1, p.190. Murray's implication that the meeting took place on 10 September is undermined by Durham's log, which shows that Durham was back with his ship by that date.

15 PRO ADM 51/1640, Log, HMS *Defiance*.

16 *Ibid.*; PRO ADM 36/16244, Muster-roll, HMS *Defiance*; Oman, *op.cit.*, p.526; Desbrière, *op.cit.*, vol.1, p.189. See also Chapter Nine, note 61.

17 Julian S. Corbett, ed., *Fighting Instructions 1530–1816*, London, 1905 (NRS Publications, vol.29), pp.290-91.

18 *Ibid.*, pp.291-92.

19 James, *op.cit.*, vol.4, p.22; Desbrière, *op.cit.*, vol.1, p.190; *Naval Chronicle*, vol.14, 1805, p.44; Oman, *op.cit.*, pp.531, 532;

20 'Sir Robert Calder', *op.cit.*, pp.324-5; Betsey Fremantle, journal entry, 25 October [1797], in Fremantle, ed., *op.cit.*, vol.2, pp.194-5.

21 Calder to Barham, 27 September 1805, *Barham Papers*, vol.3, pp.268-9.

22 *Naval Chronicle*, vol.17, 1807, p.102.

23 Calder to Barham, 22 September 1805, *Barham Papers*, vol.3, pp.268-9; Calder to Barham, 30 September 1805, *ibid.*, p.270.

24 Nelson to Marsden, 2 October 1805, Nicolas, *op.cit.*, vol.7, pp.64-5.

25 PRO ADM 51/5371, Transcript, Calder Court Martial; Annual Register, 1805, p.577.

26 PRO ADM 51/1640, Log, HMS *Defiance*; Thomas Fremantle to Betsey Fremantle, 6, 7 October 1805, in Fremantle, ed., *op.cit.*, vol.3, p.212, where Durham's name has been mistranscribed as 'Buckham'; Charles Newbolt to his mother, 15 October 1805, E. Hallam Moorhouse, ed., *Letters of the English Seamen 1785-1808*, London, 1910, p.273.

27 PRO ADM 51/1640, Log, HMS *Defiance*; cf. Allen, *op.cit.*, pp.100-1.

28 Oliver Warner, *Trafalgar*, London, 1959, pp.610-61; Dudley Pope, *England Expects*, London, 1959, p.165.

29 Durham to Nelson, 7 October 1805, BL Add. MS 34931, Nelson Papers, fo.277.

30 Fremantle to Betsey Fremantle, 8 October 1805, in Fremantle, *op.cit.*, vol.3, p.212.

31 'Secret Memo', 9 October 1805, NAS GD 172/637; cf. *Fighting Instructions*, pp.316-20.

32 'Secret Memo', NAS GD 172/637; *Fighting Instructions*, p.320; Nelson to Collingwood, 10 October 1805; Nicolas, *op.cit.*, vol.7, p.110; Collingwood to Nelson, 10 October 1805, *ibid.*, p.110.

33 *Ibid.*; Murray, *op.cit.*, p.64.

34 Calder to Nelson, 10 October 1805, Nicolas, *op.cit.*, p.119n.

35 Murray, *op.cit.*, p.60; Durham, quoted in Allen, 'The Defiance', *op.cit.*, p.104; Durham seems to have sent Allen a letter, since lost, describing these events.

36 Calder to Nelson, 11 October 1805, Nicolas, *op.cit.*, vol.7, pp.119n-120n.

37 Same to same, 10 October, 12 October 1805, in Nicolas, *op.cit.*, vol.7, p.120n.

38 Quoted in 'Sir Robert Calder', pp.336-7, cf. Nelson to Barham, 13 October 1805, Barham Papers, vol.3, p.323; Nelson to Lady Hamilton, quoted in Warner, *A Portrait of Lord Nelson*, p.293.

39 Calder to Nelson, 10 October 1805, Nicolas, *op.cit.*, vol.7, p.119n; Nelson to Alexander Davison, 13 October 1805, in Nicolas, *op.cit.*, vol.7, p.118.

40 Thomas Fremantle to William Fremantle, 13 October 1805, Ann Parry, *The Admirals Freemantle*, London, 1971, p.72; Edward Codrington to Jane Codrington, 30 September 1805, *Memoirs of the Life of Admiral Sir Edward Codrington*, ed. Lady Bourchier, vol.1, pp.51-2; the editress excised Durham's name, but there is no doubt that the reference is to him.

41 St Vincent to Viscount Garlies, 31 August 1801, *Letters of Admiral of the Fleet the Earl of St Vincent,* ed. David Bonner Smith, London, 1922 (NRS Publications, vol.55), p.350; Byam Martin, *op.cit.*, vol.3, pp.281-2.

42 Quoted in Warner, *A Portrait of Lord Nelson*, p.297.

43 PRO ADM 51/1640, Log, HMS *Defiance*; Schom, *op.cit.*, p.293, Murray, *op.cit.*, pp.60-61; Charles Newbolt to his mother, 15 October, 1805, in Moorhouse, *op.cit.*, p.273.

44 Nelson to Barham, 13 October 1805, *Barham Papers*, vol.3, p.323.

45 Desbrière, *op.cit.*, vol.2, pp.198-9; Robert Holden McKenzie, *The Trafalgar Roll*, London, 1913, pp.1 *et seq.*, where, *inter alia*, Rotheram's name is mistakenly spelled Rotherham. T. Sturges Jackson, ed., *Logs of the Great Sea Fights 1794–1805*, vol.2, London, 1900 (NRS Publications, vol.18), p.144, mistakes or misspells the first or middle names of Durham, Laforey, Redmill and Rutherford, and erroneously asserts that the *Entreprenante* was commanded by Lieutenant John Puver, a mistake originating in the *Naval Chronicle*, vol.14, 1805, p.410.

46 Nelson to Collingwood, 9 October 1805, Nicolas, *op.cit.*, vol.7, p.95.

47 James, *op.cit.*, vol.4, p.31; Corbett, *op.cit.*, p.398; PRO ADM 51/1640, Log, HMS *Defiance*; Sturges Jackson, *op.cit.*, vol.2, pp.145-6; Colin Campbell to Walter Campbell of Shawfield, 3 December 1805, *Scottish Historical Review*, vol.20, 1923, p.117. Campbell may have been acting as a master's mate.

48 Oman, *op.cit.*, p.539; Sturges Jackson, *op.cit.*, vol.2, pp.146-7.

49 *Ibid.*, pp.147-8; George Browne to his parents, 4 December 1805, *ibid.*, p.194.

50 *Ibid.*, p.195.

51 I am basing the number of guns on Collingwood's despatch, 4 November 1805, printed in the *London Gazette*, 27 November 1805, and reprinted in the *Naval Chronicle*, vol.14, 1805, pp.434-5; see also Desbrière, *op.cit.*, vol.2, p.299; Paul Harris Nicolas, marine lieutenant, quoted in Joseph Allen, comp., *Life and Services of Admiral Sir William Hargood*, Greenwich, 1841, pp.278-9; James, *op.cit.*, vol.4, p.28. According to Desbrière, *op.cit.*, vol.1, p.105, the *Santissima Trinidad* bore 136 guns, while according to Collingwood she bore 140.

52 Paul Harris Nicolas, quoted Allen, *Hargood*, pp.278-9; *Naval Chronicle*, vol.14, 1805, p.495.

53 Sturges Jackson, *op.cit.*, vol.2, p.149; Robert Moorsom to Richard Moorsom, 1 November 1805, in *ibid.*, p.243.

54 *Ibid.*, vol.2, p.238; Collingwood to Marsden, 22 October 1805, *Naval Chronicle*, vol.14, p.423; Paul Harris Nicolas, in Allen, *Hargood*, pp.279, 280.

55 Henry Walker to his mother, 22 November 1805, in Sturges Jackson, *op.cit.*, vol.2, p.323; Moorsom to Moorsom, 1 November 1805, *ibid.*, p.244; Murray, *op.cit.*, p.61. The accounts of Trafalgar by Sir John Knox Laughton and Sir Henry Newbolt agree only on the relative positions of the *Victory*, *Téméraire*, *Neptune*, *Africa*, *Royal Sovereign* and *Achille*. Laughton accepts Collingwood's account of the position of the *Defiance*; Newbolt places her last in her column. See Desbrière, *op.cit.*, vol.1, p.254; Corbett, *op.cit.*, p.354; Frederick Hoffman, *A Sailor of King George: the Journals of Captain Frederick Hoffman RN 1793-1814*, London, 1999, p.109.

56 John Terraine, *Trafalgar*, London, 1998 (first published 1970), pp.146, 204-5; Moorsom to Moorsom, 1 November 1805, in Sturges Jackson, *op.cit.*, vol.2, pp.242-3; Paul Harris Nicolas, in Allen, *Hargood*, p.279.

57 Corbett, *op.cit.*, pp.382-3.

58 Clowes, *op.cit.*, vol.5, p.136; Corbett, *op.cit.*, p.378; Oman, *op.cit.*, p.544; Allen, *Hargood*, pp.119-20; Murray, *op.cit.*, p.64.

59 NMM, WAL/31, Walter Collection, Carpenters' Expenses, *Defiance*, 1805; Holden McKenzie, *op.cit.*, pp.138-9. The relative seniority of the lieutenants given in *ibid.*, p.129, is incorrect. Hellard was first lieutenant, Simons second, Henry J.S. Hargrave third, Andrew Bowden Pidgley fourth and James Uzuld Purches fifth. See Allen, 'The Defiance', *op.cit.*, p.104.

60 Mordecai M. Noah, *Travels in England, France, Spain and the Barbary States in the years 1813-14 and 1815*, New York, 1819, p.11. In 1847 Jane (and two women who had been aboard the *Goliath* at the battle of the Nile) applied for a medal which was to be awarded to those still living who had been at the major battles from 1793 to 1840. The admirals evaluating the claims initially decided to award the medals, but reneged on the grounds that 'There were many women in the fleet equally useful' and that if those three were decorated the army would be inundated with similar applications. See W.J. Rowbotham, 'The Naval General Service Medal, 1793-1840', *Mariner's Mirror*, vol.23, 1937, pp.366-67.

61 PRO ADM 51/1640, Log, HMS *Defiance*; Schom, *op.cit.*, p.367; Henry Blackwood to Harriet Blackwood, 22 October 1805, Moorhouse, *op.cit.*, pp.290-1; Paul Harris Nicolas in Allen, *Hargood*, p.280; Lieutenant John Barclay, Sturges Jackson, *op.cit.*, vol.2, p.213.

62 Campbell, *op.cit.*, pp.117-8.

63 Corbett, *op.cit.*, pp.374-5; Moorsom to Moorsom, 1 November 1805, in Sturges Jackson,

op.cit., vol.2, p.243; George Browne to his parents, 4 December 1805, *ibid.*, p.283; Collingwood, journal entry, 21 October 1805, *ibid.*, p.202; *Naval Chronicle*, vol.14, 1805, p.375, vol.15, 1806, p.371.

64 Collingwood to Sir Thomas Pasley, 16 December 1805, Edward Hughes, ed., *The Private Correspondence of Admiral Lord Collingwood*, London, 1957, p.168; Sturges Jackson, *op.cit.*, vol.2, pp.202-3.

65 Clowes, *op.cit.*, vol.5, p.137; Holden McKenzie, *op.cit.*, p.26.

66 Allen, *Hargood*, pp.123-31, 280-1; Henry Walker to his mother, 22 November 1805, in Sturges Jackson, *op.cit.*, vol.2, p.243; Clowes, *op.cit.*, vol.5, 150-1; Holden McKenzie, *op.cit.*, pp.26, 94.

67 *Ibid.*, p.121; Clowes, *op.cit.*, vol.5, pp.151-2; Sturges Jackson, *op.cit.*, vol.2, p.246; James, *op.cit.*, vol.4, pp.48-9.

68 Clowes, *op.cit.*, vol.5, p.152; Sturges Jackson, *op.cit.*, vol.2, p.237; Hoffman, *op.cit.*, pp.115-6; James, *op.cit.*, vol.4, p.50; Holden McKenzie, *op.cit.*, pp.50-51.

69 James, *op.cit.*, vol.4, pp.50-51; Hoffman, *ibid.*, p.116.

70 Oman, *op.cit.*, p.543; Clowes, *op.cit.*, vol.5, p.134, seems to have placed this signal too early; see also *ibid.*, pp.139-40; Corbett, *op.cit.*, p.375, James *op.cit.*, p.29.

71 Clowes, *op.cit.*, pp.140-3; Nelson's 'exact' words are given in *Naval Chronicle*, *op.cit.*, vol.15, 1806, p.28; according to Holden McKenzie, *op.cit.*, p.20, two midshipmen claimed to have shot his killer. The *Gibraltar Chronicle*, 2 November 1805, quoted in the *Naval Chronicle*, vol.14, 1805, p.485, names one, Midshipman Pollard, and asserts that Nelson's murderer 'was seen to fall out of the mizen-top'.

72 PRO ADM 51/1640, Log, HMS *Defiance*.

73 Murray, *op.cit.*, p.61; Allen, 'The Defiance', *op.cit.*, p.104; Desbrière, *op.cit.*, vol.1, p.301 and vol.2, p.429 (Falcon's report, which is confusing regarding times). James, *op.cit.*, vol.4, p.75 and Nicolas, *op.cit.*, vol.7, p.204 claim that the *San Juan Nepomuceno* struck to the *Dreadnought*, an impression given by her captain's log as well as her master's: see PRO ADM 51/1549 and ADM 52/5600. The master's log misnames her the 'St James'. There is no mention of the capture in the *Defiance's* logs.

74 PRO ADM 51/1640, Log, HMS *Defiance*; Moorsom to Moorsom, 1 November 1805, in Sturges Jackson, *op.cit.*, vol.2, p.243; James, *op.cit.*, vol.4, p.75.

75 Campbell, *op.cit.*, p.118.

76 PRO ADM 51/1640, Log, HMS *Defiance*; Sturges Jackson, *op.cit.*, vol.2, p.229; James, *op.cit.*, vol.4, pp.75-6; Nicolas, *op.cit.*, vol.7, pp.202-3; Desbrière, *op.cit.*, vol.1, p.301. James and Nicolas may have mistimed the *Principe de Asturias'* encounter with the *Revenge*, placing it before rather than after that with the *Defiance*.

77 Campbell, *op.cit.*, p.118; Henry Walker to his mother, 22 November 1805, Sturges Jackson, *op.cit.*, vol.2, p.324; Nicolas, *op.cit.*, vol.7, p.172n; Murray, *op.cit.*, p.61; James, *op.cit.*, vol.4, pp.51-52; Desbrière, *op.cit.*, vol.2, p.242.

78 Nicolas, *op.cit.*, vol.7, p.172n; James, *op.cit.*, vol.4, p.52; Desbrière, *op.cit.*, vol.2, p.242; *Naval Chronicle*, vol.15, 1806, p.284n, vol.17, 1807, pp.361-2.

79 Desbrière, *op.cit.*, vol.2, p.243; Lieut. E. [*sic*; i.e. G.L.] Saunders, Sturges Jackson, *op.cit.*, vol.2, p.273. According to some historians the *Revenge* then raked the *Aigle*.

80 Campbell, *op.cit.*, p.118; Desbrière, *op.cit.*, vol.2, p.242.

81 PRO ADM 51/1640, Log, HMS *Defiance*; *Gibraltar Chronicle*, 11 January 1805, quoted in *Naval Chronicle*, vol.15, 1806, p.193; O'Byrne, *op.cit.*, pp.1105, 1105n; *United Service Journal*, February 1836, pp.172-3; Murray, *op.cit.*, p.62 must have been mistaken in stating that all the *Defiance's* boats were shot through, since they were used later in the action.

82 Campbell, *op.cit.*, p.118; Desbrière, *op.cit.*, vol.2, p.243.

83 Allen, 'The Defiance', *op.cit.*, p.104; PRO ADM 51/1640, Log, HMS *Defiance*; O'Byrne, *op.cit.*, p.1105; Campbell, *op.cit.*, p.118; Nicolas, *op.cit.*, vol.7, p.204 mistakenly says the *Defiance* sheered off to 'a half-pistol-shot-distance'.

84 Countess of Elgin to Earl of Elgin, 3 December 1805, Broomhall MSS 20/1/62; Murray, *op.cit.*, p.62; Campbell, *op.cit.*, p.119; PRO ADM 51/1640, Log, HMS *Defiance*; Desbrière, *op.cit.*, vol.2, pp.242-3, 243n.

85 PRO ADM 36/16244, Muster-roll, HMS *Defiance*; PRO ADM 51/1640, Log, HMS *Defiance*; Desbrière, *op.cit.*, vol.1, p.297, vol.2, p.243; James, *op.cit.*, vol.4, p.53; Campbell, *op.cit.*, p.119; Allen, 'The Defiance', *op.cit.*, p.104; cf. Holden McKenzie, *op.cit.*, p.129, which is incorrect.

86 *Naval Chronicle*, vol.15, 1806, pp.15, 39, 409; according to the *Gibraltar Chronicle*, 2 November 1805, quoted *ibid.*, vol.14, p.485, Nelson knew only that twelve enemy ships had struck, said he was counting on fifteen or sixteen, but added that 'twelve are pretty well!'

87 Campbell, *op.cit.*, p.119; PRO ADM 51/1640, Log, HMS *Defiance*; Nicolas, *op.cit.*, vol.7, p.204.

88 Campbell, *op.cit.*, p.119; James, *op.cit.*, vol.4, p.77; *Naval Chronicle*, vol.36, 1816, p.372; Desbrière, *op.cit.*, vol.1, p.297.

89 James, *op.cit.*, vol.4, p.92; Desbrière, *op.cit.*, vol.1, pp.298, 301; Schom, *op.cit.*, pp.354-5; Holden McKenzie, *op.cit.*, p.168.

90 Desbrière, *op.cit.*, vol.1, p.295; *Naval Chronicle*, vol.14, 1805, pp.436-38; Collingwood to Sir Peter Parker, 1 November 1804, 'Letters from Vice-Admiral Lord Collingwood, 1794-1809', ed. C.H.H. Owen, in *The Naval Miscellany*, vol.6, ed. Michael Duffy, London, 2003 (NRS Publications, vol.146), p.184; Allen, 'The Defiance', *op.cit.*, pp.104-5; cf. Holden McKenzie, *op.cit.*, pp.129, 138; Brown's name is given as Robert in Collingwood's returns, and James in NAS GD 172/637: 'A List of Officers and Men killed and wounded on board HM Ship Defiance in the Battle of Trafalgar'.

91 Murray, *op.cit.*, p.64.

92 'General Memorandum', 22 October 1805, NAS GD172/637.

93 John Barrow, *An Auto-Biographical Memoir of Sir John Barrow, Bart.*, London, 1847, pp.283-5.

CHAPTER 7: TRAFALGAR'S WAKE

1 Allen, 'The Defiance', *op.cit.*, p.105; Corbett, *The Campaign of Trafalgar*, pp.387-99.

2 *Ibid.*, p.397; PRO ADM 51/1640, Log, HMS *Defiance*; *Naval Chronicle*, vol.15, 1806, p.373.

3 PRO ADM 51/1640, Log, HMS *Defiance*; Allen 'The Defiance', *op.cit.*, p.105.

4 Report of Lieutenant Asmus Classen, 1 November 1805, Desbrière, *op.cit.*, vol.2, p.243; cf. *ibid.*, vol.1, p.294n.

5 PRO ADM 51/1640, Log, HMS *Defiance*; Master's log, HMS *Defiance*, Sturges Jackson, *op.cit.*, vol.2, p.255; Campbell, *op.cit.*, p.119; see also Allen, 'The Defiance', *op.cit.*, p.105.

6 Collingwood to Hugh Elliot, 24 October 1805, Nicolas, *op.cit.*, vol.7, p.231, quoted in Corbett, *The Campaign of Trafalgar*, pp.398-99; Desbrière, *op.cit.*, vol.2, p.244.

7 James, *op.cit.*, vol.4, p.90; Clowes, *op.cit.*, vol.5, pp.162-3; Sturges Jackson, *op.cit.*, vol.2, pp.155-6, 205-6.

8 Collingwood, 'Journal', 23 October 1805, Sturges Jackson, *op.cit.*, vol.2, p.206.

9 Desbrière, *op.cit.*, vol.1, pp.296-301.

10 Campbell, *op.cit.*, p.120; Allen, 'The Defiance', *op.cit.*, p.105, mistakenly records it as the

French *Argonaute*, an impression derived from Durham's log, PRO ADM 51/1640.

11 Campbell, *op.cit.*, pp.119-20; *Gibraltar Chronicle*, 9 November 1895, quoted in *Naval Chronicle*, vol.14, 1805, p.460.

12 Campbell, *op.cit.*, p.120; *Gibraltar Chronicle*, 9 November 1895, quoted in *Naval Chronicle*, vol.14, 1805, p.458.

13 Collingwood to Barham, 26 October 1805, *Barham Papers*, vol.3, p.327; that Collingwood regretted this judgment as too hasty is suggested by his letter of 1 November 1805 to Admiral of the Fleet Sir Peter Parker, in Owen, ed., 'Letters from Vice-Admiral Lord Collingwood, 1794–1809', p.184.

14 Sturges Jackson, *op.cit.*, vol.2, p.173; Allen, 'The Defiance', p.105, mistakenly giving the ship as the French *Argonaute* (see note 10 above).

15 Murray, *op.cit.*, p.64.

16 Collingwood to Marsden, 28 October, 1805, in *London Gazette*, 16 November 1805, reprinted in *Naval Chronicle*, vol.14, 1805, p.429; see also note 13 above.

17 Murray, *op.cit.*, p.65.

18 PRO ADM 51/1640, Log, HMS *Defiance*; Holden McKenzie, *op.cit.*, p.49; Eliab Harvey to Lady Louisa Harvey, 23 October 1805, Sturges Jackson, *op.cit.*, pp.226-27.

19 Same to same, *ibid.*, p.228; Murray, *op.cit.*, p.63; O'Byrne, *op.cit.*, p.1105.

20 Campbell, *op.cit.*, p.120; Countess of Elgin to Earl of Elgin, 3 December 1805, Broomhall MS 202/1/62.

21 *Ibid.*; Murray, *op.cit.*, p.62.

22 PRO ADM 1/5371, Proceedings of the Court Martial on Vice-Admiral Sir Robert Calder; see also *Naval Chronicle*, vol.15, 1806, pp.79-86. Seater's name is given in Syrett and DiNardo, *op.cit.*, p.399, as either James or John.

23 PRO ADM 1/5371, Proceedings, Calder Court Martial; Nicolas, *op.cit.*, vol.7, p.64n, where Lechmere is spelled 'Lechemere'.

24 PRO ADM 1/5371, Proceedings, Calder Court Martial.

25 *Naval Chronicle*, vol.15, 1806, pp.85-6. The transcript of the proceedings, PRO ADM 1/5371, does not include this material pertaining to Durham.

26 *Annual Register... 1805*, pp.576-77.

27 *Ibid.*, 570-1, 578.

28 PRO ADM 1/5371, Proceedings, Calder Court Martial.

29 *Naval Chronicle*, vol.15, 1806, p.173.

30 *Ibid.*, pp.174-5.

31 Calder to Barham, 28 November 1805, *Barham Papers*, vol.3, pp.271-2; *Annual Register... 1805*, pp.436-7.

32 Edward Codrington to Jane Codrington, 20 January 1806, Codrington, *op.cit.*, vol.1, p.93; Roddam to Barham, 18 November 1805, *Barham Papers*, vol.3, p.336; 'Lines on Sir Robert Calder', BL Add. MS 39898, fo.84, Warren Hastings Papers.

33 *Naval Chronicle*, vol.25, 1811, pp.16-17.

34 Collingwood to Patience Stead, 1 January 1805 [*sic*, i.e. 1806], Edward Hughes, ed., *The Private Correspondence of Admiral Lord Collingwood*, London, 1957, p.169.

35 Minto to Lady Minto, 10 November 1805, Minto, *op.cit.*, vol.3, p.374; Corbett, *The Campaign of Trafalgar*, p.207. See also Codrington, *op.cit.*, vol.1, p.81n.

36 *Naval Chronicle*, vol.14, 1805, pp.465-66.

37 *Ibid.*, pp.48-52; *Scots Magazine*, vol.68, 1806, p.65.

38 O'Byrne, *op.cit.*, pp.912, 939-40.

39 *Naval Chronicle*, vol.15, 1805, p.142; cf. *ibid.*, p.139, which erroneously states that Durham was in the water procession.

40 *Gentleman's Magazine*, vol.76, 1806, p.67.

41 *Ibid.*, pp.68-69; *Naval Chronicle*, vol.15, 1806, pp.146-47.

42 *Gentleman's Magazine*, vol.76 1806, p.72; *Naval Chronicle*, vol.15, 1806, pp.46, 149.

43 *Gentleman's Magazine*, vol.76, 1806, p.69.

44 *Ibid.*, p.69; *Naval Chronicle*, vol.15, 1806, p.223.

45 *Ibid.*, pp.232-33.

46 Corbett, *The Campaign of Trafalgar*, pp.450-1. This print was probably the item listed in Durham's effects as 'Launch of Trafalgar'. A version of the print can be seen on wall tiles at the Trafalgar Square entrance to Charing Cross underground station.

47 Countess of Elgin to Earl of Elgin, n.d., ca. December 1805, Broomhall MS 20/1/62; Fergusson, *Henry Erskine*, pp.376, 386. Henry Erskine had first served as Lord Advocate in 1783.

48 Clowes, *op.cit.*, vol.5, pp.157-60; Collingwood to Patience Stead, Hughes, ed., *op.cit.*, 5 March 1806, p.173. The first lieutenant of the *Royal Sovereign* was John Clavell.

49 Edward Codrington to Jane Codrington, 15 November 1805, 22 February 1806, Codrington, *op.cit.*, vol.1, pp.72-96.

50 Collingwood to Sir Thomas Pasley, 16 December 1805, Hughes, ed., *op.cit.*, p.168; *Naval Chronicle*, vol.15, 1806, p.207; Codrington to Jane Codrington, 23 February 1806, Codrington, *op.cit.*, vol.1, pp.99-100. Codrington's editor, his daughter Lady Bourchier, coyly concealed the names of Harvey and Durham, but there is no doubt that they were the captains mentioned.

51 Collingwood to Patience Stead, 5 March 1806, Hughes, ed., *op.cit.*, p.173.

52 Barham to Collingwood, 8 November 1805, *Barham Papers*, vol.3, p.332; Collingwood to Barham, 28 March 1806, *ibid.*, p.355.

53 'Clerk of Eldin: A Statement of Facts', *Mariner's Mirror*, vol.20, 1934, pp.475-95.

54 Corbett, *Fighting Instructions*, p.285; Durham to Clerk, 29 October 1805, 'Clerk of Eldin', *op.cit.*, p.491.

55 NRAS 63, Adam of Blair Adam Papers, Bundle No.B1805A; Hardy to anon.; *Barham Papers*, vol.3, p.398.

56 Durham to Major Ferrier, n.d. and draft, Edinburgh University Library Special Collections, MS La.II.79. Durham's statement, 15 February 1806, Stirling Council Archives, GD 189/2/478/4; George Callander of Craigforth to Sir Alexander Campbell of Ardkinglas (his cousin), 20 April 1805, Stirling Council Archives, GD 189/2/478/2; Dennistoun ed., *Coltness Collections*, p.387.

CHAPTER 8: RULING THE WAVES

1 Collingwood to Walter Spencer-Stanhope, 20 January 1806, Owen, ed., *op.cit.*, p.189; St Vincent to Durham, 22 May 1806, NAS GD 172/637; Harvey to Durham, 10 October 1806, *loc.cit.*; Durham to Harvey, 11 June, 18 July 1806, *loc.cit.*

2 Durham to Howick, 10 August 1806, *ibid.*

3 Fergusson, *Henry Erskine*, p.338; Durham to Howick, 31 August 1806, NAS GD 172/637.

4 Murray, *op.cit.*, p.66.

5 Durham to St Vincent, 26 November, 11, 14, December 1806, 18 January 1807, NAS GD 172/637.

6 Murray, *op.cit.*, p.66; Durham to Rathborne, 30 January 1807, NAS GD 172/637; Durham to St Vincent, 26 November, 14 December 1806, *loc.cit.*; Durham to Baker, 11 December 1806, *loc.cit.*

7   Durham to St Vincent, 28 January, 16 February 1807, *loc.cit.*

8   Same to same, 28 February 1807, *loc.cit.*

9   James Cockburn (Under Secretary for War) to Durham, 21 January 1807, *loc.cit.*; St Vincent to Durham, 21 January 1807, *loc.cit.*; Durham to Rathborne, 30 January 1807, *loc.cit.*

10 Durham to Henry Hotham, 8 March 1807, *loc.cit.*

11 St Vincent to John Markham, 17 March 1807, Sir Clements Markham, ed., *Selections from the Correspondence of Admiral John Markham*, London, 1904 (NRS Publications, vol.28), p.65; St Vincent to Lord Thomas Grenville, 20 March 1807, *The Naval Miscellany*, vol.4, ed. Christopher Lloyd, London, 1952, pp.490-1 (NRS Publications, vol.92); Dowager Countess of Elgin to Durham, 28 February 1807, University of Edinburgh MS La.II.79.

12 Murray, *op.cit.*, p.67; Durham to Commissioner of the Navy, 17 March 1807, NAS GD 172/637; Durham to Rear-Admiral Sutton, 17 March 1807, 'Report of the Reconnoitre of a French Squadron, 20th April 1807', *loc.cit.*

13 Thomas Alexander to Commissioner Fanshawe, 26 September 1807, NAS GD 172/637.

14 See St Clair, *op.cit.*, pp.144 *et seq.*; Checkland, *op.cit.*, pp.65 *et seq.*; Queen Charlotte to Lady Charlotte Durham, 8 February 1808, NAS GD 172/1072/6.

15 *Ibid.*

16 NRAS 3215, Durham of Largo Papers, Bundle 72, Appendix, vol.1, pp.146-7; 'Register of Burials of Parish of Largo', NAS SC 20/34/5, fo.277-80, and SC 20/34/1, fo.184-91; *Edinburgh Advertiser*, 22 April 1808l; *Scots Magazine*, vol.70, 1808, p.399.

17 *The British Almanack, and Universal Scots Register for 1808*, Edinburgh [1808]; *Naval Chronicle*, vol.20, 1808, p.336; see also *ibid.*, vol.9, 1803, pp.425-39.

18 *Ibid.*, vol.19, 1808, pp.55-57; *Edinburgh Advertiser*, 5 January 1808.

19 Murray, *op.cit.*, pp.67-68.

20 Dillon, *op.cit.*, vol.2, pp.111, 119; Hill, *op.cit.*, pp.203-9.

21 *Ibid.*, pp.68-71.

22 *Ibid.*, p.69; Stanley Lane-Poole, *The Life of Lord Stratford de Redcliffe K.G.*, London, 1890. p.14. Abraham Crawford, *Reminiscences of a Naval Officer*, London, 1999 (first pub. 1851), p.22, describes the Burlings as 'ship-like'.

23 Murray, *op.cit.*, p.70; see also Sir Robert Adair, *Mission to Constantinople*, 2 vols., London, 1845.

24 Collingwood to Patience Stead, 13 August, 28 December 1809, Hughes, ed., *op.cit.* pp.289-90, 310-11; Byam Martin, *op.cit.*, pp.304-5; Crawford, *op.cit.*, pp.162-3.

25 Purvis to Durham, 16 October 1808, NAS GD 172/637; Durham to Purvis, 14 October 1808, *loc.cit.*; Durham to Collingwood, 18 November 1808, *loc.cit.*; Murray, *op.cit.*, p.71.

26 *Ibid.*, p.72; Marquis di Circello to Durham, 14 November 1808, NAS GD 172/637; Purvis to Durham, 18 September 1808, *loc.cit.*; Martin to Durham, 17, 24 November 1808, *loc.cit.*; Durham to Collingwood, 3 December 1808, *loc.cit.*

27 Circello to Durham, 31 January 1809, *ibid.*

28 Murray, *op.cit.*, p.72; Durham to Circello, 7 March 1809, NAS GD 172/637.

29 Collingwood to Durham, 7 April 1809, *loc.cit.*; Durham to Collingwood, 7 April 1809, *loc.cit.*

30 Murray, *op.cit.*, pp.72-74; Durham to Collingwood, 3 May 1809, NAS GD 172/637.

31 Murray, *op.cit.*, p.75; Durham to Collingwood, 4 May 1809, NAS GD 172/637; Collingwood to Durham, 4 May 1809, *loc.cit.*; *Naval Chronicle*, vol.22, 1809, p.85. Murray

  op.cit., p.100, mistakenly gives the number of guns aboard the *Champenoise* as sixteen.

32 Collingwood to Durham, 2 August 1809, NAS GD 172/637; Durham to Collingwood, 6 August 1809, *loc.cit.*; Durham to J. Lavers (Assistant Agent Victualler, Mahon), 6 August 1809, Durham to Ross Donnelly, 6 August 1809, *loc.cit.*

33 Crawford, *op.cit.*, p.185; Collingwood to Durham, 13 October 1809 and 'Order of Battle' (same date), NAS GD172/637; Ralfe, *op.cit.*, vol.3, p.42; Murray, *op.cit.*, p.75.

34 Collingwood to Durham, 18 September 1809, NAS GD 172/637; Crawford, *op.cit.*, pp.83–84; James, *op.cit.*, vol.5, p.142.

35 *Ibid.*, 'Untitled document [October 1809]', NAS GD 172/637; Crawford, *op.cit.*, pp.185–6.

36 'Untitled document', *loc.cit.*

37 *Ibid.*; Crawford, *op.cit.*, pp.186–7; James, *op.cit.*, vol.5, p.42.

38 Crawford, *op.cit.*, p.186; Murray, *op.cit.*, pp.75–76.

39 Crawford, *op.cit.*, p.187.

40 *Ibid.*

41 *Ibid.*, p.188; 'Untitled document', NAS GD 172/637; James, *op.cit.*, vol.5, p.143.

42 'Untitled document', NAS GD 172/637; James, *op.cit.*, vol.5, p.143; Crawford, *op.cit.*, pp.188–9.

43 *Ibid.*, 'Untitled document', NAS GD 172/637; James, *op.cit.*, vol.5, p.143.

44 Crawford, *op.cit.*, p.190–1; James, *op.cit.*, vol.5, p.644; Murray, *op.cit.*, p.76; Hill, *op.cit.*, p.203. The *Borée* was later floated and got into Toulon.

45 Crawford, *op.cit.*, p.191; James, *op.cit.*, vol.5, pp.145–6; Durham to Collingwood, 3 November 1809, NAS GD 172/637.

46 Murray, *op.cit.*, p.76.

47 *Ibid.*, pp.76–77; J.S. Yorke to Charles Yorke, 8 October [1786], *loc.cit.*

48 Elizabeth, Countess of Elgin, 'Slight Recollections', Broomhall MSS. See also Checkland, *op.cit.*, pp.72, 74–76.

CHAPTER 9: SAILOR OF FORTUNE

1 *Naval Chronicle*, vol.25, 1811, p.260; Lords Commissioners to Durham, 2 April 1811, NAS GD 172/638; Saumarez to Durham, 3, 18 April, 2 September 1811, *loc.cit.*; A.N. Ryan, ed., *The Saumarez Papers*, London, 1968 (NRS Publications, vol.110), pp.173–6; Byam Martin, *op.cit.*, pp.29–30.

2 Young to Durham, 18 September 1811, NAS GD 172/638; same to same, 3 October 1811, Edinburgh University MS La.II.79; *Naval Chronicle*, vol.30, pp.361 *et seq.*; Murray, *op.cit.*, pp.78–9; cf. James, *op.cit.*, vol.5, p.350.

3 Murray, *op.cit.*, pp.80–1; Durham to Carden, 22 July 1812, NAS GD 172/638; John Surman Carden, *A Curtail'd Memoir*, Oxford, 1912.

4 Melville to Durham, 24 September 1812, NAS GD 51/198/10/69; Elgin to Sir John Henderson, 27 September 1812, GD 172/1037; Durham to James Black, 18 December [1812], GD 172/640/8; *Caledonian Mercury*, 15, 24 October 1812; *Edinburgh Advertiser*, 16, 20, 23 October, 3 November 1812.

5 For details see Edinburgh University MS La.II.79 and NAS GD 172/638; Durham to Black, 18 December [1812], GD 172/640/8.

6 Anon. to Melville, 8 May 1813 and Keith to Melville, 16 May 1813, NLS MS 3420, Dalrymple Papers, fos. 92–5; Keith to Durham, 5 June 1813, NAS GD 172/639.

7 Durham to Keith, 29 November 1812, in Christopher Lloyd, ed., *The Keith Papers*, vol.3, p.223; Noah, *op. cit.*, p.10.

8 Murray, *op.cit.*, pp.83–5; NAS GD 172/637; Log, HMS *Venerable*, PRO ADM 51/2958;

Durham to Croker, 31 December 1813, 16 January 1814, *Naval Chronicle*, vol.31, 1814, pp.255-6.

9 Same to same, 20 January 1814, *ibid.*, p.256; Murray, *op.cit.*, pp.86-90; Clowes, *op.cit.*, vol.5, p.543, gives incorrect casualty figures. The Admiralty renamed the frigates *Gloire* and *Immortalité*.

10 Murray, *op.cit.*, pp.87 *et seq;* Durham to Merchants and Underwriters of St Thomas, 2 July 1814, Durham to the members of the Legislature, St Vincent's, 8 June 1814, and Durham to Thomas Pierrepoint *et. al.*, n.d., and Pierrepoint to Durham, NAS GD 172/637; NRAS 832, Lauderdale Papers, Bundle 64/26/3.

11 *Naval Chronicle*, vol.31, 1814, p.507 and vol.32, 1814, p.436; NAS GD 172/637.

12 Durham to his captains, 26 November 1814, Byam to Durham, 12 December 1814, Byam to Croker 19 December 1814, PRO ADM 1/3902; Durham to Byam, 3 January 1815, Scott to Croker, 16 May 1815, PRO ADM 1/3903; Durham's Journal, 26 August 1815, PRO ADM 50/77; James and Michael Cavan to Durham, 22 February 1816, NAS GD 172/637.

13 *Naval Chronicle*, vol.31, 1814, p.508; Croker to Durham, 3,7, January 1815, NAS GD 172/637; Durham to Cochrane, 14 February 1814 (sic., i.e. 1815), NLS MS 2574, Cochrane Papers, fo.97.

14 Durham to Sir James Leith, 'Sunday 17 [June? 1815]', NAS 225/1044, Leith Hay Muniments; Durham to Cochrane, 28 June 1815, NLS MS 2327, fo.135; Murray, *op.cit.*, pp.94-5; 'Diary of General James Durham', NRAS 3246, Dundas of Arniston Papers, Box 24, no.14.

15 Quoted in Murray, *op.cit.*, pp. 95-6

16 Bathurst to Leith, 10 April 1815, PRO ADM 1/366.

17 Leith to Bathurst, 10 June 1815, NAS GD 172/637; 'A Statement of the Services of Sir Charles P. Durham', *loc.cit.*

18 Murray, *op.cit.*, p.96; Leith to Durham, 30 June 1815 [two letters], Durham to Leith, 1 July 1815, PRO ADM 1/336; Raife, op.cit., vol.3, pp.44-5.

19 Leith to Durham, 2, 6 July 1815, Durham to Leith, 3, 7 July 1815, PRO ADM 1/336.

20 Murray, *op.cit.*, pp. 96-7; Durham's Journal, 25, 27 July 1815, PRO ADM 50/77.

21 *Naval Chronicle*, vol.34, 1815, pp.340-1.

22 Murray, *op.cit.*, pp.97-8; Durham to Croker, 15 August 1815, *Naval Chronicle*, vol.34, 1815, pp.338-9; Durham's Journal, 22 July, 8,9,10 August 1815, PRO ADM 50/77.

23 Durham to Croker, 15 August 1815, *loc.cit.*; Marshall, *op.cit.*, vol.1, part 2, p.869n (which misdates the fort's surrender); Durham's Journal, 10, 16 August 1815, PRO ADM 50/77; Ralfe, *op.cit.*, vol.3, pp.45-6.

24 *Ibid.*, p.46; 'Published at Barbadoes with the ratification of the Treaty of Peace' and Christopher Letard *et. al.* to Durham, 18 August 1815, NAS GD 172/637. The sword is displayed at the National War Museum, Edinburgh.

25 NRAS 3215, Durham of Largo Papers, Bundle 72, Appendix, vol.2, p.353; 'Diary of General James Durham', *loc.cit.*

26 The remainder of this chapter draws extensively on the voluminous Henderson of Fordel Papers, consisting of numerous collections within NAS GD 172.

27 Durham to James Chalmer, 5 November 1816, NAS 172/1101/2; Lauderdale to Chalmer, 13 January 1817, GD 172/1091/22; cf Durham's own statement, GD 172/585/7; for half-pay rates see *Naval Chronicle*, vol.31, 1814, p.498.

28 Durham to Anne Henderson, 31 December 1816, NAS GD 172/1082/30, cf. same to same, 1 February 1817, GD 172/1101/5; Vicomte du Bouchage to Durham, 13 March 1817 and Durham to Charles Stuart, 7 April 1817, NLS 6174, fo.789; Richelieu to Stuart,

24 May 1817 and Stuart to Castlereagh, 26 May 1817, NLS MS 6175, fo.585.

29 See, *inter alia*, NAS GD 172/1091/22,23,29,35 and GD172/999/103 and 109; *The Scotsman*, 20, 27 September 1817. Sir John died in December 1817.

30 Murray, *op.cit.*, pp.105-7.

31 Lady Durham to Douglas Mercer, 26 October 1842,22 October, 22 November 1843, NAS GD 172/1112/35,36,37; 'Rental... Fordel... 1845', GD 172/649; Lady Durham to Douglas Mercer, 26 October 1842, 22 October, 22 November 1843, GD 172/1112/35, 36, 37.

32 Durham to Lady Durham, 30 December 1834, 1 January 1835, n.d., NAS GD 172/1101/95, 95, 123; James Durham to Sir Philip Durham, 26 April 1834, GD 172/1116/14; NRAS 3215, Durham of Largo Papers, Bundle 72, Appendix, vol.5, nos.12-30; Hansard's Parliamentary Debates [19 March 1835], vol.26, London, 1835, pp.1130-31; NRAS 3246, 'Autobiography of General Durham'.

33 *United Service Journal*, July 1836, p.408, September 1836, pp.115-6, October 1838, pp.258-9, May 1839, p.116, November 1839, p.418; 'Sir Philip and White at the Main', NAS GD 172/2807/2 and 3; J.S., *op.cit.*, p.181. Durham is seated with the 'spyglass' in a portrait by John Wood, who had earlier depicted him standing.

34 Durham to Lady Durham, n.d. [ca. 1 March 1829], NAS GD 172/1101/124; R. Keppel Craven to George Mercer, 3 April 1845, GD 172/1141/11; James Denniston to George Mercer, 6 April 1845, GD 172/12135/11; Murray, *op.cit.*, p.118; *Fifeshire Journal*, 5 June 1845; *Illustrated London News*, 3 May 1845. Durham's niece Lilly succeeded him in possession of Largo and Polton. His daughter Ann married teacher Peter Mathison in 1832 and died childless in 1858.

Illustration List

Index

Quacks Fakers and Charlatans in Medicine
ROY PORTER

'A delightful book'
The Daily Telegraph
£12.99
0 7524 2590 0

The Tudors
RICHARD REX

'Up-to-date, readable and reliable. The best introduction to England's most important dynasty'
David Starkey
£9.99
0 7524 3333 4

The Kings & Queens of England
MARK ORMROD

'Of the numerous books on the kings and queens of England, this is the best'
Alison Weir
£9.99
0 7524 2598 6

The Covent Garden Ladies
Pimp General Jack & the Extraordinary Story of Harris's List
HALLIE RUBENHOLD

'Has all the atmosphere and edge of a good novel… magnificent'
Frances Wilson
£20
0 7524 2850 0

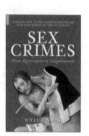

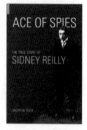

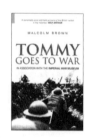

Okinawa 1945
GEORGE FEIFER

'A great book… Feifer's account of the three sides and their experiences far surpasses most books about war'
Stephen Ambrose
£17.99
0 7524 3324 5

Sex Crimes From Renaissance to Enlightenment
W.M. NAPHY

'Wonderfully scandalous'
Diarmaid MacCulloch
£10.99
0 7524 2977 9

Ace of Spies The True Story of Sidney Reilly
ANDREW COOK

'The most definitive biography of the spying ace yet written… both a compelling narrative and a myth-shattering *tour de force*'
Simon Sebag Montefiore
£12.99
0 7524 2959 0

Tommy Goes To War
MALCOLM BROWN

'A remarkably vivid and frank account of the British soldier in the trenches'
Max Arthur
£12.99
0 7524 2980 4

If you are interested in purchasing other books published by Tempus, or in case you have difficulty finding any Tempus books in your local bookshop, you can also place orders directly through our website

www.tempus-publishing.com